TIMAEUS IN PARADISE

Timaeus in Paradise

METAPHORS AND BEAUTY FROM PLATO TO DANTE AND BEYOND

PIERO BOITANI

TRANSLATED BY
JANE WILKINSON

PRINCETON UNIVERSITY PRESS
PRINCETON & OXFORD

Published by Princeton University Press
41 William Street, Princeton, New Jersey 08540
99 Banbury Road, Oxford OX2 6JX

press.princeton.edu

GPSR Authorized Representative: Easy Access System Europe - Mustamäe tee 50, 10621 Tallinn, Estonia, gpsr.requests@easproject.com

ISBN 9780691276144
ISBN (e-book) 9780691277264

Library of Congress Control Number: 2025940493

British Library Cataloging-in-Publication Data is available

Editorial: Ben Tate and Josh Drake
Production Editorial: Nathan Carr
Jacket/Cover Design: Heather Hansen
Production: Danielle Amatucci
Publicity: William Pagdatoon and Charlotte Coyne
Copyeditor: Francis Eaves

Jacket Credit: Giovanni di Paolo, *The Creation of the World and the Expulsion from Paradise*, 1445, tempera and gold on wood. Courtesy of Robert Lehman Collection, 1975 / The Metropolitan Museum of Art, New York.

This book has been composed in Arno

Printed in the United States of America

10 9 8 7 6 5 4 3 2 1

MIX
Paper | Supporting responsible forestry
FSC® C008955
www.fsc.org

For Pat and Lino

χαλεπὰ τὰ καλά

(beautiful things are difficult)

TIMO grece, latine dicitur flos vel floreo, unde hoc timum generaliter dicitur flos, specialiter tamen quedam herba dicitur timum et eius flos timum vel timus [. . .]; item a timo timinus -a -um, idest floridus vel dulcis et suavis, unde et timinum dicitur mel suave et odoriferum. Et hic Timeus, liber Platonis quasi floridus vel quasi flosculus, quia ibi flosculi totius philosophie comprehenduntur [. . .] vel timo sive timos grece, latine dicitur mens, inde Timeus liber Platonis, quia ibi multa de divina mente continentur.

(*TIMO*, in Greek, in Latin *flos* or *floreo*, whence *timo* generally means a flower, but specifically a certain herb called *timum*, and its flower thyme or *timus* [. . .]; from *timo* came *timinus -a–um*, meaning flowery or sweet and pleasant, whence thyme honey is called sweet and fragrant. And here comes Plato's book, *Timaeus*, almost as if it were flowering, or a little flower, because it includes the flowers of the whole of philosophy [. . .]; but also *timo* or *timos* in Greek, in Latin *mens*, because Plato's *Timaeus* contains so many things about the divine mind.)

HUGUTIO OF PISA, *DERIVATIONES*

CONTENTS

ILLUSTRATIONS

Illustration section follows page 198

PREFACE

THE ORIGIN OF THIS book lies in the fascination Plato's *Timaeus* continues to hold for its readers two thousand four hundred years after it was written. My initial idea was to read it in the light of what the anonymous author of *On the Sublime* says about Plato, then to view it through the eyes of Proclus, the Neoplatonic philosopher of the fifth century of our era. Nearly eight hundred years had gone by since the appearance of the *Timaeus*, but it still held its own even in a culture increasingly dominated by Christianity.

Both Longinus, reputed to be the author of *On the Sublime*, and Proclus highlighted two main qualities of the *Timaeus*, one being its logical, rational reasoning, and the other its metaphorical language: its 'verisimilar' discourse or myth—the *eikòs lógos* Plato used in so many of his works. This is the very same language of which Dante speaks in the fourth canto of *Paradiso* [fig. 1], seeing it as equivalent to that of the Bible. In that canto, Beatrice tells Dante that '[q]uel che Timeo de l'anime argomenta' ('what Timaeus argues about the souls': that is, about their return to their stars after death) is not true, as he can now himself see with his own eyes; unless, that is, Plato is speaking like the Bible, which 'piedi e mano / attribuisce a Dio e altro intende' (endows God with hands and feet but means something else)—in other words, unless Plato speaks by metaphors like Scripture. For some time, this line of Beatrice's was my title. This was because I wanted to travel along the paths of figurative language that lead from Plato to Dante: paths that are not always straight, not always recognisable at first sight, but often oblique, hidden, camouflaged. After the definitive affirmation of Christianity, this language had to find new justifications: while it was possible to read Christianity with Plato, it was necessary to find the right way to do it. And all the more so in that the *Timaeus* confronted two central nodes: Creation and Beauty.

Boethius and the so-called School of Chartres were the direct heirs to this mentality, often achieving quite extraordinary poetic and philosophical results. But there was also a series of indirect descendants and passages that needed to be considered: Ovid, who received several stimuli from the *Timaeus*, and his commentators; Plotinus, with his devotion to the Beautiful; Augustine, who spent thirty years struggling with the problem of the Creation and who founded a new vision of the Scripture as humble and sublime at one and the same time; Gregory, the narrator, exegete and poet pope. And then, how was the Beauty of the *Timaeus*, the *Phaedrus*, the *Symposium*, the *Enneads*, to be related to the beauties of the Hebrew Bible, and to the lilies of the field preached by Jesus of Nazareth—and to those, finally, of the Transfiguration?

The relationships existed; all that was necessary was to bring them to light. So, my aim was to establish a family tree for the *Timaeus*, but also to turn it upside down so as to produce a view like the one Dante claims can be gained from the highest Heaven, directing the gaze towards the biblical trunk and the leafy boughs of the Beautiful and the Sublime. Here it was impossible to avoid an encounter with the work of the personage called Dionysius the Areopagite, the only Athenian to be converted by Paul the Apostle, reputed later to be the same person as Saint Dionysius, bishop of Paris: the Saint Denis of the abbey that houses the graves of the kings of France and to which Suger applied the new criteria of the Beautiful [figs. 4 and 5]. Dionysius—known as Pseudo-Dionysius, recalling Longinus's rebaptism as Pseudo-Longinus—arrived in Saint-Denis in 827, delivered into the hands of King Louis the Pious in the form of a Greek manuscript sent as a gift by the emperor of Constantinople. Its effect was immense. Translated immediately by a team led by Abbot Hilduin—who invented the French part of the Dionysius legend—it was retranslated shortly afterwards by John Scotus Eriugena, the Irish director of the Palace School of Charles the Bald at Aachen (or Aix-la-Chapelle), and then again by John Sarrazin in the twelfth century, before being taken in charge by Marsilio Ficino.

In his foundation of Christian mysticism, Dionysius used Plato's weapons to address certain fundamental themes: first and foremost Beauty, the angelic hierarchies and the names to be given to God: the metaphorical language, in other words, with which to speak of the unnameable and indescribable Absolute. Almost all the best minds of the Middle Ages, starting with John Scotus himself, commented on one or other, or all, of the Areopagite's works. After Eriugena, I choose three among the greatest of these authors: Bonaventure of Bagnoregio (the Franciscan 'Doctor Seraphicus'), and the Dominicans Albert the Great and his pupil Thomas Aquinas.

Timaeus and Boethius, Dionysius and the Bible, are never separate; interlaced together, they weave a fascinating, multi-nuanced text, charting an intellectual adventure that is unique in the history of Western culture, beginning with the little less than miraculous fate that befell the *Timaeus* itself. Partially translated into Latin by Cicero, it survived the catastrophe of the ancient world in the incomplete version and commentary of Calcidius, a fourth-century century Christian [fig. 2]: the only dialogue of Plato known in the West for a thousand years! It remained so until Marsilio Ficino translated the entire Platonic corpus in the fifteenth century.

This is the adventure I wanted to recount in my essay—for it is nothing less than an intellectual, philosophical, aesthetic and literary adventure. A reader of the twenty-first century is not obliged to believe what my main actors believed, but people did so believe for over one thousand, five hundred years. One might express it, metaphorically, as Chaucer did, when at the beginning of Book 2 of *Troilus and Criseyde* he justified the language—and hence the thinking—of his characters thus (with my emphasis):

> Ye knowe eek, that in forme of speche is chaunge
> With-inne a thousand yeer, and wordes tho
> That hadden prys, now wonder nyce and straunge
> Us thinketh hem; *and yet they spake hem so,*
> And spedde as wel in love as men now do;
> Eek for to winne love in sondry ages,
> In sondry londes, sondry ben usages.

Giacomo Leopardi, great lover of Plato as he was, and always thoroughly radical and perfectly clear-minded in his thinking, wrote in the *Zibaldone* that Plato's system is not 'chimerical, bizarre, whimsical, arbitrary, and fantastical', but in fact capable of attaining 'the ultimate depths of abstraction'. Plato, according to Leopardi, discovered that our opinion of things, that which considers them absolute, could not be saved but by means of eternal, necessary images and reasons, and that if you take away the Ideas, you will have destroyed the Absolute, or God.

He was, I think, right, and I am quite prepared to admit that one can live without the Absolute. But again, most people a thousand years ago, say, were not able to do so, and quite a few cannot even today. One may also believe, with Karl Popper, that Plato was a totalitarian thinker and politician. If it were so (to echo Shakespeare's Antony), it was a grievous fault, and grievously hath Plato answered it, in his reputation. But I would humbly reply that more than half of this planet still lives under totalitarianisms far worse than Plato's; and that if there is one thing of which one cannot accuse Plato, it is of being a conservative. He was potentially far more open to such future developments as evolution theory and quantum theory—as A. N. Whitehead and Werner von Heisenberg have shown—than were either his predecessors or most of his successors.

I wanted to narrate this story first of all to myself, and therefore in terms that could be understood even by a non-philosopher and non-theologian. Several friends I asked to read the typescript—among them Federico Giuntoli, Rosita Copioli, Paolo Febbraro, Jill Mann, Franco Ferrari, Stephen Halliwell—expressed their appreciation. The greatest support, however, I received from Patrick (Pat) Boyde and Lino Pertile, to whom this book is therefore dedicated. Nor can I forget the shade of Pietro Citati, for many years my *maestro* and great friend in reading. One of my early readers, Jane Wilkinson, liked the book to the point of accepting my invitation to translate it into English, for which I am more grateful than I can say.

I hope I have succeeded in conveying to my reader the enthusiasm—Plato would say the *mania*—with which I have approached the story, and which was the result of the excitement of discovery. I have provided the book with the flashbacks and flashforwards, analepses and prolepses, any self-respecting narrative makes use of—particularly in the last sections, devoted to Dante (and Ezra Pound). The last section, which begins with chapter 22, '"We must lose ourselves"', retraces the path taken in many of the previous stages, moving in the opposite direction: starting, that is, with Dante and going back to Boethius, Dionysius, the writers of Chartres. For the convenience of the reader, I have divided my tale into short chapters with a title alluding to a theme—but without mentioning an author, to keep a little mystery about it and pique curiosity. To this end, I recommend my audience to read the story slowly and carefully, paying attention to the wide bends and steep rises of its itinerary. Finally, the book has an Epilogue, which recounts the adventures of the *Timaeus* tradition *after* Dante, from the early modern age of Italian Humanism and Raphael to the new science of Kepler, and on into the twentieth century of Whitehead and Heisenberg. An Afterword devoted mostly to the parallel developments of the Creation motif in the visual arts, 'The Unmoved Mover Begins to Move', forms a conclusion to the volume.

I have chosen thirty-two spectacular colour pictures to illustrate the book. They cover over a thousand years of iconography relevant to my themes, so that the fare for this banquet might satisfy the appetite not only of the reader's mind, but also that of her or his eyes. The final picture, by Turner, offers, with Moses writing *Genesis,* surrounded by blinding light, a modern view of Creation.

The bibliography for each of these steps is of course immense. The essential references are in the notes, but I also wanted to compile a final conspectus of the most important works that I do not mention, but that lie behind my thinking in this essay, and that might be welcomed as further reading.

Before I wrote this book, I composed a poem in English (why in English, I still don't know) entitled *Plato's Poem,* which recounts part of the story as narrated here, but with sections that are different, or absent, from this volume (as vice versa). It appeared, with facing Italian translation and introduction by poet Paolo Febbraro, in September 2024, published by Elliot of Rome. Terence Cave who, with Michael Longley, has been untiringly supportive of my poetic efforts, called *Timaeus in Paradise* 'the scholium to *Plato's Poem*'. I have long thought he was right to name it so.

Rome, June 2024

NOTE ON TRANSLATIONS

QUOTED EXTRACTS FROM the *Timaeus* are from Benjamin Jowett's translation in *The Collected Dialogues of Plato,* edited by Edith Hamilton and Huntingdon Cairns (Princeton University Press, Bollingen Series 71, 1961), with occasional changes for greater closeness to the original. Jowett's text is included in this volume as an Appendix. All other translations are mine where not otherwise indicated.

TIMAEUS IN PARADISE

1

One, Two, Three

'ONE, TWO, THREE': the *Timaeus* opens simply with the enumeration of the three guests—Critias, Hermocrates and Timaeus—who have accepted Socrates's proposal to meet for a discussion. The tone is light, almost an echo of the joking song of the protagonist of Mozart's *Marriage of Figaro*: 'Five, ten, twenty, thirty, thirty-six, forty-three'. But Plato is not beginning an *opera buffa*. He is opening one of his most important dialogues. And one of the most beautiful. The early Socratic works, the *Apology*, *Crito* and *Phaedo*, staging the trial and death of Socrates while he preaches justice, the duty of the citizen and the immortality of the soul, have unparalleled dramatic force. *Phaedrus* and the *Symposium*, dedicated to love and beauty, are bedazzling. The *Republic* has the merit of admirable completeness. But the *Timaeus* has a fascination all its own, the fascination of a text that replaces Hesiod's myths and Parmenides's accounts with its own view of the creation of the cosmos, its structure, its soul and body, the generation of man. The *Timaeus* recounts our origins and destiny; it enchants us with images of the model, the triangles, the order and beauty that reign supreme in the universe; of our souls descending from the stars and returning to them after death.[1] In his introduction to the splendid most recent Italian edition of the *Timaeus*, Franco Ferrari summarises in a few lines what has been traced in this work since ancient times: 'the lineaments of a unitary project able to combine the main aspects of philosophy, namely ontology, theology, cosmogony, ethics, anthropology and psychology, enriched by its engrafting of a complex set of specialised branches of knowledge, ranging from astronomy to medicine, from biology to optics and the theory of music'.[2]

In short, the *Timaeus* is a sort of *summa* of Platonic thought and imagination (the whole of the first part speaks, among other things, of Atlantis, a theme that always guarantees success). In addition, it has in its favour its form: varied and multiple, yes, yet for the most part no longer dialogical but monological, and always original in its verbal formulation. Supreme, too, in its creation and presentation of the rational, reasonable, 'verisimilar' myths by which it is distinguished. Often considered obscure, its very difficulty generates attraction and the desire to understand it. But no reader can escape the bubbly vivacity of Socrates's opening line—what I call its almost Mozartian enumeration: 'One, two, three, but where, my dear Timaeus, is the fourth of those who were yesterday my guests and are to be my entertainers today? Few will remain insensitive to this simple, clear and solemn announcement of the preliminary theme and how it should be understood:

> First then, in my judgment, we must make a distinction and ask, What is *that which always is and has no becoming*, and what is *that which is always becoming* and never is? That which is apprehended by intelligence and reason is always in the same state, but that which is conceived by opinion with the help of sensation and without reason is always in a process of becoming and perishing and never really is.[3]

Reverberations of the most famous passages of the *Timaeus* would continue, not for centuries, but for millennia; first and foremost, the consideration of sight as a gift from the gods, founding the human conception of time, research into the nature of the cosmos, and ultimately philosophy, 'than which there is no greater good':

> [S]ight in my opinion is the source of the greatest benefit to us, for had we never seen the stars and the sun and the heaven, none of the words which we have spoken about the universe would ever have been uttered. But now the sight of day and night, and the months and the revolutions of the years have created number and have given us a conception of time, and the power of inquiring about the nature of the

> universe. And from this source we have derived philosophy, than which no greater good ever was or will be given by the gods to mortal man.[4]

A passionate and fundamental proclamation of the raison d'être of science and thought, this must be seen together with the passage on the Demiurge and the model he used to shape the universe:

> But the father and the maker of all this universe is past finding out, and even if we found him, to tell of him to all men would be impossible. This question, however, we must ask about the world. Which of the patterns had the artificer in view when he made it—the pattern of the unchangeable or of that which is created? If the world be indeed fair and the artificer good, it is manifest that he must have looked to that which is eternal, but if what cannot be said without blasphemy is true, then to the created pattern. Everyone will see that he must have looked to the eternal, for the world is the fairest of creations and he is the best of causes.[5]

And also together with the *Timaeus*'s last proclamation, the one that concludes the work with the celebration of the living cosmos, the beautiful and perfect god:

> We may now say that our discourse about the nature of the universe has an end. The world has received animals, mortal and immortal, and is fulfilled with them, and has become a visible animal containing the visible—the sensible God who is the image of the intellectual, the greatest, best, fairest, most perfect—the one only-begotten heaven.[6]

Plato's preoccupation with the beautiful and the good emerges forcefully here, and it is a force that dominates the whole of the *Timaeus* in all its articulations and that inevitably brings with it the discussion of the kind of language and imagery that should be used in contexts such as this. Plato is well aware that 'beautiful things are difficult', as he repeats several times in his works: 'khalepà tà kalá'.[7] Our accounts, consequently, 'need only be likely and analogous to the former words'. Those that concern what is stable, fixed and evident to the intellect will thus be stable, irrefutable, 'invincible'. Those, on the other hand, that we give of that which has been formed to be like that reality, since they are accounts of what is a likeness, are themselves likely, and stand in proportion to the previous accounts: 'as being is to becoming,' that is, 'so is truth to belief.[8]

Here, then, are the *eikòs lógos* and the *eikòs mýthos*, likely accounts and myths, which will serve to illustrate, for example, 'gods and the coming to be of the universe', and which, after all, are the inevitable consequence of the fact that both speaker and listener are human. The conclusion of the piece is great:

> Let me tell you then why the creator made this world of generation. He was good, and the good can never have any jealousy of anything. And being free from jealousy, he desired that all things should be as like himself as they could be. This is in the truest sense the origin of creation and of the world, as we shall do well in believing on the testimony of wise men. God desired that all things should be good and nothing bad, so far as this was attainable. Wherefore also finding the whole visible sphere not at rest, but moving in an irregular and disorderly fashion, out of disorder he brought order, considering that this was in every way better than the other. Now the deeds of the best could never be or have been other than the fairest, and the creator, reflecting on the things which are by nature visible, found that no unintelligent creature taken as a whole could ever be fairer than the intelligent taken as a whole, and again that intelligence could not be present in anything which was devoid of soul. For which reason, when he was framing the universe, he put intelligence in soul, and soul in body, that he might be the creator of a work which was by nature fairest and best. On this wise, using the language of probability, we may say that the world came into being—a living creature truly endowed with soul and intelligence by the providence of God.
>
> This being supposed, let us proceed to the next stage. In the likeness of what animal did the creator make the world? It would be an unworthy thing to liken it to any nature which exists as a part only, for nothing can be beautiful which is like any imperfect thing. But let us suppose the world to be the very image of that whole of which all

> other animals both individually and in their tribes are portions. For the original of the universe contains in itself all intelligible beings, just as this world comprehends us and all other visible creatures. For the deity, intending to make this world like the fairest and most perfect of intelligible beings, framed one visible animal comprehending within itself all other animals of a kindred nature. Are we right in saying that there is one world, or that they are many and infinite? There must be one only if the created copy is to accord with the original. For that which includes all other intelligible creatures cannot have a second or companion; in that case there would be need of another living being which would include both, and of which they would be parts, and the likeness would be more truly said to resemble not them, but that other which included them. In order then that the world might be solitary, like the perfect animal, the creator made not two worlds or an infinite number of them, but there is and ever will be one only-begotten and created heaven.[9]

I wanted to quote the whole of this passage so that its unparalleled *claritas,* the unusually elevated style of its reasoning and the range of its rhythm could appear as clearly as possible, even in translation. Over two thousand years later, it impressed Friedrich Schelling, who noted that the idea of the creation of the cosmos by the Demiurge 'free of jealousy' and as similar as possible to himself was something that had never occurred to Moses or any of the Jews.[10] But it did not impress the greatest of Plato's disciples, Aristotle, who quoted it in the *De caelo* in order to use it against the author: 'This is held in the *Timaeus,* where Plato says that the heaven, though it was generated, will none the less exist to eternity': which is obviously contradictory.[11] Aristotle, moreover, will consider the universe ungenerated and existing since the beginning of time, and when he reaches Plato in his account of the succession of theories on the principle of the cosmos at the beginning of the *Metaphysics,* he ignores the *Timaeus* and turns decisively towards the Platonic world of Ideas. Finally, the man who loved myth, as is clear from the *Poetics* and his other works, was obviously not going to be persuaded by the 'verisimilar' myths proposed by Plato.

2

Emulator of Homer

FEW REPROACHED THE author of the *Timaeus* for having a shifting register and a style that was not always elevated. Cicero, who translated a not insignificant section, spoke of Plato's *inconstantia* in the *Timaeus*, but regarded him as almost divine, the prince and—in the words of Panaetius—the 'Homer of philosophers'.[1] Francis Cornford, one of the three or four most authoritative and profound twentieth-century commentators on the *Timaeus*, proclaimed it 'no less than the *De rerum natura* of Lucretius, and indeed more so in certain respects'.[2] Almost five hundred years earlier, Torquato Tasso had not hesitated to call Plato a 'poet' when he 'presents Timaeus narrating how God the father, calling the other gods lesser, created the world'.[3] But the strongest reaction came from the author of the treatise *On the Sublime*, a Greek who most probably lived in Rome, or partly in Rome, perhaps at the beginning of the first century CE, about five hundred years after Plato's lifetime. 'Longinus', as he was once called and will also be called here for the sake of brevity, devotes the central chapters of his *Perì hýpsous*, and in particular the ninth, to the sublimity produced by greatness of mind, dwelling on famous scenes from the *Iliad* and the *Odyssey* (as well as on the beginning of the biblical *Genesis*), and then on Sappho's 'In My Eyes That Man Is a Match for the Gods'. After this, he focuses on 'amplification', contrasting the sublime of Demosthenes with that of Cicero as two different kinds of fiery greatness:

> Demosthenes' greatness depends mostly on a precipitous sublimity, while Cicero's has a copious flow; our Greek author, given the force,

> speed, strength, vehemence with which, as it were, he burns and plunders everything, might be compared to lightning or a thunderbolt, while Cicero, like a widespread conflagration, I think, broadens and swells in every direction, with a strong, persistent heat that keeps perpetuating and renewing itself through varying forms in successive stages.[4]

Leaving those who are of Latin language and culture, like his addressee Terentianus, to judge between the two, Longinus finally reaches Plato, whom he had mentioned earlier (he will soon add Thucydides 'in history' to his list of sublime authors such as Demosthenes and Plato). It goes without saying, he argues, that Plato draws on sublimity, and anyone who has read the *Republic* realises this perfectly well:

> That Plato (to whom I return) flows silently with a stream of words of this kind, yet achieves no less greatness, is a hallmark of his which you yourself know from reading in the *Republic*: 'Those lacking wisdom and virtue, perpetually engaged in feasting and the like, sink lower, it seems, and wander through life at that level; they never raise their sight to the truth nor are lifted upwards; they taste no lasting, pure pleasure, but like cattle look constantly downwards, stooped over the ground and their tables, filling up with fodder and copulating; and to maximize their share of these things, they kick and butt one another to death with iron horns and hooves in their insatiability.'[5]

There is in fact another route that leads to the sublime, differing from those examined previously: 'the imitation and emulation of great writers and poets from the past'. Tradition itself, in short, becomes—or can become—a source of sublimity. Longinus explains:

> Many are divinely possessed by another's spirit, in the same way as the Pythia, we are told, when she approaches the tripod, where a cleft in the earth breathes out, it is said, a divine vapour, is at once impregnated with supernatural power, and immediately chants oracles by inspiration; and likewise the genius of older writers releases certain emanations, as if from sacred apertures, into the minds of those who

> emulate them; inspired by these, even those whose temperament is not vatic share in the rapture of others' greatness.[6]

Inspiration is not necessarily of the first degree; it can also be 'derivative', so to speak, or second degree: coming in other words from the spirit of another author, like the inspiration of the Sibyl who is impregnated with the power of the divinity as soon as a 'divine vapour' reaches her. From the genius of the ancients springs emulation, which leads to a 'shar[ing] in the rapture of others' greatness': a sublimity, as it were, handed down. And if everything in Greek literature goes back to Homer, Homer will be the greatest source of this kind of sublimity. It was not only Herodotus, Longinus continues, who was 'highly Homeric', but also Stesichorus and Archilochus, '*but more than anyone else Plato, who drew off into his own work innumerable side channels from that great Homeric stream*'.[7]

This is not plagiarism, the author of the *Sublime* specifies; it is similar to 'the way that statues or other artworks incorporate the fine character of their models':

> I do not think so many Homeric features would have blossomed around Plato's doctrines or that he would so often have become absorbed in poetic matters and language if he had not pitted himself with all his heart against Homer for first prize, like a young competitor facing an acknowledged master—doing so perhaps with too much competitiveness, in a kind of jousting contest, but nonetheless fruitfully; 'this strife', in Hesiod's words, 'is good for mortals'.[8]

Plato is sublime—and Adelard of Bath in the twelfth century will continue to judge him to be 'one of them, borne aloft by the sublimity of his mind and by those wings which he strenuously attempted to don'[9]—because he competes with Homer, vies with the greatest poet, draws inspiration from him. This is an extraordinary, enormous statement. Plato is not a poet on a par with Lucretius, as Cornford would have it; he is on a par with the creator of the *Iliad*, the *Odyssey* and the *Hymns*. Longinus has no doubt about this: he speaks explicitly of *poietikàs hýlas*, of 'poetic matters and language'.

Now it so happens that the most extensive Platonic passage quoted in *On the Sublime* comes precisely from the *Timaeus*. Not from the so-called Proemium, nor even from the cosmogonic section where one would expect to find it, but in the part that speaks of the construction and articulation of the human body. Plato had no models in the earlier tradition to refer to here, so the invention is basically his own. And what an invention! Longinus summarises it as follows, quoting its most striking expressions:

> Furthermore, in set-piece descriptions and accounts nothing is so incisive as a connected sequence of tropes. This is what makes the depiction of the human body's anatomy in Xenophon so splendid, and Plato's even more inspired. The latter calls the head the body's 'acropolis', the neck an 'isthmus . . . built across' between head and chest, and says that vertebrae are set beneath one another 'like pivots', that pleasure is 'evil's snare' for humans, the tongue a 'testing implement' for taste, that the heart is 'a knot in the veins' and 'the spring of the blood that circulates vigorously, stationed in the guardhouse'; he calls the body's system of channels 'alleyways'; he declares that the gods 'when devising assistance for the heart's throbbing in anticipation of fearful things or for the arousal of its anger in an inflamed state, planted the arrangement of the lungs, soft and bloodless and with cavities, serving like a cushion, in order that when anger boiled up in the heart, it would throb against something yielding' and not be harmed. And he described the appetites' dwelling as women's quarters, that of the spirited part as like men's quarters; the spleen he called a 'cloth' to clean the inner parts, 'which makes it fill up with the removed impurities and swell to a large, festering size'.
>
> 'Next', he writes, 'they screened everything with flesh', placing the flesh as a 'defence' against the external world, 'like felt covering'; he called the blood 'the flesh's pasturage'. 'For purposes of nourishment', he says, 'they made channels through the body, as if cutting irrigation channels in gardens, so that from the advancing stream', with the body as a narrow 'conduit', 'the streams of the veins might flow'. When the end of life is imminent, 'the soul is like a ship whose cables are untied, and it is set free'.[10]

Hippocrates and his followers, who looked to material bodies for symptoms of disease, would have considered such descriptions more pertinent to 'painting' than to anatomy or medicine, as indeed they did with works of this kind by Empedocles.[11] Longinus, however, is not interested in establishing precise boundaries between the language of science and that of art. To him what is important is to point out how a passage like the one he has just quoted attains sublimity. What emerges here is the essential role of figurative language ('tropes') and metaphors, most particularly in emotional and descriptive passages, ones that 'are by their nature imposing', contributing decisively to the development of the sublime.

Longinus could have recalled, in this regard, the famous pronouncement on the use of metaphor in the *Poetics*: 'by far the greatest asset is a capacity for metaphor'. This alone, Aristotle comments—as one who frequents, and increasingly as an old man, traditional myth, and even claims that the lover of myth (*philómythos*) is in a sense a lover of wisdom (*philósophos*)[12]—Aristotle, as I say, comments, with his customary acumen and depth of thought, that metaphor 'cannot be acquired from another, and it is a sign of natural gifts: because to use metaphor well is to discern similarities'.[13] Instead, Longinus prefers to recall Aristotle's and Theophrastus's recommendations on mitigating 'bold metaphors' with expressions like 'as if' or 'as it were' and so on: a principle he accepts. However, he insists that 'timely, intense emotions and authentic sublimity are special antidotes for numerous, bold metaphors, because these qualities naturally sweep and propel along everything else with the spate of their momentum', making the listener forget to count the metaphors employed by the speaker.[14]

Dionysius of Halicarnassus and Caecilius of Caleacte, Longinus's main targets, criticise Plato for often being 'carried away by a sort of frenzy of language into extreme, abrasive metaphors and intemperate metaphor' and abandoning himself to heavily inflated allegory. 'It is not easy to grasp', Longinus says, referring to Plato's statement in the *Laws*,[15] that 'a city should be mixed like a wine bowl, in which the wine boils into madness when poured in, but when rebuked by a second, sober god, and when it accepts a beautiful partnership, it produces a healthy, balanced drink'. His critics maintain in fact that '[t]o call water "a sober god" [. . .] and mixing a "rebuke", is the language of a poet who is himself really not sober'. Fastening on such defects, Caecilius even goes so far as to declare that Lysias is altogether superior to Plato, because he is always 'pure', while Plato is not. But suppose we concede that Theocritus and Apollonius Rhodius are faultless, while Homer makes mistakes; would you rather be Apollonius or Homer? Would you choose Bacchylides rather than Pindar, Ion of Chios rather than Sophocles? The former are 'impeccable, specimens of utterly polished beauty', as against Pindar and Sophocles who 'sometimes ignite everything with their power, though they often unexpectedly lose their heat and crash disastrously'. But no one endowed 'with fine judgement could think all the works of Ion, taken together, worth as much as one single play, *Oedipus*', Longinus concludes.[16]

Plato is sublime because he competes with Homer, emulates him and commits excesses like him. Indeed, perhaps he *is* Homer. John of Salisbury, the great English scholar of the twelfth century—secretary to Thomas Becket, several times ambassador to the Pope, correspondent with all the most important figures in Europe, the author of works such as the *Metalogicon* and the *Policraticus*, and finally bishop of Chartres, the place where he had studied—discusses the *Timaeus* at length and then takes up a statement by Valerius Maximus, that Homer died as a result of his despondency at not being able to answer a question put to him by some fishermen.[17] Some say the same of Plato, John asserts. Therefore, the opinion spread that 'Homer' was *aequivocus*, synonymous with Plato for the elevation of his knowledge, the elegance of his speech and the breadth of his chest'. After all, 'uiros nobiles certum est polynomios extitisse': noblemen were known to be *polynomioi*, to have more than one name. Plato, the *philosophorum princeps*, perceived truth by flying as high as John the Evangelist: it is uncertain whether he should be called god or demigod.[18]

It's a good story, that of an interchangeable Homer and Plato. But let us limit ourselves, with Longinus, to considering the philosopher a sublime emulator of the poet. He uses 'likely' myths and accounts, and tells them by means of figurative and metaphorical language. And the *Timaeus* is one of his greatest masterpieces.

3

Pythagorean and Socratic

NOT ENTIRELY DIFFERENT considerations are put forward, albeit for quite different purposes, by the greatest of Plato's commentators to be known in late antiquity (we are now in the fifth century CE): Proclus.[1] Proclus, who dwells at length on the relationship between Plato and Homer in his *Commentary on the Republic* and calls Plato *zelotés,* the emulator and rival of Homer,[2] immediately discusses the 'genre' and 'character' of the *Timaeus*: its literary nature, in other words.[3] He takes it for granted that Plato had taken his work from the book on the universe composed by the 'Pythagorean' Timaeus and therefore decided to 'to do Timaeus-writing' (*timaiográphein*)—that is, to write a *Timaeus* in the manner of Pythagoras. It is, however, generally agreed that the *Timaeus*'s quintessentially Platonic 'character' (*ethos*) is 'Socratic' (*philánthropon kaì apodeiktikón,* 'considerate and demonstrative'). In the *Timaeus,* as in other dialogues, Plato combines the characteristics of both approaches: the Pythagorean 'tradition' and the Socratic manner.[4]

The former contains 'loftiness [or "sublimity": *to hypselónoun*] of mind, intuition [*to noerón*], inspiration [*to éntheon*], a tendency to link everything with the intelligibles, to depict the Whole in terms of numbers, to give an indication of things in a symbolic and mystical fashion [*symbolikòs kaì mystikós*], to lead upwards [*to anagogón*], to remove one's focus on the particulars, to state with affirmation [*to apophantikón*]'. The latter brings with it 'approachability [*to eusynousiastón*], gentleness [*to heméron*; 'bonhomie' for Festugière], a tendency towards demonstration, to studying reality through images, to moral content, and so on'. As a result, Proclus concludes, 'the dialogue is elevated (*semnós*), and derives its conceptions from above, from the very first originative principle. It mixes the demonstrational method with the revelational, and it prepares us to understand physical things not only from the point of view of physics, but also from that of theology'.[5]

Proclus knows his stuff. His analysis of the two approaches adopted in the *Timaeus* is extremely acute, and it finds confirmation in the *Theologia platonica*, where the *Timaeus* is considered—along with *Phaedo, Phaedrus, Symposium, Philebus, Sophist, Politicus* and *Cratylus*—one of the dialogues ' which principally unfold to us the mystic discipline about the Gods'.[6] He is even ready to admit that Plato distinguishes 'poetic talent inspired by the gods from that gained by means of art' and that 'he makes the gods responsible for the magnificence of language and the sublimity that come from divine possession [*enthousiasmoû*]'.[7] In the *Theologia*, Proclus also dwells on the 'likely' myths that we have seen Timaeus indicate as those to be preferred in philosophical reasoning. Plato could not, Proclus argued, employ for the gods the myths of the ancient poets, which with their rapes and adulteries, their tearing divisions and wars, were more suited to tragedy. Consequently, he considers 'those mythological discourses about the Gods, as more persuasive, and more adapted to truth and the philosophical habit, which assert that a divine nature is the cause of all good, but of no evil'. All of Plato's mythical narratives, which hold 'the truth in concealment [. . . ,] bring with them an image of the mundane composition, in which both the apparent beauty is worthy of divinity, and a beauty more divine than this, is established in the unapparent lives and powers of the Gods'[8]—beauty:Beauty. The *kalon*, what the young Schelling called *Vollkommenheit*: perfection, completeness, *plenitudo*.[9]

4

Parens, fabricator, artifex

DEMOGORGON AND PHAETHON

WE SHALL NOW TAKE an oblique and at the same time circular route. It will lead us from Plato to Ovid, to the medieval commentaries on the *Metamorphoses*, to Boccaccio, and back to Plato. When Cicero translated the *Timaeus* into Latin, instead of the original *poietès kaì patér*, maker and father, he used the expressions *parens* and *fabricator*, or *artifex* and *opifex*, for the Demiurge.[1] They became the true marks of Plato's presence in the cosmogonic accounts of later ages. Even in the very different, multi-layered and original narrative of Ovid in the *Metamorphoses*, mingling Hesiod with Lucretius, and Empedocles with Virgil, and where absence prevails over presence (there was no sun, no earth, no sea, or everything was unstable), the signals of the *Timaeus* are unmistakable.[2] We see the *mundi fabricator* assigning a place of origin to the winds, and shortly afterwards, as *opifex rerum* and *mundi melioris origo*, creating man—unless he was moulded by Prometheus with earth that still kept some traces of the 'seed divine', mixing it with rainwater 'in effigiem moderantum cuncta deorum' ([in] likeness of the gods that govern the world).[3]

The combination of Platonic terminology (which will of course also return in Apuleius, where the Demiurge is called *fabricator*)[4] and an annotation that corresponded perfectly to the words of the biblical Genesis, in which man and woman were made 'in the image and likeness' of God, ensured the fortune of Ovid's story for centuries to come, from Giovanni del Virgilio to Boccaccio, from Francis Bacon to George Sandys. A wide range of commentators devoted themselves to interpreting the *integumenta Ovidii*, the veils that even in the perturbing, pagan *Metamorphoses* were meant to conceal the truth, with Plato as their guide. In the twelfth century, for example, Arnulf of Orléans has no doubts about this in his *Allegoriae*, where he declares, 'Quod caos *in species* in rei veritate fuit, hoc Moyse etiam dicente, unde non indiget expositione' (That chaos was transmuted into forms truly took place—even Moses says so. So, this does not need explanation.) The same applies to man created in the image of God.[5] John of Garland, in the twelfth century, calls the Demiurge, philosophically, *natura generans*.[6] The Third Vatican Mythographer knows much more. He quotes directly from Calcidius's *Timaeus* on the generation of the soul, and contrasts it with the *Phaedo*,[7] referring more than once to Platonic doctrines.

One often has the impression of close hand-to-hand combat between the reasons of myth and poetry on the one hand, those of philosophy on the other, and those of theology on yet another. Giovanni del Virgilio, the scholar of Latin who taught at Bologna and kept up a correspondence in the form of Eclogues with Dante, limits himself to noting that there are, at the beginning, two *transmutationes*: the first, from chaos to the four elements, was performed by the 'lord of nature' while shaping the whole 'summe pietatis amore', for love of supreme piety; the second, from earth to man, by Prometheus. On this, however, Giovanni offers two possible explanations, one theological, where 'Prometheus' is interpreted as the *provisio* 'of the mind of God'; the other, between philosophy and Scripture, according to which Prometheus is a 'philosopher who thought man came from the earth and a soul was breathed into him from heaven'.[8] Pierre Bersuire, the Benedictine humanist who knew Petrarch and placed an *Ovidius moralizatus* at the end of his *Reductorium morale*, is much more 'pious' in his interpretations, which oscillate continuously between the moralising and the mystical. On the Beginning, the only point of particular curiosity is his claim that Ovid treated the Creation according to 'the belief of Anaxagoras'.[9]

At the beginning of the fifteenth century, in England, Thomas Walsingham composed a *De archana deorum* inspired fundamentally by

Ovid, in which he has very little to say about his cosmogony other than to reiterate, in the words of the Creed, his faith 'in unum deum celi et terrae, rerum omnium visibilium et invisibilium creatorem'.[10] Much more articulate is his compatriot George Sandys, who in 1632 published a complete translation of the *Metamorphoses* accompanied by a substantial English commentary for which he declared he was 'much indebted to *Plato*, the poeticall Philosopher'.[11] It is worth reading at least part of the first chapter of the commentary to understand how the *Timaeus* is at the centre of his inspiration:

> Then hee proceeds to the description of that confused Masse, which the Platonists call the undigested World, as the world the digested *Chaos*: ordered, as they say by *Love*; who raised the heavy, illuminated the obscure, quickned the dead, gave forme to the deformed, and perfection to the imperfect: which was no other then that harmony in Nature created by the Almighties *Fiat*. And although by not expressing the originall he seemes to intimate the eternitie of his *Chaos*: yet appeares in the rest so consonant to the truth, as doubtlesse he had either seene the Books of *Moses*, or receaved that doctrine by tradition. He confesseth God, not disguizing his name (as observed by *Lactantius*) to be the Creator of the World & maker of all things: and by that word *Commanded*, so often reiterated, that hee made them by his Word only.[12]

The most fascinating and even amusing case is that of Giovanni Boccaccio, who tackles the problem of the first divinities with firm determination at the beginning of his *Genealogie deorum gentilium*. Boccaccio possessed a culture of classical myths and texts greatly superior to that of most of his contemporaries and he had studied the authors and texts in depth. He placed at the end of his *Genealogies* two books, the fourteenth and fifteenth, devoted to a 'Defence of Poetry', in which he went so far as to claim that poetry has a divine origin and that pagan poets are theologians of myth.[13] At the beginning of the book, he has the brilliant idea of reproducing the second chapter of Aristotle's *Metaphysics* in dramatic form, pretending he is meeting the earliest philosophers and asking them who they believe was the first god. Thales replies that it was water;

Anaximenes, air; Alcmaeon, the sky and the stars. Macrobius, the youngest, replies, 'The sun.' The modern Theodontius(?), 'Earth'. Then Boccaccio considers the poets. But the candidate supported by those who believe in water with Thales is Ocean. Those who follow Anaximenes and Chrysippus think rather of Jupiter as the origin of fire and air. However, each of these indications runs into one or more objections. Ocean, for example, is held by some to be the son of Caelus, Jupiter of Ether or Saturn: they cannot therefore be the first gods. Boccaccio then accepts Theodontius' proposal: the divine mind mixed with the earth that produces everything is Demogorgon.[14]

Demogorgon: a terrible name (*daemon* + *gorgon*) for a hideous being, shrouded in mist and darkness, smelling strongly of damp earth. He was invented, says Theodontius, by the ancient peasants of Arcadia, and his name, according to Leontius Pilatus, means 'God' or 'wisdom of the earth'. Well, this Demogorgon is none other than the Demiurge of the *Timaeus*. The deity whose name it is unlawful to know appears in two passages by Lucan and Statius.[15] Lactantius, commenting on the *Thebaid*, declares, 'Dicit deum *demiourgon*'.[16] But the copyist, ignorant of Greek, transcribes it as 'demogorgon'. And so, as C. S. Lewis noted, this was perhaps 'the only case in which a scribe's blunder gave rise to a true apotheosis'.[17]

Boccaccio is known, as Bacon would later be in *De sapientia veterum*, for arguing that allegories are not always fictitious, imposed from the outside: 'parables', Bacon writes, have a dual function, for they 'serve as well to instruct or illustrate as to wrap up and envelop', to disguise and veil the meaning, and they serve also to clear and throw light upon it'.[18]

And it is Plato himself, and precisely in the *Timaeus*, who provides us with an example. We are in the first part of the dialogue. Socrates asks Critias about the strange story he had promised to reveal to them. So Critias recounts what his grandfather had told him, when he was ten, of Solon's visit to Egypt and his conversation with Egyptian priests. He tells them about Phoroneus, 'the first human being, it is said', and about the flood and Deucalion and Pyrrha. Speaking of the most ancient things the Greeks remember, Solon tries to lead the priests on to do the same. One of the oldest interrupts him to exclaim, 'Ah, Solon,

Solon, you Greeks are never anything but children, and there is not an old man among you.' Then, pressed, he continues, 'I mean to say [. . .] that in mind you are all young.' The Greeks have no remembrance of any 'old opinion handed down among you by ancient tradition', no 'science which is hoary with age'. Many disasters, mostly brought on by fire or water, says the old man, have struck men in the past and will strike them again in the future.

> There is a story which even you have preserved, that once upon a time Phaethon, the son of Helios, having yoked the steeds in his father's chariot, because he was not able to drive them in the path of his father, burned up all that was upon the earth, and was himself destroyed by a thunderbolt. Now this has the form of a myth [mythoû skhêma], but really signifies [to de alethes esti] a declination of the bodies moving in the heavens around the earth, and a great conflagration of things upon the earth which recurs after long intervals.[19]

Plato knows how to play the part of Ovid, who narrates the myth of Phaeton in Book 2 of the *Metamorphoses,* adding the Egyptian patina of 'learning made hoary by time'. He also knows how to be a commentator on Ovid *avant la lettre*. And Ovid, who has Pythagoras, Plato's ancestor, give a lengthy speech at the end of the *Metamorphoses,* seems to have understood what Plato meant. After Plato, it would take almost one thousand five hundred years for someone to explain Phaeton's fable 'scientifically' in this way; and then it would not be in one of the various *Integumenta Ovidii,* but in William of Conches's commentary on the *Timaeus.*[20]

5

Descendants and Intermediaries

FROM THE *TIMAEUS* comes almost everything worth remembering: the way the cosmos came into being and was organised, its characteristic union of beauty and goodness. What could Aristotle and Philo of Alexandria, Augustine and Boethius, and many, many others up to modern times, have written without the *Timaeus*? I will provide a brief initial family tree, which will later expand into a leafy canopy.

Philo of Alexandria, the Jewish exegete who was the first to build up a systematic allegorical interpretation of the Bible, defines God the creator in Genesis with the words used by Plato for the Demiurge in the *Timaeus*: *poietès kai patér*, 'maker and father'.[1] In fact he platonises, or, if I may use this expression, 'timaeises' the whole of Creation.[2] Lactantius, Constantine's advisor and a key figure in early Christianity, repeats three times in the *Divinae institutiones* that Plato, 'considered by all the wisest of all philosophers', 'openly affirms the rule of one (*monarchiam*) and calls him neither aether, nor reason nor nature, but god, and that by him this perfect, wonderful world was created'.[3] From Philo the method and details of the operation are handed down to the Christian authors of the first centuries—I will skip some of the intermediate stages for now—and on to reach Augustine.[4] He reads the *Timaeus* in Cicero's version and is familiar with Calcidius's commentary. After meditating for nearly thirty years on the many problems of the Creation—from *De Genesi contra Manicheos* to *De Genesi ad litteram imperfectum*, from books 11–13 of the *Confessions* to *De Genesi ad litteram*—Augustine returns to them one last time in books 11–12 of *De civitate Dei*, and focuses among other things on Plato's chronology. 'Moreover some of those who are our fellows in the grace of Christ', he writes, 'are astonished when they hear or read that Plato had views about God which they can see are in close agreement with the truth of our religion.' This led them to think the philosopher must have met and listened to the prophet Jeremiah and read the books of the prophets during his journey to Egypt. Instead, according to a more accurate calculation, Augustine continues, there is a difference of one hundred years between the prophet and the philosopher (at least twice as many, in reality), and furthermore, the Greek translation of the Bible ordered by Ptolemy II Philadelphus, the so-called Septuagint or Bible of the Seventy, was still a long way off. So Plato could not have met Jeremiah or read the Scriptures. At least unless, 'perhaps, because he was an eager student, he studied them by means of an interpreter', as he had for the writings of the Egyptians:

> Hoc ut existimetur, illa suadere videntur indicia, quod liber geneseos sic incipit: *In principio fecit Deus caelum et terram. Terra autem erat invisibilis et incomposita, et tenebrae erant super abyssum, et spiritus Dei superferebatur super aquas*; in Timaeo autem Plato, quem librum de mundi constitutione conscripsit, Deum dicit in illo opere terram primo ignemque iunxisse. Manifestum est autem quod igni tribuat caeli locum: habet ergo haec sententia quandam illius similitudinem qua dictum est: *In principio fecit Deus caelum et terram*. Deinde ille duo media, quibus interpositis sibimet haec extrema copularentur, aquam dicit et aerem; unde putatur sic intellexisse quod scriptum est: *spiritus Dei superferebatur super aquam*.

> (Certain indications seem to support this supposition. For example, the book of Genesis begins with the words: 'In the beginning God created the heaven and the earth. And the earth was invisible and without form, and darkness was over the abyss, and the spirit of God moved over the waters.' Moreover, in the *Timaeus,* his treatise on the formation of the universe, Plato says that God in this operation first united earth and fire. But it is clear that he assigns to fire the region of heaven. So this opinion bears a certain resemblance to the statement: 'In the beginning God created the heaven and the earth.'

> Next Plato speaks of the two elements, water and air, which by their intermediate position form a bond between the two extremes. This prompts the thought that he so understood the scriptural words: 'The spirit of God moved over the waters.')[5]

In fact, air is also called spirit, so Plato may have thought that the verse in Genesis referred to all four of the elements. Then there is the fact that Plato goes on to affirm that the true philosopher is one who loves God,[6] 'and nothing is put with more burning eloquence in those sacred scriptures'. Finally, one particular passage inclines Augustine almost to think that Plato was not unaware of the Bible: this is when Moses who had asked the name of the God who was ordering him to go to Egypt to deliver his people receives the anwer, 'I AM THAT I AM: and he said, Thus shalt thou say unto the children of Israel, I AM hath sent me unto you.'[7] As if, Augustine comments, 'in comparison with him who really is because he is unchangeable, things which have been created subject to change have no being. This tenet Plato strenuously upheld and most earnestly urged upon others.'[8]

In short, Augustine really believes Plato may have known the Bible, and is ready to interpret the sacred text in such a way that it agrees with the *Timaeus*. At least thirty times in his works he quotes from this particular dialogue in Cicero's version,[9] and uses it as a yardstick in addressing a whole series of difficult problems such as the eternity of God, time, and matter.[10]

6

Rachel's Beauty

AT THE END OF THE LAST three days of Creation, God looks at what he has done and decides it is 'good'. The Hebrew for that is *tov*, meaning primarily 'good' but including the notion of 'beautiful' in a sort of *kalokágathon avant la lettre*. But when the Seventy translated the Bible into Greek in Alexandria, the word they chose was simply *kalón*, which privileges beauty over goodness. Jerome restored the original *bonum*, but the *pulchritude* of the universe had been affirmed once and for all, and its history goes down the millennia, to Dante, as we shall see, and beyond.

The Hebrew Bible, contrary to what most people think, teems with beauty. Extraordinarily beautiful, in fact literally 'wonder-ful', is the cosmos created by God. And some human beings, both women and men, have the special gift—natural, but clearly mirroring a supernatural blessing—of beauty, generally expressed by a word related to *yāpheh*. Five ladies stand out in this respect—Sarah, Rebekah, Rachel, Esther and the Bride of the Song of Songs. To the first two, comeliness causes quite a few problems. Sarah, Abraham's wife, is *y*[e]*phat-mar'eh*, which the Seventy translate as *euprósopos*, and in the Vulgate is simply *pulchra*. Robert Alter uses 'beautiful', too, and the occasion is a memorable one, because the word is spoken by Abraham as he and Sarah go to Egypt to find food in a time of famine. Abraham says,

> Look, I know you are a beautiful woman, and so when the Egyptians see you and say, 'She is his wife', they will kill me while you they will

> let live. Say, please, that you are my sister, so that it will go well with me on your count and I shall stay alive because of you.[1]

The erotic undertones of the story are pretty obvious, and the text plays on them with great subtlety. Pharaoh's courtiers don't fail to notice Sarah's beauty and praise her to him, so that Sarah is 'taken into Pharaoh's house'. All does indeed go well with Abraham, and he receives sheep, cattle and camels. But God afflicts the house of Pharaoh with plagues because of Sarah. Things get clearer only at the end, for Pharaoh summons Abraham and reproaches him for saying Sarah was his sister, 'so that I took her to me as wife'. 'Now, here is your wife. Take her, and get out.' Genesis doesn't tell us what exactly happened in Pharaoh's harem, and we can speculate at leisure on alternative sequences of events, from the most to the least erotic.

Something similar happens to Isaac and Rebekah, even though she is not beautiful, but 'very comely to look at', as the narrator describes her on her first appearance, with a jug on her shoulder.[2] When, again because of a famine, Isaac and his wife go to Gerar, to Abimelech king of the Philistines, he tells the locals Rebekah is his sister for fear they would kill him seeing his wife is 'comely to look at' (ṭōbat mar'eh).[3] Things, however, go differently this time. One day, King Abimelech looks out of the window, and 'there was Isaac playing with Rebekah his wife'. There can be no possible doubt as to what kind of 'playing' they are engaged in,[4] such that Abimelech reprimands Isaac: 'What is this you have done to us? One of the people might well have lain with your wife and you would have brought guilt upon us.' He then commands his subjects upon pain of death not to touch the couple. Isaac, meanwhile, prospers.

Once more there is fear, once more there is eros—actually, this time, sex proper. Nothing of the kind with the most fascinating young woman of the Bible, Rachel. The beginning of her story is enchanting. Jacob, obeying Isaac's orders, travels all the way from Canaan to the land of his relatives, Paddan-Aram, to the house of Bethuel, his mother's father, 'to take from there a wife from the daughters of Laban', his mother's brother. He has already stolen the blessing from Esau and they have separated. On the way to Haran, he has a momentous dream—a ladder reaching from the ground to the heavens, with angels going up and down, and God poised over him, blessing him with the words, 'I, the Lord, am the God of Abraham your father and the God of Isaac. The land on which you lie, to you I will give it and to your seed.'[5] This is a second, and greater, blessing Jacob receives.The following day, as he approaches Paddan-Aram, he sees a well, and flocks of sheep waiting to be watered, and men who should remove the huge stone on the well's mouth. He addresses them, and Rachel appears:

> And Jacob said to them, 'My brothers, where are you from?' And they said, 'We are from Haran.' And he said to them, 'Do you know Laban son of Nahor?' And they said, 'We know him.' And he said to them, 'Is he well?' And they said, 'He is well, and, look, Rachel his daughter is coming with the sheep.' And he said, 'Look, the day is still long. It is not time to gather in the herd. Water the sheep and take them to graze.' And they said, 'We cannot until all the flocks have gathered and the stone is rolled from the mouth of the well and we water the sheep.' He was still speaking with them when Rachel came with her father's sheep, for she was a shepherdess. And it happened when Jacob saw Rachel daughter of Laban his mother's brother and the sheep of Laban his mother's brother that he stepped forward and rolled the stone from the mouth of the well and watered the sheep of Laban his mother's brother. And Jacob kissed Rachel and lifted his voice and wept.[6]

The scene is quietly pastoral from beginning to end. But nothing in it is left to chance even though it might appear otherwise. To Jacob's first questions, the men around the well answer briefly and precisely: they are from Haran, they know Laban, he is well. As they say this: they add, 'and, look, Rachel his daughter is coming with the sheep'. This comes as a surprise, though it doesn't seem to have any effect on Jacob, since he goes on to suggest it is too early to gather in the herd and the sheep should be left to graze. While he is still speaking, Rachel the shepherdess enters the scene. Not a word is said of her physical appearance, but her presence changes everything. Jacob forgets his earlier suggestions and, now that all the flock is gathered, accomplishes what Alter calls the

'Homeric feat' of lifting the huge stone from the mouth of the well all by himself. He kisses Rachel (the text, we are told, is punning on 'kissing' and 'watering') and bursts into tears. His emotions are revealed only indirectly: first, it is only when he sees Rachel that, suddenly Herculean, he lifts the stone, as if shot through by a discharge of lightning; then the reactions of kiss and tears follow—natural releases for having finally met one of Laban's daughters, the original purpose of his long journey. Or is there something else?

Something has happened to Jacob during that meeting which will become clear only afterwards, when, the sequence of events now accelerating, Rachel runs to Laban to give him the news and Laban runs out to meet his nephew. It is at this point only that the narrator sees fit to allude to Rachel's physical appearance. When Laban offers to pay wages to Jacob even though he is his kin, the text tells us, 'And Laban had two daughters. The name of the elder was Leah and the name of the younger Rachel. And Leah's eyes were tender, but Rachel was comely in features and comely to look at, and Jacob loved Rachel.'[7]

So, it's finally out. Rachel is, the text asserts, 'yᵉphat-tō'ar wîphat mar'eh'. The Seventy translate 'kalè tô eídei kaì horaía tê ópsei'. Jerome opts for 'decora facie et venusto aspectu', a pretty weak rendering. Rachel is *beautiful*. The Greek makes this explicit, but the Hebrew specifies that her comeliness is a question both of 'features' or 'forms' and of looks. She is doubly beautiful. Rachel, a mere shepherdess, is the Hebrew Bible's Helen, or Cassandra, but without any of the fearsome aspects associated with them, and without the golden aura conferred on them by Aphrodite. In a way, she resembles the equally beautiful, but more human and frailer, Andromache. Her beauty has the appeal of homeliness and tenderness.

And love. Within the same sentence, Genesis also states that Jacob loved her. It reminds one of Pierre Bezuhov's realization, at the end of Tolstoy's *War and Peace*, when he sees Natasha again after a long time: 'It was Natasha, and he loved her.'[8] Jacob loves at first sight, one might say, but for that love he is prepared to work for Laban fourteen years, and he will treasure it in his heart forever. And Rachel's beauty will be transmitted to her son Joseph, 'comely in features and comely to look at', a fact that will undoubtedly help his rise in Egypt but which will also provoke the assault by Potiphar's wife immediately afterwards in the narrative.[9] Rachel is beautiful, but sterile for a long time, and short-lived, for she dies giving birth to her second son, Benjamin. Beauty exacts a terrible price.

Rachel's beauty is supreme, though humble. It is shared by Esther—the Ishtar and the Star of Israel—in almost exactly the same terms,[10] but her story is far too complex and dramatic to be examined here. Bathsheba and Queen Vashti share some of the same qualities,[11] but the erotic implications of their stories are so strong as to ruin them. David passionately loves Bathsheba as soon as he sees her, makes her pregnant and has her husband Uriah killed in battle by asking for him to be positioned in the front line against the enemy. King Ahasuerus, protagonist of the Esther story, is half drunk one night and voyeuristically wants Vashti, his first queen, to show off her beauty 'to the peoples and the ministers'. When she refuses to comply, she is banished. Saul, David and Adonaijah are also beautiful, the first being 'goodlier' than all the Israelites, the second a lad 'with good looks', the third 'very goodly of appearance'.[12] Considering their subsequent careers, this kind of beauty will turn out to be, as for Bathsheba and Vashti, a curse rather than a blessing.

The beauty of the universe praised in the Septuagint translation of *tov* in Genesis emerges powerfully in the Wisdom Books, with a proper cosmic resonance in the 'wonders' performed by God; for instance in Psalms 19, 78 and 104:

> The heavens tell God's glory,
> and his handiwork sky declares.
> Day to day breathes utterance
> and night to night pronounces knowledge.
> There is no utterance, and there are no words,
> their voice is never heard.[13]

Psalm 19 begins with a marvellous paradox: the heavens celebrate God's glory by speaking, but in total silence. The firmament doesn't need a voice, it 'pronounces knowledge' simply by displaying its beauty. It will acquire a sound—and what sound!—only in Haydn's oratorio *The*

Creation, where Psalm 19 is sung by the choir of angels and archangels immediately after the creation of sun, moon and stars on the fourth day.

In Psalm 78 the perspective is historical rather than astronomical, for the poetry sums up the *Heilsgeschichte*, the sacred history above all of Exodus. I quote only a few lines from this long narrative (seventy-two verses) recounting the 'wonders' performed by the Lord for Israel's salvation and survival:

> He split open the sea and let them pass through,
> He made water stand up like a heap
> And He led them with the cloud by day
> and all night long with the light of fire.
> He split apart rocks in the wilderness
> and gave drink as from the great deep.[14]

Yet the cosmic magnificence, the 'grandeur and glory', returns fully in Psalm 104, where imagination and language are perfectly matched:

> Wrapped in night like a cloak,
> stretching out heavens like a tent cloth.
> Setting beams for His lofts in the waters,
> making His chariot the clouds,
> He goes on the wings of the wind.
> He makes His messengers the winds,
> His ministers, glowing fire.[15]

This type of 'Wisdom Sublime' returns in the *mirabilia Dei* celebrated by Elihu in the Book of Job,[16] and is magnified with thundering voice out of the whirlwind by God himself for two entire chapters.[17] What prevails here is the 'terribilità of things and of God that Michelangelo was to represent in the Sistine Ceiling, according to Vasari,[18] and the properly 'awesome' quality of the cosmic beauty created by the Almighty.

The quieter, but equally sublime conclusion of the Wisdom Books on beauty is to be found in the third chapter of Ecclesiastes, the one which famously begins with 'a time to be born and a time to die'. Verse 11 sums it all up with ''et-hakkōl 'āśāh yāpheh b^{e}'ittō', where the Seventy catch both the beauty and the *kairós*, or right time, dear to classical

Greek culture: 'sỳn tà pànta epoíesen kalà en kairô autoû'. Jerome replaces both *yāpheh* and *kalá* with *bona*: 'cuncta fecit bona in tempore suo'. He, too, doesn't seem aware that Ecclesiastes is stressing the pulchritude of the cosmos created, and being continuously created 'at the right time', by God.[19]

However, the Wisdom Books contain one more kind of beauty, more similar to Rachel's than to the marvels of God. It is the unforgettable beauty of the Bride in the Song of Songs, to which I will also return in a later chapter: 'O you are fair, my friend, O you are fair'. Once more the original, 'hinnāk yāphāh, ra'yātî, hinnāk yāphāh', has the key word for beauty, *yāphāh,* and for once the Vulgate and the Seventy get it straight: 'quam pulchra es amica mea quam pulchra es', writes Jerome; 'idoù eî kalé, he plesíon mou, idoù eî kalé', the Seventy translate.[20] It is one of the most poignant, moving and beautiful lines of the Hebrew Bible, and one doesn't need an exegete to understand the attributes of that beauty—eyes like doves, lips like a scarlet thread, cheekbones like cut pomegranate, breasts 'like two fawns, twins of a gazelle, that graze among the lilies'. Whatever allegorical interpretation one wishes to superimpose on the text, the Bride's beauty spreads around it a pure, perfumed feeling of eros which any human being can perceive as inherent to beauty and even—were she or he thus inclined—translate it into mystical *agape* or *charitas*. One can for a moment imagine Jacob singing that song to Rachel![21]

One final example from the Prophets will round up this short 'aesthetic' review of the Hebrew Bible. This is a passage in Isaiah 52, where the feet of the messenger are praised as 'lovely': 'mah-nā'wû 'al-hehārîm raglê m^{e}baśśēr mašmî^{a}' šālôm':

How lovely on the mountains
the steps of the bearer of good tidings,
announcing peace, heralding good things,
announcing triumph,
saying to Zion: Your God reigns.[22]

Many years ago, in a seminal essay significantly entitled 'What is Beautiful?', Harold Fisch maintained that 'beauty in the Bible is an elusive quality' and, after discussing some of the passages I myself have cited, came to examine Isaiah 52. He quoted critics who had considered it 'a scene of breathtaking beauty', then offered his own comment. 'If we think of this scene in terms of the art of painting', he wrote, 'then the figure representing the messenger will have to be striving for something outside the painting, some yet-to-be disclosed image of glad tidings.' Words like 'peace', 'good' and 'victory', he continued, intimate something of the nature of the tidings, but the ultimate climax is in the final phrase, 'saying to Zion: Your God reigns'. 'This is not merely beyond the frame of the picture; it seems to set aside all mere pictures', Fisch goes on; 'it transcends and, in a manner, it abolishes the category of the beautiful.' This is not 'because we are beyond visible beauty in some region of abstraction', since in the following verse we are told, 'For with their very eyes they shall see when the Lord comes back to Zion'. Visibility, in other words, remains, but 'beauty is the thread on which salvation is strung'.[23]

I don't agree that 'beauty in the Bible is an elusive quality', and I have tried to show that it is not: Sarah, Rebekah, above all Rachel and Esther, are real characters. The Bride's beauty is perfect. The staggering, at times terrible, beauty of the cosmos is shown to us many times. It might all be less obviously visible than in Greek culture, yes. It is 'the thread on which salvation is strung', yes. But that is precisely it: the beauty of the messenger's feet running over the mountains was clearly appreciated by Georg Friedrich Handel, who, superimposing Romans 10:15 on Isaiah 52:7, turned it into one of the sweetest, most moving arias in the second part of the *Messiah*: 'How beautiful are the feet of those that preach the gospel of peace and bring tidings of good things!' But Isaiah's passage itself has a kinematic quality in both space and time, absent elsewhere, and projects itself from the present to the future, when the tidings become announcement. Perhaps the announcement of Prince Myshkin in Dostoevsky's *The Idiot*: 'mir spaset krasota'—Beauty will save the world.[24]

7

The Lilies of the Field

'FROM WHAT SOURCE, then, did the beauty of Helen whom men fought for shine out, or that of all the women like Aphrodite in beauty?' Plotinus wondered. 'Then again, what is the source of the beauty of Aphrodite herself, or of any other beautiful human being or of any god of those who appear visibly, or even of those who do not appear but have in themselves a beauty which could be seen?' After discussing sensible beauty, Plotinus begins to address the issue of intelligible beauty, answering the question he has just put as follows: 'In all these is it not the Idea, something of that realm but communicated to the produced from within the producer just as in works of art, we held, it is communicated from the artists to their creations?'[1] Plotinus, the Neoplatonist who settled in Rome and whose work has reached us thanks to his disciple Porphyry; Plotinus, who speaks of the many times when, after waking from his slumber and estranging himself completely from all external things, he has had a vision of divine beauty: 'I have seen a beauty wonderfully great and felt assurance that then most of all I belonged to the better part'; that he had 'come to identity with the divine'.[2] On the very same page he evokes Heraclitus, Empedocles and above all 'the illustrious Plato' and his theory of the soul's descent from heaven in the *Timaeus*.

Plotinus, who alludes specifically to the *Timaeus*, or quotes it continuously, is the great theoriser of the One, the Soul, the Intelligence and rapture: a thinker and mystic who places Beauty at the centre of his reflections and devotes dazzling pages to the subject. Like this, in which he takes a sharp jab at his venerated Plato, turning his positions upside down:

> But if anyone despises the arts because they produce their works by imitating nature, we must tell him, first, that natural things are imitations too. Then he must know that the arts do not simply imitate what they see, but they run back up to the forming principles from which nature derives; then also that they do a great deal by themselves, and, since they possess beauty, they make up what is defective in things. For Pheidias too did not make his Zeus from any model perceived by the senses, but understood what Zeus would look like if he wanted to make himself visible.[3]

Plotinus is a master in using Greek myth and poetry to support his theories. When, in the first *Ennead,* he discusses Beauty in depth, he preaches flight from the beauty of bodies towards 'that which they image'. If someone wanted to clutch the image as if it was real he would be like Narcissus, who through his desire to grasp a beautiful image reflected in the water ended up by sinking into the stream and disappearing. No, one must act not like Narcissus, but like Ulysses:

> 'Let us fly to our dear country'. What then is our way of escape, and how are we to find it? We shall put out to sea, as Odysseus did, from the witch Circe or Calypso—as the poet says (I think with a hidden meaning)—and was not content to stay though he had delights of the eyes and lived among much beauty of sense. Our country from which we came is there, our Father is there.[4]

No, not like Narcissus: not the grandeur of the object, but the contemplation of wisdom. Of course, nature too is beautiful:

> But certainly nature which produces such beautiful works is far before them in beauty, but we, because we are not accustomed to see any of the things within and do not know them, pursue the external and do not know that it is that within which moves us: as if someone looking at his image and not knowing where it came from should pursue it. But the beauty also in studies and ways of life and generally

> in souls makes clear that what is pursued is something else and that beauty does not lie in magnitude: it is truly a greater beauty than that when you see moral sense in someone and delight in it, not looking at his face—which might be ugly—but putting aside all shape and pursuing his inner beauty.[5]

Plotinus is at the origin of medieval aesthetics:[6] as André Grabar has convincingly demonstrated, especially but not only of Byzantine aesthetics, especially but not only of its realisation in works of art that were actually produced. I wonder then how Plotinus would have reacted to the two ideals of beauty implicitly proclaimed by the Christian Gospels, that of the lilies of the field, and that of the Transfiguration?

To start with, let us consider the first of these. In the synoptic Gospels of Matthew and Luke, there is a point in which Jesus dwells, with exceptional delicacy and tenderness, on the lilies of the field. In Matthew, this occurs after the Beatitudes, after his speech on the fulfilment of the Law, after his teaching of the 'Our Father', in the midst of a series of recommendations to the disciples:

> Therefore I say unto you, Take no thought for your life, what ye shall eat, or what ye shall drink; nor yet for your body, what ye shall put on. Is not the life more than meat, and the body than raiment? Behold the fowls of the air: for they sow not, neither do they reap, nor gather into barns; yet your heavenly Father feedeth them. Are ye not much better than they? Which of you by taking thought, can add one cubit unto his stature? And why take ye thought for raiment? Consider the lilies of the field, how they grow; they toil not, neither do they spin: And yet I say unto you, That even Solomon in all his glory was not arrayed like one of these. Wherefore, if God so clothe the grass of the field, which today is, and tomorrow is cast into the oven, shall he not much more clothe you, O ye of little faith?[7]

It is clear that the main concern in Jesus's words is to recommend abandoning oneself to Divine Providence and renouncing any thought of foreseeing and providing for one's material needs: food, drink and clothing. But an aesthetic touch is also present: the lilies of the field possess a *dóxa* superior to that of Solomon, adorned in kingly splendour. Their 'glory' is naked, elementary, natural: it is a simple, primal beauty. And transient; because the Gospel adds, with an eye to Psalm 90, that the grass of the field 'is today, and tomorrow is cast into the oven'.

The exegesis of the passage must have begun very early, if we find it recalled in a passage from Clement of Alexandria's *Paedagogus*, which focuses above all on luxury in clothing.[8] 'What, I ask, [is] more graceful, more gay-coloured, than flowers?' Clement wonders. 'What, I say, [is] more delightful than lilies or roses?'[9] The word Clement uses for 'more graceful', *horaióteron*, comes from the *horaiótes* of Isaiah 44:13, where it indicates the beauty of a man.

The lilies of the field take on an aesthetic quality. This is achieved conclusively in a passage from Ambrose's *Exaemeron* where they appear in a comment on a verse in Genesis (1:11): 'Let the earth bring forth grass, the herb yielding seed, and the fruit tree yielding fruit after his kind.' Citing Virgil, Cicero and Pliny the Elder, Ambrose launches immediately into a lengthy technico-poetical explanation of the transformation of seed into grain, and then green shoot into leaf and ear. The *Georgics* are not far away. In the end, his speech becomes a veritable paean to the field in full bloom:

> Quae uero species pleni agri, qui odor, quae suauitas, quae uoluptas agricolarum! Quid digne explicare possimus, si nostro utamur adloquio? Sed habemus scripturae testimonia, quibus agri suauitatem benedictioni et gratiae sanctorum aduertimus comparatam dicente sancto Isaac: *Odor filii mei odor agri pleni.*[10] Quid igitur describam purpurescentes uiolas, candida lilia, rutilantes rosas, depicta rura nunc aureis, nunc uariis, nunc luteis floribus, in quibus nescias utrum species amplius florum an uis odora delectant? Pascuntur oculi grato spectaculo, longe lateque odor spargitur, cuius suauitate complemur. Vnde digne dominus ait: *Et species agri mecum est.*[11] Cum ipso est enim quam ipse formauit; quis enim alius artifex posset tantam rerum singularum exprimere uenustatem? *Considerate lilia agri*, quantus sit candor in foliis, quemadmodum stipata ipsa folia ab imo ad summum uideantur adsurgere, ut scyphi exprimant formam, ut auri quaedam

species intus effulgeat, quae tamen uallo in circuitu floris obsaepta nulli pateat iniuriae. Si quis hunc florem decerpat et sua soluat in folia, quae tanti est artificis manus, quae possit lilii speciem reformare?

Quis tantus imitator naturae, ut florem hunc redintegrare praesumat, cui dominus tantum testimonium tulit, ut diceret: *Nec Solomon in omni gloria sic uestiebatur sicut unum ex istis*? Rex opulentissimus et sapientissimus inferior iudicatur quam huius floris est pulchritudo.

(When the land, in fact, is completely stocked, how can we, if we are to rely on our tongue, satisfactorily describe the pleasant sights and scents and the joys of the countryman? But we have the testimony of the Scripture, wherein we note that the delights of the countryside are compared to the blessing and grace of the saints, for Isaac, a holy man, says: 'The smell of my son is the smell of a plentiful field.' How can I describe the violets with their shades of purple, the lilies of brilliant white, and the roses with their shades of red? How describe the landscape painted with flowers, sometimes of a golden hue or of varied colors or of bright yellow, among which you cannot decide whether their beauty or their fragrant scent gives more delight. Our eyes revel in this pleasant spectacle as that fragrance which fills us with its sweetness is spread far and wide. Whence the Lord has justly said: 'And with me is the beauty of the field.' This beauty is with Him because He has created it. What other artist could so depict such charm in each and every object? 'Consider the lilies of the field,' what brilliance in their petals, how they appear to arise in packed rows all the way to the top so as to form a goblet! Note how within it gleams like gold, and, furthermore, how around its edge as a defense against any injury a kind of rampart is constructed! If any one were to pluck this flower and take each petal apart, what craftsman's hand is so expert as to be able to restore the form of the lily? Who is such an effective imitator of nature as to presume to reconstruct this flower, to which the Lord has so borne testimony as to say: 'Not even Solomon in all his glory was so arrayed like one of these'? A king so rich and wise was deemed inferior to the beauty of this flower!)[12]

This is a masterly exercise in rhetoric and poetry, which even includes a double comparison between human artist and divine Creator. When he reaches the lilies, Ambrose turns painter, and lo and behold, the white petals take the shape of a chalice, gleaming like gold inside. At the end, the *testimonium*, God's recognition, seals the whole with its last word: *pulchritudo*, beauty.

Pulchritudo, yes: as humble as you like, but not too humble either, as we see from reading Ambrose. What of Plotinus, then? Where has the Neoplatonic philosopher gone, the passionate devotee of Beauty? Plotinus did not disdain the humble beauty of flowers; in the third *Ennead* he proclaims with great clarity that in the universal order even the most insignificant details matter and that

> the art is wonderful which appears, not only in the divine beings but also in the things which one might have supposed providence would have despised for their smallness, for example, the workmanship which produces wonders in rich variety in ordinary animals, and the beauty of appearance which extends to the fruits and even the leaves of plants, and their beauty of flower which comes so effortlessly, and their delicacy and variety.[13]

Augustine, shrewd and sagacious, grasped the coincidence without a moment's hesitation and transformed Plotinus's beauty into the *pulchritudo* of his own master, Ambrose. This is what he wrote in *De civitate Dei*:

> De providentia certe Plotinus Platonicus disputat eamque a summo Deo, cuius est intelligibilis atque ineffabilis pulchritudo, usque ad haec terrena et ima pertingere flosculorum atque foliorum pulchritudine comprobat; quae omnia quasi abiecta et velocissime pereuntia decentissimos formarum suarum numeros habere non posse confirmat, nisi inde formentur, ubi forma intelligibilis et incommutabilis simul habens omnia perseverat. Hoc Dominus Iesus ibi ostendit, ubi ait: *Considerate lilia agri, non laborant neque nent. Dico autem vobis, quia nec Salomon in tota gloria sua sic amictus est, sicut unum ex eis. Quod si faenum agri, quod hodie est et cras in clibanum mittitur, Deus sic vestit: quanto magis vos, modicae fidei?*

(Providence is without doubt a subject that the Platonist Plotinus discusses. He demonstrates that providence reaches down from the most high God, to whom belong intellectual and inexpressible beauty, all the way to things here on earth and proves it by the beauty that is seen in tiny flowers and in leaves. All these, he maintains, inasmuch as they are so lowly and fade so fleetingly, could not possibly have such perfectly designed harmony in their proportions, should they not derive from a region where intellectual and immutable beauty continues to exist while at the same time it dwells in all things. This is what the Lord Jesus points out when he says: 'Consider the lilies of the field; they neither toil nor spin; yet I tell you, even Solomon in all his glory was not arrayed like one of these. But if God so clothes the grass of the field, which today is alive and tomorrow is thrown into the oven, will he not much more clothe you, O men of little faith?')[14]

8

'Mira profunditas'

THE BEAUTY OF AMBROSE AND AUGUSTINE is not only that of the lilies of the field. For the latter, as also for Boethius, a mathematico-musical approach is in order, as emerges forcefully in their respective *De musica* and *De institutione musica* and as has been attentively examined by Edgar De Bruyne.[1] But it is not this that interests me here.[2] It is much more important to me to take another look at Augustine's consideration of Scripture. As is well known, and as Erich Auerbach has reminded us, Augustine is the writer who established once and for all the Christian reaction to the contempt shown by cultured pagans for the low, even sloppy, style of the Bible. Its style is *humilis*, Augustine pointed out, but its content is *sublimis*.[3] The most balanced and articulate passage he wrote on this subject is the final, forty-second chapter of Book 2 of his *De doctrina christiana*, in which he compares the knowledge that may be obtained from pagans to the treasures the Israelites managed to take away from Egypt, and then goes on to extol the riches of Scripture, its admirable depth and its admirable humility, its unfamiliar and ambiguous signs:

> Quantum autem minor est auri, argenti vestisque copia, quam de Aegypto secum ille populus abs tulit, in comparatione divitiarum quas postea Hierosolymae consecutus est, quae maxime in Salomone rege ostenduntur, tanta fit cuncta scientia quae quidem est utilis, collecta de libris Gentium, si divinarum Scripturarum scientiae comparetur. Nam quidquid homo extra didicerit, si noxium est ibi damnatur,

si utile est, ibi invenitur. Et cum ibi quisque invenerit omnia quae utiliter alibi didicit, multo abundantius ibi inveniet ea quae nusquam omnino alibi, sed in illarum tantummodo Scripturarum *mirabili altitudine et mirabili humilitate* discuntur. Hac igitur instructione praeditum cum *signa incognita* lectorem non impedierint, mitem et humilem corde, subiugatum leniter Christo et oneratum sarcina levi, *fundatum et radicatum et aedificatum in caritate quem scientia inflare non possit,* accedat ad *ambigua signa* in Scripturis consideranda et discutienda, de quibus iam tertio volumine dicere aggrediar, quod Dominus donare dignabitur.

(The insignificance of the amount of gold, silver, and clothing which that people took away with it from Egypt, in comparison with the wealth that it later attained in Jerusalem, as shown particularly in the reign of Solomon, is the measure of the insignificance of all knowledge, I mean useful knowledge, that is collected from pagan books, when compared with the knowledge contained in the divine scriptures. For what a person learns independently of scripture is condemned there if it is harmful, but found there if it is useful. And when one has found there all the useful knowledge that can be learnt anywhere else, one will also find there, in much greater abundance, things which are learnt nowhere else at all, but solely in *the remarkable sublimity and the remarkable humility* of the scriptures. Readers furnished with such an education will not be held back by *unfamiliar signs*. Gentle and lowly in heart, peacefully subject to Christ, laden with a light burden, *founded and rooted and built up in love, and incapable of being puffed up by knowledge,* they should now proceed to consider and analyse the *ambiguous signs* in the scriptures, on which I will now endeavour to present, in my third book, such learning as the Lord deigns to deliver to me.)[4]

The biblical *mirabilis altitudo* seems to have nothing to do with Longinus's *Perì hýpsous,* where, however, the beginning of Genesis is proclaimed to be comparable to the sublimity of Homer,[5] paving the way for Robert Lowth's *De sacra poesi hebraeorum* and Coleridge's assertion: 'Sublimity is Hebrew by birth.'[6] But Augustine follows a route of his own towards the new biblical poetics. First, cautiously but with great intelligence, he approaches the figurative language of Scripture, its *figurata locutio*, and its *submissa locutio*, its simple style, recommending extreme prudence in literal and allegorical interpretation.[7] Then, he takes an unexpected leap. We are now in Book 12 of the *Confessions*, the penultimate book of the work, dedicated, like the previous and following ones, to the beginning of Genesis. Once again, Augustine is facing the text that has preoccupied him for decades: in particular, the mystery of the 'heaven of heavens' that Genesis seems to indicate with its very first verse: 'In the beginning God made heaven and earth.' For while the second entity, earth, is certainly material, 'heaven' can indicate both a corporeal and a spiritual dimension: *caelum caeli*, as it is called in the Psalms.

While he passionately debates this issue, along with others, Augustine launches into an exclamation concerning Scripture itself:

> Mira profunditas eloquiorum tuorum, quorum ecce ante nos superficies blandiens parvulis: sed mira profunditas, Deus meus, mira profunditas! Horror est intendere in eam, horror honoris et tremor amoris.
>
> (What extraordinary depth there is in your eloquent words! And look—right in front of us is a surface meaning to charm the immature, but still what extraordinary depth, O my God, what extraordinary depth! It is terrifying to look into that depth, but it is a terror born of reverence, and a trembling born of love.)[8]

An initial distinction, which appears frequently in the *Confessions*, between two levels of Scripture, the *profunditas* and the *superficies*, certainly corresponds 'to the duality between hidden meaning and apparent meaning' commented on by Manlio Simonetti and Jean Pépin.[9] This distinction, already presented and explained in Book 6 (5.8), is not enough, however, to erase the impression that what is being emphasised strongly now is above all depth: a notion that is frequently invoked in relation to the Bible in Augustine, as is confirmed at least twice in his *Enarrationes in Psalmos*. In Scripture, there is a surface that enchants its readers as if they were children, and an abyss of mystery that confounds and terrifies. Indeed, it is looking into this abyss—this *profunditas*—that provokes horror: the 'holy terror' of respect and the trembling of love. Moreover, the sense of horror returns frequently in the *Confessions*: an *effroi* that reflects the pole of the 'tremendum' in Rudolf Otto's famous formula 'mysterium tremendum et fascinans' that defines the sacred.[10]

This, then, is the new Christian sublime of Scripture for Augustine: *profunditas* and *horror*. As it happens, however, there is again a precedent in Plotinus, in the first *Ennead,* dedicated specifically to the Beautiful. If anyone sees the Good, writes Plotinus,

> what passion will he feel, what longing in his desire to be united with it, what a shock of delight! The man who has not seen it may desire it as good, but he who has seen it glories in its beauty and is full of wonder and delight, enduring a shock which causes no hurt, loving with true passion and piercing longing; he laughs at all other loves and despises what he thought beautiful before.[11]

Ascertaining philologically whether Augustine was deliberately echoing Plotinus when he wrote the lines on the *profunditas* and *horror* of Scripture is of little importance. The subjects are after all different. But the emotion is the same—the feeling of being divided when facing the sublime. Hans Urs von Balthasar was right to end his chapter on Augustine by quoting a sentence from his Epistle 138 'ad Marcellinum'. The Creator, wrote von Balthasar, is he who 'guides the ages until the beauty of the universe, whose individual parts consist of the things appropriate to each period, combines in the great song of an incomparable composer: *veluti magnum carmen ineffabilis modulationis*'.[12]

Augustine, the advocate of biblical sublimity, outlines a theology of beauty. When, in Book 11 of the *Confessions,* he addresses the beginning of the Scriptures in Genesis and John, he confesses to God his burning desire to meditate upon his law, admitting both his knowledge and his ignorance of it, the first signs of divine light and the remaining darkness. His chaste delights will therefore be the Scripture: full of unfathomable mysteries, but not without purpose, for God did not want so many pages of 'dark secrets' to be written in vain. Thus, Augustine prays the Lord to reveal these enigmas himself: Moses, who wrote them, is no more, and cannot be questioned. He, Augustine, will listen and understand how, in the beginning, God created heaven and earth, because Truth itself will tell him. Heaven and earth cry out that they were made, because they have changed from what they were before. They cry out, too, that they did not make themselves. Therefore, it is the Lord who created them: 'tu ergo, Domine, fecisti ea, qui pulcher es: pulchra sunt enim; qui bonus es: bona sunt enim; qui es: sunt enim': 'So, Lord, you have made them; and you are beautiful, so they are beautiful; and you are good, so they are good; and you exist, so they exist.' Yet they are neither as beautiful, nor as good, nor as truly real as their Creator. The truth of Moses and of the Scriptures can only be verified by divine Truth. Beauty and goodness are simply an aspect of being: but the dazzling beauty of heaven and earth is not as complete as that of their Creator, because their being is not as complete: 'quid enim est, nisi quia tu es?' This is why God *spoke*, and heaven and earth were created *in* his Word.[13]

Augustine is struggling with the irreducible absoluteness of Scripture, behind which he senses the massive and elusive hand of the beauty, goodness and being of God. This feeling is not so different from the one Pindar gives voice to in the 'Hymn to Zeus' or that Plato articulates in the *Timaeus*, in that it simply expresses the common human perception of the immense force that lies behind the visible universe and that appears to move it. Many exegetes have spoken of the profundity of God and the Scriptures, starting with Jerome, who saw 'the ocean of the Scriptures and the mysteries of God as a labyrinth.'[14] 'Deep sky', 'unfathomable abyss', 'immense sea', 'ocean of mystery': these are expressions of Autpertus, Honorius, Rupert of Deutz, Ambrose, Gregory.[15] In fact, Augustine writes about this very mystery: with both knowledge and ignorance, with the exaltation of one who has understood and the frustration of one who cannot fully comprehend. In him there is none of Pindar's miraculous measure; instead, what we find in him is the tremendous lack of measure of the Bible: the *pavor* and *formido*, the 'fear' and 'terror' that perhaps only Origen had articulated, in his *Homilies on Genesis*:

> Quantum legentes progredimur, tantum nobis sacramentorum cumulus augetur. Et ut si quis exiguo vectus navigio ingrediatur mare, donec terrae vicinus est minus metuit, cum vero paulatim in altum fuerit progressus et undis intumescentibus vel in excelsum attolli coeperit vel iisdem dehiscentibus in ima deduci, ibi vero mentem pavor ingens et formido percurrit, quod exiguam ratem tam immensis fluctibus credidit: ita etiam nos pati videmur, qui exigui meritis et ingenio tenues inire tam vastum mysteriorum pelagus audemus.
>
> (The further we progress in reading, the greater grows the accumulation of mysteries for us. And just as if someone should embark on the sea borne by a small boat, as long as he is near land he has little fear. But, when he has advanced little by little into the deep and has begun either to be lifted on high by the swelling waves or brought down to depths by the same gaping waves then truly great fear and terror permeate his mind because he has entrusted a small craft to such immense waves. So also we seem to have suffered, who, small in merits and slight inability, dare to enter so vast a sea of mysteries.)[16]

However, Augustine is the only one to use the formula that unites *mira profunditas* with *horror* and *tremor*: the abyss with wonder, horror with understanding, terror with respect, trembling with love.

9

Compunction and Transfiguration

GREGORY THE GREAT WAS truly a man for all seasons. A descendant of an ancient Roman patrician family, he was *praefectus urbi*, papal legate to Constantinople, monk and founder of the monastery on the Caelian Hill in what was formerly his father's palace, initiator of the Anglo-Saxon mission, to convert England, reorganiser of the liturgy and founder of what was later called the Gregorian chant, historian, preacher, exegete' finally, bishop of Rome, and Pope, from 590 to 604. In Rome, on the Caelian Hill, one can still visit the great late Baroque basilica dedicated to him, part of the huge monastery building from which Gregory's monk Augustine (not to be confused with Augustine of Hippo, whom I discussed in the previous chapter) left for Kent, with its three small chapels, in one of which one can still see the marble table from which Gregory distributed bread to the poor.

Gregory interests me for three reasons besides that of having decisively and definitively Romanised the Church, which I cannot comment on here for lack of space. The first is his exegetical intelligence, as in the following, quite remarkable example. In his *Homilies on Ezekiel*,[1] when he reaches the vision of divine majesty that occupies the first chapters of the prophet's book he comes across a verse describing how, the moment a voice from above the firmament descends upon the heads of the four beasts, they lower their wings. Gregory maintains that the voice Ezekiel speaks of in his vision is the 'sound of intelligence', but that what our senses perceive is at times the voice of the flesh, at times that of the soul, at times that of the firmament, and at times, finally, a voice from above the firmament. So we must 'transcend' the voice of the flesh and of the soul and seek that of the firmament: in it we will find the infinite multitude of angels in the presence of the Lord, the happiness (*festivitas*) they find in the vision of God, the 'faultless joy', the ardour of love which does not harm but delights, both satiety and the desire to contemplate God, beatitude: the endless contemplation of eternity, which makes the angels themselves eternal; their union with light, which turns them into light; their gaze steadily fixed on the immutable, which makes them immutable.

And yet, in all these thoughts about angels, it is still the voice of the firmament that is speaking. But the soul must move beyond, 'transcend all that has been created', fix the eyes of faith on the Creator's light alone, as John did, like the eagle gazing at the sun. 'Let us then set before the eyes of the mind', Gregory writes, 'the being that holds, fills, embraces, exceeds and sustains all.' When the spirit is caught up in that being and considers its power, the voice comes from above the firmament, because it is able to conceive an idea of He who transcends the intuition of the angels with His incomprehensibility. At this point, the flying ends: here, Ezekiel's creatures lower their wings; men may no longer transcend, but must 'tremble with great fear' and 'humble' their own virtues. Abraham laid down his wings when, speaking with the Lord, he acknowledged he was dust and ashes: Moses did the same, in front of the burning bush; as did Isaiah when the burning coal of the altar touched his mouth; Jeremiah, who exclaimed 'Lord God! Behold, I cannot speak for I am a child'; Daniel, who fell sick after his vision; Job, who recognised his own ignorance after hearing the Voice from the whirlwind.[2]

Gregory uses the image of flight to depict the wondrous sequence of contemplation: first transcending and then folding wings in recognition of finiteness and ignorance. This is precisely the *occulti iudicii profunda cogitare*: thinking about the depths of secret wisdom. This, properly speaking, is mysticism in the guise of exegesis. And Gregory is undoubtedly a mystic, of the first magnitude. One need only read the wonderful pages Jean Leclercq devoted to this aspect to be spellbound by the inventiveness he possessed, despite being burdened by his duties as an ecclesiastical administrator.[3] To begin with, it is he who theorises *compunctio*, compunction, the divine gift we cannot comprehend.[4] Between the compunction of penitence and fear, and that of the desire for God and indeed even the possession of God, is the *compunctio cordis et animi*, a compunction that always tends to become one of love, delight and contemplation, says Leclercq. The path of humility soars high.

To describe this ascent, Gregory resorts to the figurative language I have been discussing since the beginning of this essay: palate of the heart, inner song, benevolent murmuring, silent word—the Holy Spirit as the 'finger of God'.[5] And then the language of desire: *anhelare, aspirare, suspirare*. Breathtaking insights, between philosophy and theology: 'know not by faith, but by love'; 'in contemplatione Dei homo sibi vilescit' (in God's contemplation man humbles himself); 'do not consider yourselves for what you have, but for what you are'.[6] A defender of images in the controversy over iconoclasm ('pictura ut scriptura', he used to say), Gregory is an expert storyteller. His *Dialogues* contain exemplary tales of all kinds: Paulinus of Nola and Benedict of Norcia, but also peasants slain by the Lombards and bishops mutilated by the Visigoths; and above all the survival of the soul after the death of the body, exemplified positively and negatively in a host of stories. An endless sequence of miracles great and small, of both important and humble saints, of devils engaged in acts of provocation and disturbance. The everydayness of the supernatural dominates the world.[7]

Finally, it is to Gregory that we owe, at least indirectly, the consecration of the other pole of the Christian sublime. The *Commentary on the First Book of Kings*, for eight centuries considered the work of the pontiff, is now attributed to Peter Divinacellus, or Peter de Cava, a twelfth-century cleric, who left us the only manuscript of the work. The highest point of the book is when the author explains the events of the call of Samuel and combines them with the Transfiguration recounted in the Synoptic Gospels.

The biblical episode, recounted in 1 Samuel 3, is in itself a story with formidable theological and poetic force, a narrative based on the Voice and on a misunderstanding. The call of Samuel (whose name means 'his name is God', or 'the name of God') is the first call of a prophet-judge since Moses was entrusted with his mission in Exodus,[8] and is therefore of particular importance; all the more, as the text takes care to emphasise, since 'the word of the Lord was precious in those days; there was no open vision'. 'Vision', in this context, actually means 'prophecy', and the whole episode signals 'the transition from priestly to prophetic authority'.[9] The 'call' to Samuel is repeated four times, because Samuel is ignorant: 'Now Samuel did not yet know the Lord, neither was the word of the Lord yet revealed unto him.' The tragic irony of the episode lies in the fact that it is the old priest Eli who enables Samuel to hear the Lord: the very man whose house, as Samuel reveals, Yahweh will 'judge for ever', because he did not restrain his sons who 'made themselves vile'.

In his interpretation, Peter of Cava adopts a plain style method of literal exposition, devoid of Pindaric or mystical flights until the moment when Samuel replies to the mysterious Voice that has already spoken to him twice while he was sleeping: 'Speak; for thy servant heareth.' He maintains that it is only by the grace of the Lord that we can say 'Speak!'; nevertheless, 'we cannot say it with the sentiments which are those of the perfect elect when they say it to him': 'for what belongs to an ineffable desire cannot be expressed in reasonable language'. This, the exegete continues, is identical to the sentiment expressed by Peter when he witnessed the Transfiguration: 'Lord, it is good for us to be here.' The feelings of Samuel and Peter are the same, even if their words are different. The evangelist reproaches Peter not for his feeling, but for his reasoning: Peter did not know what he was saying, 'but he burned with love for what he saw'. Yet, even as he rebukes the apostle, the evangelist also explains the reason for his ignorance: 'He wist not what to say; for they were sore afraid':

> Illa enim internae maiestatis ineffabilis pulchritudo electam mentem, cui se delectabiliter ostendit, aliquando mirabili pauore concutit; ne de uisionis magnitudine ad elationem prosiliat, si eam, quam blanda contemplatio ad tam summa euehit, prouector suus spiritus timoris moderamine non refrenat. In una quidem et eadem reuelatae gloriae uisione et bonitas creatoris adspicitur ineffabiliter blandiens et

> aequitas ipsius inaestimabiliter terrens; ut, quo uidentis animus de respecta dei bonitate dulcius pascitur, consideratione aequitatis territus caueat, ne inaniter satietur.
>
> (The ineffable beauty of divine majesty sometimes strikes wondrous fear into the chosen soul to whom it so delightfully manifests itself; for the grandeur of the vision might fill it with pride at being raised to such heights by this alluring contemplation, had the Spirit that moves it not restrained it with the restraint of fear. In one and the same vision of the glory that is revealing itself, it contemplates both the unspeakably attractive goodness of the Creator and his incomparably terrifying justice, so that the more the seer's soul delights in the sight of God's goodness, the more, terrified by the thought of his justice, it avoids sating itself in vain.)[10]

Here, once again, is Augustine's *ineffabilis pulchritudo*. Here, again, are terror and attraction, contemplation and vision: the Transfiguration of Christ in glory.

10

'O qui perpetua mundum ratione gubernas'

NOW LET US RETURN to where I left this discussion, taking it up from Proclus, who was naturally attentive not only to philosophy, but also, and above all, to the theology of Plato. The writer who seems to me to put into practice his theory of the two 'veins' of the *Timaeus* is the last Latin thinker of antiquity: Boethius. Boethius comes, admittedly, after Philo had transfused Platonic images and concepts into the Hebrew Bible, especially with regard to the Creation, and after Calcidius had translated into Latin and commented on much of the *Timaeus*. However, I am not interested here in examining the problem of his knowledge of his two predecessors (or three, counting Proclus).[1] It will suffice me to take Boethius's Christianity for granted, but also his Platonism, albeit tinged at times with Aristotelian traits (his ambition was to reconcile the latter two currents of thought). If one reads the *Consolation of Philosophy*—this 'Book of Job', as Lev Shestov once said, 'written by a man who, though a Christian, belonged to the Graeco-Roman culture'[2]—carefully, but all in one go, one gets the distinct impression that the prose passages are clearly inspired by the 'Socratic' current, and the lyrics by the 'Pythagorean'.

The most striking example is found in Book 3, prose and metre 9. The prose passage is all about the search for happiness (*beatitudo*) and its definition; after a series of reasonings on the impossibility of achieving self-sufficiency with wealth, power with kingdoms, respect with office, fame with glory, and joy with pleasures, it ends with two wonderful paragraphs:

> 'You know, then,' she said, 'both the form of false happiness, and its causes. Now turn your mind's gaze in the opposite direction; for there you will at once see true happiness, as I promised.' 'It is indeed clear', I said, 'even to a blind man, and you have shown it to me just now, while you were seeking to display the causes of false happiness. For unless I am wrong, that is true and perfect happiness which makes a man sufficient, powerful, respected, famous and joyful. And so that you may know that I have inwardly understood this, that which can truly provide one of these—since all are really the same—that I recognize unequivocally as full happiness.'[3]

Philosophy realises, delightedly, that her pupil has understood at last. So she persists, enabling the logical conclusion to be reached, a conclusion indicated precisely by Plato's *Timaeus*:

> 'O my pupil,' she said, 'I should call you happy in this opinion, if you but added this.' 'What, please?' I asked. 'Do you think that there is any among these mortal and impermanent things which could produce a condition of this kind?' 'I most certainly think not,' I replied, 'and that has been so demonstrated by you that no further argument is desired.' 'These things, therefore, seem to give mortals images of the true good, or certain imperfect goods, but they cannot confer the true and perfect good.' 'I agree,' I said. 'Then since you have recognized what is the true happiness, and what things counterfeit it, it now remains for you to recognize whence you can seek this true happiness.' 'That indeed', I said, 'is what I have long been eagerly hoping for.' 'But since,' said she, 'as is my Plato's opinion in the *Timaeus*, we ought to implore God's help in even the least of matters, what do you think we should do now, that we may be worthy to discover the abode of that highest good?' 'We must call upon the Father of all things,' I said, 'for if this is omitted no beginning can be rightly and properly based.'[4]

Agreeing with him completely, Philosophy bursts into song. This is the most beautiful lyric of the entire *Consolation*, worth quoting in full in the original as well as in translation:

O qui perpetua mundum ratione gubernas
Terrarum caelique sator qui tempus ab aevo
Ire iubes stabilisque manens das cuncta moveri,
Quem non externae pepulerunt fingere causae
Materiae fluitantis opus, verum insita summi
Forma boni livore carens, tu cuncta superno
Ducis ab exemplo, pulchrum pulcherrimus ipse
Mundum mente gerens similique in imagine formans
Perfectasque iubens perfectum absolvere partes.
Tu numeris elementa ligas ut frigora flammis
Arida conveniant liquidis, ne purior ignis
Evolet aut mersas deducant pondera terras.
Tu triplicis mediam naturae cuncta moventem
Conectens animam per consona membra resolvis.
Quae cum secta duos motum glomeravit in orbes,
In semet reditura meat mentemque profundam
Circuit et simili convertit imagine caelum.
Tu causis animas paribus vitasque minores
Provehis et levibus sublimes curribus aptans
In caelum terramque seris quas lege benigna
Ad te conversas reduci facis igne reverti.
Da pater augustam menti conscendere sedem,
Da fontem lustrare boni, da luce reperta
In te conspicuos animi defigere visus.
Dissipe terrenae nebulas et pondera molis
Atque tuo splendore mica! Tu namque serenum,
Tu requies tranquilla piis, te cernere finis,
Principium, vector, dux, semita, terminus idem.

(O you who in perpetual order govern the universe,
Creator of heaven and earth, who bid time ever move,
And resting still, grant motion to all else;

Whom no external causes drove to make
Your work of flowing matter, but the form
Within yourself of the highest good, ungrudging; from a
heavenly pattern
You draw out all things, and being yourself most fair,
A fair world in your mind you bear, and forming it
In the same likeness, bid it being perfect to complete Itself
In perfect parts. *You* bind its elements with law, so that the cold
Come together with flames, the dry with liquids, lest the fire too
pure
Fly off, or lest its weight pull down the overwhelmed earth.
You, binding soul together in its threefold nature's midst,
Soul that moves all things, then divide it into harmonious parts;
Soul thus divided has its motion gathered
Into two circles, moves to return into itself, and the Mind
deep within
Encircles, and makes the heaven turn, in likeness to itself.
You then bring forth, with the same bases, lesser living souls,
And giving them light chariots fitting their heavenly nature,
Broadcast them in the heavens and on earth, and by your
bounteous law
Make them, turned towards you, with returning fire come back.
Grant, Father, to my mind to rise to your majestic seat,
Grant me to wander by the source of good, grant light to see,
To fix the clear sight of my mind on you.
Disperse the clouding heaviness of this earthly mass
And flash forth in your brightness. For, to the blessed, *you*
Are clear serenity, and quiet rest: to see you is their goal,
And you, alone and same,
Are their beginning, driver, leader, pathway, end.)[5]

'Ut in Timaeo Platoni nostro placet'—'as is my ['our' would perhaps be a better translation] Plato's opinion in the *Timaeus*', Philosophy says in the prose passage cited above. The song that follows, the centre and heart of the *Consolation*, is a hymn to Plato's dialogue,[6] as William of

Conches was aware in devoting over thirty very beautiful pages (in the modern edition) to this passage.[7] With its beginning linked to the hymnographic tradition (to Cleanthes, Proclus and Lucretius among others), a tripartite structure of invocation, aretalogy and supplication takes shape in Boethius's lyric. All the key images and ideas of the cosmogonic section of the *Timaeus* recur, in particular those of a creation driven not by external causes, but, 'ungrudging' (*livore carens*), by the form of the highest good inherent within the creator; and its derivation from the supreme model. The perpetual *ratio* governing the world, the impulse given to time to move perennially, the beauty and perfection of the Creator becoming the beauty and perfection of the cosmos, made in his image like man in Genesis. For a moment, the Aristotelian icon of the unmoved Mover appears, accompanied by the echo of the praise of Wisdom in the Bible,[8] then the originally Pythagorean idea of the link between the elements established by means of numbers, and that of the harmony and balance imposed on the elements themselves by means of *philía,* take hold. There then arises, to give life to the whole, the tripartite *anima mundi,* in circular motion around the divine 'deep mind', as in Plotinus and Proclus, and the cause of movement in the heavens. Finally, the notion of 'lesser living souls' in their 'light chariots', as in the *Timaeus* and *Phaedrus,* leads to Plotinus's 'return' with the mystical image of the 'returning fire' that closes the aretalogy. The final seven lines are a crescendo culminating in the 'your' and thrice 'you', then in the summation of '*tu* namque serenum, / *tu* requies tranquilla piis, *te* cernere finis, / principium, uector, dux, semita, terminus idem': '*you* / Are clear serenity, and quiet rest: to see *you* is their goal, / And *you,* alone and same, / Are their beginning, driver, leader, pathway, end.'[9]

There is no other lyrical version of the *Timaeus* of equal concentration and splendour in the entire European tradition [fig. 3].

11

Beauty

THE LIFE, WORKS AND ADVENTURES of Dionysius the Areopagite burst upon the European West with a deflagrating blaze in the ninth century, when the Byzantine emperor Michael II sent a manuscript copy of all his works to the king of the Franks, Louis the Pious. Hilduin, the abbot of Saint-Denis, was immediately ordered to translate them into Latin. We are in the year 827, and Hilduin, assisted by Hincmar, set to work at once, as well as drawing up a *Passio Sancti Dionysii* to accompany the work with the necessary biographical background. Dionysius was already a well-known figure both, by reputation, in the Latin West, and, with more direct knowledge, in the Byzantine East, where his writings had appeared in the sixth century among the works of Severus of Antioch and his identity had been endorsed shortly afterwards by Maximus the Confessor.[1]

A fictitious identity, this, since Maximus holds, like many others before and after, that this self-styled 'Dionysius' was the disciple mentioned by Luke in the Acts of the Apostles, the only one of all the local sages converted in Athens by Paul.[2] In a letter to the evangelist John in exile on Patmos, he writes of Dionysius's affirmation: 'at Heliopolis he witnessed the eclipse of the sun that occurred at the death of Jesus and was present, together with the apostle Peter and with James, "the brother of the Lord", at the death of the Virgin Mary'.[3] He is thus supposed to have been an apostolic witness. In the hands of Hilduin, and as the crowning achievement of a glorious career, after being proto-bishop of Athens,[4] he finally becomes the same person as Saint

Dionysius, the first bishop of Paris and martyr: the Saint Denis of the abbey of which Hilduin himself was titular.[5]

The legend which grows around his figure—the 'historical' figure of the Dionysius mentioned in the Acts of the Apostles—is a sequence of stupefying adventures, which leave real chronology out of account and can be summed up as follows. Dionysius, bishop of Athens, is accused of not following tradition properly. He leaves for Rome, where he establishes strong ties with Pope Clement I (r. 88–97). Clement sends him off as missionary to Gaul. But another version maintains that he left Rome to escape Trajan's persecutions (Trajan was emperor from 98 to 117). He barely has time to become bishop of Paris before he is captured by local 'pagan' priests and beheaded (in 250!). He picks up his head, washes it and walks for several miles until he reaches the place where a basilica in his honour—in honour of Saint Denis—will eventually be built.

This is all *fictio,* and *fictio* is also the story of his writings. As a matter of fact, the author of these, 'Dionysius the Areopagite', may have been a nameless Greek-speaking Syrian, who lived in the sixth century and was therefore a contemporary of Boethius. Strongly influenced by Proclus,[6] he was the author of an admirable corpus of treatises and epistles, which with their mysticism, figurative language and exaltation of the *via negativa* constitute for all Christianity an explosive event that has endured for centuries. He has long been called 'Pseudo-Dionysius the Areopagite'. Fiction, however, acts upon reality. When another abbot of Saint-Denis, Suger, a firm believer in the identity of the two Dionysuses, set himself the task of reconstructing, decorating and embellishing the abbey against the advice of Bernard of Clairvaux, he used the theories of light and beauty of Dionysius the Areopagite, mediated by the works of John Scotus Eriugena and Hugh of Saint-Victor.[7]

It would be inappropriate here to enter into a discussion of the infinite complexities of the entire corpus. I would like just to indicate a few passages that are central to my theme, in which Dionysius seems ideally to combine the metaphorical language of the *Timaeus* and Proclus with the exaltation of beauty in the *Phaedrus* and the *Symposium,* recreating them in a Christian key.[8] In his *Mystical Theology* Dionysius offers a description of his own work that is a useful introduction to the themes that interest me most: 'In my *Theological Representations*,' he writes,

> I have praised the notions which are most appropriate to affirmative theology. I have shown the sense in which the divine and good nature is said to be one and then triune [. . .]. In *The Divine Names* I have shown the sense in which God is described as good, existent, life, wisdom, power, and whatever other things pertain to the conceptual names for God. In my *Symbolic Theology* I have discussed analogies of God drawn from what we perceive. I have spoken of the images we have of him, of the forms, figures, and instruments proper to him, of the places in which he lives and of the ornaments he wears. I have spoken of his anger, grief, and rage, of how he is said to be drunk and hung-over, of his oaths and curses, of his sleeping and waking, and indeed of all those images we have of him, images shaped by the workings of the symbolic representations of God.[9]

Neither the *Theological Representations* nor *The Symbolic Theology* have come down to us, but Dionysius's description is clear: both works, as well as part of the treatise on *The Divine Names* (*De divinis nominibus*), presented 'kataphatic', affirmative theology. Now, however, 'as we plunge into that darkness which is beyond intellect', Dionysius writes,

> we shall find ourselves not simply running short of words but actually speechless and unknowing. In the earlier books my argument travelled downward from the most exalted to the humblest categories, taking in on this downward path an ever-increasing number of ideas which multiplied with every stage of the descent. But my argument now rises from what is below up to the transcendent, and the more it climbs, the more language falters, and when it has passed up and beyond the ascent, it will turn silent completely, since it will finally be at one with him who is indescribable.[10]

This is the proclamation of the 'apophatic', negative path, which dominates the *Mystical Theology* and which will have so great a following in the centuries to come. But let us cast a glance at the 'kataphatic' approach, and the names of God it is good to use. Dionysius distinguishes a 'dual aspect' in theological tradition, almost as if he were Proclus with Plato's two voices in the *Timaeus*, the Pythagorean and the Socratic: 'the ineffable and mysterious on the one hand, the open and more evident on the other. The one resorts to symbolism and involves initiation. The other is philosophic and employs the method of demonstration.'[11] In the same context he offers a wonderful list of the 'incredible and contrived fantasy' of which Scripture is full, including a number of examples: 'Regarding the transcendent generation of God, scripture speaks of God's womb begetting God in a corporeal way. It speaks of the Word coming like a breath of air from a human heart. It depicts the Spirit as breathed out from a mouth':

> For physical imagery it resorts to trees, leaves, flowers, roots, bubbling fountains of water, radiant sources of shining light, together with all those other revealing depictions in the transcendent Word of God. In the domain of the mind, in the area of God's providence, whether it be with respect to his gifts, his appearances, his powers, his attributes, his dispositions, his abodes, his processions, his distinctions, or his unions, these are all variously represented in the forms of men, of wild or domestic animals, of plants, and of stones. God is clothed in feminine adornments or in the armour of barbarians. He is given the attributes of an artisan, be he potter, or refiner. He is put on horses, or chariots, on thrones. Well-laid feasts are put on for him. He is represented as drinking, as inebriated, as sleeping, as someone hung-over.[12]

Summarizing the whole of the Bible in their search for anthropomorphic symbols, these magnificent paragraphs would continue for centuries to spur commentators to follow the same path, producing justifications and allegories. 'Symbols', Dionysius says: even angels express themselves through 'riddles', and Jesus 'by means of parables'.[13] The 'war of the giants' in Genesis, the council held in heaven to deceive Ahab, the 'passionate longings fit only for prostitutes' in the Song of Songs are symbolic figurations, not the 'materialistic and impassioned [. . .] stories of the poets'.[14]

Theologians, Dionysius writes in *The Divine Names*, praise the 'supra-essential being of God—transcendent Goodness transcendentally there [. . .] by every name—and as the Nameless One'. However, since '[it] is the cause of everything', it must be celebrated, recalling for example, how 'the supreme Deity, during a mysterious revelation of the symbolical appearance of God', rebuked the man who asked, 'What is your name?'—a reference to Jacob, during his nocturnal struggle with the deity at Jabbok.[15] So Scripture gives the Deity many names, firstly by having it say 'I am he who is' or 'I am being'—this time to Moses, from the burning bush[16]—but then also 'life', 'light', 'God', 'the Truth', or, in celebrating it as 'the Cause of everything that is', by using names 'drawn from all the things caused':

> good, beautiful, wise, beloved, God of gods, Lord of Lords, Holy of Holies, eternal, existent, Cause of the ages. They call him source of life, wisdom, mind, word, knower, possessor beforehand of all the treasures of knowledge, power, powerful, and King of Kings, ancient of days, the unaging and unchanging, salvation, righteousness and sanctification, redemption, greatest of all and yet the one in the still breeze. They say he is in our minds, in our souls, and in our bodies, in heaven and on earth, that while remaining ever within himself he is also in and around and above the world, that he is above heaven and above all being, that he is sun, star, and fire, water, wind, and dew, cloud, archetypal stone, and rock, that he is all, that he is no thing.[17]

Thus, skilfully quoting from several passages in the Old and New Testaments, Dionysius employs names that are essentially metaphors: traditional, but absolutely original in their summing up: adjectives, attributes, names of things that are intelligible: that is, open to the intellectual understanding of one and all.

In addition to names for God 'drawn from universal or individual acts of Providence', the 'scripture writers' also employ others originating in 'spiritual visions which enlightened initiates or prophets in the holy places or elsewhere':

> For all sorts of reasons and because of all sorts of dynamic energies they have applied to the divine Goodness, which surpasses every name and every splendor, descriptions of every sort—human, fiery, or amber shapes and forms; they praise its eyes, ears, hair, face, and hands, back, wings, and arms, a posterior, and feet. They have placed around it such things as crowns, chairs, cups, mixing bowls, and similar mysterious items of which I will do my best to speak in *The Symbolic Theology*.[18]

It is clear that here the anthropomorphism of images is going in a different direction from before. These are images that touch the senses as organs of perception, and objects, or organs, that have symbolic value. To represent God by means of forms and figures such as these is to make Him more familiar and comprehensible and at the same time to understand that one's individual strength is not enough for the task and that the objects are mere signs, metaphors that are more mysterious than ever, 'arcane': *mystiká*, as the original says.

It is passages such as these, as we shall see, that will be debated for centuries by the philosophers and theologians of the West, in that they tell of the possibility of using figurative language when attempting to speak of the ineffable Absolute. There was, however, another aspect of Dionysius's writings that must have irresistibly attracted his readers: that of beauty. At the centre of the *De divinis nominibus* are two pages occupied entirely by this subject. 'The Good is described as the light of the mind', writes Dionysius, 'because it illuminates the mind of every supra-celestial being with the light of the mind', and dispels all darkness, flooding the souls with light with its 'beam and spring', and 'overflowing radiance'. This is why the Good that is 'above all light is given the name "light of the mind" [. . .]. The sacred writers lift up a hymn of praise to this Good. They call it beautiful, beauty, love, and beloved.' Dionysius, who must have in mind famous verses from the Song of Songs and the Psalms, sentences from the Gospels and passages from the Epistles of John and Peter,[19] now turns to Plato, Plotinus and Proclus and quotes the *Symposium*, his language swelling from a slender stream into an impetuous torrent and then gradually turning into the ample and majestic flow of a great river:

> But do not make a distinction between 'beautiful' and 'beauty' as applied to the Cause which gathers all into one. [. . .] But the 'beautiful' which is beyond individual being is called 'beauty' because of that beauty bestowed by it on all things, each in accordance with what it is. It is given this name because it is the cause of the harmony and splendour of everything, because like a light it flashes onto everything the emanations that make all things beautiful of its own beautiful spring-ray. Beauty 'bids' all things to itself (whence it is called 'beauty') and gathers everything into itself. And they name it beautiful since it is the all-beautiful and the beautiful beyond all. It is forever so, unvaryingly, unchangeably so, beautiful but not as something coming to birth and death, to growth or decay, not lovely in one respect while ugly in some other way. It is not beautiful 'now' but otherwise 'then', beautiful in relation to one thing but not to another. It is not beautiful in one place and not another . . . Ah no! In itself and by itself it is the uniquely and eternally beautiful.[20] It is the superabundant source in itself of the beauty of every beautiful thing. [. . .] From this beauty comes the existence of everything and is the source of all things. It is the great creating cause which bestirs the world and holds all things in existence, each being exhibiting its own way of beauty.[21]

This is but the first wave, a single paragraph of more than ten lines. Immediately there comes a sort of shorter undertow, in which the wave turns back and rushes forward again with only slightly diminished impetus. All beings have attained beauty precisely from this Beauty, the 'great creating cause which bestirs the world and holds all things in existence by the longing inside them to have beauty'. We seem to hear echoes of the *Timaeus*, of Aristotle and Boethius: instead it is Dionysius, blending them with the Bible to create a single whole. Efficient cause, the Beautiful is also the final cause, because it is the Goal of all things and is worthy of being loved as such—'since it is a longing for beauty which actually brings them into being', Dionysius adds, in an extraordinary aside; and an formal cause: 'a model to which they conform'. Beautiful and, of course, Good: *kalokágathos*, according to the classical Greek formula. Now, however, comes a second wave, regarding nothing less than non-being:

> And I would even be so bold as to claim that nonbeing also shares in the Beautiful and the Good, because nonbeing, when applied transcendently to God in the sense of a denial of all things, is itself beautiful and good. This—the One, the Good, the Beautiful—is in its uniqueness the Cause of the multitudes of the good and the beautiful. From it derives the existence of everything as beings, what they have in common and what differentiates them, their identicalness and differences, their similarities and dissimilarities, their sharing of opposites, the way in which their ingredients maintain identity, the providence of the higher ranks of beings, the interrelationship of those of the same rank, the return upward by those of lower status, the protecting and unchanged stability of all things amid themselves. Hence, the interrelationship of all things in accordance with capacity.[22]

He could go on like this for ever, Dionysius; he's following Proclus now, with variations. And we can imagine the almost terrified awe pages like this must have inspired in his first readers: the same awe that seizes us, one thousand five hundred years after they were written. In the introductory chapters of his commentary on the *Mystical Theology* and the *Divine Names*, Marsilio Ficino did indeed state that 'our inebriated Dionysius runs riot everywhere: he pours forth enigmas, he sings in dithyrambs'; he speaks in an 'Orphic manner'. Hence, to translate and interpret him one needs *divinus furor*, 'divine frenzy'.[23]

The immense labour of translation and commentary in Western Europe began immediately. After the version coordinated by Hilduin came that of John Scotus Eriugena, also in the ninth century; then, in the twelfth, the translation by John Sarrazin, requested by John of Salisbury among others, and used, for example, by Albert the Great.[24] The finest version would arrive with Marsilio Ficino in the late fifteenth century.[25] All the sharpest and most profound minds of at least three centuries measured themselves against the beauties and asperities of Dionysius's texts: from Robert Grosseteste to Hugh of Saint-Victor, from Thomas Gallus to Bonaventure, from Albert the Great to Thomas Aquinas, up to Hugues de Balma, Meister Eckart and Jean Gerson.[26] Finally, a truly striking episode comes when the *Corpus* enters vernacular literature with *The Cloud of Unknowing*, by a fourteenth-century English author who also composed *Deonise Hid Diuinite*, or the *Mystica* [hidden, secret] *theologia*. He explicitly employs Thomas Gallus's commentary in his version, and writes a *Book of Privy Counselling*, and the *Epistle of Prayer*.[27]

There are also, of course, some strange and incomprehensible gaps: for example, regarding the great Richard of Saint-Victor. His knowledge and use of Dionysius are disputed,[28] while it seems that at least one passage (4.22) in his *Beniamin maior* is a reworking of the *Mystical Theology* (1.3). And Dionysius is less present in Peter Lombard's *Sentences* (in 1.22, on the names of God, there is no mention of him) and in the commentaries on them, as generally in Abelard—so much so that it suggests an alternative tradition might be traced, apparently with no communication with the former, outlined here, even within the work of a single author.

Overall, however, one could conclude with the words of Maximus the Confessor, which provide an admirable summary of Dionysius:

> The beautiful and the good are one and the same thing, since everything looks towards the beautiful and the good as the cause of its being, and there is no being without a share of the beautiful and the good. The beautiful and the good, truly worthy of admiration, are for all beings the object of desire, of love, of pleasure, of choice and of delight. Observe how divine passion, pre-existing in the good, has generated in us a passion for good thanks to which we tend to the beautiful and the good; as someone once said: '*I yearned for her beauty*', and '*Yearn for her and she shall keep you; exalt her and she will extol you*.'[29]

12

Metaphorá

DIONYSIUS IS THE LINK between Christianity and medieval Platonism in the West.[1] Here I want to take up a couple of observations by Peter Dronke, who more than anyone else, from *Fabula* onwards, has studied medieval Platonism with his usual sharp and wide-ranging gaze.[2] They are related most especially to the introduction of the terms *metaphor* and *integumentum* in the Platonic meditations of John Scotus Eriugena and William of Conches. Dronke writes about the former,

> The Greek word *metaphorá* (which Eriugena knew in particular through Origen) had its Latin counterpart, *translatio*, which he uses just as often. The two words essentially convey the idea of a transfer—for Eriugena in particular, the transfer of language from the created world to the creator. Moreover, like Dionysius, he speaks of 'words [that are] symbols' (*symbolica verba*, 456a)—words that, utterly inadequate to express the inexpressible, at least concede something to the aspiration of human minds. It is this acute sense of the failure of language to understand the divine that leads to a wider discussion, based on Dionysius, of the two human ways of approaching God through language—the affirmative and the negative or, in Eriugena's Hellenising terms, the Cataphatic and Apophatic (458a–461c).[3]

Scotus develops a series of considerations on the metaphorical language of Scripture in Book 1 of the *Periphýseon*. They are of particular interest to us. One must believe that true authority and rational deduction derived from right contemplation, argues the 'Nutritor', the Master of the

Periphýseon, are not at odds with each other, because both 'flow from the same source, the Wisdom of God'.

> The one has conceded and conferred to pious inquirers the ability to think and say many things about the incomprehensible and ineffable Nature, so that the study of true religion should not be silent on all matters, but nourish those who are as yet ignorant in the simplicity of the teaching of their faith, and that, instructed [and armed<and> fortified by divine defences], it may have an answer for those who challenge the Catholic Faith; while the purpose of the other is to correct, by the instillation of religion and piety, those simple people who thus far have been nourished in the nursery of the Church, lest they should either believe or think anything unworthy of God, or should suppose that everything that Holy Scripture predicates of the Cause of all things is predicated properly, whether it is a question of the most glorious and exalted names such as Life or Virtue or the names of the other virtues; or intermediate names such as Sun, Light, Star, or anything from the higher regions of this visible world which is predicated of God; or those (taken) from the lower motions of the visible creature, such as Breath, Cloud, Brightness, Sunrise, Thunder, Dew, Shower, Rainfall; also Water, River, Earth, Stone, Log, Vine, Olive, Cedar, Hyssop, Lily, Man, Lion, Ox, Horse, Bear, Panther, Worm; also Eagle, Dove, Fish, Monster, and the numberless other names which are taken from the created nature and applied to the Creative Nature by a kind of metaphor and figurative manner of expression [transformatione quadam figurataque significatione]; and, what is more strange, not only from the created nature did Scripture in its ingenuity make these transpositions [translationes] to the Creator, but even from things which are contrary to nature, namely. Frenzy, Drunkenness, Intoxication, Forgetfulness, Anger, Rage, Hatred, Concupiscence, and other similar terms, by which the minds of the uninstructed are less seriously deceived than by the aforementioned metaphors [transfigurationibus] which are taken from nature.[4]

Scripture, which Scotus brilliantly personifies in *artifex,* or artist,[5] roots its metaphors in divine Wisdom. The 'names' of God come from

Dionysius and are those of everyday things, but also those proposed by the Wisdom Books of the Bible.

With even greater intensity, Eriugena returns to these concepts when, in Book 3, he attempts to explain Genesis and its first verses.[6] The biblical text, for example, mentions the earth that produced verdant plants and fruit trees: Scotus comments, 'You see how the divine Scripture reveals most clearly the genera and the species in which there subsist causally and invisibly whatever things break forth through generation in quantities and qualities into the knowledge of the corporeal senses?' Then, however, the Master gets carried away:

> But if it seems to anyone that this account which we have given to the best of our ability of the three first days is not in accordance with history but with the laws of allegory, let him carefully consider the fourfold division of wisdom. And first is ΠΡΑΚΤΙΚΗ, practical; second ΦΥCΙΚΗ, natural; third ΞΕΟΛΟΓΙΑ, which discusses God; fourth ΛΟΓΙΚΗ, rational, which shows by what laws each of the other three parts of wisdom should be discussed. One investigates the virtues by means of which the vices are replaced and are entirely eradicated; the second the reasons of natures whether in their causes or their effects; the third what should piously be thought of the Cause of all things. Who is God; but how to conduct a rational inquiry into virtue and nature and God is, as we have said, what the fourth teaches and carefully considers. To this [division] of the four aforesaid parts of wisdom he ought to apply the historical account of the establishment of things, and if he is not entirely ignorant of philosophy, he will attach it to none but the physical. And if this is so, let him look for anything that has been said by us by way of allegory and, as I think, he will not find it. For in the case of the first day we said that the procession, comprehensible to senses and intellects, of the primordial causes into their effects is signified in general by the creation of light. [Now, that the primordial causes of all things are substances established in Divine Wisdom St. Ambrose is witness when he says in his Hexemeron, 'The man who is full of knowledge', Moses, that is, 'observes that the substance of things visible and

invisible and the causes of things are contained in the Mind of God alone.'] In the case of the second we decided, not inappropriately as *I think*, that the triple constitution of this world, made up, that is, of its reasons, and of the incomposite elements, and of the composite bodies, is described by the word 'waters', and the firmament that was made in the midst of them; but we judged that the third consideration of this world, consisting in the separation of the things that are mutable in it from those which, protected by the support of their own nature, remain immutably in the same [state], that is, in the distinction which a logical observation draws between all the mutable accidents and the immutable solidity of the substantial forms, was what the divine Scripture intended by the gathering together of the waters and the appearing of the earth. Not unreasonably; for it is a very common practice of the Holy Oracles to signify by words which signify visible things the natural existences and reasons of invisible things, to exercise devout philosophers. Nor is this surprising; for very often they are in the habit of denoting corporeal and sensible things by the names of the spiritual and invisible. But to load the present discussion with examples of this reciprocity of metaphor, since they are many and innumerable and very well known to those who are practised in Holy Scripture, would be a long and superfluous task. Nevertheless, let us use a few examples: 'That which is born of flesh is flesh'—here the whole man born in original sin is called by the name of flesh—'and that which is born of the spirit is spirit'—the whole man reborn by regeneration in Christ is expressed by the word 'spirit'. And if anyone shall say: Not the whole man is born of flesh but only the flesh of man, I shall reply: Then not the whole man is born of the spirit but only the soul, and if so it follows that the grace of baptism is of no benefit to bodies. But if the whole man, namely, soul and body, is reborn in Christ and is made spirit, the whole man necessarily is born in Adam of the flesh and is flesh, and so it is concluded both that flesh is called spirit and spirit flesh. The Word of God is called flesh, and flesh the Word, and (there are) similar cases in which there is understood both CYNEKΔOXH and METAΦORA.[7]

No, the Master is right, this is not allegory, it is *metaphorá*. But what frustration lies behind his words! Explaining Scripture in human words is an impossible task. The modern commentator, Peter Dronke, can only recall the words of the *Timaeus* in Calcidius's translation: this is 'the imaginary tale of an image as the simulacrum of a rational discourse which borrows from it a superficial element of likeness' (utpote imaginis imaginaria simulacrumque rationis, perfunctoriam imaginem mutuatur).[8]

This defines the way Master and Disciple construct their *imago mundi* together. Yet while they can offer an account of it that is as likely as it is imaginary, they can say nothing about 'the purpose of the Divine Wisdom [divinae sapientiae propositum]'. They are ready to admit that the 'how or why [quomodo aut qua ratione] the Word of God is made in all things which are made in Him eludes the sharpness of [their] mind [mentis nostrae aciem fugit]'.[9]

Scotus, however, sticks to metaphor. The word, and its cognates, are used in his commentary on Dionysius's *Celestial Hierarchy*.[10] And one wonders if he would have considered one of his masterpieces, the *Homily on the Prologue to John's Gospel*, as belonging to the metaphorical, rather than the allegorical genre. There, he sees the John of the Prologue as a spiritual bird, flying swiftly, with the eyes of one who can behold God, transcending every visible and invisible creature, penetrating every object of intellection, and 'deified, achieving his entry into God who deifies him'. From the very start of his *Homily*, Eriugena sings the Prologue's praises with unusual fervour: 'The voice of the spiritual Eagle', he writes, 'resounds upon the Church's ears. Turned outwards, may the senses grasp its fleeting sound, may the inner soul penetrate its unchanging meaning.' It is the voice, he continues, of the 'bird of heights', which flies not only above the physical element of the air to the very limits of the known universe in its totality, but succeeds in transcending every 'theory', beyond all things which are and are not, 'with the swift wings of the most inaccessible theology, with the expressions of the most shining contemplation, and the loftiest'.[11]

13

Integumenta; Esthétique du Timée

ONCE AGAIN WE RETURN to the *Timaeus* and its *lògos eikós*. References to the *Timaeus* as well as to Dionysius are also made by William of Conches, who cites the Areopagite's *De divinis nominibus* and Letter 9 in his commentary on Plato.[1] Lucidly sensing the joint importance of the *Timaeus* and the *Consolation*, William composes the *Glosae super Platonem* and the *Glosae super Boetium*, which are of central importance in his work [fig. 6].[2] It is William who launches the 'derivation' of 'timaeus' from *timo*, 'flower', in his comparison of the words, a derivation shared by Hugutio of Pisa, as is evident in the epigraph to this book. William differs from Hugutio over the meaning of 'timaeus', however: while Hugutio links it to the Greek *thymós* and to the divine mind Plato knew so much about, William argues that many believe it refers to *tymo*: to the 'living creature', that is—the 'animal'; because the *Timaeus* deals with 'the great animal that is the world'.[3]

Plato wanted to discuss natural justice; and to do so, writes William in his Prologue, he decided to address the problem of Creation. But I am skipping these opening pages, which have been analysed to perfection by Peter Dronke,[4] in order to focus instead on a passage from Book 2 that was translated into Italian by Tullio Gregory and taken up by Dronke himself.[5] It is in this passage that the notion of 'integumentum'—a word long familiar to exegetes—is employed.[6] William writes that when Plato, in the *Timaeus*, says that 'God chose as many souls as there are stars, [...] some people, expounding this literally, say that Plato here taught heresy, for Scripture [diuina pagina] says that God creates new souls each day.'[7] But we must look not only at Plato's words, but also his sense and mind. This will reveal that there is no heresy here, 'but the most profound philosophy, under the cover of mythopoetic language [integumentis uerborum tectam], which we who love Plato shall show. When he said that the stars are the vehicles of the soul [. . .] Plato meant that souls are set on stars causally, not spatially: they are the soul's vehicles in that, through the effect of the stars, the body becomes apt for a soul to be created in it.'[8]

More than a century later, Albert the Great, in contrast to the view that would be held by his disciple Thomas Aquinas,[9] gave a favourable interpretation of the Platonic idea that 'every soul descends from a star and after death returns to its own star'. This is for four main reasons, he says, and above all because the soul is 'caused' by the intellect and the light of intelligence 'which universally moves through nature'; and this motion is impossible without that of the stars. Albert dwells for a whole paragraph on this relationship between souls and stars, then—without in any way mentioning either *metaphor* or *integumentum*, but clearly implying the former—he concludes, 'Plato meant that the soul comes from the first cause in the same way as the light of celestial intellects. Its *inductio* in the body occurs through the movement of the cosmos, and therefore after death it returns to heaven.'[10]

The so-called School of Chartres is particularly sensitive to the reasoning of Dionysius and Plato. According to Edgar De Bruyne, it elaborates a veritable *esthétique du Timée* which is mirrored even in the sculpture of one of the portals of Chartres Cathedral and whose echoes, as we shall see, reach the *Roman de la rose*. In the portal of the north transept of the great church (reconstructed 1194–1230) the two sets of reliefs representing the First Day of Creation are placed one on top of the other. In both, the bearded God is seated, but in the lower one he lifts his hand high up towards the sky (and all the other scenes) as if to initiate the work of creation, while in the upper one he leans his head on his hand while a book lies on his knees. A 'Timaeic' God appears in the posture of the Demiurge, thinking intensely of the model he is going to adopt, and therefore consults a volume (probably the *Liber vitae*). In the lower scene, this very book has seemingly become a scroll, as if God, holding the universe in one hand, were ready to unroll it. The scene is repeated in inverted manner in the Creation of Day and Night, where the lower section presents the Creator with his head inclined resting on his left arm and a volume on his knees, while in the upper one he lifts his right arm towards his chin, turning his gaze upwards.

'Not the exalting wonder of sensible forms considered in themselves,' De Bruyne wrote of the 'esthetics of the *Timaeus*', 'nor the subtle enjoyment (*jouissance*) of their correspondences and allegorical meanings', but instead 'the joy of an inclusive vision in the light of certain simple principles, of certain very general notions, of fundamental causes and certain primary relations'.[11] William himself, in his commentary on Plato, speaks of *exornatio mundi* as 'kósmos, consentiens conspirans continuata cognatio' supported by a divine principle, as Tullio Gregory noted.[12] The beauty of the world, the *ornatus mundi*, lies, and appears, in individual elements, 'such as stars in the sky, birds in the air, fish in water, men on earth': 'est ornatus mundi quidquid in singulis videtur elementis, ut stellae in coelo, aves in aere, pisces in aqua, homines in terra'.[13] In this regard, De Bruyne recalls a passage from the *Beniamin maior* by Richard of Saint-Victor, for whom the 'second kind of contemplation' resides in the imagination but is shaped and developed 'according to reason': if, in the first, 'we look at, explore and marvel at things themselves; in the second kind we do the same with the reason, order, and disposition of these things, and the cause, mode and benefit of any one thing'.[14]

The poetry of Chartres, moreover, also celebrates this beauty.[15] Alain de Lille, in *De planctu Naturae*, speaks of Creation in aesthetic terms. God, who has given admirable form to the palace of the world, is for him 'like an elegant cosmic architect, like a goldsmith creating a work of gold, like the highly gifted artist of an astonishing piece of art, like the skilled producer of an admirable work': 'Deus tamquam mundi elegans architectus, tamque aureae fabricae faber aurarius, velut stupendi artificii artificiosus artifex, tamquam admirandi operis operarius opifex, mundialis regiae admirabilem speciem fabricavit'.[16] And it is enough to read poem 5, 'Floriger horrentem Zephyrus', in the same work, to understand what expressive power is to be found in a philosopher poet of his kind, able precisely 'in singulis elementis', as William says, to see the achievement of the divine *artifex*. An ability also demonstrated in his longer *Anticlaudianus* as well as in his poems, *The Book of Creation (Omnis mundi creatura)* and *On the Incarnation*, and finally in that miracle of a Sermon that focuses on the 'intelligible sphere'.[17]

Bernardus Silvestris, the poet of the *Cosmographia* quoted and studied by Gregory, Dronke, Stock and Wetherbee,[18] presents himself as the cantor of the Megacosmus and the Microcosmus, of Nature and Noys, of Endelechia, Silva and Mundus, of the creation of the Universe and of Man. His are not cold allegories, but personifications full of life and thought, as in the following passage, from the *Megacosmus*, in which it is possible to see, 'sustained by the gift of vivifying Soul, the ordered progression of created life unfolded from the nurturing womb of Silva':

Ergo sideribus levis ether, sidera celo,
Celum secessit aere, terra freto.
In celo divina manus celique ministris
Omne creature primitiavit opus.
Celi forma, teres; essentia, purior ignis;
Motus, circuitus; numina, turba deum—
Dico deos quorum ante deum presentia servit,
Quos tenet in vero lumine vera dies,
Pacis enim locus etheree, totoque tumultu
Aeris exceptus, sepositusque sibi,
Separat archanas sedes; super, immo superne,
Extramundanus creditur esse deus.

(Thus the subtle ether grew separate from the stars, the stars from the firmament, the heavens from the atmosphere, the earth from the waters.

In heaven and in the heavenly powers the hand of God produced the first fruits of the entire work of creation: the rounded form of the celestial sphere, its essence a purer fire, circular motion, heavenly powers, the host of the gods.

I call 'gods' those beings whose presence is attendant upon God, those whom true day retains in its true light. For a region of ethereal calm, eempt from all the tumult of the atmosphere, secluded unto

> itself, sets apart their secret dwelling places. Belief holds that God exists far above, indeed above all, beyond the limits of the universe.)[19]

The passage seems even more extraordinary when one sees how it continues, unveiling the grandiose panorama of what the stars inscribe in the firmament, prefiguring: 'all that can come to pass through decree of fate [. . .]. That sequence of events which long ages and the measured course of time will unfold appears first in the stars'—natural disasters such as Deucalion's Flood and Phaeton's celestial fire; historical events such as the war of the Seven at Thebes and the birth of Christ; individuals with a predictable character such as Pollux the boxer, Tiphys the helmsman of the Argonauts, Thales 'the geometer', Plato who 'intuits the principles of existence', Milo the sculptor, Cicero the orator, Virgil the poet; nations, then, and empires, Persia, Egypt, Greece, Rome; finally, the entire historical-mythical *historia* consecrated by the Greeks and Romans: Paris, Priam, Achilles, Ulysses, Turnus.[20]

Conversely, in the 'Microcosm', once chaos has been dismembered, Silva acquires full beauty and the name of 'world', and becomes a 'figure of things', addressing to Nature a discourse whose inspiration comes from the *Timaeus*. It is the moment of *exhornatio*, the moment, that is, in which the *ornatus mundi*, the beauty of the world, fully emerges:

> Iam sectum per membra chaos, iam Silva, decorem
> Nacta suum, vero nomine mundus erat;
> Siquid adhuc ruris vetus importabat origo,
> Expulit artifices usque secuta manus,
> Et nichil obtrectans operi rerumque figuris,
> Continuam sese morigeramque dedit.
> 'In laudem titulosque meos, Natura, repono
> Tam bene materias excoluisse rudes:
> Induxi rebus formas, elementa ligavi,
> Concordem numero conciliante fidem;
> Ascripsi legem stellis, iussique planetas
> Indeclinatum currere semper iter;
> Substrinxi mare limitibus; ne terra labaret,

In medio sedit pondere fixa suo.
Mandavi, calor ethereus produceret herbas—
Quas calor ethereus parturit, humor alat;
Corpora cuncta creet Tellus, resolutaque rursus
Excipiat placido mater amica sinu;
Ex Endelichia mundi res queque creata
Sementem vite principiumque trahat.'

(Now chaos had been divided into parts; now Silva had attained her proper beauty, there existed a Universe worthy of the name. If her ancient origin intruded any trace of rusticity, she banished it, ever submissive to the shaping hand; offering no resistance, she presented herself, coherent and obedient, to the work of Noys and the formation of creatures.

'I count it to my praise and glory, O Nature, that I have so well cultivated my coarse materials. I have brought form to creatures and yoked the elements by a proportion which has elicited peace and trust. I have given a law to the stars, and ordered the planets always to pursue an undeviating course. I have curbed the sea with boundaries, and lest the earth should totter, it rests, fixd by its own weight, at the center of things. I have decreed that ethereal warmth should bring forth vegetation, and that moisture should sustain what this ethereal warmth has produced; that the earth, loving mother, should give birth to all things, and at their dissolution receive them back again into her tranquil bosom; that every creature should derive the seed and principle of its vitality from Endelechia, soul of the Universe.')[21]

'I have brought form to creatures and yoked the elements', 'I have given a law to the stars, and ordered the planets [. . .]. I have curbed the sea with boundaries': the *Timaeus* and the Book of Job converge in the poetic writing of the School of Chartres. Their echoes will be heard again in the poetry of the thirteenth century, in Jean de Meun's continuation of the *Roman de la rose,* begun by Guillaume de Lorris. Thus, Plato's *Timaeus,* Boethius's *Consolation,* the Dionysian aura of the thinking and images of Chartres re-emerge in the words with which Nature makes her confession to her priest, Genius:

> 'cil Diex, qui de biautez habonde,
> quant il tres biaus fist ce biau monde
> don il portoit en sa pansee
> la bele fourme porpansee
> toujorz en perdurableté
> ainz qu'ele eüst dehors eté
> car la prist il son exemplaire
> et quan que li fu necessaire
> [. . .]
> Et le fist au commencement
> une masse tant seulement,
> qui toute iert an confusion,
> sanz ordre et sanz distinction;
> puis le devisa par parties,
> qui puis ne furent departies,
> et tout par nombres assoma'

> ('When that most fair God who abounds in beauty created the world of beauty whose fair form of fairness, pondered upon forever in eternity, He carried within His thought before it ever existed outside, nothing ever moved Him to do so except His own sweet-tempered will, broad, courteous, free of envy, the fountain of all life; He took His exemplar and whatever was necessary from His thought [. . .]. In the beginning He created only a mass that was in confusion, without order or distinction, and then divided it into parts that afterward were not split up. He enumerated everything by number, and He knows how many there are altogether.')[22]

Jean speaks of beauty four times in the first lines of this passage (in French, *biautez, biaus, biau, bele*). This is enough to give us an idea of the context in which his vision developed and the direction it was taking.

However, since I started this chapter with Chartres Cathedral, I will conclude it with another cathedral, this time in Anagni, south of Rome, constructed in austere Romanesque style between the late eleventh and the thirteenth centuries. A crypt in honour of Saint Magnus was built at the same time, which has been called the Sistine Chapel of the Middle Ages.[23] On the precious cosmatesque floor, the crypt (next to a chapel devoted to Saint Thomas Becket)[24] is divided into three naves, and every single square inch of it is covered by frescoes, attributed to three unknown masters (and their assistants) succeeding each other in time [fig. 7]. The total effect is that of finding oneself inside an enchanted jewel box of all colours, with gems blue, red, green and golden responding to each other, with geometrical patterns, circles, diagrams, inscriptions, human figures, animals, stories from the Old and New Testaments, tales of Saint Magnus, and much more.

The reading of these hundreds of images has never been easy, but most interpreters agree the general scheme is typological. Not, however, a linear kind of typology, but a complex one, operating on various levels and through several cycles—scientific/cosmic, eucharistic, apocalyptic, prophetic, historical, political, christological, mariological, hagiograpic.[25] Since the beginning of the twentieth century, the decoration of the crypt has been said to begin with the Creation and end with Apocalypse. Artistically speaking, some of the most effective scenes appear to be those with Christ or Mary at the centre, but the judging God of the Last Day is also very vivid, and most of the episodes on the Ark of the Covenant, the stories of Saul and Samuel, the ascent of Elijah and the vicissitudes of Saint Magnus are true masterpieces [figs. 11–13, 15].

A couple of books would be necessary to illustrate the crypt properly and interpret both its single episodes and the whole.[26] I shall limit myself here to the most fascinating features of the Beginning scenes. Here, the traditional representations of the creating God have been replaced by a series of frescoes depicting the nature of the universe and of man (Macrocosm and Microcosm) from a scientific point of view, according to the theories expounded in Plato's *Timaeus* and in Calcidius's commentary.[27] Thus, we have a Zodiac, then the Four Ages of Man, the elements and their combinations [figs. 10–12]. In other words, the universe has already been created, and the painters devote themselves to illustrating its inner and outer structure in Platonic terms. No greater triumph had yet been celebrated for the *Timaeus*.

14

The Three Days

HUGH OF SAINT-VICTOR (ca. 1096–1141) opened his *Didascalicon* with a quotation of Plato's *Timaeus* and devoted a substantial commentary to Dionysius's *Celestial Hierarchy*. He preached beautiful homilies on Ecclesiastes, composed a *Soliloquy on the arrha* [earnest money] *of the Soul*, analysed in detail the mysteries of Christian faith in the *De sacramentis*, structured three treatises around Noah's ark—*Libellus de formatione arcae, De arca Noe morali, De arca Noe mystica*—, created the *De vanitate rerum mundanarum* and the *Dialogus de creatione mundi*, and wrote a short but precious book *On the Three Days* (*De tribus diebus*). His works, of which the ones I have listed are just the most important, occupy three entire volumes of Migne's Patrologia Latina, and some still lack a modern critical edition.[1] Of 'Saxon'—probably German or Franco-German—origin, he lived most of his life in the Abbey of Saint-Victor in Paris, teaching, meditating and praying, and became a cardinal two years before his death. Called 'second Augustine' and recognised as 'Master' by Bernard of Clairvaux, he was perhaps the greatest Neoplatonist and mystic of the twelfth century, transmitting his passion for mysticism (but not, apparently, for platonism) to his disciple Richard of Saint-Victor (d. 1173).

It would obviously be impossible to discuss here even a handful of the most important of Hugh's works, but the short treatise on the *Three Days*, considered in the past as the last book of the *Didascalicon*, deserves some closer scrutiny, for it is there, in the mere seventy pages of its modern critical edition,[2] that Hugh's passion for beauty and the beautiful emerges most fully and becomes a true theory, virtually the only real aesthetic theory that has come down to us from the Middle Ages.

The three days of the title, to begin with, are the first three days of Creation as recounted in Genesis 1, the days in which God, by the power of his word alone, creates light, the firmament, the sea and the dry land. There is a certain amount of naming and separating which accompanies this primary creation: for instance, the division between light and darkness and the names which are conferred upon them, 'day' and 'night', or again the placing of the firmament between two layers, as it were, of waters, those above and those under it, with the firmament itself being now named as 'heaven'. From the third day onwards, God contemplates the work he has done and sees it as 'good'.

Hugh opens his exposition in a solemn way, enunciating the principles which will inspire the entire work:

> Verbum bonum et uita sapiens quae mundum fecit contemplato mundo conspicitur. Et Verbum ipsum uideri non potuit, et fecit quod uideri potuit, et uisum est per id quod fecit.
>
> Invisibilia enim ipsius a creatura mundi per ea quae facta sunt intellecta conspiciuntur. Tria sunt inuisibilia Dei: potentia, sapientia, benignitas. Ab his tribus reguntur omnia, in his tribus consistunt omnia.
>
> (The good Word and wise Life that made the world is perceived when the world is contemplated. The Word itself cannot be seen, but the Word both made what can be seen and is seen through what He made.
>
> From the creation of the world the invisible realities of God are beheld through what is understood of the things which are made. The invisible things of God are three: power, wisdom and kindness. From these three proceed all things. In these three all things subsist.)[3]

The intonation, the style, and some of the words themselves derive from John's Prologue to the Fourth Gospel, the Prologue exalted by Augustine, Gregory and John Scotus as the sublime flight of God's eagle. But the quotation in the second part of the passage comes from Paul's Epistle to the Romans,[4] where the Apostle affirms one of the central tenets of Hugh's belief: that invisible things pertaining to God are seen clearly if understood through created beings.

What seems essential is the constant dialectic between things visible and things invisible. Beauty belongs to both in a mirror-like way, as Hugh delves with particular joy into the marvels of creation and what lies behind them. He does quote a Psalm and Isaiah to make clear where the source of beauty lies:

> How great Your works, O LORD,
> Your designs are very deep.
> The brutish man does not know,
> Nor does the fool understand this.

> Who with his hand's hollow has measured the waters,
> the heavens has gauged with a span,
> And meted earth's dust with a measure,
> Weighed with a scale the mountains,
> And the hills with a balance?[5]

But he possesses the very special gift, both psychological and rhetorical, of feeling the beauty of nature, as in the following passage, equal in poetic power to the one from Ambrose I quoted in chapter 7 above:

> Quod luce pulcrius, quae cum colorem in se non habeat, omnem tamen colorem rerum ipsa quodammodo illuminando colorat? Quid iucundius ad uidendum caelo cum serenum est, quod resplendet quasi saphirus et gratissimo quodam suae claritatis temperamento uisum excipit et demulcet aspectum? Sol sicut aurum rutilat, luna pallet quasi electrum, stellarum quaedam flammeo aspectu radiant, quaedam luce rosea micant, quaedam uero alternatim, nunc roseum, nunc uiridem, nunc candidum fulgorem demonstrant.

> (What is more beautiful than light, which, although it does not have colour in itself, in some ways gives colours to all the things that it illumines? What is more delightful to behold than a clear sky; resplendent like a sapphire, it draws one's gaze by the extremely pleasing mildness of its glow and softens the view? The sun shines like gold;

> the moon is pale like electrum. Certain stars radiate a flaming appearance; others sparkle with a rosy light; others alternately display a rosy glow, then green, then white.)[6]

The colours of the sky are not enough for Hugh, who now launches onto gems and precious stones, flowers of diverse kind, and finally the new green shoots which stand up on their stalks and bud forth into the light 'in a symbol of future resurrection'. God's wisdom produces beauty from the dust of the earth, beauty 'enraptures the minds of those who see it'.[7] And there is a way in which even 'monsters' such as a crocodile or a salamander possess their own uncanny beauty, for the observer wonders at the fact that the former doesn't move its lower jaw while eating and the latter survives undamaged in fire. Wonder, *admiratio*, astonishment, stupor are the feelings from which the perception of the *mirabilia Dei* arises and beginning with which the sense of beauty takes shape. When he talks about *magnitudo*, Hugh outlines a mechanism relying on wonder and leading, through wonder, from meditation to contemplation of beauty:

> Sed fortasse qui tot fecit, parua fecit, multa simul et magna facere non potuit. Quanta tamen! Metire moles montium, tractus fluminum spacia camporum, altitudinem Caeli, profunditatem abyssi. *Miraris quia deficis, sed melius deficiendo miraris.* Meditantibus de creaturarum immensitate, quasi seminarium quoddam iecimus; nunc ad contemplandam earum pulchritudinem transeamus.
>
> (However, perhaps he who made so many things made small things, but could not make many and great things at the same time. On the contrary, what great things there are! Measure the masses of the mountains, the channels of the rivers, the expanses of the fields, the height of the heaven, the depth of the abyss. *You are amazed for you fall short, but your amazement is better because you fall short.* For those meditating on the immensity of creatures we have, as it were, laid out a seed plot. Now we move on to contemplate the beauty of these things.)[8]

We are now in the section devoted by Hugh to 'species', itself one of the four features which characterise creatures' *pulchritudo*: structure, motion, appearance (*species*), and quality. On each of these Hugh expands, distinguishing its various aspects with extraordinary lucidity. Structure (*situs*) is for instance further divided into 'disposition of places', 'of times' and 'of parts'. Movement is fourfold: 'local, natural, biological, rational'. Finally, to quality is added 'utility'. All these distinctions (and there are several more), each reasoned out exhaustively, constitute as it were the elements on the basis of which the central thesis of the *De tribus diebus* is proved: that every invisible light is refracted in material lights and beauty is the multiplicity and variety of all things, themselves being the products of the diffusion of divine light. All depends on God's wisdom, and wisdom, power and benignity (*sapientia, potentia, benignitas*) are the three invisible qualities of God from which everything proceeds. The 'immensity' of creatures shows the power, beauty is the work of wisdom, utility highlights benignity: 'potentia creat, sapientia gubernat, benignitas conservat' is the supreme formula. The sensible universe is a book written by God's finger, and single creatures figures are sketched to signify divine wisdom.

These ideas and these images recur in the *De sacramentis*, the *Didascalicon*, the *De arca Noe mystica*, the homilies on Ecclesiastes. They are the theological bricks upon which Hugh builds an aesthetics that tries to bridge the gap between visible and invisible, a true vertiginously vertical Gothic cathedral where the space between floor and vault is enormous but measurable.[9] An aesthetics that is scriptural, Trinitarian, Neoplatonic and Dionysian, but at bottom a unique, original amalgam of different strains. It is not I think by chance that Dante places Hugh in the crown of *sapientes* led by Bonaventure in *Paradiso* 12 [fig. 18].

15

Towards the *altitudo terribilis*

THEY WERE BORN WITHIN TEN years of each other, in the last quarter of the twelfth century, and they died within five years of each other, in the third decade of the thirteenth century. One was Spanish, from Castille, Dominic de Guzmán; the other was Italian, from Umbria, Francis of Assisi. Their personalities, their preaching, the orders they founded, revolutionised the Church and the whole of Europe. Dante, as usual extremely perceptive of cultural and religious novelties, invents in *Paradiso* 10–12 a nice dramatic fiction structured like a chiasmus whereby it is a Dominican, Thomas Aquinas, who tells the story of, and praises, Saint Francis, while it is Bonaventure of Bagnoregio, a Franciscan, who celebrates Saint Dominic [figs. 17 and 18]. Dante attributes to Divine Providence the birth of these two 'princes' who would guide the 'Bride of Christ', the Church, to her Beloved (the language being borrowed from the Song of Songs), and characterises each of them in three famous lines:

> L'un fu tutto serafico in ardore;
> l'altro per sapïenza in terra fue
> di cherubica luce uno splendore.

> (One prince was all seraphic in his ardor;
> The other, for his wisdom, had possessed
> The splendor of cherubic light on earth.)[1]

Francis was a seraph because of his mystical ardour. Dominic was a cherub for his *sapientia*, his knowledge and wisdom. Both produced a noble progeny, notably Bonaventure among the Franciscans, and Albert the Great and Thomas Aquinas among the Dominicans. Of the two, the one who interests me here is Francis, the seraph, who maintained openly he was 'ignorans et ydiota', but who nevertheless taught the beauty of creatures as if he had read plenty of traditional theology and contemporary mystical writings, at the same time renovating both.

Reading the two *Vitae* by Tommaso da Celano—once considered the author of the 'Dies irae'—and the later *Legenda maior* of Bonaventure, one becomes acquainted with the episodes which have turned Francis into a myth: his stripping off of his clothes and remaining naked, giving up the wealth of a merchant, in Assisi's public square; his preaching to birds and taming of the Gubbio wolf; his venturing to go all the way to Palestine during the Fifth Crusade to talk to the sultan of Egypt; his invention of the Greccio Christmas Crib—which started with just the Child in the manger and soon grew into a whole world of shepherds, angels, mountains, rivers and villages; his receiving in the wilderness of La Verna the stigmata—the wounds resembling those the nails of the Cross had driven into Christ's hands. And even without reading anything, it would be enough for anyone to gaze at Giotto's beautiful frescoes in Assisi's upper basilica of San Francesco.

Nothing, however, would prepare us fully for the 'Canticle of the Creatures', or 'Canticle of Brother Sun', which Francis composed, one of the earliest and most beautiful lyrics in vernacular Italian. One of the greatest, most original mystics of the Middle Ages,[2] more original even than Hugh of Saint-Victor, writes in his 'Canticle' the equivalent of a Psalm or of an entire section in a Wisdom Book of the Bible:

Laudato sie, mi' Signore, cum tucte le tue creature,
spetialmente messor lo frate sole,
lo qual è iorno, et allumini noi per lui.
Et ellu è bellu e radiante cum grande splendore:
de te, Altissimo, porta significatione.

Laudato si', mi' Signore, per sora luna e le stelle:
in celu l'ài formate clarite et pretiose et belle.

Laudato si', mi' Signore, per frate vento
et per aere et nubilo et sereno et onne tempo,
per lo quale a le tue creature dài sustentamento.

Laudato si', mi' Signore, per sor'aqua,
la quale è multo utile et humile et pretiosa et casta.

Laudato si', mi' Signore, per frate focu,
per lo quale ennallumini la nocte,
et ello è bello et iocundo et robustoso et forte.

(Praised be you, my Lord, with all your creatures,
especially master brother Sun,
who is the day and you give us light through him.
And he is beautiful and radiant with much splendour:
he signifies and manifests you, Most High.

Praised be you, my Lord, for sister Moon and the stars:
in the sky you shaped them, clear, precious, and beautiful.

Praised be you, my Lord, for brother wind
and for the air, cloudy and serene and all weather,
by whom you give sustenance to all your creatures.

Praised be you, my Lord, for sister water,
who is very useful and humble and precious and chaste.

Praised be you, my Lord, for brother fire,
by whom you illuminate the night,
and he is beautiful and joyful and vigorous and strong.)

Everything is chosen with care and simplicity. The beauty and the radiance of the sun dominates the opening, but is followed by the especially evocative *claritas* of stars and moon, the humbleness and precious chastity of water, the jocundity and robustness of fire, the acceptance of 'onne tempo', all weather. Francis is an accomplished, strong poet.

Having acknowledged, as would any good theologian at the time, that the sun 'signifies and manifests' the Lord, Francis praises cloudy and serene sky, water, and fire, then earth with its fruits, grass and flowers—that is, all living things—as beautiful.[3] He then turns from Ecclesiasticus (Sirach), and the Psalms,[4] to the Beatitudes preached in Matthew's and Luke's Gospels ('blessed are those who forgive for love of God and those who suffer illness and tribulation, for they shall be crowned by the Most High', he says), and finally surprises the reader by praising 'our sister bodily death,[5] which no living human can escape'. The contrast, and at the same time the close kinship, between 'brother' Sun and 'sister' death is indeed a sublime stroke of genius.[6] And while, shortly before the end, Francis sternly warns those who will die in mortal sin, he immediately adds, 'Blessed are those whom death shall find in the will of God, for second death shall not harm them.'

Francis reinvents the language of Scripture and exalts the beauty of the world. Indeed, he *blesses* the universe, life, and death after having opened the 'Canticle' by saying that all praise, glory, honour and *benediction* are in the first place due to the 'Altissimu, onnipotente, bon Signore', the most high, almighty, good Lord.

Francis's disciple Bonaventure will move towards that highness, calling it 'altitudo terribilis'. 'Of all the great scholastics,' wrote Hans Urs von Balthasar, 'Bonaventure is the one who offers the widest scope to the beautiful in his theology: not merely because he speaks of it most frequently, but because he clearly thereby gives expression to his innermost experience and does this in new concepts that are his own.'[7] Entrusted by his mother to Francis of Assisi in person as a child when he fell seriously ill, Bonaventure studied in Paris with Alexander of Hales and Jean de la Rochelle,[8] became a friar minor at the age of twenty-six, composed the famous *Legenda maior* on Saint Francis,[9] was for a long time general of the Franciscan order, and finally became a cardinal. As can be seen in his *Vitis mystica, De triplici via, Soliloquium, Lignum vitae, De perfectione vitae, De sex alis Seraphim* and even his *Collationes in Hexaemeron,* among others, his thought was profoundly marked by the mystical experience of Francis, which he wished to repeat by going on a retreat to the mountain of La Verna at the age of thirty-three.[10]

A Franciscan, yes, but also with an inclination for Augustine and ultimately Plato, whom he clearly prefers to Aristotle,[11] Bonaventure follows the exalted vision of the Beautiful of Dionysius, whose *Mystical Theology* he cites at the beginning and end of his best-known work, the *Itinerarium mentis in Deum*.[12] It is in this short, very dense treatise that he provides the fullest outline of his aesthetics. At the most elementary level, beauty 'is nothing but numerical equality' or 'a certain distribution of parts and suitable colour', as the *Itinerarium* repeats from Augustine. This entails not merely the 'relationship of the parts', von Balthasar observes, but also 'an impulse of that which enchants and casts a spell'.[13]

On the other hand, the supreme beauty, the *summe pulcrum* of sight, as well as the *summe harmonicum* of hearing, the *summe odoriferum* of smell and the *summe delectabile* of taste and touch, are attributes of God. And in God, according to the *De triplici via*, we find unity, truth, goodness, the first of his 'appropriated attributes'; power, wisdom, will, the second; sublimity, beauty and sweetness, the third. Sublimity belongs to the Father, beauty to the Son, sweetness to the Holy Spirit. 'Est igitur in Deo', Bonaventure concludes, opening up a perspective that can only be called sublime, 'altitudo terribilis, pulcritudo mirabilis, dulcedo desiderabilis': 'in God there is awesome *sublimity*, marvelous *beauty*, desirable *sweetness*'.[14] In the Prologue of the *Soliloquium*, following the doctrine of the Epistle to the Ephesians, Bonaventure speaks rather of the four 'dimensions' of God, corresponding to the four directions of the Cross, its length, breadth, height and depth: *longitudo, latitudo, sublimitas* and *profundum*, an articulation also proposed in the *Breviloquium* for the attributes of Scripture.[15]

God and Scripture are sublime and unfathomable. But the world also possesses fascinating beauty for Bonaventure. He repeats this many times: for example, in the *Itinerarium*, the *Breviloquium* and the *Collationes in Hexaemeron*, each time with important variations, but above all in his imitation of the supreme model, Francis of Assisi, of whom he says in the *Legenda maior*:

Vt autem ex omnibus excitaretur ad amorem diuinum, *exultabat in* cunctis *operibus manuum* Domini et per iucunditatis spectacula in uiuificam consurgebat rationem et causam. Contuebatur in pulchris Pulcherrimum et per impressa rebus *uestigia prosequebatur* ubique *Dilectum,* de omnibus *scalam* faciens, per quam conscenderet ad apprehendendum eum qui est *desiderabilis totus.*

(Aroused by all things to the love of God, he rejoiced in all the works of the Lord's hand and from these joy-producing manifestations he rose to their life-giving principle and cause. In beautiful things he saw Beauty itself and through his vestiges imprinted on creation he followed his Beloved everywhere, making from all things a ladder by which he could climb up and embrace him who is utterly desirable.)[16]

In his *De reductione artium ad theologiam* Bonaventure translates this characteristic of Francis into a general rule, according to which 'every sense seeks its proper sense object with longing, finds it with delight, and never wearied, seeks it again and again'; because 'the eye is not filled with seeing, neither is the ear filled with hearing'.[17] In the same way, our spiritual senses must seek with longing, find with joy, and time and again experience the beautiful, the harmonious, the fragrant, the sweet, or the delightful to the touch: 'per hunc etiam modum sensus cordis nostri sive pulcrum, sive consonum, sive odoriferum, sive dulce, sive mulcebre debet desideranter quaerere, gaudenter invenire, incessanter repetere'.[18] This is the beauty that 'our eyes will never tire of seeing and that does not lead us to perdition but is the way to wellbeing'.[19]

'Since all things are beautiful and in some way delightful, and since beauty and delight do not exist without proportion, and proportion exists primarily in numbers,' Bonaventure declares in the *Itinerarium,* following Augustine's *De vera religione* and *De musica,* 'all things are subject to number. Hence "number is the foremost exemplar in the Maker's mind" and in things, the principal vestige leading to wisdom.'[20] 'Est enim pulcritudo magna in machina mundana': 'There is indeed great beauty in the fabric of the world', affirms the *Breviloquium,* but there is even more in the Church, which 'is adorned with the splendour of the holy charismatic gifts; and greater beauty still in the heavenly Jerusalem;

and the greatest beauty of all in the supreme and most blessed Trinity. Not only, then, do the Scriptures have a MOST LOFTY subject, which procures delight and raises on high the vision of the mind; they are also MOST BEAUTIFUL, delighting our intellect in a certain special way.' There is indeed great beauty in the fabric of the world; but there is one that is greater, a greatest one—'et sic magis ac magis delectando assuefacit ad divinorum spectaculorum contuitus et anagogias'—'and as they deepen this delight more and more, they prepare our souls for the heavenly vision of God's exalted marvels'.[21] The world is shown in the Scriptures 'to run in a most orderly fashion from beginning to end, like a beautifully composed poem'—'ad modum cuiusdam pulcherrimi carminis ordinati'—'in which every mind may discover, through the succession of events, the diversity, multiplicity, and justice, the order, rectitude, and beauty, of the countless divine decrees that proceed from God's wisdom ruling the universe'.[22]

Then, in his *Collationes in Hexaemeron*, Bonaventure tells his readers that 'in the contemplative soul the sphere of the universe is described, and a certain heavenly spirit that has inscribed within it the whole sphere. There is also described in it the supersubstantial radiation which contains both the sphere of the universe and the universe of the spirits.' As a result, 'within the contemplative soul there are marvellous lights and a marvellous beauty'. And so, 'as the world, beautiful from top to bottom, from beginning to end, described in the soul produces a mirror'—'sic ergo mundus, pulcher a summo ad imum, ab initio ad finem, descriptus in anima facit speculum'—and any spirit is a mirror, 'so also in the soul there is a marvellous multiplicity, supreme order, and supreme proportionality'. When this happens, 'as often as there is reflected in the soul the disposition of the earthly sphere, and of the spirits of the blessed, and of the supersubstantial radiation, so often is there within it a marvellous refulgence: and because of this, it is more beautiful than the sun': 'toties in ea est mira refulgentia. Et ex hoc est speciosor sole.'[23]

Bonaventure's cosmos is made of light, as was that of Grosseteste,[24] and for him light is in fact the 'substantial form' of bodies.[25] Above all, it is a universe that shines with the light of Scripture, which he quotes in all his works, always with formidable passion. A single example will suffice to illustrate the aesthetic importance the Bible assumes for him. In the thirteenth of his *Collationes in Hexaemeron*, Bonaventure sets himself to explaining Genesis 1:9–11: 'Let the waters below the heavens be gathered into one place and let the dry land appear. And so it was. God called the dry land Earth and the assembled waters Seas. And God saw that it was good. Then God said, Let the earth bring forth vegetation: seedbearing plants and all kinds of fruit trees that bear fruit containing their seed [etc.]' His exposition is divided into two parts, the first dedicated to the multiplicity of the spiritual senses of Scripture, the second to its four senses. The first, consistent with the subject matter of the biblical verses, is entirely dominated by the image of water: from the drop to the fountain, from the rivers to the sea.

In the work of the third day, says Bonaventure, 'the third vision of understanding instructed by Scriptures' is figured. There might seem to be a contradiction between the earth, the last and lowest of the elements, and Scripture, which is instead the loftiest (*sublimissima*). But this is not the case, because the earth receives from heaven all that is excellent in it: 'it receives the influences of heaven, and brings forth the most beautiful swarms of beings': 'facit pulcherrimas pullulationes'. Scripture itself has three fundamental aspects:, spiritual meanings (the gathering of the waters); symbolic figures (the germinations of the earth); and manifold interpretations (the seed). But of course its senses are infinite, because 'forests of forests' are enclosed in a seed, and the seeds themselves are 'infinite'. 'Hence, in relation to the interpretations yet to be drawn, we may compare to a single drop from the sea all those that have been drawn so far'.[26]

The icon of water now takes shape, with the evocation, one after the other, in crescendo, of Psalm 32, Ecclesiastes (Qohelet), Psalms 92 and 106, the Gospel of Matthew, Ecclesiastes again, Luke, Isaiah, Esther, Lamentations, Ezekiel, Gregory the Great and Revelation: an impressively brilliant outburst of authorities and images. I will dwell on just a few. The first and the last point the way: the verse from Psalm 32, 'He gathers the waters of the sea as in a flask', signifies the universality of spiritual interpretations, their origin, and the 'most profound depth' and 'abundantly overflowing multiformity' of spiritual meaning they entail; the two quotations from Revelation, 'I heard a voice from heaven, like a voice of many waters', and the voice 'of harpers', indicate the multitude of intelligences and their agreement: 'for they agree in such a marvellous way [miro modo] that the resulting harmony is wonderful [et mira est harmonia]'. Between the first and the last, I choose the second and the third. They are two sublime moments, based primarily on Ecclesiastes and Psalms 92 and 106. Bonaventure, it must be remembered, wants to illustrate how the verse 'He gathers the waters of the sea as in a flask' in Psalm 32 represents and 'gathers together' 'spiritual meanings'. He then proceeds as follows:

> De primo in Ecclesiaste: *Omnia flumina intrant in mare, et mare non redundat; ad locum, unde exeunt, flumina revertuntur, ut iterum fluant*; sic omnes intelligentiae spirituales a Scriptura divina. Intelligentiae spirituales dicuntur flumina—et etiam viri intelligentes spiritualiter—quia originem habent a Scriptura et per Scripturam confirmantur, et per illas aliae intelligentiae habentur; unde in Psalmo: *Elevaverunt flumina, Domine, elevaverunt flumina vocem suam. Elevaverunt flumina fluctus suos a vocibus aquaruin multarum.* Quare? *Quia mirabiles elationes maris.* Quare? Quia *mirabilis in altis Dominus,* vox Dei debuit esse magna.
>
> Secunda ratio, propter profundissimam altitudinem; in Psalmo: *Qui descendunt mare in navibus, facientes operationem in aquis multis.* Ille descendit cum navibus in mare, qui cum spiritu summae reverentiae accedit ad exponendum Scripturas. Cum navibus descendit qui habet manuductionem lignum crucis; quia qui sine isto ligno vult intrare mare Scripturae submergitur, in maximos errores cadens; nisi enim sit Petrus, demergitur. Unde, alta profunditas; *quis inveniet eam*? Sapientia gloriatur, quae profundum abyssi penetravit et vidit mirabilia Dei in profundo; Ecclesiastici vigesimo quarto: *Ego in altissimis habitavi, et thronus meus in columna nubis. Gyrum caeli circuivi sola et profundum abyssi penetravi, in fluctibus maris ambulavi.* Haec dicit Sapientia incarnata: *Ego in altissimis habitavi,* in

creatione; *thronus meus in columna nubis,* in incarnatione; *in fluctibus maris ambulavi,* in passione; *profundum abissi penetravi,* in penetratione Scripturarum, quia aperuit illis sensum post resurrectionem, ut intelligerent Scripturas. Propter fidem crucis Petrus super mare ambulavit.

(In relation to the first, it is written in Ecclesiastes: *All rivers go to the sea, yet never does the sea become full. To the place where they go, the rivers keep on going:*[27] and it is the same with all the spiritual meanings that flow from divine Scripture. The spiritual meanings are called rivers—and also those men who understand in a spiritual manner—because they have their origin from the Scriptures and are confirmed by the Scriptures, and because, from these [spiritual meanings] other meanings are derived. Hence in the Psalm: *The floods lift up, O Lord, the floods lift up their voice; the floods lift up their tumult.*[28] *More powerful than the roar of many waters.* Why? Because *powerful on high is the Lord,*[29] God's voice had to be loud.

In relation to the second—the most profound depth [of spiritual meanings]—the Psalm reads: *They who sailed the sea in ships, trading on the deep waters.*[30] The man goes down to the sea in ships who approaches the Scriptures in a spirit of extreme reverence in order to explain them. He goes down with ships who takes as support the wood of the cross: for anyone who seeks to enter the sea of Scriptures without this wood is submerged, for he sinks into the greatest errors. Unless he is Peter himself, he founders. Hence, *it is very deep: who can find it out?* Wisdom is glorified, which penetrated the profound abyss and saw God's marvels in the deep. *I dwelt in the highest places, and My throne is in a pillar of a cloud. I alone have compassed the circuit of heaven, and have penetrated into the bottom of the deep, and have walked in the waves of the sea.*[31] This is what incarnate Wisdom says: *I dwelt in the highest heavens,* in the creation; *My throne is in a pillar of cloud,* in the incarnation; *I have walked in the waves of the sea,* in the passion; *I have penetrated into the bottom of the deep,* in the penetration of Scriptures, for after He arose, *He opened their minds,*

> *that they might understand the Scriptures.*[32] By faith in the cross, Peter walked on the sea.)[33]

He doesn't miss a beat, Bonaventure, does he? All the texts, except the last, come from the Wisdom literature of the Bible; all have water at their centre; all are read through a continuous interlacing of scriptural exegesis and Scripture. A Scripture that shines like a sun in the centre of the exegetical system. Its depth and its loftiness, its wonder and its marvels—the drop taken from the sea and the *mirabiles elationes maris*: the wondrous 'roar of many waters'—will remain within us.

16

The Names of God

ALBERT AND HIS PUPIL THOMAS: a fundamental moment in the history of the Beautiful. Both are bent over Dionysius's *De divinis nominibus*: Thomas even acts as an amanuensis for all Albert's commentaries on Dionysius, including the *Ecclesiastical Hierarchy*, the *Celestial Hierarchy* and the *Mystical Theology* with the *Epistles*.[1] There are differences between them, of course. Albert thinks that 'Dionysius follows Aristotle nearly everywhere, as is clear to one who diligently examines his books', a phrase of Thomas's in his *Commentary on the Sentences*, which objectively reflects Albert's thinking more than his own.[2] The Master is a 'peripatetic Dionysian', according to Wayne Hankey's definition, the pupil a 'Platonic Dionysian': the former uses Augustine and Aristotle; the latter, Aristotle and Proclus, or rather the *Liber de causis* traditionally attributed to Aristotle, but which Thomas realises cannot be by the Stagirite, for in the wake of William of Moerbeke he scents behind it the hand and doctrine of Proclus.[3]

There are also differences in their treatment of the names attributed to God, with Thomas appearing to be more open to 'sensibiles similitudines' and anthropomorphic images than his predecessor. But Albert, who dedicates page after page to *pulchrum* and *pulchritudo* in his commentary on the *De divinis nominibus*, must have transmitted to his disciple the enthusiasm for the beautiful that Dionysius, as we have seen, had celebrated more than all the Neoplatonists. To convince ourselves of this, all we have to do is to compare their expositions on the *De divinis nominibus*, perhaps under the expert guidance of Umberto Eco, who studied the aesthetics of both extensively.[4]

Albert and Thomas share a formal approach to the Beautiful. 'Ratio pulchri in universali consistit in resplendentia formae super partes materiae proportionatas vel super diversas vires vel actiones': 'The universal essence of beauty', says Albert, 'consists in the resplendence of form on the proportioned parts of matter or over the different powers or actions.'[5] Thomas agrees. 'Dicit ergo primo quod *ex pulchro isto* provenit *esse omnibus existentibus*: claritas enim est de consideratione pulchritudinis, ut dictum est; omnis autem forma, per quam res habet esse, est participatio quaedam divine claritatis': '[Dionysius] says, first, that from *that beautiful* [God] there comes forth *being for all existing things*: for clarity is of the consideration of beauty, as has been said; yet every form, through which a thing has being, is a certain participation of divine clarity.'[6]

Albert insists that what counts is form. In one of the passages transcribed by Thomas himself he writes,

> Dicendum quod pulcrum in ratione sui plura concludit: scilicet splendorem formae substantialis vel actualis supra partes materiae proportionatas et terminatas, sicut corpus dicitur pulcrum ex resplendentia coloris supra membra proportionata.
>
> (It must be said that beauty in its *ratio* contains many things: namely, the splendour of its substantial or actual form in the proportioned and bounded parts of matter, just as a body is said to be beautiful because of the resplendence of its colours shining over its well proportioned limbs.)[7]

All knowledge, Albert continues, pertains to form, which determines the multiplicity of the powers of matter: 'Omnis enim cognitio pertinet ad formam, quae est determinans materiae potentiarum multiplicitatem'. 'It is clear that beauty is attributed here to all things,' Eco comments. 'But more than this, beauty is guaranteed by metaphysics, not by mere lyrical excitement. Beauty exists in a thing as the splendour of its form, the form which orders the matter according to canons of proportion, and which in shining forth reveals the ordering activity. "Beauty", he writes, "does not subsist in material parts, but in resplendence of form".'[8]

Albert is absolute: 'all beautiful things are uniformly in God,' he states, and 'all beauty comes from the First Beauty, and is caused by God': 'beauty is in God and is the supreme and primal beauty, from which emanates the nature of the beauty of all beautiful things, the form of beauty'.[9] Albert is well aware that beauty 'omnia rapit ad desiderium sui' (draws everything to desire its self), and, conversely, that all things desire the beautiful and the good because together they form a whole, the *kalokágathon*, 'the good-and-beautiful'. He also proposes 'consonantia' and 'claritas' as the 'rationes' of beauty.[10] Albert reads and cites the *Timaeus* several times in his commentary on *De divinis nominibus*, but he does not dwell in any way on the use of myths or 'verisimilar' accounts, while in his commentary on the *Mystical Theology* he argues that Scripture 'describes divine things for us by means of symbols'.[11]

Thomas goes further. When Dionysius, quoting Plato's *Symposium*, describes supreme beauty as that which is 'neither made nor destroyed, nor increased nor diminished',[12] he (Thomas) attributes it, of course, to God, distinguishing it from that of his creatures. He states, however, in a quietly sensational phrase, that 'all things are made in order that they might imitate the divine beauty in whatever way': 'omnia enim facta sunt ut divinam pulchritudinem qualitercumque imitentur'.[13] Thomas also adopts a subjective approach with his famous 'pulchra sunt quae visa placent' (beautiful things are those which please when seen),[14] and he too reiterates: 'Requiritur enim ad pulchritudinem et claritatem forma et commensuratio quae ad ordinem pertinet' (For there is required for beauty and clarity form and the commensuration that pertains to order).[15] In the *Summa*, he then develops the three formal criteria for beauty echoed by Stephen Dedalus in Joyce's *Portrait of an Artist as a Young Man*:[16]

> Ad pulchritudinem tria requiruntur. Primo quidem, integritas sive perfectio: quae enim diminuta sunt, hoc ipso turpia sunt. Et debita proportio sive consonantia. Et iterum claritas: unde quae habent colorem nitidum, pulchra esse dicuntur.
>
> (For beauty includes three conditions, *integrity* or *perfection*, since those things which are impaired are by the very fact ugly; due *proportion*

> or *harmony*; and lastly, *brightness* or *clarity*, whence things are called beautiful which have a bright color.')[17]

Albert displays stringent theological and philosophical arguments and considerable scientific knowledge when he speaks of the sun as the 'name' of God and enters into a discussion about all the celestial bodies and their movements.[18] Equally rigorous, Thomas nevertheless maintains a certain openness to figurative language, to metaphor. God, he writes, in his exposition on *De divinis nominibus*, can be called 'lumen sensibile', even to the point of giving him the metaphorical name of *Solar lumen*, or Sun: 'nomen luminis Solaris metaphorice Deo attribuitur' (304). The reason, he then explains, is that Dionysius

> [d]icit ergo primo, quod sicut praedicta ex divina Bonitate habent esse et bene esse, ita et radius solaris per se consideratus, est ex Bonitate Dei et est quaedam *imago*, idest expressa similitudo divinae Bonitatis. Inde est quod ipsum *Bonum*, quod est Deus, *laudatur nominatione* Solaris *luminis*, eo quod manifestatur Bonitas divina in tali lumine, *sicut archetypum*, idest principalis figura vel principale exemplar in impressa imagine. Dicitur enim Malach. 4: 'Vobis timentibus nomen meum, orietur sol iustitiae'.

> ([Dionysius] says, first, that just as the aforementioned things have being and wellbeing from the divine goodness, so also the solar ray, considered through itself, is from the goodness of God and is a certain *image*, that is, an expressed likeness, of the divine goodness. Thence it is that *the good* itself, which is God, *is praised by the naming* of solar *light*, because the divine goodness is manifested in such light, *as an archetype*, that is, a principal figure or principal exemplar, *in* the impressed *image*. For it is said in Malachi 4:2: *For you fearing my name, the sun of justice shall rise.*)[19]

This is the justification that was needed not only by theologians, but also poets, especially those who dare to mix poetry and theology, or to treat the latter *metaphorice*, in poetic form.

In commenting on Dionysius's Epistles 7 and 9, Albert pronounces sentences of condemnation, albeit reasonably argued, against poetry and poets. Poets 'are not philosophers if not *secundum quid*', as he declares in his commentary on the seventh epistle, because the poets' aim is to persuade or dissuade, leaving rational judgment aside and inducing terror or abhorrence of the things used by *fabulae* to produce the very same effect: 'fictiones poetarum' is what Albert calls everything that in idolatrous cults cannot be proved by means of reason: for example, metamorphosis into the sun or a star.[20] The same concept is repeated in his commentary to Epistle 9, where however he accentuates his condemnation of poetry: 'modus symbolicae theologiae' Albert writes, 'est alius a modo poetriae, quia modus poetriae est falsus': the mode of poetry is false because 'the poet's intention is to bind the soul to his *figmenta*, in which he conceives either the horror or delight' of what he intends to persuade or dissuade, in an exclusively human sphere, whereas that of theology does not propose symbols for the soul to cling to, but intends instead to 'remove them from us and to guide us by way of the similarities they contain to that which is beyond human proportion'.[21]

Thomas, perhaps because he also composed poetry, is more cautious. In the *Summa*, he even devotes an article of the very first Quaestio of the Prima Pars to the problem 'utrum sacra Scriptura debeat uti metaphoris' and calmly replies that there is a difference in the use of metaphor by poetry and that of the 'sacra doctrina': the poet employs metaphor for representation, which is 'naturally delightful for the human being', Scripture 'out of necessity and utility'. Finally, it is 'convenient' for Scripture to express itself 'through bodily similitudes', because our *cognitio* begins with the senses. I will return to this in a moment, but in the meantime it is worth noting that for both points, Thomas openly quotes Dionysius's *Celestial Hierarchy*.[22]

For Thomas, there is even a similarity between 'poetics' and Scripture. In Quaestio 101 of the Prima Secundae he examines the problem of 'ceremonial precepts', whether they are 'figurative' or not, and finally admits, 'Sicut poetica non capiuntur a ratione humana propter defectum veritatis qui est in eis, ita etiam ratio humana perfecta capere non potest divina propter excedentem ipsorum veritatem' (Just as human reason fails to grasp poetical expressions on account of their being lacking in truth, so does it fail to grasp Divine things perfectly, on account of the sublimity of the truth they contain.)[23]

It is a comparison that attributes failure to sublimity, but it says a lot, it seems to me, about the way Thomas looks at poetry: that it is representation *naturaliter homini delectabilis*. 'It is natural to man to be pleased with representations',[24] and where natural feelings are involved there can be no completely negative judgment.

17

Decor, altitudo, gloria

THOMAS HAD IN FACT COMPOSED an *Expositio super Iob ad litteram*, a 'literal' commentary on the Book of Job, in which he makes frequent use of metaphorical parlance. In chapter 37, for example, while explaining Elihu's speech on light, atmospheric phenomena and God's construction of the heavens, Thomas inserts a clear reference to the *Timaeus* and the *Somnium Scipionis* on the descent of souls from the stars and their return to them after death—a passage far more open to the possibilities of 'metaphorical' interpretation than that of the *De anima* he had evoked before:

> quamvis etiam hoc posset exponi de luce corporali: posuerunt enim Platonici quod animae hominum derivabantur ab animabus stellarum, unde quando animae humanae suam dignitatem servant secundum rationem vivendo, revertuntur ad claritatem stellarum unde defluxerunt; unde in somnio Scipionis legitur quod civitatum *rectores et servatores hinc profecti,* scilicet a caelo, *huc revertuntur.* In quo etiam dat intelligere quod non ponebat ultimam remunerationem virtutis in temporalibus bonis sed in bonis spiritualibus post hanc vitam.

> (However, one can also say this about corporeal light. For the Platonists posited that the souls of men are derived from the souls of the stars. Therefore, when human souls guard their dignity by living according to reason, they return to the clarity of the stars from which they flowed down, and so Macrobius says in the *Dream of Scipio* that *rectors and guardians of cities come from above,* namely, from heaven,

and return there. In this, he gives us to understand that he does not put the ultimate reward of virtue in temporal goods, but in spiritual goods after this life.)[1]

A similar attitude appears again in the same chapter when Elihu explains the construction of the heavens,[2] and even more strongly when Thomas addresses the great speech uttered by God himself in chapters 38–41 of the Book of Job. For example, Thomas takes issue with the celestial harmony and music of the spheres postulated by the 'Pythagoreans' (and the Platonists), which he contrasts with the pure and simple word of Aristotle, making him regard the earlier opinions as interpretable only by way of metaphor:

> Considerandum autem est hic quod ex motu caelorum Pictagorici posuerunt sonitum harmonizatum provenire propter convenientissimam proportionem caelestium motuum, et quia ponebant corpora caelestia animata ideo talis consonantia sonorum possit concentus caeli vocari; sed Aristotiles probat in II de caelo quod ex motu caelestium corporum nullus sonitus procedit, et ideo hic concentum accipere possumus metaphorice positum pro sola convenientia caelestium motuum qui numquam requiescunt. Huiusmodi autem inspiratio sapientiae vel intelligentiae aut etiam concentus caeli ab initio fundationis terrae fuit, unde subdit *quando fundabatur pulvis in terra,* quod refertur ad situm terrae quae in imo ponitur sicut in fundamento, *et glebae compingebantur,* quod refertur ad humorem continentem in unum partes terrae, ne scilicet terra propter sui siccitatem in pulverem resolvatur.
>
> (Consider here that the Pythagoreans thought that a harmony of sounds came forth from the motion of the heavens because of the very fitting proportion of the heavenly motions, and since they posited that celestial bodies had souls, therefore, such a harmony of sounds can be called the harmonious singing of heaven. But Aristotle proves in Chapter II of *On Heaven* that no sound comes forth from the motion of the heavenly bodies,[3] and so we can take this harmonious singing metaphorically, as posited from the unique property of

> the heavenly motions, which never cease. This inspired wisdom or intelligence, or even this harmonious singing of heaven, existed from the beginning of the foundation of the earth, and so he says, *when the dust was established on the earth*, which refers to the position of the earth, placed on the deep as on a foundation, *and the clods of the earth held fast together*,[4] which refers to the humidity which holds the parts of the earth together, namely, so that the land may not return to dust because of its dryness.)[5]

Thomas then provides a survey of the animals celebrated by God in chapters 38–39—cock, lioness, crows, mountain goats, deer, wild ass, rhinoceros or unicorn, oxen, ostrich, horse, hawk, eagle—and dwells for several pages on Behemoth, identified with the elephant, and Leviathan, a whale covered with impenetrable scales. These can also be interpreted figuratively, he writes, as metaphors for the devil.[6] But the most fascinating passages are those devoted to the wisdom, beauty, sublimity and glory of God, in which the voices of the Psalms, Isaiah, Jeremiah and Luke resound, together with those of Ambrose, Augustine and Dionysius. It is evident that divine *decor* and *altitudo* find in Thomas a particular response, both emotional and intellectual:

> Ex huiusmodi autem effectibus excellentiam divinam demonstrat quantum ad tria: primo quidem quantum ad decorem cum dicit *circumda tibi decorem*, quasi dicat: si tam potens es in effectibus sicut Deus, attribuas tibi eius decorem, unde signanter dicit *circumda tibi*: Deus enim non habet circumdatum decorem quasi superadditum eius essentiae sed ipsa essentia eius est decor, per quem intelligitur ipsa claritas sive veritas, et puritas sive simplicitas, et perfectio essentiae eius; sed homo non potest habere decorem nisi circumdatum, quasi participando ipsum a Deo ut superadditum suae essentiae. Secundo tangit divinam altitudinem cum subdit *et in sublime erigere*: attenditur autem divina sublimitas non loco quia Deus loco non comprehenditur, sed perfectione et virtute quia quicquid de eo dicitur convenit ei in summo; huiusmodi immobiliter manet; homo autem secundum suam naturam est infimae condicionis, unde ad illam sublimitatem divinam pervenire non posset nisi se supra se

> sublevando, et ideo signanter dicit *in sublime erigere*. Tertio tangit eius gloriam . . .
>
> (From effects of this kind he demonstrates the divine excellence as to three things. First, as to beauty when he says, *deck yourself with dignity*, as if he should say, 'If you were as powerful in your works as God, you should attribute his beauty to yourself,' and so he clearly says, *deck yourself*, for God does not surround himself with beauty as something added beyond his essence, but his essence itself is beauty. This beauty includes his clarity or truth, his purity or simplicity, and the perfection of his essence. But man cannot have beauty unless he is decked with it, by participating in it from God as something added beyond his essence.
>
> Second, he treats the divine majesty when he says, *and lift yourself on high*. The divine majesty is not in a place, because God is not understood in a place, but consists in his perfection and power, because whatever is said about him is fitting to him in the highest degree. Majesty befits God essentially, and so he does not lift himself up to it, but it remains in him immovably. Man is in a weak condition according to his nature, and so he cannot arrive at that divine height except by lifting himself up above himself, and so he clearly says, *lift yourself on high*.
>
> Third, he treats of his glory . . .)[7]

The image of God immovable in sublimity is significant. It is certainly influenced by the Aristotelian conception of the Unmoved Mover, but it more closely follows Boethius's formulation in the famous ninth song of the third book of the *Consolation*: 'stabilisque manens'. It is a Byzantine-style icon like those painted by Cimabue: powerful, beautiful, sublime—motionless in its eternity.

18

Philomythía and Poetry

A VERY DIFFERENT ANGLE IS taken by Albert and Thomas in relation to the idea of *philomythía* proposed by Aristotle at the beginning of the *Metaphysics*, an idea that for both, in different ways, touches on the conception of the poet and poetry.[1] Aristotle held that the origin of 'philo-sophia', the love of knowledge, is wonder. But wonder establishes a kinship between the lover of knowledge (*philósophos*) and the lover of myth (*philómythos*), since myths are constructed out of wonder, so that the *philómythos* is 'in a sense' a philosopher, a *philósophos*.[2] This statement makes both Albert and Thomas take a giant leap forward.

In his *Metaphysica*, Albert affirmed that philosophy shared its origin with all the other arts and sciences because 'they seek by wondering [admirando] what is extraordinary in humans'. He then proposes his own definition of wonder, basing it, surprisingly, not on philosophical speculation but, for the first time, on physiology: 'Admirationem autem vocamus agoniam et suspensionem cordis in stuporem prodigii magni in sensum apparentis, ita quod cor systolem patitur' (And we call wonder the agony and suspension of the heart in astonishment at a great prodigy apparent to the senses, making the heart experience a systole.)[3] Wonder has some resemblance to fear, in the movements of the heart, since both derive from a 'suspension': in wonder from a suspension of the desire to know the portent appearing before the senses. That is why it is an *agonia* and why the heart has a systole, or contraction. *Agonia* is ignorance (*ágnoia*), as Albert says elsewhere, taking the idea from Averroes and playing on the similarity of the words.[4] The Aristotelian mechanism can therefore be reestablished: he who is in a state of ignorance entertains doubt, first about simpler phenomena (for Albert, the Pythagoreans' questions about number), then the more complex ones (astronomical phenomena):

> Similiter autem proficientes in physicis plus et plus admirari coeperunt de generatione universi, quaerentes utrum mundus esset factus vel non? Qui autem dubitat et admiratur, ignorans videtur: est enim admiratio motus ignorantis procedentis ad inquirendum, ut sciat causam eius de quo miratur: cuius signum est, quia ipse Philomithes secundum hunc modum Philosophus est: quia fabula sua construitur ab ipso ex mirandis.
>
> (Similarly, as they progressed in physics, they began to wonder more and more about the generation of the universe, asking whether the world had or had not been created. He who doubts and wonders seems ignorant, for wonder is the impulse moving the ignorant person to inquire so that he may know the cause of that at which he wonders, the sign of which is that in this way the Philomythes is himself a Philosopher: because he composes his *fabula* out of wondrous things.)[5]

Here *Poetics, Metaphysics* and *Timaeus* are being brought together. The lover of the *fabula,* the *philómythes* 'fingit fabulam' to arouse wonder, Albert writes referring to the *Poetics,* and that wonder stimulates further 'inquirendum', thereby generating philosophy: 'as is the case when Plato speaks of Phaethon, and of Deucalion'. By myth 'is meant the urge to wonder at the causes of the two deluges, of water and fire, which result from the orbit of the wandering stars (the planets), so that by means of wonder one seeks the cause and gets to know the truth'. 'Poesis modum dat philosophandi sicut aliae scientiae logices' (Poetry provides a way of philosophizing, like the other logical sciences): if the latter do it by means of reason, poetry does it through the impulse to inquiry produced by wonder.

This is a striking result, which suddenly overturns Albert's negative positions on poetry. Reading a passage like this, a poet-philosopher like

Dante must have leapt up from his bench. Thomas, who also asserts that 'as the proverb says: the poets tell many lies', avoids taking positions of this kind, but shifts the focus from Albert's present tense ('poetry gives way') to the past, when poetry and theology (not philosophy, as for Aristotle and Albert) were confused. He acquires the process through which *admirari* generates philosophy from Aristotle and treats the love of myth, *philomythía*, in the same way, ending up, however, in poetry:

> Et ex quo admiratio fuit causa inducens ad philosophiam, patet quod philosophus est aliqualiter philomythes, idest amator fabulae, quod proprium est poetarum. Unde primi, qui per modum quemdam fabularem de principiis rerum tractaverunt, dicti sunt poetae theologizantes, sicut fuit Perseus, et quidam alii, qui fuerunt septem sapientes.
>
> (And since wonder was the motive which led men to philosophy, it is evident that the philosopher is, in a sense, a philomythes, that is, a lover of myth, as is characteristic of the poets. Hence the first men to deal with the principles of things in a mythical way, such as Perseus and certain others who were the seven sages, were called the theologizing poets.)[6]

The fact that Thomas reverses Aristotle's model, writing that it is the philosopher who is similar to the poet, may depend on his use of a manuscript from a different family than the 'Vulgate' of the *Metaphysics*.[7] In any case, his reading of the text leads him to the identification of the 'theologizing poets' of earlier times, Perseus and the Seven Sages. Later, in his commentary on Book Lambda of the *Metaphysics* and the construction within it of a First Cause as the Unmoved Mover that moves all things, Thomas returns to those defined by Aristotle as 'the cosmologists who generate everything from night',[8] calling them 'theologizing poets' and including among them Orpheus 'and certain others, who maintained that the world is generated from night, that is, from a simple pre-existing privation': 'et quadam alii, qui ponebant mundum esse "generatum ex nocte", idest simplici privatione praeexistente'.[9] Then, following Aristotle, he mentions the 'physicists', those who, like Anaxagoras, claimed that in the beginning 'all things were together in a kind of mixture, which they called Chaos', hence their belief 'that all things exist potentially and not actually'. He then goes on to speak of Leucippus, Democritus and Plato, who claimed that 'movement had always existed even before the world': for Leucippus, in atoms, 'which are mobile in themselves, from which he supposed the world was composed'; for Plato—the Plato of the *Timaeus*—in 'the elements, which he said were moved by disorderly motions before the formation of the world, and afterwards were brought into order by God'.[10]

The commentary on the *Metaphysics* is thus for Albert and Thomas the occasion for a reappraisal of myth and poetry. For the former this even 'provides a way of philosophizing, like the other logical sciences'; for the latter it leads back to the time when poetry and theology coexisted in a single person, that of the poet, as perhaps it did in Parmenides and Hesiod, whom Thomas is keen to define a 'poet'. Hesiod, however, also made a decisive contribution to postulating Chaos as 'primo omnium' and establishing at the very beginning of things Love, 'qui condocet omnia immortalia', 'who instructs all the immortals' (i.e., for Thomas, the celestial bodies or the material principles themselves):[11] 'as though there had to be in existing things', he concludes, taking up the Aristotelian text,[12] 'not only a material cause of their motions, but also an efficient cause that moves and unites them'. That Love 'unites things', writes Thomas, 'is clear from this: love itself is a certain union between the lover and the thing loved, seeing that the lover regards the beloved as himself'.[13]

Albert and Thomas, therefore, in the thirteenth century, were stimulated to come to these conclusions by their reading of Aristotle.[14] But a thousand years earlier, a Greek-speaking intellectual of the late Antonine age, who declared that he was 'persuaded' by Homer, 'believed' in Plato and 'pitied' Epicurus, seemed to have figured it all out already. Maximus of Tyre, a Middle Platonist who lived in Rome under Commodus, left a work variously called *Diálexeis* or *Philosophoúmena,* but generally known as *Dissertations,* in the course of which he quotes from Plato's *Timaeus, Symposium* and *Phaedrus.* At the beginning of his fourth dissertation, dedicated to the problem of whether poets or philosophers had 'better conceptions about the gods', he writes as follows:

> Human beings are terribly contentious. Not only do they quarrel about consitutions and political power and about the evils that afflict us all; they have even extended this habit to those most peaceable of all pursuits, poetry and philosophy. Now, 'poetry' and 'philosophy' are two names for what is, in reality, a single thing [haploûn katà tèn ousían], differing within itself only to the extent that, as one might hold, day is distinct from the light of the sun falling on the earth, or the sun its course over the earth as distinct from day. Such is the relationship between poetry and philosophy. What is poetry if not a more venerable form of philosophy, composed in metre [harmonìa émmetros] and mythological in expression [gnòme mythologiké]? What is philosophy if not a younger form of poetry, less formal in composition and more lucid in expression? If then these two differ from each other only in age and in superficial form, how ought one to understand the difference in what the two kinds of composer—poet and philosopher—say about the gods?[15]

Maximus has clear ideas, though perhaps a bit simplistic if compared to those of Plato and Aristotle. He can see the importance of age, compositional structure, and above all myth, in the difference, or equality, between of philosophy and poetry. Almost five hundred years after Aristotle, a thousand before the Scholastics. One wonders what Marcus Aurelius, the philosopher emperor under whom Maximus most likely grew up, would have thought of this: he, a Stoic, who said he had learnt from one of his masters, Rusticus, to 'eschew [aposténai] rhetoric, and poetry, and fine language'.[16]

Times really had to change to allow us to reach the appreciation of Maximus's theories shown by Tasso in his *Discourses on the Heroic Poem*, where, in his comment on them in Book 1, he first declares they are not to be despised and then opposes to them his own more considered opinion:

> Ma io estimo che 'l modo di considerare le cose faccia l'una da l'altra differente, perciò che la poesia le considera in quanto belle, e la

> filosofia in quanto buone, come accenna il medesimo autore in un altro luogo, dicendo ch'Omero ebbe da far due cose, l'una appartenente a la filosofia, l'altra a la poesia; ed in quella ebbe risguardo a la virtù, in questa a l'effigie de la favola. È dunque la poesia investigatrice e quasi vagheggiatrice de la bellezza.
>
> (But I believe that the way of considering things leads to their being different one from the other, since poetry considers them in as much as they are beautiful, and philosophy in as much as they are good, as the same author mentions elsewhere, saying that Homer's poetry had a twofold scope; according to poetry arranged into the form of a fable, but according to philosophy, co-ordinated to the emulation of virtue, and the knowledge of truth. Poetry is therefore an investigator and coveter of beauty.)[17]

'È dunque la poesia investigatrice e quasi vagheggiatrice de la bellezza': Tasso's words will be echoed by another poet, several centuries later:

> 'Beauty is truth, truth beauty'—that is all
> Ye know on earth, and all ye need to know.[18]

19

'I love those who love me'

OUR WEB OF INTERSECTING STRANDS crosses a multiplicity of eras and cultures at this point of the story. The actors coming into play are not only the pagan gods and what they represent, but also Cicero, Philo and Seneca, then—interrelated but also entirely different—Wisdom and Proverbs from the Bible, and finally that wonderful love song, the Song of Songs. Let us begin, once again, with the *Timaeus*. According to Timaeus, '[t]hus far and until the birth of time the created universe was made in the likeness of the original, but inasmuch as all animals were not yet comprehended therein, it was still unlike. Therefore, the creator proceeded to fashion it after the nature of the pattern in this remaining point.'[1] I leave the floor to Federico Petrucci:

> In the generation narrative [. . .] the spiritual beings are the last living creatures to be produced directly by god, who in these pages will charge the gods he has begotten with the task of generating mortal living things following his own rational and providential plan (40d6–41d3). In order however to enable the generated gods to produce human beings, the Demiurge must still generate what is immortal and divine in them, namely the rational soul, and instruct it by showing it the laws of fate (41d4–42d4). In this way, the generated gods are able to fulfil the necessary providential plan that leads them to implant the rational soul in the body, an incorporation which in turn determines, according to a natural and mechanical necessity, the emergence of the irrational components of the soul and the passions they entail (42e5–43c7).[2]

Here, then, are the 'generated gods', but Plato carefully avoids discussing them in detail, merely providing a few hints:

> To know or tell the origin of the other divinities [*daimónes*] is beyond us, and we must accept the traditions of the men of old time who affirm themselves to be the offspring of the gods—that is what they say—and they must surely have known their own ancestors. How can we doubt the word of the children of the gods? Although they give no probable or certain proofs, still, as they declare that they are speaking of what took place in their own family, we must conform to custom and believe them. In this manner, then, according to them, the genealogy of these gods is to be received and set forth.
>
> Oceanus and Tethys were the children of Earth and Heaven, and from these sprang Phorcys and Cronus and Rhea, and all that generation, and from Cronus and Rhea sprang Zeus and Hera, and all those who are said to be their brethren, and others who were the children of these.[3]

Traditional genealogies were certainly insufficient, however, to satisfy Plato's successors and allow them to avoid giving more scientifically precise indications. To begin with, they had to try and harmonise this view with the general panorama of the beginnings of philosophy presented by Aristotle in the first book of the *Metaphysics*. Thus Cicero, for example, in *De natura deorum*, argues that 'Thales of Miletus [. . .] said that water was the first principle of things, but that god was the mind that moulded all things out of water' and that the 'view of Anaximander is that the gods are not everlasting but are born and perish at long intervals of time, and that they are worlds, countless in number'. He then addresses all the other Pre-Socratics, from Anaxagoras to Alcmeon, from Pythagoras to Xenophanes, Empedocles, Antisthenes and Socrates, each with his own 'god': the infinite mind, the sun and the stars all, the soul, the mind and all that is infinite, the four elements. He also engages with Plato:

> Iam de Platonis inconstantia longum est dicere, qui in Timaeo patrem huius mundi nominari neget posse, in Legum autem libris, quid

> sit omnino deus, anquiri oportere non censeat. [. . .] Idem et in Timaeo dicit et in Legibus et mundum deum esse et caelum et astra et terram et animos et eos, quos maiorum institutis accepimus. Quae et per se sunt falsa perspicue et inter se vehementer repugnantia.
>
> (The inconsistencies of Plato are a long story. In the Timaeus he says that it is impossible to name the father of this universe; and in the Laws he deprecates all inquiry into the nature of the deity. [. . .] Yet both in the Timaeus and the Laws he says that the world, the sky, the stars, the earth and our souls are gods, in addition to those in whom we have been taught to believe by ancestral tradition; but it is obvious that these propositions are both inherently false and mutually destructive.)[4]

Such statements could confuse anyone, learned and less learned, sceptics and believers in the ancient pantheon when, says Dante, 'all the gods were lying cheats'. The author of the Wisdom of Solomon—almost certainly an Alexandrine Jew living in the Augustan period—put it this way:

> Surely vain are all men by nature, who are ignorant of God, and could not out of the good things that are seen know him that is: neither by considering the works did they acknowledge the workmaster;
>
> But deemed either fire, or wind, or the swift air, or the circle of the stars, or the violent water, or the lights of heaven, to be the gods which govern the world.
>
> With whose beauty if they being delighted took them to be gods; let them know how much better the Lord of them is: for the first author of beauty hath created them.
>
> But if they were astonished at their power and virtue, let them understand by them, how much mightier he is that made them.
>
> For by the greatness and beauty of the creatures proportionably the maker of them is seen.
>
> But yet for this they are the less to be blamed: for they peradventure err, seeking God, and desirous to find him.[5]

It is remarkable that the author of Wisdom should so strongly emphasise in particular the beauty of created things, taken for 'gods' because of their beauty, and even more remarkable is his stressing that it was 'the first author of beauty' who created them. Indeed, this writer manifests a particular sensitivity to beauty, praising Wisdom in terms reminiscent of Plato's enthusiasm for beauty in the *Symposium*:

> For wisdom, which is the worker of all things, taught me: for in her is an understanding spirit, holy, one only, manifold, subtil, lively, clear, undefiled, plain, not subject to hurt, loving the thing that is good, quick, which cannot be letted, ready to do good,
>
> Kind to man, steadfast, sure, free from care, having all power, overseeing all things, and going through all understanding, pure, and most subtil, spirits.
>
> For wisdom is more moving than any motion: she passeth and goeth through all things by reason of her pureness.
>
> *For she is the breath of the power of God, and a pure influence flowing from the glory of the Almighty: therefore can no defiled thing fall into her.*
>
> *For she is the brightness of the everlasting light, the unspotted mirror of the power of God, and the image of his goodness.*
>
> [...]
>
> *For she is more beautiful than the sun, and above all the order of stars: being compared with the light, she is found before it.*
>
> *For after this cometh night: but vice shall not prevail against wisdom.*[6]

Beautiful beyond words, this *Sophía*, who is Wisdom and Knowledge together, possesses attributes that in the first two verses (22–23), comments Luca Mazzinghi, bring her close to the 'spirit of the world' described by the Stoic philosophers—in Cleanthes's *Hymn to Zeus* for example—'without slipping into the pantheism that characterises them'. She thus remains 'distinct from both God and creation'. The five metaphors of the central verses (25–26), 'inspired by Greek philosophy, describe the mediating nature of wisdom, the point of contact between God, the world and human beings'.[7]

Let us return for a moment to the *Timaeus*, going back to a passage I quoted at the very beginning of this essay. Timaeus said,

> This question, however, we must ask about the world. Which of the patterns had the artificer in view when he made it—the pattern of the unchangeable or of that which is created? If the world be indeed fair

> and the artificer good, it is manifest that he must have looked to that which is eternal, but if what cannot be said without blasphemy is true, then to the created pattern. Everyone will see that he must have looked to the eternal, for the world is the fairest of creations and he is the best of causes. And having been created in this way, the world has been framed in the likeness of that which is apprehended by reason and mind and is unchangeable.[8]

Engaging, centuries later, with the creation of the world in his *Quod Deus*, Philo of Alexandria returned to this passage from the *Timaeus*, adding qualifications that were not present in the original. 'The man of worth,' he stated, 'being zealous in inquiring and eager to learn, in all his inquiries found this to be the highest truth, that all things are the *grace* or gift of God—earth, water, air, fire, sun, stars, heaven, all plants and animals.' Since however God himself had no need of grace, he 'bestowed no gift of grace on Himself, [. . .] He has given the world to the world, and its parts to themselves and to each other, aye and to the All':

> But He has given His good in abundance to the All and its parts, not because He judged anything worthy of grace, but looking to His eternal goodness [agathótes], and thinking that to be beneficent was incumbent on His blessed and happy nature. So that if anyone should ask me what was the motive for the creation of the world, I will answer what Moses has taught, that it was the goodness of the Existent [toû óntos agathótes], that goodness which is the oldest of His bounties and itself the source of others.[9]

Plato, however, had never used either the term 'grace' or the word *agathótes* (goodness). Instead, it is the Latin Seneca who employs it, translating this very passage from the *Timaeus* in one of his *Epistles to Lucilius*. 'Quaeris quod sit propositum deo?' (Do you ask what God's purpose is?), he asked. 'Bonitas'—goodness—was his simple answer. 'Plato, at any rate, says: "What was God's reason for creating the world? God is good, and no good person is grudging of anything that is good. Therefore, God made it the best world possible."'[10] This was evidently the prevailing exegetical trend among the Stoics, or simply in the cultured circles of imperial Rome.

The celebration of goodness went hand in hand with that of beauty: 'without blemish is the root of discernment', of *phrónesis,* proclaims the Wisdom of Solomon, using an adjective, *adiáptotos,* 'without imperfection', which we have already found in the *Sublime*. Moreover, long before, Proverbs had already employed poetic imagery of uncommon strength:

> Doth not wisdom cry? and understanding put forth her voice?
> For wisdom *is* better than rubies; and all the things that may be desired are not to be compared to it.

> I was set up from everlasting, from the beginning, or ever the earth was.
>
> When *there were* no depths, I was brought forth; when *there were* no fountains abounding with water.
>
> Before the mountains were settled, before the hills was I brought forth: While as yet he had not made the earth, nor the fields, nor the highest part of the dust of the world.
>
> When he prepared the heavens, I *was* there: when he set a compass upon the face of the depth:
>
> When he established the clouds above: when he strengthened the fountains of the deep:
>
> When he gave to the sea his decree, that the waters should not pass his commandment: when he appointed the foundations of the earth:
>
> Then I was by him, *as* one brought up *with him*: and I was daily *his* delight, rejoicing always before him;
>
> Rejoicing in the habitable part of his earth; and my delights *were* with the sons of men.[11]

The cosmic inspiration, the originality of the imagery—like that of Wisdom, here her own orator, at play in God's presence at the time of Creation—go hand in hand, in other verses of Proverbs 8, with the celebration of her links with justice and the government of the world.[12] Sensitive to the poetic power and significance of these chapters of Proverbs and Wisdom, Dante reacted in Book 3 of the *Convivio*, with the lines of 'Amor che ne la mente mi ragiona' (Love, that speaks to me within my mind) that celebrate the eyes and 'sweet laughter' of his new noble Lady, Philosophy.

The composition begins with a general praise of the Lady, so 'noble' that the sun, 'which circles the whole world', cannot see another who could vie with her in any place. The commentary, always precise, will not let the apparently banal notation pass without launching into geographical-cosmological discussion that makes use of the highest authorities. Not the entire universe, Dante specifies, but only this part of sea and earth, 'this world':

> Questo mondo volse Pittagora—e li suoi seguaci—dicere che fosse una de le stelle e che un'altra a lei fosse opposita, così fatta, e chiamava quella Anticthona; e dicea ch'erano ambe in una spera che si volvea da occidente in oriente, e per questa revoluzione si girava lo sole intorno a noi, e ora si vedea e ora non si vedea. E dicea che 'l fuoco era nel mezzo di queste, ponendo quello essere più nobile corpo che l'acqua e che la terra, e ponendo lo mezzo nobilissimo intra li luoghi de li quattro corpi simplici: e però dicea che 'l fuoco, quando parea salire, secondo lo vero al mezzo discendea. Platone fu poi d'altra oppinione, e scrisse in uno suo libro che si chiama Timeo, che la terra col mare era bene lo mezzo di tutto, ma che 'l suo tondo tutto si girava a torno al suo centro, seguendo lo primo movimento del cielo; ma tarda molto per la sua grossa matera e per la massima distanza da quello. Queste oppinioni sono riprovate per false nel secondo De Celo et Mundo da quello glorioso filosofo al quale la natura più aperse li suoi segreti; e per lui quivi è provato, questo mondo, cioè la terra, stare in sè stabile e fissa in sempiterno. E le sue ragioni, che Aristotile dice a rompere costoro e affermare la veritade, non è mia intenzione qui narrare, perchè assai basta a la gente a cu' io parlo, per la sua grande autoritade sapere che questa terra è fissa e non si gira, e che essa col mare è centro del cielo.

> (Pythagoras and his followers maintained that this world was one of the stars and that there was another opposite it that was identical, which he called Antichthon; and he claimed that both were on a single sphere which turned from west to east, and that because of this revolution the Sun circled around us, and was alternately visible and invisible. He also claimed that fire was present between these two

masses, asserting that it was nobler than both water and earth, and that the center was the noblest among the places of the four simple bodies; and therefore he said that fire while seeming to rise was in reality descending toward its own center. Plato, coming later, was of a different opinion and wrote, in a book of his called *Timaeus,* that the earth with the sea was indeed the center of everything, but that its whole globe circled its center, following the primary movement of the heavens, but very slowly because of its dense matter and its extreme distance from that movement. These opinions are repudiated in the second book of *Heaven and Earth* as false by that glorious philosopher to whom nature most revealed her secrets; and there he proves that this world, that is the earth, stands in itself still and forever fixed. It is not my intention here to relate the proofs that Aristotle gives in order to refute those men and affirm the truth, because it is quite enough for those whom I am addressing to know on his great authority that this earth is fixed and does not turn, and that with the sea it is the center of heaven.)[13]

Pythagoras, Plato—once more the Plato of the *Timaeus*—and finally Aristotle. A few centuries of Greek 'wisdom' summed up in a dozen lines. It is against this cosmic background that the eyes and the smile of she who explores and studies it, Philosophy, stand out. Her nature and her features, however, transcend that same background, showing the delights of Paradise—making clear, in other words, that *sophía* is both human and more than human:

Cose appariscon ne lo suo aspetto,
che mostran de' piacer di Paradiso,
dico ne li occhi e nel suo dolce riso,
che le vi reca Amor com'a suo loco.
Elle soverchian lo nostro intelletto
come raggio di sole un frale viso.

(In her countenance appear such things
As manifest a part of the joy of Paradise.
I mean in her eyes and in her sweet smile,

For here Love draws them, as to himself.
They overwhelm our intellect,
As a ray of sunlight does weak vision.)[14]

To these he then added three of the densest and most moving verses he ever composed, all centred on the beauty of philosophy and what rains down from it, probably playing on earlier lines by Guinizzelli, but above all on the account of Pentecost in the Acts of the Apostles:[15]

Sua bieltà piove fiammelle di foco,
animate d'un spirito gentile
ch'è creatore d'ogni penser bono.

(Her beauty rains down little flames of fire,
Enkindled by a gentle spirit,
Who is the creator of all good thoughts.)[16]

And then he commented, with one of the most resonant proclamations of the beauty of Philosophy,

> Ne lo precedente capitolo questa gloriosa donna è commendata secondo l'una de le sue parti componenti, cioè amore. Ora in questo, ne lo quale io intendo esponere quel verso che comincia: *Cose appariscon ne lo suo aspetto,* si conviene trattare commendando l'altra parte sua, cioè *sapienza*. Dice adunque lo testo 'che ne la faccia di costei appariscono cose che mostrano de' piaceri di Paradiso'; e distingue lo loco dove ciò appare, cioè ne li occhi e ne lo riso. E qui si conviene sapere che li occhi de la Sapienza sono le sue demonstrazioni, con le quali si vede la veritade certissimamente; e lo suo riso sono le sue persuasioni, ne le quali si dimostra la luce interiore de la Sapienza sotto alcuno velamento: e in queste due cose si sente quel piacere altissimo di beatitudine, lo quale è massimo bene in Paradiso [. . .]. E in questo sguardo solamente l'umana perfezione s'acquista, cioè la perfezione de la ragione, de la quale, sì come di principalissima parte, tutta la nostra essenza depende; e tutte l'altre nostre operazioni—sentire, nutrire, e tutto—sono per quella sola, e questa è per sè, e non per altri; sì che, perfetta sia questa, perfetta è quella, tanto cioè che

l'uomo, in quanto ello è uomo, vede terminato ogni desiderio, e così è beato. E però si dice nel libro di Sapienza: 'Chi gitta via la sapienza e la dottrina, è infelice': che è privazione de l'essere felice [. . .]. Dunque si vede come ne l'aspetto di costei de le cose di Paradiso appaiono. E però si legge nel libro allegato di Sapienza, di lei parlando: 'Essa è candore de la etterna luce e specchio sanza macula de la maestà di Dio.'

(In the preceding chapter this glorious lady is praised according to one of her constituent parts, namely love. Now in the present one, in which I intend to explain the stanza that begins *In her countenance appear such things*, it is necessary to take up the praise of the other part, namely wisdom. The text says then 'that in her face there appear things which manifest some part of the joy of Paradise,' and it identifies the place where it appears, namely her eyes and her smile.

Here it is necessary to know that the eyes of wisdom are her demonstrations, by which truth is seen with the greatest certainty, and her smiles are her persuasions, in which the inner light of wisdom is revealed behind a kind of veil; and in each of them is felt the highest joy of blessedness, which is the greatest good of Paradise. [. . .]

It is in this gaze alone that human perfection is acquired (that is, the perfection of reason), on which, since it is our foremost part, all our being depends; and all of our other activities (feeling, nutrition, and the rest) exist only for the sake of this, and this exists for its own sake and not for the sake of anything else. Therefore if this is perfect, so is the other, to the extent that man, insofar as he is man, sees all his desires brought to their end and is thereby blessed. This is why it is said in the book of Wisdom: 'He who casts away wisdom and learning is unhappy,' for that is the deprivation of the state of happiness. [. . .] Consequently we see how some of the things of Paradise appear in her countenance. So we read in the book of Wisdom just cited, where it speaks of her: 'She is the brightness of the eternal light and the flawless mirror of the majesty of God.')[17]

If the author of Wisdom declares in the Bible that 'I loved her, and sought her out from my youth, I desired to make her my spouse, and

I was a lover of her beauty,'[18] Dante devotes the whole of his *Convivio* to his love of philosophy, which for him is 'a loving use of the wisdom which exists in the greatest measure in God, since supreme wisdom, supreme love, and supreme actuality are found in him'. *Philo-sophia* means 'love of wisdom', and Dante, following Aristotle, places its origin in wonder. When, in the *Convivio*, he writes that 'awe is the amazement of the mind [lo stupore è uno stordimento d'animo] at seeing or hearing, or in some way perceiving, great and marvellous things. Insofar as they seem great, they instil reverence for them in him who perceives them; insofar as they seem marvellous they make him yearn for knowledge about them,' the echo of the *Metaphysics* is transparent.[19] Wisdom too, however, is linked to wonder. 'He hath garnished the excellent works of his wisdom,' Sirach proclaims,[20] and all the Wisdom Books of the Bible are full of the wonders wrought by God, especially with Creation. But the most resounding proclamation of this love of wisdom comes from Proverbs:

> I love those who love me; and those that seek me eagerly shall find me.[21]

All Dante does is to quote the first part of the verse, preceding it with a brief introduction based on Aristotle's *Ethics* and placing it in a position of absolute prominence, almost as if it were the climax of the vision of the *Convivio*:

> Sì ch'omai qui si può dire, come la vera amistà de li uomini intra sé è che ciascuno ami tutto ciascuno, che 'l vero filosofo ciascuna parte de la sua sapienza ama, e la sapienza ciascuna parte del filosofo, in quanto tutto a sé lo riduce, e nullo suo pensiero ad altre cose lascia distendere. Onde essa Sapienza dice ne li Proverbi di Salomone: 'Io amo coloro che amano me'.

> (So now we can say here that as true friendship among men exists when each person loves the other in full measure, so the true philosopher loves every part of wisdom, and wisdom every part of the philosopher, since she draws him to herself in full measure and does not allow his thoughts to stray to other things. This is why wisdom herself says in the Proverbs of Solomon: 'I love those who love me'.)[22]

It is clear that by using the term 'Wisdom' Dante is hinting at the two aspects, 'the speculative-rational or philosophical, and the mystical-religious, proper to scriptural revelation, identified in the one certainty of a divine, absolute and eternal truth. Constituting the proper object of human perfection, it is the source of a beatitude, already on this earth, that heralds that of the future life.' This is from Cesare Vasoli's comment on the *Convivio*, concluding with a statement on this passage that is of fundamental importance: 'the love of God and the love of knowledge [. . .] *are one and the same*.'[23]

From the *Timaeus* we have moved on to Wisdom, then to Philo and Seneca, finally to Proverbs, Aristotle and Dante. One last step remains to be taken. In the *Convivio*, Dante himself refers on several occasions to the Song of Songs, that sweet and intense poem of love between a bride and her bridegroom that we have already encountered in chapter 6 and which contains some of the most beautiful verses ever written, together with constant exaltations of beauty:

> Behold, thou art fair, my love; behold, thou art fair; thou hast
> doves' eyes.
> Behold, thou art fair, my beloved, yea, pleasant: also our bed
> is green.
> The beams of our house are cedar, and our rafters of fir.[24]

In the treatise, Dante's only departures from the traditional interpretations of the Song are when he combines references to it with quotations from Wisdom and Sirach, as when, speaking of divine philosophy, he exclaims, 'O most noble and excellent is that heart which directs its love toward the bride of the Emperor of heaven, and not the bride alone but the sister and the most beloved daughter!' She who is 'the most beautiful and honourable daughter of the Emperor of the universe, to whom Pythagoras gave the name of Philosophy';[25] she who was the first to be created by the most High in Ecclesiasticus (Sirach), the sister and spouse in the Song of Solomon.[26] When, after abandoning the *Convivio* and embarking on the *Commedia*, Dante imagines his meeting with Beatrice, at long last, so many years after her death, he invents a phantasmagorical procession on top of the mountain of Purgatory, with a chariot (the Church) pulled by a gryphon (Christ) and a veiled woman standing on it. Twenty-four 'elders' (the books of the Old Testament) accompany him, all of whom are singing the Angel's greeting to Mary in Luke's Annunciation—to which Dante significantly adds the 'beauty' of the Virgin:

> Tutti cantavan: '*Benedicta* tue
> ne le figlie d'Adamo, e benedette
> sieno in etterno le bellezze tue!'

> (And all of these were singing: 'You among
> the daughters born to Adam are *benedicta,*
> your beauty blessed to all eternity.')[27]

The chariot stops. One of the elders, as if he were a messenger 'sent from heaven', intones, shouting three times, with the others following on, 'Veni, sponsa, de Libano', verse 8 of chapter 4 of the Song of Songs:

> Come with me from Lebanon, my spouse, with me from
> Lebanon.

This is how Dante announces the appearance of Beatrice: Divine Science, glimpsed already in the *Convivio*: 'la colomba mia e la perfetta mia', 'my dove and my perfect one'.[28] 'Io amo coloro che amano me.' I love those who love me.[29]

20

'What Timaeus argues about the souls'

FROM HERE, MY ROUTE CANNOT but lead once again to the writer who best knew how to celebrate this love, combining Aristotle and Boethius: that is, Dante, who seems to me, with all his characteristic originality, to be the true heir to the tradition outlined up to now.[1] That Dante is bound to Boethius from the very depths of his soul is testified by the passage in the *Convivio* in which he declares that his conversion to philosophy is due precisely to his reading of the *Consolation*.[2] He quotes Boethius several times elsewhere in the treatise, and then, in the *Commedia*, he repeatedly inserts expressions, ideas and images he draws from the *Consolation*, often combining them with passages from the *Timaeus* of Calcidius.[3] His use of Dionysius is explicit in the 'retraction' of *Paradiso* 28 regarding the celestial hierarchies.[4] That Dante knew Bonaventure, Albert and Thomas does not even need to be said. I will only observe that Thomas, Albert and Boethius are all three to be found in the first *corona* (crown) of the wise spirits of *Paradiso* 10, while Bonaventure leads the second.

There is one aspect in particular of Canto 4 of *Paradiso* that I want to discuss now.[5] The encounter with Piccarda Donati in Canto 3 raises a series of questions that might seem idle but are instead essential to the very setting and structuring of the third cantica: the location of souls in heaven, the kind of speech used in the Scriptures, absolute and relative will, and the possibility of compensating for not keeping a vow, or obtaining dispensation. I deliberately neglect most of them here, particularly the first, third and fourth, so as to concentrate on the second, the kind of speech used in the Scriptures, because it is here that the particular *pulchritudo* of *Paradiso* takes shape.

Beatrice explains to Dante that the souls of the blessed do not in fact return to heaven, as Plato seems to be declaring in the *Timaeus,* and that the shadows of Piccarda and Constance do not reside in the Heaven of the Moon, but only appear there. In reality they are in the Empyrean like 'the most in-god-ed of the Seraphim, Moses and Samuel—and either John you care to mention', and Mary. It is that they show themselves in this heaven, in order to 'signify' their condition:[6]

Ancor di dubitar ti dà cagione
parer tornarsi l'anime a le stelle,
secondo la sentenza di Platone.

Queste son le question che nel tuo velle
pontano igualmente; e però pria
tratterò quella che più ha di felle.

D'i Serafin colui che più s'india,
Moïsè, Samuel, e quel Giovanni
che prender vuoli, io dico, non Maria,

non hanno in altro cielo i loro scanni
che questi spirti che mo t'appariro,
né hanno a l'esser lor più o meno anni;

ma tutti fanno bello il primo giro,
e differentemente han dolce vita
per sentir più e men l'etterno spiro.

Qui si mostraro, non perché sortita
sia questa spera lor, ma per far segno
de la celestïal c'ha men salita.

Così parlar conviensi al vostro ingegno,
però che solo da sensato apprende
ciò che fa poscia d'intelletto degno.

Per questo la Scrittura condescende
a vostra facultate, e piedi e mano
attribuisce a Dio e altro intende;

e Santa Chiesa con aspetto umano
Gabrïel e Michel vi rappresenta,
e l'altro che Tobia rifece sano.

Quel che Timeo de l'anime argomenta
non è simile a ciò che qui si vede,
però che, come dice, par che senta.

Dice che l'alma a la sua stella riede,
credendo quella quindi esser decisa
quando natura per forma la diede;

e forse sua sentenza è d'altra guisa
che la voce non suona, ed esser puote
con intenzion da non esser derisa.

S'elli intende tornare a queste ruote
l'onor de la influenza e 'l biasmo, forse
in alcun vero suo arco percuote.

Questo principio, male inteso, torse
già tutto il mondo quasi, sì che Giove,
Mercurio e Marte a nominar trascorse.[7]

(A further reason for your doubt is this:
our souls return, or so it may appear,
as Plato in his teaching says, to stars.

These are the questions that, with equal weight,
point, in volition, hard upon your mind.
I'll first treat that which is more poisonous.

The most in-god-ed of the Seraphim,
Moses and Samuel—and either John
you care to mention—even Maria,

none is enthroned in any other sphere
than those souls are who've just appeared to you.
Nor are their years, existing, more or less.

All add in beauty to the highest gyre.
Some sense the eternal breathing more, some less.
So life is sweet to all in differing ways.

They did, here, show themselves, but not because
this sphere has been allotted them as theirs.
They signify celestial power least raised.

To speak in this way fits the human mind.
For you can only grasp through things you've sensed
what mind will then present as fit for thought.

For this same reason, Scripture condescends
to your capacities, and says that God
has hands and feet—though meaning otherwise.

So, Holy Church will also represent
Michael and Gabriel with human face,
the other, too, who helped heal Tobit's sight.

But Plato in *Timaeus* 'On the soul'
argues a case at odds with that seen here.
For what he says, it seems, has literal force.

He says that souls go back to their own stars,
believing them to be excised from these,
when Nature granted each its proper form.

This doctrine, though, perhaps conceals a sense
quite other than these words of his pronounce,
with implications we should not deride.

If Plato means that, back to join these wheels,
there comes the blame or honour of their power,
perhaps his bow shot hits upon some truth.

And yet, misunderstood, this principle
wrenched almost all the world off course.
So Jove and Mars and Mercury were named as gods.) [See fig. 1]

The passage from Plato that Dante has in mind here is *Timaeus* 41d–42b:

> Thus he spoke, and once more into the cup in which he had previously mingled the soul of the universe he poured the remains of the elements, and mingled them in much the same manner; they were not, however, pure as before, but diluted to the second and third degree. And having made it he divided the whole mixture into souls equal in number to the stars and assigned each soul to a star, and having there placed them as in a chariot he showed them the nature of the universe and declared to them the laws of destiny, according to which their first birth would be one and the same for all—no one should suffer a disadvantage at his hands. They were to be sown in the instruments of time severally adapted to them, and to come forth the most religious of animals, and as human nature was of two kinds, the superior race was of such and such a character, and would hereafter be called man. Now, when they should be implanted in bodies by necessity and be always gaining or losing some part of their bodily substance, then, in the first place, it would be necessary that they should all have in them one and the same faculty of sensation, arising out of irresistible impressions; in the second place, they must have love, in which pleasure and pain mingle—also fear and anger, and the feelings which are akin or opposite to them. If they conquered these they would live righteously, and if they were conquered by them, unrighteously. He who lived well during his appointed time was to return and dwell in his native star, and there he would have a blessed and congenial existence. But if he failed in attaining this, at the second birth he would pass into a woman.

Of course, this is what the text of the *Timaeus* says in Benjamin Jowett's translation. But Dante must have taken the doctrine from Calcidius, or perhaps Macrobius,[8] as, later, in *Paradiso* 7.64–66, where '[l]a divina bontà, che da sé sperne' (the generosity of God which scorns all spite) is probably drawn from Calcidius 29, with echoes of Boethius.

In fact, Dante's tercets link the *Paradiso* to the Scriptures and the practice of the Church. Beatrice is referring explicitly to the description in Canto 3, where souls appear in order 'to signify', while the lines that follow deal with the Bible and with images, particularly those of angels, used in churches both as visual representations and as examples in preaching. They are first and foremost a declaration of cultural belonging—to the long ecclesiastical tradition that justifies icons,[9] and to the culture of the visual representation of the divine, which experienced a new, quite exceptional expansion in thirteenth- and fourteenth-century Italy. But they are also the distillation of 'symbolic' theories ranging from Dionysius to the great Scholastics.

Thomas Aquinas, who comments on the whole of the final part of the *Divine Names* with appellations ranging from 'I am who I am' to anthropomorphic expressions in his exposition,[10] summarises and extends the meditation in his *Summa Theologiae*.[11] 'It is befitting ['conveniens est': Dante's 'conviensi'] Holy Writ to put forward divine and spiritual truths by means of comparisons with material things. For God provides for everything according to the capacity of its nature. Now it is natural to man to attain to intellectual truths through sensible objects, because all our knowledge originates from sense ['quia omnis nostra cognitio a sensu initium habet': in Dante, 'al vostro ingegno, / però che solo da sensato apprende / ciò che fa poscia d'intelletto degno' (you can only grasp through things you've sensed / what mind will then present as fit for thought)]'. Thus it is also fitting that the Scriptures should expound spiritual truths to us 'by means of figures taken from corporeal things, in order that thereby even the simple [rudes] who are unable by themselves to grasp intellectual things may be able to understand'. Moreover, '[t]he ray of divine revelation is not extinguished by the sensible imagery wherewith it is veiled, as Dionysius says in the first chapter of the *De coelesti hierarchia*; and its truth so far remains that it does not allow the minds of those to whom the revelation has been made, to rest in the metaphors, but raises them to the knowledge of truths'. Thus, he continues, 'it is more fitting that divine truths should be expounded under the figure of less noble than of nobler bodies [vilium corporum quam corporum nobilium]'. In this way, 'men's minds are the better preserved from error. For then it is clear that these things are not literal descriptions of divine truths, which might have been open to doubt had they been expressed under the figure of nobler bodies', but also 'because this is more befitting the knowledge of God that we have in this life' and 'because thereby divine truths are the better hidden from the unworthy [indigni]'. Thus, for example, '[w]hen Scripture speaks of God's arm, the literal sense is not that God has such a member, but only what is signified by this member, namely operative power [virtus operativa]'.

Dante accepts these indications only in part. In claiming that the Bible gives God human limbs 'though meaning otherwise', and in adding that Plato's 'doctrine', when he says that the soul returns 'to its star', conceals perhaps 'a sense quite other than these words of his pronounce', Dante is echoing typical medieval definitions of allegory, which, as Isidore writes, for example, 'says one thing and other thing is understood' (aliud enim sonat et aliud intelligitur).[12] However, he is particularly careful not to employ similar anthropomorphic images of the divine, perhaps because 'our human form' 'painted' according to the 'very essence' of God—the Incarnation—concentrates and sums up in a perfectly Christian way all the representation and all the truth that God himself can sustain. In the entire *Commedia*, there are only five instances of anthropomorphism: the 'arms' of *Purgatorio* 3.122 (suggesting perhaps the open, outstretched arms of the crucified Christ); the 'face' of *Purgatorio* 3.126 (indicating its 'aspect', mercy); the creative 'hand' of *Purgatorio* 16.85; the 'eye' of *Paradiso* 10.12; and the 'face' of *Paradiso* 29.77.[13]

It is probably along these lines, though here he shifts more decisively onto the side of logic, that Dante 'saves' Plato's language and vision at the very point in which he denies its literal value.[14] What the *Timaeus* teaches about souls—'Quel che Timeo de l'anime argomenta'—has no counterpart in the reality of heaven, but Plato may perhaps have been implying something different, as when Scripture attributes hands and feet to God 'though meaning otherwise'. He—Plato—might mean that the celestial spheres—the stars—are entitled to the honour and the blame of influencing human affairs: 'perhaps' here 'his bow shot hits upon some truth'. It's worth noting the number of times 'perhaps' punctuates Beatrice's speech: Plato—even the Plato represented by Calcidius, Macrobius, or William of Conches—should be accorded the benefit of the doubt! 'On this *alcun vero*, the link between the souls and their stars', writes Anna Maria Chiavacci Leonardi, 'Dante will build the whole of his sensible *Paradiso*, the myth and figure of invisible reality, exactly in the way he understands Plato's *Timaeus* here.'[15]

The *Epistle to Cangrande* refers continually to Aristotle, cites the *Liber de causis* to explain the working of the *Commedia* and towards the end provides an explanation of the lines from *Paradiso* 1: 'vidi cose che ridire / né sa né può chi di là sù descende' (and saw things there that no one / who descends knows how or ever can repeat). As well as explicitly recalling the Second Epistle to the Corinthians, Matthew's Gospel on the Transfiguration, Ezekiel and Daniel, Richard of Saint-Victor and his *De contemplatione*, Bernard of Clairvaux with his *De consideratione*, and Augustine's *De quantitate animae*, the *Epistle* cites the famous metre 9 of Boethius's *Consolation*, Book 3, and invokes Plato's 'use of metaphors' 'in his books' to compensate the lack of suitable words to express his thoughts:

> Vidit ergo, ut dicit, aliqua que referre nescit et nequit rediens. Diligenter quippe notandum est quod dicit 'nescit et nequit': nescit quia oblitus, nequit quia, si recordatur et contentum tenet, sermo tamen deficit. Multa namque per intellectum videmus quibus signa vocalia desunt: quod satis Plato insinuat in suis libris per assumptionem metaphorismorum; multa enim per lumen intellectuale vidit que sermone proprio nequivit exprimere.
>
> (He saw, then, as he says, certain things 'which he who returns has neither knowledge nor power to relate'. Now it must be carefully noted that he says 'has neither knowledge nor power'—knowledge he has not, because he has forgotten; power he has not, because even if he remembers, and retains it thereafter, nevertheless speech fails him. For we perceive many things by the intellect for which language has no terms—a fact which Plato indicates plainly enough in his books by his employment of metaphors; for he perceived many

> things by the light of the intellect which his everyday language was inadequate to express.)[16]

We have reached the final paragraphs of the *Epistle*, and the author sees fit to refer to Plato's 'books'. But the only one of those books he could have known was the *Timaeus*, because the others had not yet returned to the West. It is therefore the *Timaeus* the writer of the *Epistle* is speaking of when he compares Dante's experience to that of Plato. This is no small thing, whoever the author of the *Epistle to Cangrande* may have been.[17]

21

'The hall-mark of genius'

IN 1910, IN *The Spirit of Romance,* Ezra Pound, one of the major exponents of Modernism, goes much further.[1] Pound finds an equivalent for Dante's *Paradiso,* albeit in an experience few human beings would be able to have. This time, he resorts to Plato's *Phaedrus* and the great myth of the winged chariot.[2] 'The colourless and formless and intangible essence', Plato states in Pound's translation, 'is visible to the mind, which is the only lord of the soul: circling around this in the region above the heavens is the place of true knowledge.' He then claims that 'of the heaven which is above the heavens no earthly poet has sung, or ever will sing in a worthy manner'. This, Pound retorts, is false: if we want a perfect definition of Dante's *Paradiso* we will find it in this very same dialogue: 'And this is the recollection of those things which our souls saw when in company with God—when looking down from above on that which we now call being, and upward toward the true being.'[3] For Pound, the experience described in the *Phaedrus* is corroborated by the first four tercets of Canto 1 of *Paradiso*—discussed at length in the *Epistle to Cangrande*—where Dante announces that he has been 'in that heaven which most receiveth of his light' and affirms that memory cannot follow the intellect when, 'as it draweth nigh to its desire, our intellect sinketh so deep'. 'Nowhere', Pound continues, 'is the nature of the mystic ecstasy so well described' as in Glaucus's famous tercet in Canto 1 of *Paradiso*. And again two pages later, recalling Piccarda's speech in *Paradiso* 3, he argues that it not only contains 'that philosophy with which some say the poem is over-loaded', but that it is also '*the very marrow of beauty*'.[4] In short, 'quel che Timeo de l'anime argomenta' may not be literally true, but it is perhaps an example of *eikòs lógos*, or 'verisimilar discourse': in any case the door has now been flung wide open for Dante to enter the figurative space in which to locate his *Paradiso*.

Dante himself resorts to metaphors drawn from philosophical and theological language: love, splendour, point, substance, form, matter, act, potency. In other words, he chooses the mode of speech adopted by God and that Dionysius and Thomas call 'per intelligibiles processiones'. When he opts for 'sensibiles similitudines', he uses not 'vile' but 'noble things': light, ray, fire, sea. If he uses allegory, it is once or twice removed from the experience of the *rudes*. He elevates his metaphors and 'sensitive' figures to the high and rarefied register of his own lyric poetry, already codified in the *De vulgari eloquentia* (2.7). A poet of multilingualism and *sermo humilis*, he does indeed at times choose his icons from among 'corporeal' objects, but he immerses them in *claritas*, surrounding them with Neoplatonic splendour and alternating them with discourses dominated by a mystical circularity, referring to the precise terminology of Aristotelian and Scholastic thought. Dante's is thus an allegory that is entirely 'intellectual'. Always attentive to detail, he sees it, so to speak, *sub specie integritatis*, as an element of the universal order within the perfection of the whole. He pays attention, Dante, to 'degrees', to the more and the less ('more in one part, less elsewhere'), while safeguarding the *consonantia*, the proportion of each thing to each other.

For Pound's Aristotle, 'the apt use of metaphor, arising, as it does, from a swift perception of relations, is the hall-mark of genius'.[5] Dante establishes continuous relations: not between things and words, but between two different linguistic modes. If there is a hiatus between letter and allegory, it depends on their relationship; on metaphor, in other words: the evocative gap between one sphere and the next, between our understanding and misunderstanding of 'love' or 'splendour'. The hiatus itself saves the dramatic-theological fiction of the cantica: the spirits of the First Heaven appear in the moon, but only 'to signify' their 'spiritual' destiny, which consists in being distributed in the Empyrean according to their 'degree'. Dante attributes a particular meaning, both theological and poetic, to the 'allegory of the theologians', a particular meaning that is both theological and poetic, just as he did in speaking of 'shadows' and inventing for them a physiology and metaphysics. In this sense, there is a correspondence between the theory expounded by Statius in *Purgatorio* 25, stemming from the pilgrim's doubts after meeting Forese, and that which is illustrated by Beatrice, stemming from the doubts arising after his encounter with Piccarda, Forese's sister. Meanwhile, Timaeus has ascended into Paradise, the *Timaeus* to the *Paradiso*.[6]

22

'We must lose ourselves'

SO NOW TIMAEUS IS in Paradise. But we must lose ourselves in his heavens to see how far this *Dantes Platonicus* can go. Let us take the same path as before, but in the opposite direction: that is, going back from Dante. We will start by stating the facts: up to the thirteenth century, when Aristotle returns to the field, the European Middle Ages is essentially Platonic. Therefore, in order to stray into the Platonic waters of the last cantica of the *Commedia*, it is necessary to set clear limits to a field that spans almost a thousand years and includes philosophers, theologians and Church Fathers, from Tertullian and Augustine to at least Thomas Aquinas, as well as works of *ars poetica* and *ars dictaminis*, rhetoric and mythography, such as those composed by Geoffroi de Vinsauf, Boncompagno da Signa, Brunetto Latini, or the tradition that goes at least from John of Garland to Giovanni del Virgilio and perhaps the Vatican Mythographers.[1] So, to return to my previous pages, I would like to trace a path whose points of departure and arrival are compulsory, since the names of Boethius and the *Liber de causis* are mentioned by Dante himself, while Platonism—which after all begins with Plato himself—follows instead a partly subterranean but nonetheless complex and grandiose itinerary through all the centuries under consideration and particularly in the so-called School of Chartres. In conclusion, as a true dwarf on the shoulders of more than one giant, I would like to venture an overall view. My impression is that, when he conceives his *Paradiso*, and then as he maps his own ascent towards the Empyrean, Dante is getting closer and closer to Neoplatonism.

Let us begin, then, with Plato. The Plato Dante places, together with Aristotle and many others, in the Castle of Limbo, is but a name, a shadow that together with that of Socrates is closest to the 'master of those who know'.[2] And such he will also be in *Purgatorio* 3, again together with Aristotle, in the famous speech Virgil dedicates to the constitutional incapacity of human reason to understand the Trinity:

Matto è chi spera che nostra ragione
possa trascorrer la infinita via
che tiene una sustanza in tre persone.

State contenti, umana gente, al quia;
ché, se potuto aveste veder tutto,
mestier non era parturir Maria;

(It's madness if we hope that rational minds
should ever follow to its end the road
that one true being in three persons takes.

Content yourselves with quia, human kind.
Had you been able to see everything,
Mary need not have laboured to give birth.)[3]

Virgil recommends abiding by the *quia*; accepting, that is, the fact of things, their existence: there would have been no need for the Incarnation if human beings had possessed the faculty of understanding everything. Some, he adds, including himself (as indicated by his bowing his head and remaining silent and troubled), have yearned to see 'everything', and their yearning has become their condemnation, to be 'mourned' eternally in Limbo—that is, in hell:

'State contenti, umana gente, al quia;
ché, se potuto aveste veder tutto,
mestier non era parturir Maria;

e disïar vedeste sanza frutto
tai che sarebbe lor disio quetato,
ch'etternalmente è dato lor per lutto:

io dico d'Aristotile e di Plato
e di molt'altri'; e qui chinò la fronte,
e più non disse, e rimase turbato.

('Content yourselves with quia, human kind.
Had you been able to see everything,
Mary need not have laboured to give birth.

You saw the fruitless yearning of those men
who might have had that yearning satisfied,
now given them eternally to mourn.

Plato, I mean, and Aristotle, too,
and many more with them.' He bowed his head
and said no more, remaining darkly troubled.)[4]

Here Aristotle, Plato and Virgil are mere examples of excessive desire for knowledge, like Ulysses in Canto 26 of *Inferno*. Plato has quite a different consistency, however, in *Paradiso* 4, in which Dante—as we have just seen—refers to a specific point of the *Timaeus*. Plato, as I was saying, is granted a figurative, metaphorical language not unlike that which inspires Scripture. We could even say that Dante admits Plato's use of the *eikòs lógos*, or 'verisimilar' discourse: that is, of myths; which was no mean achievement for the medieval exegesis of the prince of Greek philosophers, and thus of all his followers in later times. Moreover, Plato's 'assumptio metaphorismorum' is recalled at the end of the *Epistle to Cangrande*,[5] in the explanation of the opening lines of *Paradiso*, canto I: 'vidi cose che ridire / né sa né può chi di là su descende' (He saw, then, as he says, certain things 'which he who returns has neither knowledge nor power to relate'): 'For we perceive many things by the intellect for which language has no terms—a fact which Plato indicates plainly enough in his books by his employment of metaphors; for he perceived many things by the light of the intellect which his everyday language was inadequate to express.'

23

'Those things that cannot die and those that can'

THE *EPISTLE TO CANGRANDE* ENDS WITH a reflection on a sentence uttered by Boethius. As concerns the 'executive part' of the cantica, the letter-writer refuses to say anything except that everywhere in *Paradiso* 'the process of the narrative will be by ascent from heaven to heaven, and that an account will be given of the blessed spirits who are met with in each sphere'.[1] Since 'their true blessedness consists in the apprehension of Him who is the beginning of truth [in sentiendo veritatis principium]', 'in order to reveal the glory of the blessedness of those spirits, many things which have great profit and delight will be asked of them, as of those who behold the fullness of truth'. The explanation lies, according to the author, in John's statement, 'Haec est autem vita aeterna: ut cognoscant te, solum Deum verum, et quem misisti Iesum Christum' (This is eternal life, that they might know thee, the only true God, and Jesus Christ, whom thou hast sent); and in Boethius's brief sentence, 'Te cernere finis' (To behold thee is the end).[2] Combining Horace ('multa queruntur que *magnam habent utilitatem et delectationem*'), who is quoted at this point by the author of the Epistle, with the Vision of John and Boethius's *Consolation* is no mean feat.[3]

Let us return then to Boethius. Boethius, whose intention, as he states in *De interpretatione*, was to translate the whole of Plato and the whole of Aristotle and harmonise their philosophies,[4] is often coupled by Dante together with the former, as if in a Platonic counterpoint. The greatest example of this comes from *Paradiso* 7, which combines the *Timaeus* of Calcidius (29E) with the famous metre 9 of Book 3 of the *Consolation*, 'O qui perpetua mundum ratione gubernas':

> La divina bontà, che da sé sperne
> ogne livore, ardendo in sé, sfavilla
> sì che dispiega le bellezze etterne.
>
> Ciò che da lei sanza mezzo distilla
> non ha poi fine, perché non si move
> la sua imprenta quand'ella sigilla.
>
> (The generosity of God which scorns all spite
> and meanness burns within itself, yet, flaring out,
> unfolds eternal beauties.
>
> Whatever—without second cause—distils directly
> from the source of good can have no end.
> Stamped thus by good, the print won't move.)[5]

The expression 'which scorns all spite' comes directly from Boethius's 'livore carens', and, before that, from the *Timaeus* itself.[6] On the other hand, the distinction between that which comes directly from God, 'without second cause', and 'can have no end', and that which is not eternal, is present at the very beginning of the *Timaeus*, as we have seen in the very first chapter of this book. Immediately afterwards, Dante's pen explodes into appropriately metaphorical language, in which his striking, impressively vivid image of the eternally beautiful creatures blazing and unfolding is of purely Neoplatonic inspiration. Dante merely adds to it his particular sensitivity to the *pulchritudo* of the universe. It is the first hint of what I would call the 'continuous Creation': that is, the creative process by God as it *always* occurs.

But the poet has the same passion for Creation as that which we have found in Augustine. The Neoplatonic amalgam in *Paradiso* 7 also informs the discourse of the Scholastic Thomas Aquinas in Canto 13, once again centred on the images of splendour, light, radiance and mirroring:

> Ciò che non more e ciò che può morire
> non è se non splendor di quella idea
> che partorisce, amando, il nostro Sire;
>
> ché quella viva luce che sì mea
> dal suo lucente, che non si disuna
> da lui né da l'amor ch'a lor s'intrea,
>
> per sua bontate il suo raggiare aduna,
> quasi specchiato, in nove sussistenze,
> etternalmente rimanendosi una.
>
> (Those things that cannot die and those that can
> are nothing save the splendours of the One Idea
> that, loving, brought our Lord to birth.
>
> For Living Light, which, from the Fount of Light,
> cascades in ways that do not disunite it,
> from Him or from the Love en-three-ing them,
>
> in generosity collects its rays,
> as mirrored in nine ranks of life anew,
> itself eternally remaining One.)[7]

The whole of Creation, both that which exists forever and that which is subject to death, is therefore the splendour of an 'idea'. However, despite the Platonic language, this 'idea' is not one of those postulated by Plato, but rather the Idea of himself that God has and *ipso facto* is: his Son, he whom the Lord generates, indeed literally gives birth to, with the Spirit ('loving'). In the second tercet, the explanation revives the splendour of the first through the image of light, declining it both as object and as subject, or agent: light. The light that thus proceeds from 'the Fount of Light'—the Son from the Father—never separates itself either from it, or from love, the Spirit, which together with the other two constitutes a 'Three', the Trinity. And through its generosity or goodness (the 'divine goodness' that was the subject of the phrase in the passage from *Paradiso* 7), it collects and makes one its radiance ('collects its rays' in one, as before with its 'en-three-ing'), as if through a mirror, into the nine substances or 'ranks of life' of the angelic choirs, while remaining one in eternity. A truly unique concision translates into images the thinking of the Platonism of Chartres.

24

'To new loves Love Eternal opened out'

HERE WE MUST RETURN to Neoplatonism. When he speaks of Creation—and he does so four times in different ways in *Paradiso* alone[1]—Dante returns primarily to the Neoplatonic impulse. Thus, at the beginning of Beatrice's explanation in *Paradiso* 29, which starts with the creation of the angels and then also includes prime matter and the heavens, the images, certainly influenced by the *Liber de causis* that Dante recalls several times in the *Convivio*,[2] unfold onto the shining splendour and the opening of the 'Love Eternal' in 'new loves':

> Non per aver a sé di bene acquisto,
> ch'esser non può, ma perché suo splendore
> potesse, risplendendo, dir 'Subsisto',
>
> in sua etternità di tempo fore,
> fuor d'ogne altro comprender, come i piacque,
> s'aperse in nuovi amor l'etterno amore.
>
> (Not seeking any good that He had not—
> there can be none—but so his shining-out
> could in return shine back and say: 'I am',
>
> in His eternity beyond all time,
> beyond our understanding, as He pleased,
> to new loves Love Eternal opened out.)[3]

The last, memorable line of these tercets summarises God's Creation of the angels by emanation, by 'parthenogenesis', as if it were the opening of a rose with all its petals, making a powerful distinction between the first, 'eternal love' pertaining to the creator, and the second, 'new love', that pertains to the created. This comes at the end of a movement starting with the prime purpose of the 'shining-out' of the originating splendour: that of allowing the reflected splendours, in imitation of God, to shine back as they proclaim their own being. As God said to Moses, from the burning bush of Exodus 3:14, 'Ego sum qui sum', 'I am that I am', so now the reflected essences can proclaim, 'Subsisto', 'I am': they are, in fact, the 'nine subsistencies' or 'ranks' of *Paradiso* 7.

Then comes the only biblical reminiscence in the entire passage. In order to deny that 'before' Creation God lay idle, in total laziness, Beatrice declares that no time existed, either 'before' or 'after': 'for neither "then" nor "now" could come before / the flowing-forth of God above these waves'. That last line is all that remains in *Paradiso* 29 of Genesis 1, of the 'spiritus Dei ferebatur super aquas' that is often interpreted as the will of the Artificer, of his readiness to create: 'ché né prima né poscia / procedette lo discorrer di Dio sovra quest'acque'.[4]

The Creation narrative is then completed in a third stage, by means of Aristotelian categories, almost as if it were implementing Boethius's attempt to fuse Plato and Aristotle in a supreme effort to bring together form and matter, potency and act. The first stage of Creation was the opening of eternal love in the new loves, the angels. The second showed God moving over the upper waters ('these' waters, those of the crystalline heaven, where Dante and Beatrice now find themselves). The third, probably prompted by Augustine,[5] summarises the whole of the Creation of the angels, the heavens and prime matter according to the articulation of pure form (the angels), pure matter (the unformed prime matter), form and matter together (the heavens) and, conversely, of pure act (the angels), pure potency (prime matter) and act and potency together (the heavens).

A grandiose articulation, which replaces the paratactic list of individual species or beings in Genesis 1 (after light, the firmament, the earth, the sea, the stars, plants, living beings, man) with the different formal gradations of the *first* beings; while to the Bible's articulation of the time of creation in six days it opposes the instantaneous and simultaneous Creation of everything, already hypothesised, for example, by Thomas.[6] Here the dominant image is that of the three-string bow simultaneously shooting three arrows (one each for angels, prime matter and the heavens), and then that of the ray of light passing uninterruptedly through glass, amber or crystal (the notion of the speed of light being unknown at the time). Everything was radiated 'all as one' together, 'without distinction in that opening word'. Thus 'rank and relationship' in the cosmos were 'co-created', structured from top to bottom according to a scale of being that has at its summit the fullness of pure act and at its lowest point pure potency, while 'between these two an intertwining binds pure potency to act—and never disentwines'. Dante even finds a way to rebuke Jerome,[7] who had postulated a long lapse of time between the creation of the angels and of the rest of the universe, objecting that reason itself proves the contrary, since the angelic intelligences could not have lain idle, without accomplishing the tasks they were appointed to perform, for very long. Let us reread the passage calmly, enjoying the transitions that link the individual phases with the change of philosophical-theological setting and language, as if it were the succession of different motifs in a piece of music:

Non per aver a sé di bene acquisto,
ch'esser non può, ma perché suo splendore
potesse, risplendendo, dir 'Subsisto',

in sua etternità di tempo fore,
fuor d'ogne altro comprender, come i piacque,
s'aperse in nuovi amor l'etterno amore.

Né prima quasi torpente si giacque;
ché né prima né poscia procedette
lo discorrer di Dio sovra quest' acque.

Forma e materia, congiunte e purette,
usciro ad esser che non avia fallo,
come d'arco tricordo tre saette.

E come in vetro, in ambra o in cristallo
raggio resplende sì, che dal venire
a l'esser tutto non è intervallo,

così 'l triforme effetto del suo sire
ne l'esser suo raggiò insieme tutto
sanza distinzïone in essordire.

Concreato fu ordine e costrutto
a le sustanze; e quelle furon cima
nel mondo in che puro atto fu produtto;

pura potenza tenne la parte ima;
nel mezzo strinse potenza con atto
tal vime, che già mai non si divima.

Ieronimo vi scrisse lungo tratto
di secoli de li angeli creati
anzi che l'altro mondo fosse fatto;

ma questo vero è scritto in molti lati
da li scrittor de lo Spirito Santo,
e tu te n'avvedrai se bene agguati;

e anche la ragione il vede alquanto,
che non concederebbe che ' motori
sanza sua perfezion fosser cotanto.

(Not seeking any good that He had not—
there can be none—but so his shining-out
could in return shine back and say: 'I am',

in His eternity beyond all time,
beyond our understanding, as He pleased,
to new loves Love Eternal opened out.

Nor had He lain in torpor till that time,
for neither 'then' nor 'now' could come before
the flowing-forth of God above these waves.

Real form and matter (both conjoined and pure),
issued in being where there was no flaw,
as from a three-string bow three arrows fly.

Light rays that enter amber, crystal, glass,
display such luminescence that, from when they reach,
then are there wholly, there's no pause.

Likewise, the three-fold action of light's lord
shone brightly through all being, all as one,
without distinction in that opening word.

Rank and relationship were co-created
with these true beings who, within the world
(pure act produced in them), stand at the height

where, at the lowest, there's pure potency,
between these two an intertwining binds
pure potency to act—and never disentwines.

Jerome proposed to you a long elapse
of centuries of angels from creation's point
before the other world was ever formed.

The truth is written, though, in many parts
—by writers listening to the Holy Ghost—
as you, if you look carefully, will see.

And even reason can see some of this,
refusing to concede that motive powers
should be so long without full carry-through.)[8]

What a sequence! Neoplatonic blossoming of love; biblical moving of God over the waters; Aristotelian history and structuring of the universe. It is, in short, a veritable symphony of motifs chasing one after the other until they calm down in the final order. It is philosophical and theological poetry of the first magnitude: together with the passages from *Paradiso* 7 and 8, it creates Dante's own myth of Creation.

25

'That deep mind'

ONCE AGAIN, HERE and in the two following sections, we return to Boethius. That Boethius is ultimately behind the very conception of *Paradiso* is evident from at least two essential moments in the cantica, figuring significantly at the beginning and the end. In the first case, in Canto 2, through the mouth of Beatrice, Dante expounds the very structure and operation of the heavens that constitute the third realm, claiming that their motion and 'virtue' are due, 'as hammer-skill from smith', to celestial engines or 'angelic moves'. The eighth heaven, he specifies, that of the fixed stars, 'so fine with all its lights' takes from the 'deep mind which rolls it round'—that is, from the angelic intelligence that moves it—the 'image', the exemplary idea or form, of which it becomes the 'seal' and which it will print on earthly matter:

> Lo moto e la virtù d'i santi giri,
> come dal fabbro l'arte del martello,
> da' beati motor convien che spiri;
>
> e 'l ciel cui tanti lumi fanno bello,
> de la mente profonda che lui volve
> prende l'image e fassene suggello.
>
> (Motion and virtue in these holy gyres rightly draw breath
> (as hammer-skill from smith),
> in turns deriving from angelic moves.

The sphere of stars, so fine with all its lights,
receives from that deep mind which rolls it round
the image that it has, then prints that seal.)[1]

The 'deep mind' is again an expression derived from Boethius's metre 9 of Book 3 of the *Consolation,* and the following two tercets are clearly inspired by the same metre: thereby constituting the very pivot around which the *Paradiso* is built.

Tu triplicis mediam naturae cuncta moventem
conectens animam per consona membra resolvis;
quae cum secta duos motum glomeravit in orbes,
in semet reditura meat *mentemque profundam*
circuit et simili convertit imagine caelum.

(You, binding soul together in its threefold nature's midst,
Soul that moves all things, then divide it into harmonious parts;
Soul thus divided has its motion gathered into two circles,
moves to return into itself, *and the Mind deep within*
Encircles, and makes the heaven turn, in likeness to itself.)[2]

'Deep mind': the spirit of the supreme divinity, the *divina profunditas,* in other words, which must find correspondence in the depth of those who seek the truth, as the *Consolation* will shortly affirm: 'quisquis profunda mente uestigat uerum', sings metre 11, again in Book 3, 'Whoever with deep thought seeks out the truth':

Quisquis *profunda mente* uestigat uerum
cupitque nullis ille deuiis falli
in se reuoluat intimi lucem uisus
longosque in orbem cogat inflectens motus
animumque doceat quicquid extra molitur
suis retrusum possidere thesauris;
dudum quod atra texit erroris nubes
lucebit ipso perspicacius Phoebo.
Non omne namque mente depulit lumen
obliuiosam corpus inuehens molem;

haeret profecto semen introrsum ueri
quod excitatur uentilante doctrina;
nam cur rogati sponte recta censetis
ni mersus alto uiueret fomes corde?
Quodsi *Platonis Musa* personat uerum,
quod quisque discit immemor recordatur.

(Whoever *with deep thought* seeks out the truth
And wants not to go wrong down devious ways,
Must on himself turn back the light of his inward vision,
Bending and forcing his far-reaching movements
Into a circle, and must teach his mind,
Whatever she is striving for without,
Removed within her treasury to grasp;
What the black cloud of error lately covered
Will shine then clearer than Phoebus himself.
For the body weighing upon the mind with bulky oblivion
Has not removed all light:
Assuredly there sticks within some seed of truth
Which is stirred to life by learning's breeze.
For why, being asked a question, do you rightly judge
Out of yourself, unless the kindling lived
Deep down in your heart? If *Plato's Muse* rings true,
What each man learns, forgetful he recalls.)[3]

Plato's Muse: evoked by Philosophy and immediately and 'vehemently' embraced by Boethius: 'Platoni, inquam, uehementer assentior': 'I strongly agree with Plato'.[4]

26

'Amor quo caelum regitur'

THERE WAS ALSO ANOTHER IMPASSIONED and similarly inspired poem in the *Consolation* that must have struck Dante: metre 8 in Book 2, which celebrates the love that holds together the potentially discordant elements of the universe:

Quod mundus stabili fide
Concordes uariat uices,
Quod pugnantia semina
Foedus perpetuum tenent,
Quod Phoebus roseum diem
Curru prouehit aureo,
Vt quas duxerit Hesperos
Phoebe noctibus imperet,
Vt fluctus auidum mare
Certo fine coerceat,
Ne terris liceat uagis
Latos tendere terminos.
Hanc rerum seriem ligat
Terras ac pelagus regens
Et caelo imperitans amor.
Hic si frena remiserit,
Quidquid nunc amat inuicem
Bellum continuo geret
Et quam nunc socia fide

Pulchris motibus incitant,
Certent soluere machinam.
Hic sancto populos quoque
Iunctos foedere continet,
Hic et coniugii sacrum
Castis nectit amoribus,
Hic fidis etiam sua
Dictat iura sodalibus.
O felix hominum genus,
Si uestros animos amor
Quo caelum regitur regat.

(In regular harmony
The world moves through its changes;
Seeds in competition with each other
Are held in balance by eternal law;
Phoebus brings rosy dawns
In his golden chariot
That his sister Phoebe may rule the nights
That Hesperus brings;
The waves of the greedy sea
Are kept within fixed bounds,
Nor may the land move out
And extend its limits.
What binds all things to order,
Governing earth and sea and sky,
Is love. If love's rein slackened
All things now held by mutual love
At once would fall to warring with each other
Striving to wreck that engine of the world
Which now they drive
In mutual trust with motion beautiful.
And love joins peoples too
By a sacred bond,
And ties the knot of holy matrimony

That binds chaste lovers,
Joins too with its law
All faithful comrades.
O happy race of men,
If the love that rules the stars
May also rule your hearts!)[1]

Boethius states, and reiterates, that it is love that 'binds all things to order, / Governing earth and sea and sky': 'terras ac pelagus regens / et caelo imperitans amor; amor, quo caelum regitur'.[2] His insistence had its effect on Dante,[3] who begins and ends the *Commedia* precisely with the divine love that moves everything:

Temp'era dal principio del mattino,
e il sol montava 'n su con quelle stelle
ch'eran con lui quando *l'amor divino*

mosse di prima quelle cose belle.

l'amor che move il sole e l'altre stelle.

(The time, however, was the hour of dawn.
The sun was mounting, and those springtime stars
that rose along with it when *Holy Love*

first moved to being all these lovely things.)

([the] love that moves the sun and other stars.)[4]

I am not going to dwell here on the fact that Dante is speaking explicitly of *divine* love and in both cases, one in the distant past, one in the present, of creation, whereas Boethius seems to intend cosmic love and the fact that it governs the universe.[5] There are differences. But that these words and the turns of the phrases, and of course the concepts behind them, come from Boethius's song to open and close the *Commedia* is indisputable.

This, after all, is what Dante learned from his predecessor in Ravenna: not only to endure adversity, love wisdom and turn to Philosophy, as he says in the *Convivio,* as to a second 'Donna gentile'; nor even only to conceive, on the model of the *Consolation*, a more strongly marked prosimetrum than that of the *Vita nuova*. Dante, like Boethius a passionate devotee of the stars, unable to read Lucretius, learned from the author of the *Consolation* how to give poetic form to thought, philosophy and theology: how to philosophise in song.

If he often did this by combining Plato and Neoplatonism with Boethius, and sometimes Aristotle, from whom he derived the very form of his own philosophy, the synthesis he was able to amalgamate from them is admirable. One need only look at Boethius's ninth metre in Book 3 to hear an echo of the *Timaeus* on the one hand, and of Book Lambda of the *Metaphysics* on the other.[6] In the heavenly Athens of *Paradiso* 10, Thomas Aquinas therefore rightly points to Boethius as the eighth light, giving us a glimpse of his tomb in San Pietro in Ciel d'Oro in Pavia, calling him a 'blessèd soul' who has come 'to peace' from the martyrdom and exile of earthly life.

27

'He laughed, self-mockingly'

ALL THE MORE SO, CONSIDERING how the poet liquidates, so to speak, Gregory the Great and replaces him with Dionysius the Areopagite. In the *Convivio* (2.5.6*ff.*), Dante had followed the order of the angelic hierarchies proposed by Gregory in the *Moralia in Iob*.[1] When, however, he reaches the threshold of the Empyrean, he declares that when Gregory ascended after death to the last heaven he realised he had made a mistake and 'laughed, self-mockingly',[2] evidently acknowledging that Dionysius's perspective was correct. To me this seems an elegant way for Dante to proclaim his new preference for Dionysian mysticism as against that which is also abundantly present, as we have seen, in Gregory's works: perhaps because Dionysius's mysticism possesses a strength and coherence that would obscure any rival.[3]

The order of the angelic hierarchies was no secondary matter for Dante, because it was supposed to reflect the logic that governs the organisation of the cosmos. In fact, the pilgrim asks Beatrice to explain why copy and model, 'type and prototype', or, in other words, the sensible and intelligible worlds, 'are not configured in a single mode', given that the universe is a copy of the eternal model present in the mind of God.[4] And Beatrice responds with a long syllogism indicating how, as corporeal instruments, the potential efficacy of the heavens is determined by their extension and size, which is not the case in the world of essences: 'A greater goodness means a greater health. / A greater health is held in greater limbs, / if these, throughout, are perfect equally. / Therefore this sphere—the Primum Mobile—/ which draws the universe entire along / answers the circle that most loves and knows'.[5] In the Empyrean, viewed from a terrestrial perspective, everything is reversed. At the end of the explanation Dante bursts into a wonderful simile, with truth shining like a star in a sky made 'serene, / its air bright, sparkling, clear' by the blowing of the North wind:

Come rimane splendido e sereno
l'emisperio de l'aere, quando soffia
Borea da quella guancia ond' è più leno,

per che si purga e risolve la roffia
che pria turbava, sì che 'l ciel ne ride
con le bellezze d'ogne sua paroffia;

così fec'ïo, poi che mi provide
la donna mia del suo risponder chiaro,
e come stella in cielo il ver si vide.

([. . .] when Boreas, the northern wind, blows from his milder
cheek,
our hemisphere is left serene,
its air bright, sparkling, clear.

The crusted scum of clouds that swirled there first
is freed and clarified. The whole sky laughs.
Its many beauties smile round every steeple.

So I became, as—caring for my good—
my lady answered with such clarity,
and truth was seen as stars are in the sky.)[6]

The sky smiles now with all its 'many beauties', says Dante in his simile, as if in an aside. Its smile is the shining of all the stars (as before, in canto 23, where Trivia, the Moon, smiled among the eternal nymphs): the smile, with its 'beauties', of *pulchritudo* itself. Almost in response to this celestial smile, there then begins an amazing spectacle of light and sound: the circles sparkle like boiling iron, each spark following the flame from which it has detached itself, outnumbering many thousands of thousands. Then, as hosannas resound throughout the heavens, Beatrice lists the hierarchies: Seraphim and Cherubim, Thrones, Dominations, Virtues, Powers, Principalities, Archangels, Angels, whose 'order all in wonder gaze above / and triumph so, beneath, that up to God / they all are drawn and drawn up to all'. Wonder unites them all, from top to bottom, towards God and towards one another. Thus, Beatrice concludes, 'Dionysius with such desire / set out to contemplate these nine-fold ranks / that he defined and named them as I do'. In the next Canto, after the sequence on the Creation, she will show 'the height and all the generous breadth / of God's eternal worth. These mirrors all / were made by Him, where He Himself now breaks, / one in Himself remaining as before':

> Vedi l'eccelso omai e la larghezza
> de l'etterno valor, poscia che tanti
> speculi fatti s'ha in che si spezza,
>
> uno manendo in sé come davanti.[7]

Finally, when the angelic orders are joined by the human blessed, the supreme vision will appear: 'I saw light form a river in full spate'. Dionysius would have admired the metamorphosis of circles into rivers and the triumph of sparks, flowers, rubies: because 'così parlar conviensi al vostro ingegno': 'to speak in this way fits the human mind'. Here are the three glorious tercets:

> e vidi lume in forma di rivera
> fulvido di fulgore, intra due rive
> dipinte di mirabil primavera.
>
> Di tal fiumana uscian faville vive,
> e d'ogne parte si mettien ne' fiori,
> quasi rubin che oro circunscrive;
>
> poi, come inebrïate da li odori,
> riprofondavan sé nel miro gurge,
> e s'una intrava, un'altra n'uscia fori.

(I saw light form a river in full spate,
fire-dazzle-gilded, flowing through verges
painted afresh in colours of wonderful spring.

And rising from that flood, alive, were sparks
that everywhere alighted on the flowers,
like rubies set in gold encirclements—

then all, as though the perfumes made them drunk,
plunged in that swirling miracle once more.
And yet where one sank in, still more spun out.)[8]

28

'This reason moved Augustine'

NOW LET US TURN TO AUGUSTINE. Neoplatonism dominated the whole of what C. S. Lewis called 'the seminal period', 'the age which brought the characteristically medieval frame of mind into being':[1] stretching from the fourth up to the sixth century CE and in which the most prominent figures, along with Boethius, are Macrobius and Martianus Capella. Then, in the sixth century, appeared in the East the writings on which Christian mysticism was founded, attributed to Dionysius the Areopagite. Written originally in Greek, they were translated into Latin by John Scotus Eriugena in the Carolingian era. I cannot reconstruct Dante's debts to all these authors in detail here; they were in any case less pervasive than his debts to Boethius. I will take a couple of interesting cases as examples.

Before Macrobius's *Commentary* on the *Somnium Scipionis* comes of course the *Somnium* itself, contained in the last book of Cicero's *De re publica*, a very significant document of Roman Platonism. Now, apart from the vision of the earth as a point in *Paradiso* 22, and Oderisi's considerations on the transience of fame in *Purgatorio* 11 ('The roar of earthly fame is just a breath of wind'), no images from the *Somnium* function as direct sources for the *Commedia*, while the first of the two exceptions is a commonplace, and the second has a perhaps closer precedent in Boethius himself (2 pr. 7).

The situation changes little if one examines the *Somnium* with Macrobius's *Commentary*, which is the only way Dante could read the passage from the *De re publica*. The expansion the original text undergoes in the *Commentary* is scarcely more likely to be the starting point for Dante's description in *Paradiso* 22, while the specification of 'that point within the universe where Satan sits', the 'point to which from every part all weight drags down', may go back not only to the *Somnium*, but also to the corresponding passage in the *Commentary*.[2] More surprising is the possibility that Dante's apostrophe to Virgil's shadow at the very beginning of the poem, 'So, could it be [. . .], you are that Virgil, / whose words (a river running full) flow wide?' echoes the terms used in the *Saturnalia* to render Virgil's eloquence: 'Quis fons, quis torrens, quod mare tot fluctibus quot hic verbis inundavit?' (What spring, what torrent, what sea has ever overflowed with as many waves as he did with words!).[3]

These are indeed small things. There are practically no references to Martianus Capella and his *De nuptiis Mercuri et Philologiae*. But a very different matter is the presence in Dante of the two Christian giants of the fourth and sixth centuries, Augustine of Hippo and Dionysius the Areopagite. John Freccero, with his usual energy and acumen, has defended the former's profound mental influence on Dante the man and his structural influence on Dante's work, in *Dante. The Poetics of Conversion*. Beginning already with its title, Freccero's book refers to the parallel path between Augustine's *Confessions* and the *Convivio-Commedia*, and it is truly illuminating on several specific moments of the poem. It is Dante himself who reveals the model, as the author points out, opening his book with a quotation from the *Convivio*:

> Veramente, al principale intendimento tornando, dico, come è toccato di sopra, per necessarie cagioni lo parlare di sé è conceduto: e intra l'altre necessarie cagioni due sono più manifeste. L'una è quando sanza ragionare di sé grande infamia o pericolo non si può cessare; e allora si concede, per la ragione che de li due sentieri prendere lo men reo è quasi prendere un buono. E questa necessitate mosse Boezio di se medesimo a parlare, acciò che sotto pretesto di consolazione escusasse la perpetuale infamia del suo essilio, mostrando quello essere ingiusto, poi che altro escusatore non si levava. L'altra è quando, per ragionare di sè, grandissima utilitade ne segue altrui per via di dottrina; e questa ragione mosse Agustino ne le sue Confessioni a parlare di sé, ché per

lo processo de la sua vita, lo quale fu di [non] buono in buono, e di buono in migliore, e di migliore in ottimo, ne diede essemplo e dottrina, la quale per sì vero testimonio ricevere non si potea. Per che se l'una e l'altra di queste ragioni mi scusa, sufficientemente lo pane del mio formento è purgato de la prima sua macula.

(To return to the main topic, however, I say that, as touched on above, speaking about oneself is allowed in cases of necessity, and among the several cases of necessity two are very evident. One is when great infamy or danger cannot be avoided except by talking about oneself; then it is permissible, for the reason that to take the less evil of two paths is almost the same as taking a good one. This necessity moved Boethius to speak of himself, so that under the pretext of consolation he might defend himself against the perpetual infamy of his exile, by showing it to be unjust, since no other apologist came forward. The other arises when by speaking of oneself very great benefit comes to another by way of instruction; and this reason moved Augustine to speak of himself in his *Confessions*, because by the progress of his life, which proceeded from bad to good, good to better, and better to best, he gave us an example and instruction which could not be provided by any other testimony so true as this. Consequently, if each of these reasons may serve as my excuse, the bread made from my wheat is sufficiently cleansed of its first impurity.)[4]

Boethius, again, and Augustine. The 'speaking of oneself' motif comes from the *Consolation* and the *Confessions*. Freccero, who also keeps a constant eye on the *Timaeus*,[5] then cites specific passages from other works of Augustine—the *De Genesi ad litteram*, the *City of God*, the *De doctrina christiana*—always with an eye to the general, 'ideal' setting of individual episodes or themes. In one particular case—but what a case!—he uses, echoing Giorgio Padoan, the *De beata vita* in order to examine the Ulysses episode with great attention and draw brilliant conclusions from it. The *De beata vita* begins with the Prologue:

Si ad philosophiae portum, de quo iam in beatae vitae regionem solumque proceditur, vir humanissime atque magne, Theodore, ratione

> institutus cursus, et voluntas ipsa perduceret; nescio utrum temere dixerim, multo minoris numeri homines ad eum perventuros fuisse, quamvis nunc quoque, ut videmus, rari admodum paucique perveniant. Cum enim in hunc mundum, sive Deus, sive natura, sive necessitas, sive voluntas nostra, sive coniuncta horum aliqua, sive simul omnia (res enim multum obscura est, sed tamen a te iam illustranda suscepta) veluti in quoddam procellosum salum nos quasi temere passimque proiecerit; quotusquisque cognosceret quo sibi nitendum esset, quave redeundum, nisi aliquando et invitos contraque obnitentes aliqua tempestas, quae stultis videtur adversa, in optatissimam terram nescientes errantesque compingeret?
>
> (If a course charted by reason and if the will itself could bring someone to the port of philosophy—the port from which, one is already advancing onto the region and solid ground of the happy life—the course must be founded upon rational thought and individual will, then I do not know whether or not I am rash in saying, O Theodorus, you most refined and great man, that men are going to reach it in very small numbers—though actually, as we see nowadays, the men who reach it *are* few and far between. For when either God or nature or necessity or our will or some combination of these or all of them together—for the matter is very obscure, although it is being undertaken now so that you may shed light on it—randomly tosses us into this world to and fro, so to speak, as if we were on a stormy sea, how few would ever come to know in what direction they should be striving or by what way they should be returning unless at one time or other, against their will and in spite of their resistance, some storm—which to the foolish seems adverse—should thrust the ignorant and the erroneous onto that land so devoutly to be wished?)[6]

Augustine then distinguishes between three kinds of 'seafaring men' that philosophy can receive: those who sail peacefully, without straying too far, and then settle down in tranquillity; those who, 'deceived by the utterly beguiling appearance of the sea', go out and 'dare to wander far from their homeland, often becoming forgetful of it'; and, finally, those who 'look back on certain standards and continue to remember their most sweet homeland' and return to it. But facing all these men who are 'brought to the region of the happy life no matter how, there stands a vast mountain before the port', which is extremely dangerous for all seafarers: the mountain of vainglory. All this has obvious relevance to the episode of Ulysses in the *Inferno*, where Ulysses would belong to the second category, of those who 'dare to wander far from their homeland, often becoming forgetful of it', and where a very high mountain, dark to look at in the distance, is the last piece of land Ulysses and his men sight.

However, there remains a fact of no small importance: in *Paradiso*, Augustine appears only at the end, together with Francis and Benedict, in the white rose of the Empyrean, just below John the Baptist [fig. 20]. But while Dante has spoken at length of Francis and Benedict in Cantos 11 and 22 of *Paradiso* (and even has a conversation with the latter), Augustine is barely mentioned, in Canto 10, as he who in his writings cited Paulus Orosius, 'quello avvocato de' tempi cristiani' (the one who spoke for Christian times). His absence from the crowns of the *sapientes* is indeed a fact of unusual proportion, all the more so when one considers that precise quotations from Augustine's works in the *Commedia* are extremely rare. Dante cannot simply have forgotten him, since he does indeed mention him. And it can hardly be due to the fact—as Anna Maria Chiavacci Leonardi once confided to me—that Dante had 'introjected' Augustine to such an extent that he did not need to make a place for him in the heavenly Athens. Dante had absorbed Boethius and Thomas Aquinas just as fully, yet he inserted them both into the crown headed by Thomas himself. What did Augustine of Hippo write or do such that he did not deserve to participate in the dance of the *sapientes*? It is a mystery, I fear, that we will never solve.

29

'Fountain of light, seedbed of life'

AN ESSENTIAL MOVE, now and in the next sections, takes us from Dante to the so called School of Chartres. Medieval Platonism has three capitals between the ninth and twelfth centuries: Aachen, where John Scotus worked in the court of Charles the Bald (and before him Alcuin, in that of Charlemagne); Toledo, where Gherard of Cremona studied and translated from Arabic Themistius and the *Liber de causis*; and Chartres, where a veritable centre of philosophical, theological and exegetical studies developed, with figures such as William of Conches, Thierry of Chartres, Clarembald of Arras, Alan of Lille and Bernardus Silvestris.[1] It was they who animated the scientific-philosophical debate that took place while the great dispute between Abelard and Bernard of Clairvaux was raging, and the mysticism of William of Saint-Thierry, Ivo, Aelred of Rievaulx, Bernard himself, Hildegard of Bingen and finally Hugh and Richard of Saint-Victor was developing.[2]

Among the Chartres thinkers, the last two, Bernardus Silvestris and Alan of Lille, interest us most particularly here, for they were not only important philosophers, but also remarkable poets. I begin with Bernardus, for a reason that will immediately be apparent. We do not know whether or how much Dante knew of the *Cosmographia*, the poem, in addition to his *Mathematicus*,[3] that Bernardus composed in order to sing of the Mega- and Microcosms. The first part narrates the creation of the nine angelic hierarchies, the stars, constellations and planets, and then moves on to that of living creatures and their characteristics; while in the second, the Microcosm, in order to reach the creation of man the poet engages in a wonderful narrative, summarised as follows in Bernardus' introductory *Summa operis*:

> In the second book, which is called *Microcosmus*, or the lesser universe, Noys turns to Nature, glories in the beautification now achieved and promises to create Man as the completion of her work. Accordingly she orders Nature to search carefully for Urania, who is queen of the stars, and Physis, who has deep knowledge of all created things. Nature obeys her instructress at once, and, searching for Urania through all the celestial spheres, finds her gazing in wonder at the stars. The cause of Nature's journey being already known to her, Urania promises to join her, in her journey and in her task. And so the two set out and when the circles of the planets have been traversed, and their several influences duly noted, they at last discover Physis, dwelling in the bosom of the flourishing Earth amid the odours of spices, with her two daughters, Theory and Practice, and they explain why they have come. Suddenly Noys is present there, and having made her will known to them she assigns to the three kinds of speculative knowledge, and urges them to the formation of Man. And so Physis forms Man out of the remainder of the four elements, and beginning with the head, and working limb by limb, completes her work appropriately with the feet.[4]

Bernardus's imagination is not merely allegorical: it is that of a philosophical mind dedicated to dramatic invention, a mythopoetic mind: acted on by suggestions, and sometimes real sources, ranging from Aristotle's *Physics* to Ovid's *Metamorphoses*, from the book of Proverbs to that of Wisdom, from Apuleius to Asclepius, from Cicero to Martianus Capella, from John Scotus Eriugena to Claudian.[5] The actions, and words, of his allegorical characters have considerable vigour, sometimes even ironic overtones, and, always, a cosmic horizon. If Dante had read the poem, he would undoubtedly have recognised in it the anxiety of quest and the icon of the journey, the mixture and power not only of the *Timaeus*, but also of Boethius: and he would have used it, or echoed it, in the passages on Creation that constellate the *Commedia*. In any case, Bernardus's poetry would have been a spur to the philosophical-theological construction of his poem. Boccaccio, who copied the *Cosmographia* by hand, quoted it in his *Esposizioni sopra la Comedia di Dante* in relation to the world 'which we inhabit' (the 'megacosm'), including Limbo, and to man (the 'microcosm').[6] I have already quoted a passage in verse from the *Cosmographia*,[7] but even its prose gives an idea of its imaginative and linguistic power, which would undoubtedly have struck Dante had he known the text:

> Erat fons luminis, seminarium vite, bonum bonitatis, divine plenitudo scientie que mens altissimi nominatur. Ea igitur Noys summi et exsuperantissimi Dei est intellectus, et ex eius divinitate nata est Natura, in qua vite viventis ymagines, notiones eterne, mundus intelligibilis, rerum cognitio prefinita. Erat igitur videre velud in speculo tersiore quicquid generationi, quicquid operi dei secretior destinarat affectus. Illic in genere, in specie, in individuali singularitate conscripta, quicquid Yle, quicquid mundus, quicquid parturiunt elementa. Illic exarata supremi digito dispositoris: textus temporis, fatalis series, dispositio seculorum; illic lacrime pauperum, fortuneque regum; illic potentia militaris; illic philosophorum felitior disciplina, illic quicquid angelus, quicquid ratio conprehendit humana, illic quicquid celum sua conplectitur curvatura. Quod igitur tale est, illud eternitati contiguum, idem natura cum deo nec substantia est disparatum. Huiuscemodi igitur sive vite sive lucis origine, vita iubarque rerum, Endelichia, quadam velud emanatione defluxit.

> (Noys was the fountain of light, seedbed of life, a good born of the divine goodness, that fullness of knowledge which is called the Mind of the Most High. This Noys, then, is the intellect of supreme and all-powerful God, and Nature is born of her divinity; in Noys are the images of unfailing life, the eternal ideas, the intelligible universe, predetermined knowledge of things. There, then, as if in a clearer glass, could be seen all that a secret disposition destined to come to be, to become a work of God. There were enrolled, in genus, in species, in individual uniqueness, whatever Hyle, the Universe, the elements labor to bring forth. There, inscribed by the finger of the supreme arbiter, were the fabric of time, the chain of destiny, the

> dispositition of the ages. There were the tears of the poor and the fortunes of kings, the soldier's strength and the happier discipline of the philosophers; all that angels, all that human reason comprehends, all that heaven encircles with its curving dome. What exists in such a way is closely joined to the eternal, one in nature with God and not distinct in substance. From such a source, then, whether of life or of light, there issued forth by a sort of emanation, the life and light of creation, Endelechia.)[8]

Bernardus is then generally credited with a *Commentum super sex libros Eneidos Virgilii*—cited again by Coluccio Salutati (without indicating the author's name) in *De laboribus Herculis*—which is an admirable example of a Neoplatonic allegorical interpretation of Virgil's poem.[9] The approach adopted follows the long-established tradition, starting with Fulgentius in *De virgiliana continentia,*[10] of seeing Aeneas's wanderings as an allegory of man's itinerary through the various ages of life and through a complete series of moral 'errors' (such as lust, represented by the episode of Dido). The descent into the underworld marks the beginning of maturity and signifies the discovery of true knowledge: theology. In visiting the underworld, Aeneas encounters his old 'errors', experiences them again with new awareness, and is finally able to attain the knowledge of God. Thus he reaches the contemplation of the Creator (Anchises) only after passing through five degrees of 'creaturarum agnitiones', or recognitions of creatures, from inanimate beings to men and angels.

It has long been established that Dante was aware of this allegorical pattern and that he used it as a framework for the *Commedia.*[11] In the poem, the protagonist's encounters with a series of characters exemplifying a sin or virtue or interpreting a particularly important doctrine lead him to salvation and ultimately to the vision of God. Naturally, Dante infuses the fundamentally Platonic design of the *Commentum* with a good dose of Aristotelian realism, whereby his characters are alive in themselves as individuals, embodying as it were the *tòde tí* of things. But the importance of the pattern and of the cognitive impulse that animates it is still essential.

30

'Beings and accidents and modes of life'

DIONYSIUS, AGAIN. FOR it is precisely from this threshold of the Empyrean that Dante approaches Dionysius most frequently, for example in the image of the mirrors he employs for the angels.[1] There is, however, a key moment at the end of *Paradiso* in which Dionysius's presence seems decisive. It involves no less than the vision of God *in sua essentia*, the culminating event of the entire *Commedia*:

> Nel suo profondo vidi che s'interna,
> legato con amore in un volume,
> ciò che per l'universo si squaderna:
>
> sustanze e accidenti e lor costume
> quasi conflati insieme, per tal modo
> che ciò ch'i' dico è un semplice lume.
>
> (Within in its depths, this light, I saw,
> contained, bound up and gathered in a single book,
> the leaves that scatter through the universe—
>
> beings and accidents and modes of life,
> as though blown all together in a way
> that what I say is just a simple light.)[2]

The Dionysian text, in Scotus Eriugena's Latin version of *De divinis nominibus*, declared with regard to 'Superior Goodness': 'Et sunt ex ipsa, et in ipsa, et ipsum esse, et existentium principia, et existentia omnia, et quae utcumque ab esse continentur: et hoc incommensurate, et convolute, et unite': 'From It and in It are Being itself, the source of beings, all beings and whatever else has a portion of existence. This characteristic is in it as an irrepressible, comprehensive and singular feature'[3]—a formulation that is echoed and even amplified in the *Periphyseon*.[4] Thomas's commentary moves decisively in the direction that will be taken by Dante's tercets, adding Aristotelian categories to the Neoplatonic and mystical mixture in a synthesis that once again sounds Boethian:

> Postquam Dionysius ostendit quod omnia existentia universaliter sunt a Deo, hic intendit ostendere quod omnia universaliter sunt in Ipso; et circa hoc duo facit: primo, proponit quod intendit; secundo, manifestat propositum [. . .]. Dicit ergo primo quod non solum ex ipsa Dei bonitate, sed etiam in ipsa est ipsum per se *esse*, quod est Dei participatio *et* omnia *principia existentium et omnia existentia*, tam substantiae quam accidentia *et* omnia *quocumque modo* continentur sub *esse*, sicut entia imperfecta, ut ens in potentia et motus et alia huiusmodi. Et ne aliquis crederet quod ista hoc modo sint in Deo sicut in seipsis, consequenter hoc excludit. In seipsis enim omnia causata sunt finita, in Deo autem sunt infinita, quia in Deo sunt ipsa divina essentia; et ideo dicit: *et hoc incomprehensibiliter*. Iterum, in seipsis oppositionem habent et diversitatem, in Deo autem coniunguntur simul; et ideo dicit: *et coniuncte*. Iterum, in seipsis habent multitudinem, in Deo autem sunt unum; et ideo addit: *et singulariter*, idest unite.
>
> (After Dionysius has shown that all existing things universally are from God, here he intends to show that all things universally are in him; and about this he does two things: first, he proposes what he intends; second, he manifests the proposition [. . .]. Therefore he says, first, that not only *from this* goodness of God, but also *in this* is per se *being itself*, which is the participation of God, *and* all *principles of existing things and all existing things*, both substances and accidents, *and* all *in whatever mode* are contained under *being*, as imperfect beings, as being in potency and motion and other things of this sort. And lest anyone were to believe that these are in God in the same

> mode as in themselves, consequently he excludes this. For in themselves all things caused are finite, yet in God they are infinite, because in God they are the divine essence itself; and for this reason he says, *and this incomprehensibly*. Again, in themselves they have opposition and diversity, yet in God they are joined together simultaneously; and for this reason he says, *and jointly*. Again, in themselves they have multitude, yet in God they are one; and for this reason he adds, *and singularly*, that is, unitedly.)[5]

Here we must take note of 'substantiae' and 'accidentia', the 'sustanze e accidenti' of *Paradiso* 33 ('beings and accidents' in the translation above); , while 'diversitatem', 'multitudinem' and 'oppositionem' will be rendered by Dante with 'si squaderna' ('scatter through the universe'), where 'coniunguntur simul' anticipates 'conflati insieme' ('blown all together') and 'un volume' imaginatively translates Thomas's 'unum' ('gathered in a single book'). I have always wondered what Dante would have been capable of had he read the *Periphyseon*, with its daring theological and linguistic flights.

31

The Moon Smiles Among the Eternal Nymphs

THINGS ARE MORE COMPLEX in the case of Alan of Lille, who is present with extensive excerpts in Polycarp Leyser's *Historia poetarum et poematum medii aevi*,[1] and whose complete works were still being printed in 1654.[2] A more prolific writer than Bernardus (whom he probably knew), Alan is the author not only of the two main poems, the *Anticlaudianus* and the *Planctus naturae*, but also of texts such as the *Sermon on the Intelligible Sphere* (in prose), and lyrics such as the *Rithmus de incarnatione Domini* (On the Incarnation) and the *Omnis mundi creatura* (The Book of Creation).[3] A philosopher and theologian of considerable depth,[4] he is the first in Europe to cite what Eckhart called the *Book of the Twenty-Four Philosophers*,[5] and what Dante, as I have had occasion to say a couple of times already, called the 'Libro de le cagioni': the *Liber de causis*, translated into Latin from the Arabic *Kitāb ul-īḍāḥ li-Arisṭūṭālis fi'l-khayri'l-maḥd* (The book of Aristotle's exposition on the pure good) by Gherardo da Cremona in 1180 and attributed to Aristotle until Thomas Aquinas, in the Prologue to his commentary on the text, disputed the attribution.[6] In 1268 William of Moerbeke—the translator, for the first time directly from Greek, of almost all the works of Aristotle—translated Proclus's *Elementatio theologica* and it was proved that this was the source of the *Liber de causis* (with Plotinus as a more remote source): it was thus a purely Neoplatonic work, whose influence in Europe from the late twelfth to the early thirteenth century was enormous, comparable in a way to that of the *Corpus Dionysiacum*.

I do not have room here to discuss the *Liber* and its importance for Dante, from the *Convivio* to the *Commedia*. I only indicate two significant extremes that both come from the *Epistle to Cangrande*. In explaining the first three verses of the *Paradiso*—'La gloria di colui che tutto move / per l'universo penetra e risplende / in una parte più e meno altrove' (Glory, from Him who moves all things that are, / penetrates the universe and then shines back, / reflected more in one part, less elsewhere)—the author of the *Epistle* adduces 'reason' and 'authority'. He cites Aristotle's *Metaphysics* 2, with regard to reason, but authority is represented by the first proposition of the *Liber de causis*, 'omnis causa primaria plus influit super suum causatum quam causa universalis secunda' (every primary cause has influence in a greater degree on what it acts upon than any second cause).[7] A little later in the same epistle, the *De coelesti hierarchia* of Dionysius the Areopagite and the *Liber de causis* are significantly coupled together to illustrate the search for the primal cause of essence and virtue: 'Whence it is evident that every essence and every virtue proceeds from a primal one; and that the lower intelligences have their effect as it were from a radiating body, and, after the fashion of mirrors, reflect the rays of the higher to the one below them.'[8] The principle that governs this interplay of reflections, and which accords with the Boethian metaphysics of form, is contained in proposition 10 of the *Liber*: 'omnis intelligentia plena est formis' (every intelligence is full of forms).[9]

The question of Dante's relations to Alan's work is complicated by the fact that in addition to their similarities of structure and imagery we must also consider Dante's probable or possible verbal borrowings from his predecessor. The first and most general analogy is between the journey that Phronesis (Wisdom), Reason and Prudence make through the seven heavens—on the chariot built by the seven liberal arts and guided by the five senses—and Dante's ascent into Paradise. On reaching the realm of Theology, the 'goddess' inspired directly by the Holy Spirit, Phronesis explains Nature's desire to create the perfect man and begs her to show them the way to God's 'fortress'. But only Phronesis herself can ascend to the Empyrean: Reason cannot enter. In the presence of angelic choirs and of the Virgin, Phronesis finally enters God's castle, 'where the eternal Ideas, the reason and cause of all things, are painted, and where from a resplendent fountain springs forth a river of equal nature and splendour (the generation of the Son from the Father)'.[10] God grants Phronesis's prayer and orders Noys to mould a perfect soul, on which he imprints his seal. This is followed by the return journey and Nature's construction of a perfect human body, which is then adapted to the soul. The perfect man who is born in this way, Iuvenis, now establishes the reign of Concord and Harmony, a kind of second Earthly Paradise from which 'the ancient curse that burdened the sons of Adam has disappeared'.[11]

The similarities to the *Commedia* are obvious. Passion for knowledge and an intense predilection for problems of science, philosophy and theology are equally profound in both authors. When Ernst Robert Curtius argued that Alan 'drew up the program for a new epic genre which should treat the ascent of reason into the realm of transcendent truth', and that Dante 'first and alone seized upon it once again and recast it in a new experiential material [*Erlebnisgehalt*]', he had a point.[12] Moreover, the fact that in Phronesis's journey there are three guides, as in the *Commedia*—Reason, the unnamed *puella poli*, and finally Faith, following one after the other, each being suited to that particular stage but not to those beyond it—constitutes a further reason to believe in a direct relationship between the two poems.[13]

Then there are specific analogies, of situations, concepts, images, expressions: already indicated by Andrea Ciotti in a very pertinent essay sixty years ago:[14] no need, then, to repeat them here. But there are other parallels that can be added: for *Inferno* 7, for the Earthly Paradise in *Purgatorio* 28, for the river of light in *Paradiso* 30. Taken individually, these analogies do not constitute conclusive evidence of a direct relationship, but if we take them together they do tip the balance of probability in its favour. Finally, there are the verbal correspondences, one of which Ciotti himself had already chosen.[15] This is Dante's splendid image, in *Paradiso* 23, of 'Trivia', the 'tri-form Diana' of classical myth,[16] 'at the full moon in clear skies—/ smiling among the everlasting nymphs / who decorate all reaches of the sky'.[17] The Moon 'smiles' (a verb which in Dante always indicates joyful gleaming, flashing, glowing) in all her splendour, accompanied by her 'nymphs', the stars that fill every corner of the sky—one of the most beautiful similes in the entire poem, not least because of its reference to the remote mythological names of the celestial bodies:

Quale ne' plenilunii sereni
Trivia ride tra le ninfe etterne
che dipingon lo ciel per tutti i seni

(As in the calm, clear skies of moonlit nights,
tri-form Diana smiles (eternal nymphs, around her,
paint all Heaven's curving spheres))

The first six lines of Book 5 of the *Anticlaudianus* read:

Lucis inoffense spacium fontemque nitoris,
Quo radiant stelle, quo certant fulgure multo
Astra poli propriumque diem sine fine perhennant,
Quo celi faciem depingunt, sidera, uirgo
Exhilarata subit, hausto pro parte laboris
Pondere, letaturque poli perflata sereno.

(The maiden is cheered as she enters a region of untroubled light,
a gleaming fountain, where the stars are radiant,
where the lights of the firmament compete in brilliance,
and maintain an endless day, and the constellations adorn
the heavens' face. The most burdensome part of her task
is finished, and she rejoices, caressed by the serene air of the celestial spere.)[18]

Crucial in both passages seems to me to be the presence of 'painting' in the sense of 'adorning' or embellishing: while the image of the full moon and the stars has illustrious antecedents in ancient poetry, from Homer to Sappho and the Bible,[19] the verb 'to paint' in the meaning conveyed in a context of this kind has a complex history in the Latin sphere, probably starting with Accius,[20] going down perhaps to Manilius and certainly to Seneca, and then to Festus Avienus's *Aratea* and finally to Boethius. In Manilius's *Astronomica*, lines 451–55 of Book 1, notoriously disputable from a textual point of view, read differently in two different editions, Valla and Loeb:

> Et versas frontibus Arctos
> uno distingui medias claudique Dracone
> credimus exemplo, quamvis fulgentia visus
> hunc orbem caeli vertentis sidera cursu
> cardine tam simili fultum, quam vertice, *pingunt*.
>
> (And that Bears with opposite fronts are separated
> in the middle by a single Dragon and surrounded by it,
> we believe by analogy, although the shining stars
> *paint* this invisible hemisphere of rotating sky
> supported by similar hinges and poles.)[21]
>
> [. . .] aversas frontibus Arctos
> uno distingui medias claudique Dracone
> credimus exemplo, quia mens fugientia visus
> hunc orbem caeli vertentis sidera cursu
> tam signo simili fultum quam vertice *fingit*.
>
> (We assume by analogy that Bears with faces averted from
> each other
> are separated and encircled by a single Dragon,
> since the mind *imagines* that this southern circle of heaven,
> turning in its rotation those constellations which shun our gaze,
> is supported by similar signs just as it is by a similar pole.)[22]

Seneca uses the expression twice: in the *Medea*, where the great chorus 'Audax nimium', celebrating the proto-history and future of navigation, sings, 'Not yet were the constellations known; / there was no use / of the stars that embellish the heavens [stellisque quibus pingitur aether]':;[23] and in the *Thyestes*, in which again a great chorus, the 'Quo, terrarum superumque potens' (Where, you master of earth and heaven), mentions 'earth and girdling sea / and the wandering stars of the jeweled sky [et vaga picti sidera mundi]'.[24]

For Festus Avienus, on the other hand, 'omnia quae flammis pingunt radiantibus aethram, / nox agit' (Night drives all those stars which decorate the ether with their flickering flames).[25] Lastly, Boethius, in the first metre of the fourth book of *Consolation*, celebrates his 'wings swift flying / Which can ascend the heights of heaven': the wings of his mind, which allow him dizzying flights 'beyond the highest point of fire / That burns with the rapid motion of the upper air, / Until it rise to the houses of the stars', or 'where the glittering night is painted forth' (quocumque micans nox pingitur).[26]

Whether Alan first, and Dante later, came, independently of each other, to be aware of all the links in this chain of tradition it is impossible to say, but frankly it seems unlikely. The possibility remains that they both drew on Boethius, either independently, or with one of them, Dante, reaching Boethius through the other, Alan. But Dante knew the *Consolation* too well to have to resort to an intermediary. And his moon smiles among the stars, nymph among the nymphs, serene in nights illuminated by full moons. 'A thing of beauty', one should remark with a later poet, 'is a joy for ever.'

32

'Splendour of God!'

THE QUESTION SPONTANEOUSLY arises, then, as to what exactly the poetry of the *Paradiso* is, particularly in the last cantos. I would like to suggest an answer in the vigorous and elegant phrasing used by Kenelm Foster, a great Dante scholar as well as a great theologian, when he treated this very subject seventy years ago:

> If poetry cannot have God (in some sense) for its subject-matter, then we may as well admit that this poem is a failure: some enchanting lyrics insecurely attached to a dry theological structure, as Croce maintained. But if, as I think, the Paradiso is not a failure, this must be because Dante, aspiring to the absolute, apprehended it so vividly in created analogies that this apprehension became one with his sense of his own existence and his primitive delight in life and hunger for perfect life. God is his theme and his experience. Not that Dante really saw God face to face, as though the fiction of the thirty-third canto were a literal statement of fact; but he saw, it would seem, the radiance of his own contemplative mind as a mirror of the deity; and in the Paradiso, especially in the last cantos, that radiance possessed him. And this being possessed by light in himself was not a being enclosed in himself; anything but that: it was a being moved onwards, an in-godding, as he called it, a mounting into 'l'alta luce che da sé è vera', a being transformed into
>
> luce intellettual piena d'amore,
> amor del vero ben pien di letizia,
> letizia che trascende ogni dolzore[1]

Foster's position presents several practical and theoretical advantages. In the first place, it gives interpreters a way of bypassing or surpassing Croce's view of the *Paradiso*, which held—and partly still holds—sway in general popular reception of the cantica.[2] Secondly, it combines the existential, ethical and metaphysical planes of Dante's narrative and poetry. Thirdly, and so far most importantly, it goes beyond the literal level of the vision without necessarily resorting to allegory. When Foster says that Dante 'saw, it would seem, the radiance of his own contemplative mind as a mirror of the deity', he gives an original, modern view of the mystical experience. Fourthly, this conception of the mystical experience indirectly takes into account the Dionysian, and ultimately Neoplatonic, approach. The apprehension of the absolute by means of 'created analogies' brings us back to the metaphorical language of the *Timaeus* and above all of Dionysius's *De divinis nominibus*. And indeed Dante experiments with the 'names' of God throughout the last cantos of *Paradiso*. Just to limit oneself to *Paradiso* 33, he calls God 'lumen' ten times,[3] then 'summa et prima veritas', 'lux mundi', 'liber unus omnia continens', 'virtus infinita', 'summum bonum', 'summum ens', 'intellectus intelligens et amans seipsum'.[4] Nor can we forget that in an act of extraordinary daring, he even sees the Christian God as Neptune.[5]

Foster's passage ends by quoting three famous lines of *Paradiso* 30—'pure light of intellect, all love, / the love of good in truth, all happiness, / a happiness transcending every rapture'. These lines apply to Dante's final transformation, but are actually spoken by Beatrice and are used by the poet to describe the Empyrean, to which he is finally ascending after crossing the last material heaven, the Crystalline. The light that shines here is 'intellectual', of the mind, 'but it is made substantial by love; and this love of the true good brings with it the greatest joy, which surpasses all human delight'.[6]

The Empyrean, therefore, is at one with the divine light by means of which God 'makes himself intelligible and able to be loved',[7] and specifically with the *lumen gloriae* of theology, which makes the vision of God possible: 'lume è là sù che visibile face / lo creatore a quella creatura / che solo in lui vedere ha la sua pace' (above us there, a light / that makes the All-Creator in creation seen / by those who only seeing Him have peace). That light, and with it the river of light, 'si distende in circular figura'—'becomes a circle in its form, extending its circumference so far as might a belt too generous round the sun' before the eyes of Dante.[8] Mysticism turns into poetry of the Absolute, allowing the 'isplendor di viva luce etterna' (the 'splendour of living and eternal light!') of *Purgatorio* 31 to become

O isplendor di Dio, per cu' io vidi
l'alto trïunfo del regno verace,
dammi virtù a dir com' ïo il vidi!

(Splendour of God! Through you I came to see
triumph exalting in the realm of truth.
Grant me true strength to say what then I saw.)[9]

Poet of the Absolute: of beauty, splendour, and truth. A Dante increasingly *platonicus*, fully *dionysiacus*, yet completely in love with '*created* analogies', with the things of *this* world that are the mirrors of Creation.

33

'The beauty I saw'

DANTE IS NOW APPROACHING the 'ultimo suo', as he calls it in *Paradiso* 30, the ultimate and utmost climax of his power as a poet, beyond the sources he has interiorised. On the threshold of the Empyrean he looks fixedly once again at Beatrice, as he has been doing for thirty cantos, from the top of Mount Purgatory onwards. On that summit there had already been a first epiphany, when the lady's lips and smile were revealed fully for the first time:

> O isplendor di viva luce etterna,
> chi palido si fece sotto l'ombra
> sì di Parnaso, o bevve in sua cisterna,
>
> che non paresse aver la mente ingombra,
> tentando a render te qual tu paresti
> là dove armonizzando il ciel t'adombra,
>
> quando ne l'aere aperto ti solvesti?
>
> (Splendour of living and eternal light!
> Who would not seem—though pale from studying
> deep in Parnassian shade, whose wells he drinks—
>
> still to be much encumbered in his mind,
> endeavouring to draw what you then seemed,
> where heavens in harmony alone enshadow you,
>
> as you came forth and showed yourself in air?)[1]

The glorious exclamation which opens this passage contrasts with the tiring work of the poet, the splendour of living and eternal light with the pallor of the human writer. And Mount Parnassus, in whose grottoes Statius drank, prompted by Virgil's example,[2] and where ancient poets dreamed of Eden,[3] appears as a mere shadow. The painful work of the poet becomes evanescent paleness, insubstantial shade. Paradoxically, the lightness of this image is immediately translated into heaviness: as it pales, the poet's mind becomes 'ingombra': full, encumbered, confused, inert, as if paralysed by its own weight.

Yet this poet hasn't only become pale in the shade of Parnassus—he has also drunk abundantly from its well, absorbing the true essence of inspiration with the sacred water of the Muses. Consequently, he can observe the living light and, albeit indirectly, express it in words. In the second movement of the passage, the object itself of the epiphany, the 'second beauty' manifested by the unveiling of Beatrice's mouth as 'isplendor di viva luce etterna' is at one and the same time reduced and dilated. For the Heaven now open to Dante, harmonising both with Earthly Paradise and with Beatrice's new beauty—with the supremely human and the incipiently divine—'adombra' this splendour. 'Adombra': that is to say, it foresees, preannounces, represents; but only in an inadequate manner, as a shadow does with a body. And so, at the moment in which the brilliant light of the beginning opens itself up and dissolves in the blinding light of the end, the shadow of Parnassus returns. Poetry and its objects have become the stuff dreams are made of, and not even Dante can now 'trattare l'ombre come cosa salda' (treat a shadow as a thing of weight).[4]

Things have radically changed in *Paradiso* 30, which 'fulfils' *Purgatorio* 31 even though what the pilgrim beholds now, 'the river and the glint / of topaz, in and out', and 'the smile of grass', are 'shadowed prefaces that hint at their own truth' (son di lor vero umbriferi prefazi).[5] Dante now calls that splendour 'bellezza'—'la bellezza ch'io vidi', 'the beauty that

I saw'. And he adds several notations that hint at his own biography as a poet:

Se quanto infino a qui di lei si dice
fosse conchiuso tutto in una loda,
poca sarebbe a fornir questa vice.

La bellezza ch'io vidi si trasmoda
non pur di là da noi, ma certo io credo
che solo il suo fattor tutta la goda.

Da questo passo vinto mi concedo
più che già mai da punto di suo tema
soprato fosse comico o tragedo:

ché, come sole in viso che più trema,
così lo rimembrar del dolce riso
la mente mia da me medesmo scema.

Dal primo giorno ch'i' vidi il suo viso
in questa vita, infino a questa vista,
non m'è il seguire al mio cantar preciso;

ma or convien che mio seguir desista
più dietro a sua bellezza, poetando,
come a l'ultimo suo ciascuno artista.

(If all that has, till this, been said of her
were now enclosed to form one word of praise,
it would not, even so, fulfil my need.

The beauty I saw, transcending every kind,
is far beyond us here—nor only us.
Its maker, I think, alone could know its joy.

From now on, I'll admit, I'm overwhelmed,
defeated worse than all before—in comic
or in tragic genre—by what my theme demands.

As sunlight trembles in enfeebled eyes,
calling to mind how sweet to me her smile was,
itself deprives my mind of memory.

Not since the day that I, in our first life,
first saw her face until this living sight,
has song in me been cut so cleanly short.

It is, however, right that I stand down—
as every artist, at the utmost, does—
and no more trace her beauty, forming verse.)[6]

It doesn't matter whether this is the beauty of Dionysius, or that of the *Timaeus* or of the *Phaedrus*. It no longer counts. This is Beatrice's beauty, summing them all up! It is 'trasmodata': changed, that is, in manner and figure, but not substantially, an entity that is now 'beyond us' although still human: such, in any case, that only her Creator can enjoy fully. In other words, we are witnessing a transfiguration. Using military language, Dante proclaims himself 'vinto', 'defeated' by this moment more than any writer of comedies or tragedies was by his theme. The simile makes clear how the defeat took place: as sunlight confounds uncertain, trembling eyes, so his mind is overcome by the memory of her sweet smile. But the story is ancient, Beatrice's ineffability going back at least to *Purgatorio* 31. Indeed, the poet tells us here, ever since the first day he saw her in the world of the living, and 'until this living sight', it has never been impossible for him to sing of her.[7] But now he must stop pursuing her beauty ever more closely, as does the artist who reaches 'l'ultimo suo', the furthest limit of his ability. It is a definitive farewell to the poetry that from the *Vita nuova* to the *Paradiso* has dictated Dante's agenda, the word *loda*, 'praise', employed at line 17 being a technical term for the kind of lyric fashioned for the book of his youth: 'if all that has, till this, been said of her / were now enclosed to form one word of praise [fosse concluso tutto in una loda] / it would not, even so, fulfil my need,' Dante writes.[8]

But is this really what happens? Not exactly, for Beatrice's ineffable beauty is now transferred onto the *Commedia*'s ultimate object, the Absolute: God and his 'place', God and his light. After entering the

Empyrean and being struck by a 'lightning', which leaves him 'in swaddling weaves of brilliance', Dante, 'new seeing strength kindled' in him once again,[9] is able to begin to perceive the final vision:[10]

> e vidi lume in forma di rivera
> fulvido di fulgore, intra due rive
> dipinte di mirabil primavera.
>
> Di tal fiumana uscian faville vive,
> e d'ogne parte si mettien ne' fiori,
> quasi rubin che oro circunscrive;
>
> poi, come inebrïate da li odori,
> riprofondavan sé nel miro gurge,
> e s'una intrava, un'altra n'uscia fori.
>
> (I saw light form a river in full spate,
> fire-dazzle-gilded, flowing through verges
> painted afresh in colours of wonderful spring.
>
> And rising from that flood, alive, were sparks
> that everywhere alighted on the flowers,
> like rubies set in gold encirclements—
>
> then all, as though the perfumes made them drunk,
> plunged in that swirling miracle once more.
> And yet where one sank in, still more spun out.)[11]

From now on, almost until the last line of the last canto, this—with all its metamorphoses—will be the theme of Dante's poetry.[12]

34

Neptune and Lethargy

THE LAST CANTO OF THE *Paradiso,* opening with Bernard's Prayer to the Virgin on behalf of Dante, is one of the most extraordinary feats in the history of Western poetry—because Dante's 'sustained attack on the inarticulate', his 'wresling match',[1] faces several tasks at one and the same time. To begin with, he has to remember what he saw. Then, he has to try to describe it. And finally, he has to tackle the problem of poetry. For instance, Dante's sight brings him, four times and in each instance in two parallel stages, to link his *vista* to the Absolute.[2] The Absolute itself passes through three stages (God as pure Act, containing all the elements of the universe; the Trinity as three circles; the Incarnation as the human figure within the second circle).[3] Finally, the mystical vision is suspended between memory and words. Dante states three times that it is impossible for him to remember, to speak, and to think.[4] Simultaneously, he addresses God personally three times,[5] and three times indicates that almost all, but not all, of his vision has vanished: that he might leave a gleam, at least, of God's glory to posterity, and that he believes he saw the 'universal form' of the 'knot' which joins all beings, accidents and modes precisely because he feels greater pleasure in saying so: 'This knotting-up of universal form I saw, / I'm sure of that. For now I feel, / in saying this, a gift of greater joy.[6]

The two poetically supreme moments of this contrast between ineffability and positive affirmation are represented by four tercets, three coming after Bernard's prayer, and one after the vision of the 'universal form':

> Qual è colüi che sognando vede,
> che dopo 'l sogno la passione impressa
> rimane, e l'altro a la mente non riede,
>
> cotal son io, ché quasi tutta cessa
> mia visïone, e ancor mi distilla
> nel core il dolce che nacque da essa.
>
> Così la neve al sol si disigilla;
> così al vento ne le foglie levi
> si perdea la sentenza di Sibilla.
>
> (Like those who see so clearly while they dream
> that marks of feeling, when their dreaming ends,
> remain, though nothing more returns to mind,
>
> so I am now. For nearly all I saw
> has gone, even if, still, within my heart,
> there drops the sweetness that was born from that.
>
> So, too, in sunlight, snow will lose its seal.
> So, too, the oracles the Sibyl wrote
> on weightless leaves are lost upon the wind.)[7]

The snow melting—actually, 'losing its seal'—in the sun, and the Sibyl's oracles lost in the wind like weightless leaves are the two 'objective correlatives' of something which is no longer present, but the feeling of which persists. Then, twenty-four lines later, comes the second statement:

> La forma universal di questo nodo
> credo ch'i' vidi, perché più di largo,
> dicendo questo, mi sento ch'i' godo.
>
> (This knotting-up of universal form
> I saw, I'm sure of that. For now I feel,
> in saying this, a gift of greater joy.)[8]

This means, quite simply, that Dante is authenticating his vision of the Absolute by the joy he feels in expressing it. This isn't something that happens often in poetry—or anywhere else.

But in the last canto of the *Paradiso* any single statement seems to contradict another. One second later, we encounter important analogies with texts by Boethius and Alan of Lille. The first occurs when Dante writes, immediately after the tercet I have just quoted—I translate the lines literally on purpose—that just one 'point' is greater 'lethargy' for him than twenty-five centuries are for the enterprise that made Neptune admire the *Argo*'s shadow: 'un punto solo m'è maggior letargo / che venticinque secoli a la 'mpresa / che fe' Nettuno ammirar l'ombra d'Argo'. Alan uses the same word, 'lethargy', to indicate the catalepsy in which Phronesis lies: 'laesa sopore / lethargi' (listless, stricken by her drowsy lethargy)[9].

Ernst Robert Curtius, Erich Auerbach and Peter Dronke have confronted each other on this coincidence,[10] the second adding, and the third discussing, its source in the *Consolation*,[11] when Philosophy, having seen Boethius 'not merely silent but altogether speechless and dumb', touches his breast with her hand, saying, 'He is in no real danger, but suffers only from lethargy, a sickness common to deluded minds' (lethargum patitur, communem illusarum mentium morbum). The fact is, however, that Boethius's and Alan's lethargy constitute a 'failure of vision', whereas in Dante it signals 'a supreme success'.[12]

Let us try to read the two tercets in their context. When, between two definitive (*sic*!) proclamations of ineffability, Dante describes what 's'interna' 'nel profondo'—what is contained in the depths—of eternal light, of the Infinite itself, 'lethargy' makes its appearance:

Un punto solo m'è maggior letargo
che venticinque secoli a la 'mpresa
che fé Nettuno ammirar l'ombra d'Argo.

Così la mente mia, tutta sospesa,
mirava fissa, immobile e attenta
e sempre di mirar faceasi accesa.

(One single point in trauma is far more,
for me, than those millennia since sail
made Neptune marvel under Argos-shade.

And so my mind, held high above itself,
looked on, intent and still, in wondering awe
and, lit by wonder, always flared anew.)[13]

We owe a good deal of the fascination these tercets inspire to the mystery that envelops and fills the first of them. I shall do my best to explain the reasons behind the enigma. And first of all let's notice that, as with the image of the Sibyl's leaves, the poet plunges us suddenly into the world of ancient myth, at first sight more problematically here, because Neptune, who might have appeared as the appropriate agent of Ulysses's shipwreck in *Inferno* 26, is absent there, but present here in the middle of the supreme vision of God. In these six lines Dante establishes an implicit comparison between the present of remembering and writing, on the one hand, and the past of the vision on the other ('un punto solo m'è'—'così la mente mia mirava'), as well as between Neptune's stupor then, and the rapt, fixed 'mirare' of the pilgrim's mind into the divine substance now. He maintains that a single point of that vision is for him now, as he writes, greater oblivion than twenty-five centuries are for the enterprise that made Neptune wonder at the shade of the *Argo* [fig. 19]. On the other hand, he proclaims that, as that point, now, causes him 'greater lethargy', so his mind, then, intent and still, fixed on God with wonder ('mirava'). In short, he simultaneously affirms and denies something, opening up an immense temporal abyss. The *mirari*—that is to say, the fixing something with admiration, with wonder—growing upon itself echoes a mystical mechanism proposed by Richard of Saint-Victor:

> Sed dum mens desiderio suo satisfaciens eiusmodi inquisitioni studium inpendit, iam cogitationis modum cogitando excedit, et cogitatio in meditationem transit. Solet sane simile aliquid circa meditationem accidere, nam ueritatem quidem diu quaesitam tandemque inuentam mens solet cum auiditate suscipere, mirari cum exultatione eiusque admirationi diutius inherere, et hoc est iam

> meditationem meditando excedere, et meditationem in contemplationem ergo transire.
>
> (But when the mind for the satisfaction of its own desire begins to pursue such inquiry, already, by thinking it goes beyond the mode of thinking, and thinking passes over into meditation. Certainly, it is usual that something similar occurs concerning meditation. For after a certain truth has been sought for a long while and is found at last, the mind usually receives it with strong desire, marvels at it with exultation, and for a long time clings to the wonder of it. Already, this is to go beyond meditation by meditating, and meditation passes over into contemplation.)[14]

This of course doesn't explain how a single 'point' can be 'greater' than twenty-five centuries, which in Dante's eyes must have represented almost the whole of the history of mankind. As a matter of fact, this is possible, because the point stands for 'eternity'—because it is the 'punto / a cui tutti li tempi son presenti' (the point at which all times are present time).[15] Between time, 'lethargy' and 'point', moreover, there is a mysterious tie, which Bernard had already foreshadowed in his words to Dante in Canto 32.139–40: 'Ma perché 'l *tempo* fugge che t'*assonna* / qui farem *punto*': 'but since your time of slumber races by, / at this point we shall end'. 'Time, in its being punctually crushed and reduced towards eternity, involves sleep and oblivion'.[16]

How, though, can present 'lethargy' agree with the stupefied and self-generating attention of the past and the memory of the Argonauts' enterprise, which still persists after twenty-five centuries? The fact is that 'lethargy' indicates a fairly precise disease: that which, according to Hugutio of Pisa, afflicts 'deluded minds' with sleep and oblivion,[17] yet precisely because it denotes that disease it also alludes to the symptoms accompanying it: delirium, stupor, *Entrückung*—'rapture'. 'Where the disease of lethargy suspends the mind and makes the patient gaze in a fixed, immobile fashon, so Dante's lethargy too has these effects—in precisely the opposite sense:[18] 'così la mente mia, tutta sospesa, / mirava fissa' (so my mind, held high above itself, / looked on, intent and still). Negative and positive, past and present are joined together because

Dante finds himself now 'là 've s'appunta ogne *ubi* e ogne *quando*', 'where every "when" and "where" attains its point'.[19] Hugutio, for his part, underlines the importance of oblivion, and places the lotus, the flower of forgetfulness which 'works to avoid love', firmly in the field of poetry, quoting in relation to this two lines of the *Remedia amoris* in which Ovid associates the Lotos-Eaters with the Sirens: 'Imagine in that lair are Lotos-eaters, Sirens: / add your oars' effort now to your sails.'[20]

In this fashion, the poet's present lethargy, Neptune's wonder, and Dante's 'mirare' become a series whose single terms time after time throw light on one another and are then reflected and amplified each by the other. We are therefore witnessing the supreme instant of wonder, where the magnified echo of the *Convivio*'s 'stordimento d'animo'—the 'mind's astonishment'—is pushed to the limit.[21] *Admiratio* is the subject's mental state in the moment of vision, but it immediately reverberates in the writer's 'lethargy'. Finally, it enters the recipient's field through the image of Neptune's wonder in remote times—the image which T. S. Eliot considered 'the real right thing, the power of establishing relations between beauty of the most diverse sorts', 'the utmost power of the poet', the 'master who could thus at every moment realize the inapprehensible in visual images'.[22]

We are indeed talking about poetry: because the 'shade of the *Argo*' corresponds to the 'shade of the blessed realm' Dante had promised to describe in *Paradiso* 1, and because the enterprise of the Argonauts is Dante's own in the *Paradiso* as a whole, as he had written in his address to the readers in *Paradiso* 2: 'Que' gloriosi che passaro al Colco / non s'ammiraron come voi farete, / quando Iason vider fatto bifolco' (The Argonauts, in glory, Colchis-bound, / were not so wonder-struck as you will be / when they saw Jason yoking up the plough.)[23]

The poetic keystone is precisely lethargy, this *oppressio cerebri*, an 'oppression of the brain', as Hugutio says, which identifies with *oblivionis infirmitas*, the 'illness of oblivion'. Far from preventing poetry, this oblivion to the umpteenth power generates, guards and launches it with all its mystery. Perhaps I'm wrong, but here I see at work a mechanism like that which Mallarmé—always looking for absolute beauty—outlines in *Crise de vers* when he writes,

> Je dis: une fleur! et, hors de l'*oubli* où ma voix relègue aucun contour, en tant que quelque chose d'autre que les calices sus, musicalement se lève, idée même et suave, l'absente de tous bouquets.
>
> (I say: a flower! and outside the oblivion to which my voice relegates any shape, insofar as it is something other than the calyx, there arises musically, as the very idea and delicate, the one absent from every bouquet.)[24]

This is what, in 'Le vierge, le vivace, le bel aujourd'hui',

> Va-t-il nous dechirer avec un coup d'aile ivre
> Ce lac dur *oublié* que hante sous le givre
> Le transparent glacier des vols qui n'ont pas fui!
>
> (Will a beat of its drunken wing not suffice
> To rend this hard lake haunted beneath the ice
> By the transparent glacier of flights never flown?)[25]

It is the Constellation 'froide d'*oubli* et de désuétude' which *makes* 'le Septentrion aussi Nord' in 'Un Coup de dés'.[26] Poetry rises from lethargy, from oblivion, where it incubates before coming to light.

It seems to me that in a similar way, in Dante, the 'letargo' which is oblivion evokes *Argo* the ship: the first, Ovid says, that 'ever sailed an unknown sea'.[27] This becomes the 'ship of light' of the ancient tradition,[28] the 'holy' vessel, the 'celestial ship' not by chance represented by the constellation Argo. Now, finally, this ship perhaps 'flows forth above' the heavenly waters, imitating God's primeval spirit as Dante had described it in *Paradiso* 29, as we saw in chapter 24. In the *Aratea*, underlining the lightness of the celestial vessel, Cicero had sung, 'Insequitur labens per caeli lumina Navis', and 'totaque iam supera fulgens prolabitur Argo':[29] 'the *Argo* follows, gliding among the lights of heaven', and 'all the things up there shining *Argo* brushes'. Finally, the 'other *Argo*' prophesied by Virgil in the fourth Eclogue for the new 'golden age' also appears,[30] and Seneca has the Chorus of his *Medea* foresee new Argonauts opening up a new, immense land[31]—a passage Columbus quoted in his *Libro de las prophecías* with obvious implications for his own voyages.[32] The *Argo* sails the waters of ancient myth, of astronomy and mysticism, and of early modern European history.

Dante's *Argo*, his own poetic vessel, hasn't reached a haven, but is still sailing through high waters, in the middle of the Ocean—'in the stillness between two waves of the sea', T. S. Eliot will gloss at the end of the *Four Quartets*:[33] suspended over the billows from the depths of which rises, to contemplate it, the wonder of God.

35

The Last Simile: The Geometer

THE LAST PARALLEL TOUCHES on the simile—the last one of the *Paradiso* and of the entire *Commedia*—of the geometer who 'tutto s'affige / per misurar lo cerchio, e non ritrova, / pensando, quel principio ond'elli indige'—literally, 'who fixes his whole mind in measuring the circle and cannot find again in his thought the principle he needs'. The parallel is not with the *Anticlaudianus*, but with Alan of Lille's own *Rithmus de incarnatione Christi*, where the lines concerning geometry, in the last section but one, are the following:[1]

Sue artis in censura
geometra fallitur,
dum immensus sub mensura
terrenorum sistitur.
In directum curvatura
circuli convertitur.
Speram claudit quadratura
et sub ipsa clauditur.
In hac Verbi copula
stupet omnis regula.

(Fails the geometer
in his art's judgment
when the immense
is reduced to the measure
of earthly things.

Into a straight line is transformed
the circle's curvature.
A square encloses a sphere
and is by it enclosed.
In this copula of the Word
every rule is stupefied.)[2]

We are beyond Platonism, now, in the thickest of mysteries—that, precisely, of the Incarnation, which Dante has just contemplated, in the previous tercet, in the human figure outlined within the second circle of the Trinity: 'dentro da sé, del suo colore stesso, / mi parve pinta della nostra effige', he writes: 'deep in itself, it seemed—as painted now, / in those same hues—to show our human form'. In an act of extreme synthesis, Alan is playing on the double meaning of the term *Verbum*, the Logos or Word as second person of the Trinity, and the verb of human language—the type of verb, of which the commonest is 'to be', that joins the subject of the verb to a complement or predicate as in 'he is his son'. In this particular copula of the *Verbum*-verb, 'is', it is precisely the fact that 'he is his son' that stupefies. Every rule of grammar and reason is here obliterated, contested, reduced to stupor:

Qual è 'l geomètra che tutto s'affige
per misurar lo cerchio, e non ritrova,
pensando, quel principio ond' elli indige,

tal era io a quella vista nova:
veder voleva come si convenne
l'imago al cerchio e come vi s'indova;

ma non eran da ciò le proprie penne:
se non che la mia mente fu percossa
da un fulgore in che sua voglia venne.

A l'alta fantasia qui mancò possa;
ma già volgeva il mio disio e 'l velle,
sì come rota ch'igualmente è mossa,

l'amor che move il sole e l'altre stelle.

(As some geometer may fix his mind
to find a circle-area, yet lack,
in thought, the principle his thoughts require,

likewise with me at this sight seen so new.
I willed myself to see what fit there was,
image to circle, how this all in-where'd.

But mine were wings that could not rise to that,
save that, with this, my mind, was stricken through
by sudden lightning bringing what it wished.

All powers of high imagining here failed.
But now my will and my desire were turned,
as wheels that move in equilibrium,

by love that moves the sun and other stars.)[3]

Like Alan's geometer, Dante's, too, fails. But in the *Paradiso* the defeat is followed by three more movements—the 'mind' stricken through by a sudden lightning which envelops the will; the failing of 'high imagining';[4] and the circular motion imposed on the poet's desire and will by the love that moves the sun and the other stars, a circular motion which is explicitly uniform. Dante does not understand the circle,[5] but actually himself becomes a circle—a celestial body like the sun and the other stars. He is now one of those 'cose belle', the 'beautiful things' which, *Inferno* 1 told us, God's love first moved—'l'amor divino mosse di prima quelle cose belle'.[6] Dante: a thing, a creature, a being *of beauty*.

36

Epilogue

DESCENT FROM HEAVEN, ASCENT TO ART AND SCIENCE

WE SHOULD NEVER FORGET that Dante is by no means the end of the story. In one of the great masterpieces of Renaissance art, Raphael's *School of Athens* in the Vatican Palace, where all the philosophers of antiquity are represented, Plato and Aristotle stand at the centre of the scene, next to each other, the former pointing his right index finger to the world above, the latter stretching his right hand towards the ground. Each holds a book in his left hand: Aristotle, the *Ethics*; Plato, the *Timaeus*. Plato's visage is that of Leonardo da Vinci: a stroke of genius by which Raphael shows he has grasped the entire history of Western thought and imagination [fig. 21].

Neither Dante nor the medieval thinkers I have been talking about are far away, for on the opposite wall of the Stanza della Segnatura Raphael painted a *Disputation on the Holy Sacrament* or *Triumph of Religion*. The fresco is divided into two levels; the upper one depicts *Ecclesia triumphans*, with God the Father at the centre, surrounded by angels, patriarchs of the Old Testament, and Christian martyrs and saints. Upper and lower level communicate with each other through the figure of Christ and the dove of the Holy Ghost, surrounded by the *Ecclesia militans*. Clearly visible in this lower semicircle are popes and cardinals accompanied by four Fathers—Jerome, Gregory the Great, Ambrose and Augustine. A little further away, in the row behind them, are Thomas Aquinas and . . . Dante, crowned with laurel, poet and theologian.

Dante returns a second time in another fresco, the *School of Parnassus* that occupies the wall linking the *School of Athens* to the *Dispute*. Here, on the slopes of Mount Parnassus, Apollo sits at the centre, playing the lyre and surrounded by the nine Muses, while Homer stands on the left beside Virgil and Dante, with Sappho seated on a lower slope. On the other side, the poets include Ariosto, Petrarch, Ovid, Catullus, Propertius and Tibullus, and further down Horace, Sannazaro and a seated Pindar. The two grisaille scenes at the bottom of the fresco show Augustus restraining Virgil's friends from burning the *Aeneid*, and Alexander the Great having Homer's poems laid on the tomb of Achilles.

The vaulted ceiling, occupied at the centre by an octagon surrounded by four big circles, completes this extraordinary cultural programme with icons of Theology, Philosophy, Justice, and Poetry, added to which are rectangular sections containing symbolic representations of Original Sin (between Theology and Justice); Solomon's Judgment (between Justice and Philosophy); Astronomy, with a young Wisdom as Prime Mover of the universe (between Philosophy and Poetry); and Apollo and Marsyas (between Poetry and Theology) [fig. 22].[1]

The Stanza della Segnatura constitutes an ideal *summa* of Platonic and Neoplatonist conceptions of Truth, Goodness, and Beauty, mediated by Marsilio Ficino's work of translation and interpretation of Plato, and inspired by the Pythagorean idea of Harmony.[2] In the nearby Sistine Chapel, Michelangelo, who had absorbed Neoplatonism as a young man at the Florentine court of Lorenzo de' Medici, translated it via Augustine, Savonarola, Sante Pagnini and Dante into the magnificent sequence of the Creation on the ceiling.[3] While Neoplatonism spread throughout Italian culture and poetry by way of the works of Leon Battista Alberti, Pico della Mirandola and Angelo Poliziano, the fashion of rewriting the Creation soon revived across Europe in the realm of poetry. The best examples come from France, where Maurice Scève, the Neoplatonic love poet of *Délie*, composes a fascinating *Microcosme* (1562), in which distinctive echoes of the *Timaeus*, together with quotations and references to both medieval and more contemporary writers, gathered from Gregor

Reisch's *Margarita philosophica*, are superimposed in a new kind of philosophical-scientific poem, as, for instance, in this crucial passage on the Creation of Adam, where the inspiration from Genesis 2:7 is fused with that derived from the *Timaeus* (90a–b):

Parquoy le grand Ouvrier de tout ce grand pourpris
Reduire le voulant en un seul poinct compris
Jà par mille, & mille ans en sa divine Idee
De sa grande Bonté, & Puissance guidee
Prevu, preordonné, aussi predestiné
En ce Paradis bas estre un tems confiné
Pour y multiplier infinité de Mondes
Monstrans l'immensité de ses vertus profondes:
D'argile molle, & tendre, à l'oeuvre obeïssante
Composa une masse, et de main toutpuissante
L'ebauchant presque en rond sur la terre estendue
D'un bout, et des deux flancs en branches possibles.

(For this reason the great Workman of all this
Great enclosure, wanting to reduce it to a single point
Already for thousands and thousands of years in his
Divine Idea, out of his great Goodness and Power
Guided, foreordained, and predestined as well
To have a limited time in this low Paradise
In order to multiply in it an infinity of Worlds,
Showing the immensity of his profound virtues,
With soft and tender clay obedient to the work
Composed a mass, and with almighty hands
Shaped it almost in round form over the extended
Land, with an end and two sides into possible branches.)[4]

The 'Ouvrier' of the first line—the *operarius* of Alan of Lille—conceives a 'divine Idee', and immediately afterwards (at line 125) we are told he has a *Modelle* according to which he works. The Timaean background is clear, and the passage ends with the image of man as an *arbre renversé* which comes straight out of Plato's dialogue: 'we should consider that

God gave the sovereign part of the human soul to be the divinity of each one, being that part which [. . .] dwells at the top of our body, and inasmuch as we are a plant not of an earthly but of a heavenly growth, raises us from earth to our kindred that are in the heaven'.[5]

It is simply inconceivable for an early modern poet of Europe to write about the Beginning without having recourse to Plato's *Timaeus* or the language it inaugurated and transmitted to its successors.[6] The pre-Greek and non-European 'Tales of the Beginning' of which Ellen Van Wolde has written, are still far from surfacing to the awareness of conquering Europe,[7] even though, to quote but one example, Pedro Sarmiento de Gamboa devotes two chapters of his *Historia de los Incas* to the native 'fabulas' on origins and Creation myths.[8] The only word of warning that might have kept the poets from embarking on such enterprises would have been that of Plato himself, which, following Cicero's translation, Montaigne sums up as 'il y ayt quelque vice d'impieté à trop curieusement s'enquerir et de Dieu, et du monde, et des causes premieres des choses': 'there is as it were an excess of impiety in enquiring with too much curiosity about God, the world, and the first causes of things'.[9]

Not even this, however, stopped the poets—nor, indeed, the philosophers—if Luís de Camões himself speaks of the Archetype which created the 'gran maquina del mundo'. The passage in his Lusiads is one of the most beautiful descriptions in early modern European literature. The goddess Thetys takes Vasco da Gama—the poem's protagonist and the navigator who first reached India from Europe between 1497 and 1499 by rounding the Cape of Good Hope—to a summit and shows him the (Ptolemaic) universe. It is a sphere suspended in the air and transparent, inside which are clearly visible the 'vários orbes, que a divina verga / compôs' (the orbs which the divine wand composed):

Qual a matéria seja não se enxerga,
Mas enxerga-se bem que está composto
De vários orbes, que a diuina verga
Compôs, e um centro a todos só tem posto:
Volvendo, ora se abaxe, agora se erga,
Nunca s'ergue ou se abaxa, e um mesmo rosto

Por toda a parte tem; e em toda a parte
Começa e acaba, enfim, por divina arte,

Uniforme, perfeito, em si sustido
Qual, enfim, o Arquetipo que o criou.

(Of what the globe is formed none understand,
But all can see that various orbs compose
The whole created by the magic wand,
And all of them one central point inclose.
This globe in constant gyres revolving goes,
It rises and it falls, but rise or fall.
One only face to view it doth expose
Always the same, whatever may befall,
It thus begins and ends, for art divine rules all.

Quite uniform and perfect self-sustained,
Like its great Archetype, who formed the whole.)[10]

The notion of the Archetype was already present in Sacrobosco's (John of Holywood's) famous early thirteenth-century *Tractatus de sphaera* and ultimately went back to the *Timaeus* via Cicero's version,[11] but nothing as magnificent as Camões's description had yet appeared.

One can only imagine what lesser poets would do. Among the great ones, the very special case is that of Guillaume Salluste Du Bartas, who wrote an epic hexaemeron in French, *La sepmaine, ou Creation du monde,* which, first published in 1578, turned out to be an astonishing success all over Europe, with several Latin translations, at least two into English, Italian and Spanish, several into Dutch and one into German. Torquato Tasso, having read one of the Latin versions, composed his own *Il mondo creato,* and from Latin and Italian Alonso de Acevedo produced his own *Creación del mundo.*[12] Its brilliant Continental career ended only with Milton's *Paradise Lost.* I choose only one passage to show how Du Bartas used the *Timaeus.* We are almost at the end of the Second Day, and the author has been discussing air and fire, coming next to the heavens in general. He follows Aristotle, at first, then 'soudain revenant disciple studieux / De l'Attique Platon', he places the four elements in the heavens, according to the theory proposed by the *Timaeus*.

There, Plato maintained that heaven is one and that it is the all-perfect Living Creature. Since it came into existence, it must be of bodily form, visible and tangible, yet 'nothing is visible where there is no fire, or tangible which has no solidity, and nothing is solid without earth'.[13] The Demiurge therefore began to make the universe with fire and earth. But there must always be a third thing to act as intermediary between the two and join them together; in the case of solids the elements needed as intermediaries are two, and that is the reason why the Maker used air and water to unite the other elements, as much as possible in like ratio, 'as fire is to air so is air to water, and as air is to water so is water to earth'.[14] Thus, harmonious in its proportions, the cosmos came into existence. Du Bartas used Marsilio Ficino's *Compedium in Timaeum* to fashion his own version, which reads as follows:

Puis soudain revenant disciple studieux
De l'Attique Platon je les mets dans les cieux.
C'est la terre qui fait par ses membres solides
Et visibles leur feux, et leur corps non fluides.
L'air les fait transparents, la flamme rend legers,
Chauds, prompts et lumineux, leur cercle passagers.
Et les ondes oignant les bords dont s'entrebaisent
Leur globes tournoyans, d'une humeur froide apaisent
La chaleur, qui naissant de leur prompts mouvemens
Ne feroit qu'un brandon de tous les elemens.
Non que je face esgaux les corps dont je compose
Ce corps, qui de son rond embrasse toute chose,
A ces lourds elemens, qu'ici bas les humains
Et voyent de leur yeux, et touchent de leur mains.
Il sont tous beaux, tous purs, une saincte harmonie
D'un eternel lien tient leur substance unie:
L'air est privé de cours, le feu d'embrasement,
De pesanteur la terre, et l'eau d'escoulement.
Ils ne sont tant soit peu l'un à l'aautre funestes:
Et, pour le dire court, ils sont du tout celestes.[15]

PLATE 1. Giovanni di Paolo, *Paradiso* 4, illuminated probably 1438–44 for King Alfonso V of Naples.

PLATE 2. Plato's *Timaeus* in Calcidius's Latin translation, with diagrams, first half of the tenth century.

PLATE 3. Mattia Preti, *Boethius and Philosophy*, ca. 1680.

PLATE 4. West facade of the basilica of Saint-Denis, Paris, built ca. 1135–40.

PLATE 5. Ambulatory of Abbot Suger in Saint-Denis, built ca. 1140–44.

PLATE 6. William of Conches, frontispiece of the *Dragmaticon philosophiae*, early thirteenth century.

PLATE 7. View of the crypt of Anagni Cathedral, twelfth–thirteenth centuries: frescoes by the three 'Masters' illustrating the doctrine of the *Timaeus,* and Old Testament and apocalyptic scenes.

PLATE 8. Crypt of Anagni Cathedral: the Zodiac.

PLATE 9. Crypt of Anagni Cathedral: the Four Ages of Man.

PLATE 10. Crypt of Anagni Cathedral: On the upper right hand side of the picture the figures of Hippocrates and Galen are visible. Immediately to their left, on the pillar are the elements of the Timaeus.

PLATE 11. Crypt of Anagni Cathedral: Elijah ascends to heaven in his chariot of fire.

PLATE 12. Crypt of Anagni Cathedral: the Philistines return the Ark to Israel.

PLATE 13. Crypt of Anagni Cathedral: story of Samuel.

PLATE 14. Crypt of Anagni Cathedral: the Cherubim.

PLATE 15. Anagni Crypt series of three vaults with scenes from the Ark's history; bottom wall with St. Peter and two lady saints

PLATE 16. Anagni Crypt, Apocalypse.

PLATE 17. Giovanni di Paolo, *Paradiso* 10.

PLATE 18. Giovanni di Paolo, *Paradiso* 12.

PLATE 19. Giovanni di Paolo, Paradiso 33: Neptune and the Argo.

PLATE 20. Guglielmo Giraldi and workshop, 'The Celestial Rose of the Blessed', from Dante's *Divina Commedia* (made for Federico da Montefeltro, Duke of Urbino), ca. 1474–1478.

PLATE 21. Raphael, *School of Athens* fresco: Plato holding the Timaeus under his arm, ca. 1509–11.

PLATE 22. Raphael: the creation of the universe by Wisdom as Prime Mover or Demiurge.

PLATE 23. Girona Cathedral: 'Tapiz de la Creación', eleventh century.

PLATE 24. Monreale Cathedral: mosaic, the beginning of Creation, twelfth century.

PLATE 25. Basilica of San Marco, Venice: 'Genesis' dome, ca. 1220–40.

PLATE 26. Basilica of San Clemente, Rome: apse mosaic, the 'New Creation' of Christianity, ca. 1100.

PLATE 27. Giovanni di Paolo, *Creation of the World and Expulsion from Paradise*, ca. 1450.

PLATE 28a–b. Lorenzo Lotto (designer), 'Magnum Chaos' (28a) and Creation (28b), with wood inlay by Giovan Francesco Capoferri, 1524, in the choir of Santa Maria Maggiore, Bergamo.

PLATE 29. Lucas Cranach the Elder, 'Creation', woodcut in the 1534 *Lutherbibel*.

PLATE 30. Michelangelo, 'Separation of Light and Darkness', ceiling of the Sistine Chapel, 1508–12 (detail).

PLATE 31. Michelangelo, 'Creation of Sun and Moon', ceiling of the Sistine Chapel, 1508–12 (detail).

PLATE 32. J.M.W. Turner, *Light and Colour (Goethe's Theory), The Morning after the Deluge, Moses Writing the Book of Genesis*, 1843.

Joshua Sylvester began to adapt these lines in English in the *Divine Weeks* in the following manner:

> Then sodainly, turnd studious *Platonist,*
> I hold, the Heav'ns of Elements consist:
> 'Tis Earth, whose firm parts make their Lamps apparant,
> Their bodies fast; Aire makes them all transparant;
> Fire makes their rest-les circles pure, and cleer,
> Hot, lighsom, light, and quick in their career:
> And Water, 'nointing with cold-moist the brims
> Of th' enter-kissing turning Globes extreams,
> Tempers the heat (caus'd by their rapid turning)
> Which els would set all th' elements a-burning.
> Not, that I doo compare or match the Matter*
> Whence I compose th' All-compassing Theater,
> To those gross Elements which heer belowe
> Our hand and ey doth touch and see and knowe:
> 'T's all fair, all pure; a sacred harmony
> Those bodies bindes in end-less Vnity:
> That Aier's not flitting, nor that Water floating,
> Nor Fire inflaming, nor Earth dully doating:
> Nor one to other aught offensiue neither,
> But (to conclude) Celestiall altogether.[16]

Tasso, at the end of his career (the poem was published in 1607, after his death), tried to make his *Il mondo creato* as orthodox as possible in the context of the Roman Catholic Counter-Reformation. He filled his lines with quotations from Basil of Caesarea's *Homilies on Genesis*, from Ambrose's *Exaemeron*, from Augustine and Thomas Aquinas. But of course not even he could forget Plato's *Timaeus,* for some of its expressions and definitions were so deeply embedded in the minds of Europe that they became as it were spontaneous, almost automatic reactions to certain problems. For instance, when Tasso, in the Second Day, maintains that 'Ned infiniti sono i mondi e i cieli', the reminiscence of *Timaeus* 32c is clear (together, or perhaps through, Thomas Aquinas's commentary on *De caelo et mundo*, 19.12–14), and shortly afterwards the words 'il fabro eterno' and 'il mastro' are the very words—as Tasso himself points out in his marginal notes—employed by tradition for the Demiurge, 'esempio' corresponding to 'model':

> Ma pur ne fece un solo il Fabro eterno,
> Perch'uno era l'essempio, et uno il Mastro:
> E della sua virtù formollo impresso,
> Uno è l'ordine ancora, e 'n un si volge:
> Ma in molte sfere si comparte e gira
> La somma de le spere; e 'l sommo cielo
> Che non ha moto, onde conosce il senso
> Umano e 'nfermo le sostanze eterne,
> Corpo ancora non è, ma pura forma
> Che di serena luce arde e fiammeggia:
> E questo Empireo ciel tra noi s'appella.

> (And yet one only made of these the eternal Smith,
> For one was the model, and one the Maker.
> He shaped it imprinted with his virtue,
> One is its order, and into one it turns.
> But the highest sphere divides itself
> And revolves in many spheres. And the highest
> Heaven, which has no motion—whence
> Human, infirm senses know eternal substances—
> Is not yet a body, but pure form
> Which burns and blazes with serene light.
> And this we call the Empyrean heaven.)[17]

Not long afterwards, however, we find Tasso fighting against Empedocles, Plato's *Timaeus,* Anaxagoras and Pythagoras, evidently following Aristotle's pages on the 'archaeology' of philosophy at the beginning of the *Metaphysics.*[18] Tasso is in love with the Beginning itself, adores the *Fiat lux* and the voyage of Aurora on her chariot carrying light to 'irrigate' the world, and venerates Wisdom, who danced and played before God as he accomplished the Creation. Yet at the end of the poem, the World, already exhausted on the seventh Day, sees its own destruction as imminent and implores God to accompany it towards its end. It is the cry of an anguished, dying old man:

Dove sei? Dove sei? chi mi ti asconde?
chi mi t'invola, o mio Signore e Padre?
Misero, senza te son nulla. Ahi lasso!
E nulla spero: ahi lasso! e nulla bramo.
E che posso bramar se 'l tutto è nulla,
Segnor, senza tua grazia?

(Where are you? Where are you? Who conceals
You to me? Who steals you from me, o my Lord and Father?
Without you, I, miserable, am nothing. Alas!
And nothing do I hope, alas!, and nothing I desire.
And what could I desire if all is nothing,
Lord, without your grace?)[19]

Of course, Tasso's poetry, which at times is quite powerful even in this last work, appears heavy to us—like Du Bartas's—when the philosophy and theology it contains make it difficult to follow the poetic flow of the narrative. But to read *La sepmaine* or *Il mondo creato* is still a great intellectual experience, as one realises these poets are trying to turn what they would call 'science' into verse: not by any means an easy enterprise, as Dante's *Paradiso* shows. Milton was more successful in *Paradise Lost*, because in his account of Creation in Book 7 he incorporated the philosophico-theological debate directly into the images and, as it were, the *eikòs lógos* of the Bible itself. Thus the culminating moment of that Creation, the Word's triumphal march into Chaos, and his using his golden compass to divide the world from chaotic matter, are immediately comprehensible to the reader even if he or she is unaware of its doctrinal background and the great image of Proverbs that lies behind it:[20]

On heavenly ground they stood; and from the shore
They viewed the vast immeasurable abyss
Outrageous as a sea, dark, wasteful, wild,
Up from the bottom turned by furious winds

And surging waves, as mountains, to assault
Heaven's highth, and with the center mix the pole.
Silence, ye troubled Waves, and thou Deep, peace,
Said then the Omnific Word; your discord end!
Nor staid; but, on the wings of Cherubim
Uplifted, in paternal glory rode
Far into Chaos, and the world unborn;
For Chaos heard his voice: Him all his train
Followed in bright procession, to behold
Creation, and the wonders of his might.
Then staid the fervid wheels, and in his hand
He took the golden compasses, prepared
In God's eternal store, to circumscribe
This universe, and all created things:
One foot he centered, and the other turned
Round through the vast profundity obscure;
And said, Thus far extend, thus far thy bounds,
This be thy just circumference, O World!
Thus God the Heaven created, thus the Earth,
Matter unformed and void: Darkness profound
Covered the abyss: but on the watery calm
His brooding wings the Spirit of God outspread,
And vital virtue infused, and vital warmth
Throughout the fluid mass; but downward purged
The black tartareous cold infernal dregs,
Adverse to life: then founded, then conglobed
Like things to like; the rest to several place
Disparted, and between spun out the air;
And Earth self-balanced on her centre hung.[21]

Paradise Lost was published first in ten books in 1667, then in twelve in 1674. It may contain an allusion to the theory of the *Timaeus* about the soul's return to its star in a single line of Book 7, when Raphael, recounting the creation of the stars, indicates that they are 'numerous, and every star perhaps a world / Of *destined habitation*'; and yet another indirect reference to the *Timaeus* (41e-42a) in Book 8.148–52:

> and other suns perhaps
> With their attendant moons thou wilt descry
> Communicating male and female light,
> Which two great sexes animate the world,
> Stored in each orb, perhaps with some that live.[22]

Du Bartas, Tasso, and Milton rediscovered the Longinian sublime in recounting the Creation of the cosmos,[23] and that in itself was a feat in the history of European letters, preceded in the visual arts by Michelangelo's Sistine Chapel ceiling. The final chapter of that history was to be written in music—by Franz Joseph Haydn in his oratorio, *Die Schöpfung*.

By the end of the sixteenth century, however, Plato's *Timaeus* had moved from literature and the visual arts to science proper, the 'new science'. After Copernicus's *De revolutionibus orbium caelestium* (1543),[24] the real breaking point was Galileo's announcement, in the 1610 *Sidereus nuncius*, of the four satellites of Jupiter which orbited the planet in ways that would make it extremely complicated to fit into Ptolemy's system. Kepler wrote an enthusiastic letter, with some reservations, to his Tuscan colleague, and their correspondence continued for a long time.[25] The sequence of the masterpieces of the scientific revolution in the first thirty years of the seventeenth century is staggering: Tycho Brahe's *De stella nova* (1573) preceded Kepler's *Mysterium cosmographicum* (1596); his *Astronomia nova* (1609), containing the first two laws of planetary orbits, came out just before Galileo's *Sidereus nuncius*, and the *Harmonice mundi*, with the third law, in 1619. Galileo followed suit with *Il Saggiatore* in 1623, and with the *Dialogo sopra i due massimi sistemi del mondo* in 1632. Newton's *Philosophiae naturalis principia mathematica* sealed the heroic age in 1687.

Kepler was a strong believer in the *Timaeus* and considered himself a pupil of Pythagoras and Plato, as he stated in a letter to Galileo of 13 October 1597.[26] In the *Mysterium cosmographicum* his admiration took the form of true veneration. He quoted from Cicero's version of the *Timaeus,* saying that 'it is not, and always was not, right that the best make anything but the most beautiful thing' and that therefore when the Founder of the world pre-conceived his Idea of it, it inevitably was the best.[27] 'We have a world through movement', he concluded, 'and bodies through numbers, and magnitudes: nothing is left to say but, with Plato, that the god always acts through geometry [theòn aeì geometreîn].'[28] Galileo, who advocated the absolute importance of mathematics for the interpretation of nature, would have concurred. In *Il Saggiatore* he famously wrote,

> La filosofia è scritta in questo grandissimo libro che continuamente ci sta aperto dinanzi agli occhi (io dico l'universo), ma non si può intendere se prima non si impara intender la lingua, e conoscere i caratteri, ne' quali è scritto. Egli è scritto in lingua matematica, e i caratteri sono triangoli, cerchi ed altre figure geometriche, senza i quali mezzi è impossibile a intendere umanamente parola; senza questi è un aggirarsi vanamente per un oscuro laberinto.
>
> (Philosophy [i.e., natural philosophy] is written in this grand book—I mean the Universe—which stands continually open to our gaze, but it cannot be understood unless one first learns to comprehend the language and interpret the characters in which it is written. It is written in the language of mathematics, and its characters are triangles, circles, and other geometrical figures, without which it is humanly impossible to understand a single word of it; without these, one is wandering around in a dark labyrinth.)[29]

Indeed, Kepler picked up Plato's idea of the five regular solids and maintained that 'physics should include a mathematical component because in the world are reflected the eternal archetypes, which are of geometric-mathematical nature'.[30] Finally, he crowned the first part of the *Mysterium* with a hymn over thirty lines long in praise of the Maker, Artist and Sower of the universe which recalls Boethius.[31] The climax was to come in the *Harmonice mundi*, which, while discussing the world soul, proclaims that the *Timaeus* is a commentary on the first chapter of Genesis:

> In Timeo, qui est citra omnem dubitationis aleam, commentarius quidem in primum caput Geneseos seu libri I Mosis, transformans illum in Philosophiam Pythagoricam: ut facile patet attente legenti, et verba ipsa Mosis identicum conferenti.
>
> (In the *Timaeus*, which is without the slightest shadow of a doubt a commentary on the first chapter of Genesis or the first Book of Moses, and which tranforms it into Pythagorean Philosophy, as is obvious to anyone who reads it attentively, and the words themselves of Moses import the same.)[32]

Not even Augustine or Dante had ever dared go that far. On the one hand, the *Timaeus* as the supreme commentary on Genesis; on the other, the *Timaeus* as a supreme example of mathematical, geometrical analysis of reality. Theology and physics together.

While the scientists were busy discovering the new laws that ruled the universe, Plato's philosophy continued to be discussed (and developed) as such. In Florence, Marsilio Ficino had founded, already in 1462, an 'Accademia neo-platonica' which met until 1522 in the villa at Careggi where he had translated the whole of Plato. He set the tone of subsequent interpretation by insisting that, just as in the *Parmenides* Plato 'devotes his energies to encompassing all things divine', in the *Timaeus* he 'embraces all things natural'.[33] But he was in no way blind to the way in which the *Timaeus* attains the sphere of the divine especially through mathematics, understood perfectly well what Plato was doing with the Atlantis story and the Phaethon myth, and gave due relevance to all the dialogue has to say about the world soul. Reading Ficino's *Compendium in Timaeum* is like entering the ancient world of Plato from a post-medieval, modern perspective.

In seventeenth-century Cambridge a group of thinkers called the 'Cambridge Platonists' dominated colleges and University.[34] Allegorical interpretations of Plato and his *Timaeus* meanwhile spread all over Europe. In Germany, almost every major philosopher from Leibniz to Kant, Schelling, Hegel and Schopenhauer, down to Husserl and Heidegger, had to reckon with Plato, and we have already seen snippets of young Schelling's work on the *Timaeus* earlier in this book.[35] The poets did not lag behind. All four of the major European Romantics of the second generation—Hölderlin, Shelley, Keats and Leopardi—owed something to Plato's writings, from Keats's famous 'Beauty is truth, truth Beauty', to Hölderlin's Hyperion searching for Beauty,[36] to Leopardi's remembrance of the Greeks' eternal 'fanciullezza' from the *Timaeus* in the *Zibaldone,* to his maintaining that the *Timaeus* itself contains all of Plato's philosophical system, and that Plato was 'the deepest, most vast, most sublime philosopher among the ancients', the most elegant prose writer, and a 'poet' to boot.[37]

Fascinating as this might be, I have no space here to devote the attention they deserve to all of these. I must stick to the scientific theme with which I began in this chapter. When the 'new science' became the 'newest science' in the early decades of the twentieth century, it was of course the mathematical-geometric aspect of the *Timaeus* that was emphasised. Two names stand out in this field: those of Alfred North Whitehead and Werner von Heisenberg, an English philosopher much devoted to cosmology, and a German physicist much given, in his later years, to philosophy.

Whitehead, who maintained that 'the safest general characterization of the European philosophical tradition is that it consists of a series of footnotes to Plato',[38] never hesitated to acknowledge his debt to the *Timaeus,* to the point of regretting not having been able to consult A. E. Taylor's great *Commentary* when first writing *Process and Reality*. His use of Plato's dialogue is, however, extensive and structural from the very beginning. He maintains that 'the *Timaeus* of Plato, and the *Scholium* of Newton [the essay on time, space, place and motion appended to the *Principia*] are the two statements of cosmological theory which have had the chief influence on Western thought'.[39] Of course, compared to the *Scholium*, the *Timaeus* is 'simply foolish' 'as a statement of scientific details'; 'but what it lacks in superficial detail, it makes up for by its philosophic depth'. If it is taken as an 'allegory', the *Timaeus* 'conveys profound truth', whereas the *Scholium* is immensely detailed and can be trusted, at least up to a certain point, 'for the deduction of truths at the same level of abstraction as itself'. Readers of the latter, and almost certainly Newton himself, fall into what Whitehead calls the 'fallacy of misplaced concreteness'. It presents no hint 'of the aspect of self-production, of generation, of *physis*, of *natura naturans*, which is so prominent in nature'. For the *Scholium*, 'nature is simply and completely, *there*'.

Faced by the modern theory of evolution, Newton would have been thoroughly confused, whereas the Plato of the *Timaeus* would have been 'enlightened'. On the one hand, there are in the *Timaeus* many phrases and statements 'which find their final lucid form in the *Scholium*'. On the other, the *Timaeus* possesses a metaphysical character: that is, in 'its endeavour to connect the *behaviour* of things with the *formal nature* of things'.[40] Whitehead's conclusion—which summons the difference between Newton's 'Jehovah' and the Greek deities still not completely separated from *physis* to partly explain the diversity of approach—is worth quoting in its entirety:

> Newton could have accepted a molecular theory as easily as Plato, but there is this difference between them: Newton would have been surprised at the modern quantum theory and at the dissolution of quanta into vibrations; Plato would have expected it. While we note the many things said by Plato in the *Timaeus* which are now foolishness, we must also give him credit for that aspect of his teaching in which he was two thousand years ahead of his times.[41]

Whitehead specified that Plato's chief innovations lay in his explanation of the differences between kinds of natural things as related to the 'mathematical forms of the regular solids', and in his theory, derived from music, of 'ratios between integral numbers', hence in the notions of harmony and dissonance. He also pointed out that 'Milton, curiously enough, in his *Paradise Lost*, wavers between the *Timaeus* and the

Semitic doctrine'. He quoted 'the description of Satan's journey across Chaos, where Satan discovers

> The secrets of the hoary Deep, a dark,
> Illimitable ocean, without bound,
> Without dimension, where length, breadth, and highth,
> And time and place, are lost; where eldest Night
> And Chaos, ancestors of Nature, hold
> Eternal anarchy, amidst the noise
> Of endless wars, and by confusion stand.[42]

Whitehead remarked that 'Milton is here performing for Plato the same poetic service that Lucretius performed for Democritus—with less justification, since Plato was quite capable of being his own poet'.[43] More prosaically, and more humorously, he added that 'Satan's journey helped to evolve order: for he left a permanent track, useful for the devils and the damned'.

Even from this short and simplified account, the fruitfulness of the *Timaeus*'s grand design for an interpretation of reality as 'process' will be evident. The case with Heisenberg is even more cogent. Whitehead's masterpiece had come out in 1929; Heisenberg's *Physics and Philosophy* was published in 1958. Heisenberg had already been one of the major pioneers of quantum mechanics and the man who had formulated the 'uncertainty principle'. Yet his aim in *Physics and Philosophy* is not completely different from Whitehead's, both being bent on trying to find a reconciliation between the two disciplines after the rupture of two scientific revolutions, and on establishing what the two disciplines could gain from one another.

Naturally, Heisenberg's perspective is from the beginning that of the historian of quantum theory, which he summarises and discusses in chapters 2 and 3 ('The Copenhagen Interpretation of Quantum Theory') from the beginning to the time of Erwin Schrödinger. Before passing, in chapter 5, to 'The Development of Philosophical Ideas Since Descartes in Comparison with the New Situation in Quantum Theory', Heisenberg faces, in chapter 4, the impact of quantum theory on the 'roots of atomic science'. The story, which begins with the early Greek thought of Heraclitus, Parmenides, Empedocles and Anaxagoras, has a villain and a hero—Democritus and Plato's *Timaeus* respectively.

Parmenides had posited a basic division between Being and Non-Being. This was eventually 'secularized', Heisenberg writes, 'into the antithesis of the "Full" and the "Void"'.[44] In Democritus's atomic theory, matter consists both of Full and Void (Parmenides's 'logical objection against the Void, that non-being cannot exist, was simply ignored to comply with experience'). The atoms of Democritus 'were all of the same substance, which had the property of being, but had different sizes and different shapes'. They were divisible in a mathematical, but not in a physical, sense; they could move, but had no other physical property. They lacked colour, smell and taste—in short all the properties which we perceive with our senses.[45] Now, Heisenberg says, compare with this, and with modern atomic physics, Plato's explanation of matter in the *Timaeus*.

Plato was no atomist, and indeed Diogenes Laertius maintains 'he disliked Democritus so much that he wished all his books to be burned'.[46] Plato combined ideas that were close to atomism with the doctrines of the Pythagoreans and the teachings of Empedocles.[47] Aware of the Pythagoreans' discovery of regular solids and of the possibility of combining them with the elements of Empedocles, Plato 'compared the smallest parts of the element earth with the cube, of air with the octahedron, of fire with the tetrahedron, and of water with the icosahedron', leaving only the dodecahedron without a corresponding element. 'The smallest parts of matter are not the fundamental Beings, as in the philosophy of Democritus, but are mathematical forms'—and it is clear 'that the form is more important than the substance of which it is the form'.[48]

In modern physics, the atoms are 'divisible' into elementary particles. But in the *Timaeus* the elementary particles 'are finally not substance but mathematical forms'. 'All things are numbers' is a sentence attributed to Pythagoras. The only mathematical forms available in ancient Greece were regular solids or the triangles that form their surface. In modern quantum theory 'there can be no doubt that the elementary particles will finally also be mathematical forms', although of a much more complicated nature. 'If we follow the Pythagorean'—and Timaean—'line of thought', Heisenberg concludes, 'we may hope that the fundamental law of motion will turn out as a mathematically simple law.'[49]

However, Heisenberg could not ignore the differences between Plato's and modern physics. On the very same page of *Physics and Philosophy* he continues:

> There is an enormous difference between modern science and Greek philosophy, and that is just the empiristic attitude of modern science. Since the time of Galileo and Newton, modern science has been based upon a detailed study of nature and upon the postulate that only such statements should be made, as have been verified or at least can be verified by experiment. [This idea] did not occur to the Greek philosophers [. . .]. Therefore, the statements of modern physics are in some way meant much more seriously than the statements of Greek philosophy.

The empirical method and what I would call the 'quantitative' (as opposed to 'qualitative') consideration of things is what separates Galileo, and even Kepler, from Plato. Still, the modern physicist and the ancient philosopher, Heisenberg and Timaeus, have something in common—the problem of language. In a chapter entitled 'Language and Reality in Modern Science', which also appeared separately in his *Schritte über Grenzen,* Heisenberg maintains that 'the physicist may be satisfied when he has the mathematical scheme and knows how to use it for the interpretation of the experiments. But he has to speak about his results also to non-physicists who will not be satisfied unless some explanation is given in plain language, understandable to anybody.'[50]

He, the physicist of the uncertainty principle and quantum theory, resorts, then, to poetry—a passage from Goethe's *Faust* (1.1908–41) in which Mephistopheles concludes the first part of a long list of recommendations to a young student by recommending first and foremost the study of logic. But then, 'the subtle web of thought / is like the weaver's fabric wrought, / one treadle moves a thousand lines, / Swift dart the shuttles to and fro, / Unseen the threads unnumber'd flow, / A thousand knots a stroke combines.'[51] Logic is not enough to follow and comprehend the complexities and speed of thought. Goethe, making full use of what Plato would have called 'verisimilar discourse', has Mephistopheles end this section of his speech with the lines: 'Who would describe and study aught alive, / Seeks first the living spirit thence to drive: / Then are the lifeless fragments in his hand, / There only fails, alas!—the spirit-band.' Goethe's original adds that chemistry calls this method 'encheiresis naturae', 'manual operation': 'it makes fun of itself and doesn't even know how'. 'This passage', Heisenberg comments, 'contains an admirable description of the structure of language and of the narrowness of the simple logical patterns.'

The language problem is particularly acute when the subject is quantum theory or atomic particles, something for which the scientist does not possess the words of tradition and must invent images and terms at once precise and suggestive. 'If one wishes to speak about the atomic particles themselves', Heisenberg concludes,

> one must either use the mathematical scheme as the only supplement to natural language or one must combine it with a language that makes use of a modified logic or of no well-defined logic at all. In the experiments about atomic events we have to do with things and facts, with phenomena that are just as real as any phenomena in daily life. But the atoms or the elementary particles themselves are not as real; they form a world of potentialities or possibilities rather than one of things or facts.[52]

The kind of 'figurative' language Heisenberg seems to have in mind brings him close to the *Timaeus*, and in another fundamental essay of *Across the Frontiers*, 'The Meaning of Beauty in the Exact Sciences', the physicist once more reconstructs the beginning of Greek thought from the Presocratic philosophers onwards, giving Pythagoras and then Plato the central position they deserve in the invention and development of harmony. There are, Heisenberg maintains, two basic conceptions of this, one—in a line that joins Pythagoras and Plato to Galileo and Newton—by which 'Beauty is the proper conformity of the parts to one another and to the whole'; the other, originating with Plotinus, which states that 'Beauty is the translucence, through the material phenomenon, of the eternal splendour of the "one"'. He evokes the moment when 'the true Ideas rise up' and 'there occurs in the soul of him who sees them an altogether indescribable process of the highest intensity'.

> It is the amazed awe that Plato speaks of in the *Phaedrus*, with which the soul remembers, as it were, something it had unconsciously possessed all along. Kepler says: '*Geometria est archetypus pulchritudinis mundi*'; or, if we may translate in more general terms—'Mathematics is the archetype of the beauty of the world'.[53]

Timaeus leaves Democritus several leagues behind, and Ovid was right in having Pythagoras recount the beginnings of the world and the 'causes of things', what is nature, what god, at the end of the *Metamorphoses*.[54] He, Ovid's Pythagoras, tells a 'likely', 'verisimilar' myth the way Plato's *Timaeus* had recommended and practised. Plato's *Timaeus*—a piece of writing composed almost two thousand five hundred years ago, is still providing us with inspiration: because the gods never bestowed on us a greater gift than philosophy, as Plato said—especially when the recipient is a sublime poet.

Yet the purest, most inspired proclamation of the importance of beauty in modern science was to come from the lips of another winner of the Nobel Prize for Physics, the English Paul Dirac,[55] for whom '[t]his result is too beautiful to be false: it is more important to have beauty in one's equations than to have them fit experiment [. . .]. If one is working from the point of view of getting beauty into one's equation [. . .] one is on a sure line of progress.'[56] God, Dirac used to say, 'used beautiful mathematics in creating the world'. Plato's Timaeus, as I hope this book has shown, would have been glad to see that a scientist was still prepared to believe it two thousand five hundred years after he had first conceived the idea.

Perhaps we should rely on a painting by Turner to envisage the meeting between beauty, modern physics, Scripture and Platonism [fig. 32]. In the great globe of light a tiny human figure is writing Genesis. Or is it the *Timaeus*?

37

Afterword: The Unmoved Mover Begins to Move

LITERARY AND VISUAL RENDERINGS OF THE CHRISTIAN BIBLE

THE PRIESTLY ACCOUNT OF GENESIS does not explicitly proclaim any movement of Elohim during the Creation.[1] This, in fact, takes place by direct intervention of God's word: 'And God said, "Let there be light," and there was light.' No hand is present, no physical person is carried anywhere. In the primordial nothingness only the Voice that sets the universe in motion resounds.[2] It is before the beginning of Creation, rather, that God might be said to move: 'weruaḥ 'ĕlōhîm m^{e}raḥéphet 'al-penê hammāyim', declares the second verse of Genesis, which the Seventy translate into Greek as 'pneûma theoû epephéreto epáno toû hýdatos', and Jerome in the Latin Vulgate as 'spiritus Dei ferebatur super aquas': 'and the Spirit of God moved upon the face of the waters'.

The Hebrew original has produced many interpretations.[3] In his *Homilies on the Hexaemeron*, Basil of Caesarea quotes the explanation of a 'Syrian' according to whom the word translated as 'epephéreto', that is, *m^{e}raḥéphet*, should be interpreted as 'warmed up' and 'impregnated', 'inseminated'. 'It warmed up and impregnated', Basil writes, 'the nature of the waters as a bird broods and breathes vital force into the eggs lying under its warmth: this prepared the nature of the waters for generation [pròs zoogonían]'.[4] Latin exegesis reads the Vulgate's 'ferebatur' as either 'incubabat' or 'fovebat', thus privileging the idea of brooding, or 'volitabat', which implies the idea of hovering without excluding brooding, or finally, with a decided inclination towards movement, as 'irruebat'—it 'ran'.[5]

If the Bible, as read in Greek and Latin milieux, oscillates between an immobile flitting of wings and the running of the Spirit before Creation—that is to say, logically speaking, before the Beginning—the other great Western archetype, the Greek one, does not mention any movement at the origin of things. There is no movement in the multiple generation without a creator with which the cosmos is born in Hesiod's *Theogony*,[6] nor in Ovid's later version in the *Metamorphoses*.[7] Nor is there any movement in the great mythological and philosophical account of creation-generation in Plato's *Timaeus*, which, as we have seen, is so influential in later ages.[8] Finally, Aristotle postulates the absolute immobility of the Prime Cause. In the fundamental Book Lambda of the *Metaphysics*, he demonstrates in fact that 'the Principle and the first of beings [whom he calls 'ho theós', 'the god'] is immobile both absolutely and relatively'. Immobile, the Prime Mover 'produces the first, eternal and one, movement' by moving as object of desire and love, that is to say, as an end, as Final Cause.[9]

In the Middle Ages, it is Boethius that gives poetic form to a Christian metaphysics inspired by the *Timaeus*. Metre 9 of Book 3 of the *Consolation of Philosophy* is exemplary in this respect.[10] Boethius's inspired formulation does not conceal the Aristotelian ascendancy of the immobility of him that moves everything ('stabilisque manens das cuncta moveri'), nor the platonic ascendancy of the model ('ab exemplo'), out of which the Creator shapes the world in his image. As for the ideas of goodness ('livore carens': 'free of envy', 'ungrudging') and beauty that prompt God to create the universe, they go back to both Plato and Aristotle.

Throughout the Middle Ages, the Mover remains firmly unmoved and immobile. Only that original thinker, John Scotus Eriugena, manages, in the ninth century, to catch a glimpse of his movement by placing it within the Supreme Good itself—with a stroke of genius of philosophy and imagination at once, and by means of a series of fascinating oxymora—in order to explain the passage from the One to the many.

'Summae siquidem ac trinae soliusque verae bonitatis immutabilis motus', he writes in the *Periphyseon*, 'et simplex multiplicatio et inexhausta a se ipsa in se ipsa ad se ipsam diffusio causa omnium, immo omnia sunt': 'The unchanging movement of the sovereign and veritable triune goodness, its simple multiplication and inexhaustible diffusion from itself in itself and towards itself—this movement is the cause of all things, in fact it is everything.'[11]

Already in the first book of the *Periphyseon* Scotus had reconstructed the etymology of *theós* by recurring to the Greek verbs *théo* (I run) and *theorô* (I see). If one derives *theós* from *theorô*, he said, 'one interprets it as meaning "He who sees", because God sees in himself all that exists, whilst he contemplates nothing outside himself, because nothing subsists outside God himself'. But if one derives *theós* from *théo*, one interprets it as meaning 'He who runs', because God runs through all that exists and never stops, but fills everything with his running, in accordance with this verse of Scripture: 'quickly His word races'.[12] 'Nevertheless,' Eriugena added, 'God does in no way move. This is why one predicates of Him that He is at once immobile movement and mobile rest [motus stabilis et status mobilis])'.

Divine Creation takes place precisely within this (interior: 'non extra se, sed a se ipso in se ipso ad se ipsum') movement of the Word:

> Stat enim in seipso incommutabiliter, nunquam naturalem suam stabilitatem deserens, movet autem seipsum per omnia ut sint ea quae a se essentialiter subsistunt. Motu enim ipsius omnia fiunt. Ac per hoc unus idemque intellectus est in duabus interpretationibus eiusdem nominis, quod est Deus. Non enim aliud est Deo currere per omnia quam videre omnia; sed sicut videndo, ita et currendo fiunt omnia.

(On the one hand God remains at rest in unchanging fashion, without ever abandoning the immutability of his nature, but, on the other, God moves through all that exists so that all that exists substantially by itself may exist: because all existing things are produced by this movement. And that is why one finds one identical meaning, in the two different names of God. In God, in fact, the act of running

> through everything does not differ from the act of seeing all that exists, but all that exists is the product of his running and, at one and the same time, of his seeing.)[13]

On the one hand God remains at rest in unchanging fashion, without ever abandoning the immutability of his nature, but, on the other hand, God moves through all that exists so that all that exists substantially by itself may exist: because all existing things are produced by his movement. And that is why one finds one identical meaning in the two different names of God. In God, in fact, the act of running through everything does not differ from the act of seeing all that exists, but all that exists is the product of his running and, at one and the same time, of his seeing.

Yet not even Scotus, when he comments the work of the six days, dares attribute movement to God, although he keeps open the possibility of translating the original with 'spiritus fovebat aquas' (or 'ferebatur super aquas'): the Spirit 'brooded' or 'moved' upon the waters.[14]

Visual representations of the Creation are not common in early Christian times, but they become more frequent beginning with the eleventh century.[15] I have chosen some to illustrate the complexity of visualising the passage from the immobility of God to the movement of the cosmos. The first is the 'Tapiz de la Creación' in Gerona Cathedral, Spain [fig. 23].[16] At the centre of this splendid tapestry of 3.75 by 4.70 metres is placed Christ Pantokrator (*Principium*, following John 8:25), portrayed not in Byzantine but in Roman fashion—a young, beardless man, with his right hand raised in blessing and authoritative creation, his left resting on an open book that bears the inscription *Sanctus Deus*. His majesty is underlined by the words that appear to his right and to his left, *Rex* and *Fortis*, the 'Strong King'.

The figure of Christ is inscribed within a circle that contains the verse of Genesis, *Dixitque Deus: Fiat Lux, et Lux Facta est* (And God said, Let there be light. And there was light.) This circle—the circle of the metaphysical universe—is in turn placed within a bigger circle, surmounted by a sentence that constitutes a kind of summary of the first and last verses of Genesis 1: *In Principio Creavit Deux Celum et Terram Mare Et Omnia Qua in Eis Sunt. Et Vidit Deus Cuncta Que Fecerat Et Erant Valdebona* (In the beginning God created heaven and earth, the sea, and all the things that are in them. And God saw that all He made was very good.) This bigger circle is further divided into eight sections of different sizes and into two identical halves. The upper half, from the bottom to the top, refers to the physical sky, then to the metaphysical heaven; the lower half describes the earth. The dove of the Spirit is placed directly below the Pantokrator, within a smaller circle, and is accompanied by the inscription *Spiritus Dei Ferebatur Super Aquas* (the Spirit of God moved upon the waters).

In the two nearest sections, to the right- and left-hand sides, appear two angels, those of light (*Lux*) and of darkness (*Et Tenebre Erant Sub Faciem Abyssi*: 'and darkness was under the face of the abyss'). The two sections that follow in descending order contain the creation of the firmament (the inscription *Fecit Deus Firmamentum In Medio Aquarum*, 'God made the firmament in the middle of the waters', is found within a circle surrounded by the primordial waters, the abyss of chaos), and the separation of the waters (*Vbi Dividat Deus Aquas Ab Aquis*). Here, the internal circle towers over the waters and includes, in the shape of human figures, sun, moon, and stars: (*Sol Luna Firmamentum*).

The sections of the lower part of the great circle are consecrated to the creation of living beings: directly under Christ Pantokrator, the animals; to the right, Adam before the animals; to the left, the creation of Eve. While the upper portion of the great circle is highly hieratical, the lower one vibrates with life and takes care of details. Birds, sea monsters and fish fill the panel of the creation of animals; deer and horses surround Adam; the scene of Eve's creation is full of movement. Water dominates three of the upper sections and the lower, central one—those, that is, of the Spirit, the creation of the firmament, the division, and the creation of animals. The formless sea mass of the first three sections begins to have a shape in the third one and is clearly called *Mare* in the fourth.

The theological structure of the great circle is fairly clear. Christ, that is, the Logos, inaugurates Creation. It is the divine Word that operates with the *Fiat Lux* (Let there be light). The Spirit cooperates, by breathing over the waters and brooding them. The angels, who are also created, represent light and darkness, the primeval elements of Creation, divided from the very first day. Creation manifests itself afterwards, in the lower portion, as creation of the firmament and of animals and human beings. The Logos at the centre is immobile, but it speaks and, as it finds itself within a circle, it irradiates the greater one while constituting as it were its backbone or nervous system. With this Neoplatonic irradiation the Word 'moves', to use an Aristotelian term, the cosmos. One somehow has the impression that the Pantokrator's raised hand initiates this motion.

The great circle I have described until now is in turn inscribed within a rectangle, the angles of which are occupied by winged beings that represent the winds, and the geographical zones with which they are associated: *Septentrio,* the northern wind, hence the North; *Cephirus,* the West; *Auster,* the South; and *Subsolanus,* the East. The winds become darker and blow with decreasing intensity in passing from north to south. They appear in the guise of angels, following the letter of great Psalm 104:4 on Creation: 'Who maketh his angels spirits; his ministers a flaming fire' ('spirits'—'Spiritus' in the Vulgate—here means winds). This verse is quoted much later in the Christian Bible at the beginning of the Epistle to the Hebrews, as evidence that the Son is higher than the angels in the order of Creation.[17] Here too, in the static appearance of representation, a movement surfaces on the level of theological discourse. The creating Word at the centre of the 'Tapiz' also is the Spirit, that is to say, breath, *pneûma, ruaḥ*. The four angelic winds are the Spirit's translation in the created world, as messengers and servants. The motion that Logos and Spirit set to the cosmos is a rotating one, it articulates the space already created in the section devoted to the animals (air and sea). Thus, the four elements—earth, water, air, fire—are by now also complete.

Finally, another movement is initiated in the sections that form the frame of the tapestry. The lower portion of the 'Tapiz de la Creación' has not come down to us, but what is left seems to show clearly that its four angles were occupied by the figures of the four rivers of Eden, Gihon (the name is visible in the upper left corner), Pishon, Tigris and Euphrates. The identification of the subject in the central panel of the upper band is also clear: this is the year, surrounded by the four seasons. The two figures placed immediately next to the upper angles are generally interpreted as Cain (to the left, between Gihon and Summer) and Abel (to the right, between Spring and what ought to be Tigris). The months follow each other in the vertical panels, from June to February on the left, from July to November on the right (January and December are missing, with the portion of the 'Tapiz' that has disappeared).

The last but one panel in the lower part of the frame is occupied, both on the left and on the right, by two figures, male and female respectively, who guide chariots drawn by horses. These are the sun and the moon, accompanied by the inscriptions *Dies Solis* and *Dies Lunae*—that is, the days, and probably the two equinoxes. The delimitation of geographical space continues in the frame (with the rivers of Eden), but that movement which is time also begins with the year, seasons, months and days. And perhaps history begins, too, from Earthly Paradise to Cain and Abel.

The 'Tapiz de la Creación' provides us with an extraordinary icon of the work of Creation in which the immobile Pantokrator at the centre sets the universe in motion by what I would call a 'translative irradiation'. With the Spirit, the Logos in the first place moves the first circle, which includes light, darkness, waters, earth, humankind, air, sea, and all their dwellers. Then, divine breath transforms (translates) itself into wind, fire, and space. Finally, Word and Spirit create time (Pantokrator, dove, and year are placed in a direct vertical sequence) and history.

Let me ideally follow this movement and pass from Spain to Sicily, and from the eleventh to the end of the twelfth century. We are now in Monreale, on the heights that overlook Palermo, in the cathedral begun perhaps in 1172 during the reign of William II—a Romanesque building, but with arches that are clearly inspired by Arabic fashion. In the ten thousand square metres of mosaics that cover the interior of the church and—guarded by the gigantic Christ Pantokrator of the apse—narrate on the walls of the nave the whole of Genesis and the entire story of Jesus, there are a few panels that are of particular interest in the present context.[18]

In the upper band of the wall to the right of the central nave, the stories of Genesis are depicted in bright gold, blue, white and red. The panels from the second one onwards, the most famous ones, show Christ Pantokrator—the very same who dominates the basin of the apse—creating light in the form of angels with shining wings (those of the vision in the Book of Revelation). Then, seated on a globe, he divides earth and water; breathes life into plants, reptiles, birds and animals; shapes Sun and Moon; creates man and woman; and finally rests on the seventh day. We should note that the Word here is bearded and that the entire organisation of the scenes looks Byzantine. In all the panels, it is the hand of the Logos that initiates Creation.

The first panel, however, is a narrow, vertical rectangle at the top of which Christ Pantokrator, his head crowned by a golden halo, his bust surrounded by a dark azure, white and gold circle (the cosmos he has on his mind), wearing a mantle of the same colours, stretches his hands down to impose form (to impose the hands) on the world [fig. 24]. From the breast of this God who appears as Son there flows a thin stream, a brook light blue, white and golden, that passes through a sombre band of darkness and finally hits the waves of the sea. Right at the centre of the stream, a dove flutters—the Spirit. The primordial abyss is sketched by an endless series of grey, black and white lines in the shape of waves. Just underneath the point where the brook touches and penetrates into the ocean, the greyish lines form the face of an old man, hair and beard made of billows, his eyes wide open, his tongue hanging out.

Since Son and Spirit are placed above, Trinitarian logic would have it that the old man is the Father. Yet the Pantokrator, the Almighty of the apse and of the other panels who here stands at the top of the picture, is but the incarnated version—the Word—of the Father. Besides, no biblical or Christian God has ever been plunged into the waters instead of floating or moving on them. So no, it is not the Father. It is 'the face of the abyss', as the original has it: 'w^{e}ḥōšek 'al-p^{e}nê t^{e}hôm', 'and darkness was upon the face of the deep'; 'w^{e}ru^{a}ḥ 'ĕlōhîm m^{e}raḥéphet 'al-p^{e}nê hammāyim', the Spirit (the wind, breath, spirit) of God 'moved upon the face of the waters': 'face', literally; surface, more widely. But the Byzantine artists to whom we probably owe the mosaics of Monreale sink this visage into the primeval ocean—into Chaos. For the Greek *ábyssos* translates the Hebrew word *t^{e}hôm*, and this in turn contains an allusion to Thiamat, the Babylonian monster of primordial Chaos. Hence, this is the Old Man of Chaos, the Old Man of the Sea.[19]

The God of Monreale is unmoved except in the first scenes. Seated, after the first panel, on the cosmos, he raises and stretches his hand towards the beings he wants to create: and—to paraphrase Genesis—they are. In the case of primordial Creation and in that of man, a luminous stream flows out of his breast or from his eyes to give life to the universe or to the human being. Afterwards, the Pantokrator stands up and accompanies Adam to Eve. Finally, He sits down to rest on the seventh day. It is still God's hand that creates the new cosmos in the apse of the church of San Clemente in Rome when, coming out of heaven, it stretches down towards the Cross that is Tree of Life and of the New Covenant [fig. 26].[20] And it is again his hand that sets in motion the universe in the dome of Genesis of the basilica of San Marco in Venice.[21]

The dome of San Marco [fig. 25] features a circular structure surrounded by pendentives where four flaming, six-winged cherubim appear, accompanied by the inscription, 'Here burn the Cherubim at the heat of Christ's flame and always shine with the splendour of the eternal Sun. The mystical Cherubim, in showing their six wings, praise the Lord by singing with serene voice.' At the centre of the dome lies a rosette full of golden stars on a blue background, at its top a smaller, golden circle, with a bigger, blue-green circle surrounded by four smaller circles, two red ones and two of blue-green hue. This is the Point on which the entire cosmos depends, the Point that becomes the four elements. There follow three circular, concentric bands, divided into twenty-six panels, of which five are placed in the inner circle, eight in the middle one, and thirteen in the outer circle. The five scenes of the inner band show, first, the Spirit in guise of dove fluttering on the waters; second, light divided from darkness; third, the creation of the firmament; fourth, dry land divided from the waters; and fifth, the creation of plants. In the following band, the panel directly under the Spirit shows the creation of sun and moon; then, proceeding to the right, that of birds and fish (two scenes), of animals, of man. There follows the Benediction of the seventh day, then the soul (represented as a small, winged girl) is breathed into Adam, and God leads him into the Garden. The outer band begins immediately under this scene with Adam giving animals their names, the Temptation, the Fall, and the Expulsion from Paradise.

A beardless Word—here, too, much more Roman than Byzantine—gives life to the cosmos. He stands in the inner band, that of primeval Creation, immobile, as his feet show, resting always in the same position, while his right hand stretches out towards the objects of creation. But the dove of the Spirit moves, fluttering with agility, almost whirling over the primordial waters. Movement, however, has already been impressed upon the world, as the scene with the creation of sun and moon shows. Since this is found under the panel of the Spirit—whereas it should correspond to that of the division of light from darkness—it invites the observer to spin off the second band. As one progresses along the latter, the creating Logos begins himself to move, at times seated, at times standing, bending over Adam when he puts him to sleep to create Eve, finally walking when he finds the two sinners ('walking in the garden in the cool of the day', Genesis 3:8 recounts).

The mosaics of Monreale, San Marco and San Clemente date from the twelfth to the early thirteenth century. It is impossible to determine with certainty the order in which they were executed, and some researchers go as far as to doubt a Byzantine influence, attributing a common descent from Roman mosaic. However, they present both surprising affinities and significant differences. In all three cases, the movement that is Creation is set by the Word's hand. In all three cases, the Logos is immobile in the scenes of primordial Creation. It is only in Monreale that the scene appears of the Pantokrator Son who, through the Spirit as intermediary, gives life directly to the waters with the energy that flows out of his breast.

The representations of Creation in Chartres Cathedral date back to the same period.[22] Three different works are to be considered here: the sculpted reliefs on the portal of the north transept (1194–1230), the typological glazed window of the Good Samaritan in the third bay of the central nave (1205–15), and the rose window in the skylight of the north transept (1230–35). Unfortunately, I cannot illustrate them all here, and hence I shall repeat some of the considerations of chapter 13 above, but concentrate on the representations of God in the great church. In the portal reliefs, God is always bearded, but he appears in a considerable variety of postures. In the scene of the first day, for instance, he is shown twice, both times seated. But the two depictions differ. In the lower scene he turns and raises his left hand up—that is to say, towards the work of creation he is about to accomplish. In the upper scene he rests his head on one of his hands as if he were meditating and keeps on his knees a book he reads. This may be an allusion to the model he has on his mind and will follow in creating the world. This figure creates the impression of someone making an effort to give birth to an idea. The book is very likely the *Liber vitae*, but perhaps it is the Bible itself, or Bernardus Silvestris's *Cosmographia*, which was composed in the milieu of Chartres in the middle of the twelfth century. In the lower panel, the book seems to have become a scroll, as if God were holding the cosmos rolled up in his hand.

These sculptured representations of Creation dramatically articulate very 'human' representations of the divine figure. This impression is confirmed in the Genesis scenes of the Good Samaritan window, where a bearded God creates Adam, and then Eve, by holding the former's chin and placing his hand on the latter's head. In another scene, he warns them severely, pointing his index finger to the Tree of Knowledge.

The 'human' portrayal of God in the Gothic Chartres Cathedral might suggest movement of a sort. But when one comes to the rose window in the north transept, produced later than the scenes just described, God's immobility again becomes absolute. In fact, the stress lies here on God's total might. He appears as second person of the Trinity—the Word—seated on his throne, blessing with one hand, and holding in the other the globe of the universe. Underneath him, the rolling lines represent the primordial waters, and under them a flat surface might indicate air. Above him, there is a yellow object that could represent a city. To the left, there emerges a red disk surrounded by smaller circles—the sun and the stars. To the right, a crescent surrounded by smaller, white circles appears—the moon and, again, the stars. The Gothic style cannot, in sum, give primary movement to Creation: when the intention is to represent the very Beginning, the Prime Mover is absolutely immobile, and unmoved.

When, then, does the Mover begin to move from the very beginning of Creation? I do not think it happens in the figurative arts, but in literature. And I do not know any occurrence before Dante—who has, as we have already seen, a true passion for the theme of Creation, with which he opens and closes the *Comedy*. From *Inferno* 1 to *Paradiso* 33, divine love 'moves' the universe—in other words, creates it—to the point of including Dante himself in the new Creation.

The theme is present throughout the poem's three cantiche, from *Inferno* 3 (creation of hell) to *Purgatorio* 16 (the individual soul that 'issues from the hand' of God) and *Purgatorio* 25 (God breathing rational soul into the foetus), then more and more frequently in the *Paradiso*, in cantos 7, 10, 13, 19, 29 and 32. Dante approaches Creation with a new and profound meditation, by going back to Boethius's lesson, by translating Neoplatonic images of irradiation, sparkling and mirroring splendour, by resorting to Aristotelian categories such as *potentia* and *actus*, by using the sapiential image of the compass, by underlining the order and gradations of being, or the differences between creation and generation, or the art of the supreme Artist and the harmony of the cosmos.

But there is a culminating moment when Dante clearly envisages the movement of the Prime Mover. When, in *Paradiso* 29, Beatrice presents a definitive account of the creation of angels, she begins with the image of the Eternal Love opening himself up onto 'new loves' (the angels), 'so that his splendor might, / as it shines back to Him, declare "*Subsisto*"'. She then passes on to the creation of prime matter and of the heavens—of which she says it took place at the same time as that of the angels—by going back to the Aristotelian concepts of form, matter and substance.[23]

Right at the centre of her speech, however, Beatrice picks up—and this significantly is the only time—the narrative of Genesis, and specifically chapter 1, verse 2. But she transforms it with unheard of daring: 'Né prima quasi torpente si giacque', she declares, referring to the supreme Love, God, 'ché né prima né poscia procedette / lo discorrer di Dio sovra quest'acque' (Nor did he lie, before this, as if languid; / there was no *after*, no *before*—they were / not there until God moved upon these waters). Dante replaces the Vulgate's 'ferebatur' with 'discorrer', that is to say, the 'irruebat' of some traditional interpretations: the swift, impetuous movement of God (the Spirit is now, simply, Love). 'Discorrer' allows Dante to obliquely evoke the action of the Word, but also to refer indirectly to the *Liber de causis,* as he had already done in the *Convivio,* where he wrote, 'la prima bontade manda le sue bontadi sopra le cose con uno discorrimento' (the primal goodness makes his goodnesses flow upon all things with a single flowing).[24]

God is not 'torpente': torpid, sleepy, immobile. He is extremely mobile and quick, He 'runs' over the face of the waters. A tradition going from Augustine to Thomas Aquinas, and aptly summarised by Peter Lombard, interprets this as the 'voluntas artificis quae superfertur materiae quam vult formare', the will of the creator which 'passes above' the matter it wishes to shape.[25] Dante, who was certainly at home within this tradition, is thus describing the action whereby the supreme Agent-Artisan-Artist is preparing to give shape to shapeless matter, to the *res fabricandae,* the things to be created. For him, this is the key moment of Creation—what the artists of the 'Tapiz de la Creación' represent with the movement that takes place around the creating Logos; what the artists of San Marco render with the movement that transmits itself from one concentric circle to another; what the artists of Chartres show us in passing from a thinking, reading God to the God who raises his hand; what finally the artists of Monreale represent with the flowing of the vital stream from the Pantokrator's breast down into the billowing deep. Dante attributes all this to God Himself, the Eternal Love—a bow that shoots three arrows at the same time, a ray of light that shines fully, penetrating into glass, amber or crystal. God is archer and ir-radiator. Finally, God is supremely mobile even for a poet who had confessed to Saint Peter in *Paradiso* 24 his belief 'in one God—sole, / eternal—He who, *motionless, moves all* / the heavens with His love and love for Him'.[26]

We have to wait a little more than a century before all this is transferred to painting. And it is undoubtedly not by chance that it was an Italian who introduced the novelty, and that this was too the Italian who illustrated the third cantica of the *Comedy*. Around 1445 (hence probably in the same period he did the illuminations for the *Paradiso*), the Sienese Giovanni di Paolo painted a *Creation of the World with the Expulsion from Paradise* which is now at the Metropolitan Museum in New York City [fig. 27].[27]

In his illuminations, Giovanni never illustrated the theory of Creation of *Paradiso* 29, but this must have left some trace on his imagination, because in his picture the bearded Father, his head surrounded by a halo, draped in a blue and white mantle and supported by blue cherubim, throws himself impetuously down, stretching his right arm, hand and index finger in order to set an immense zodiacal globe in motion. Inside the sphere, a nucleus contains the known earth, then the zones of water, air and fire, the circles of the seven heavenly bodies, the band of the Zodiac, and finally, on the outside, the Primum Mobile. It is in fact at the latter that God points his finger to spur the whole to move. The structure of the cosmos is the same as that in Dante's *Comedy*; the idea of the *discorrer di Dio* (of God, not of the Spirit) has obviously inspired Giovanni. The Mover has become mobile. Swift and heavy to the point of having to be supported by the cherubim, God's élan looks like lightning, an irresistible *irruere* (the wings of the cherubim stress the impetuousness) that translates into an icon the 'will of the creator which "passes above" the matter it wishes to shape'. The rapidity of God lies in the instantaneity of thought, will and action.

Giovanni's image is revolutionary. Throughout the fourteenth, fifteenth and early sixteenth centuries, Creation continues to be represented, even in Italy, according to traditional canons. Thus the Roman Jacopo Torriti, at the end of the thirteenth century in Assisi's Upper Basilica, and the Tuscan Giusto de' Menabuoi in the last decades of the fourteenth in the Padua Baptistry, do not depart from canonical models. Even in the Quattrocento, Paolo Uccello is the only painter who gives any movement to the creating God, in the Green Cloister of Santa Maria Novella, Florence (1432–48), but he does so in the scenes concerning Adam and Eve, as artists had already done in the Middle Ages.

Pietro Perugino, who painted the fresco in the vault of the Incendio di Borgo room in the Vatican between 1507 and 1508, represented a fundamentally immobile God. In the adjoining room of the Segnatura, Raphael presented, between 1509 and 1511 (so in the same years Michelangelo painted the Sistine vault), a young Sophia as Prime Mover who, though turning her body, remains substantially immobile. Lorenzo Lotto, who had almost certainly seen the work of Michelangelo and Raphael in the Vatican, prepared his extraordinary cartoons for the wooden tarsias of Santa Maria Maggiore in Bergamo between 1523 and 1532.[28] There Lotto depicted the creating God as an imperious, immobile old man who shapes the cosmos and man with the simple gesture of his two hands, and in the *coperto* (the wooden panel that covers the tarsia) he sketched the eye that stretches the two arms (of mercy and justice) through the nine concentric spheres towards the darkness of the deep (*Magnum Chaos*) by firmly resting its feet on the earth [fig. 28].[29]

In northern Europe things are even more traditional. From the Grabow Altarpiece by Bertram von Minden (1373–83) to the *Lutherbibel* (1534) illustrated by Lucas Cranach, God remains absolutely rooted to his place [fig. 29]. Even Hieronymus Bosch, who painted an extraordinarily suggestive *World* (probably on the third day of Creation) on the exterior panels of his *Garden of Earthly Delights* between 1490 and 1510, in the *Haywain* triptych (1500–1502) represented a Creator immobile on his infinitely remote summit.

It is Michelangelo, of course, in the frescoes for the Sistine vault he painted between 1508 and 1512, who consecrates once and for all the icon of the moving Mover inaugurated by Giovanni di Paolo.[30] A faithful reader of Dante, Michelangelo does not hesitate to endow his Creator with an impetuous, even spinning movement. In the panel representing the division of light and darkness, for instance, a bearded, old God as Father whirls in space, sketching an 'S' with his body and mantle, opening up his arms in a circle towards light, his head turned to darkness [fig. 30]. It is certainly not by chance that this scene also depicts God hovering over the waters, the *irruere* therefore reaching a climactic point.

Divine motion in the panel of the division of dry land and water is also very powerful [fig. 30]. Supported by two *putti* (it is difficult to believe Michelangelo did not know Giovanni di Paolo's painting), the Old Father here bends down, his arms open again in the gesture of imposition. The movement, and what has been called the 'terribility' of God,[31] are so intense in the famous double scene of the creation of sun and moon and of plants, that in the right section of the fresco God's body and arms form two arches crossed in extreme tension, as if the upper one, a bow made up of the arms, were shooting the globes of sun and moon like arrows. God's impetuousness is such that no fewer than four figures are necessary now to support and hold him. In the left section, by contrast, the Creator's body, now without any support, bends into an inverted 'S', showing his strong buttocks—the 'posteriora Dei' of Exodus.[32] The back and the knees form another arch, inverted with regard to that of the right-hand side figure, so that space itself is splayed into a dynamic depth, whereas the waving mantles wedge in two opposing flights.

Finally, nine figures support God in the enormous cloud that envelops him ('one would say', Vasari writes, 'that they support not only a figure, but the weight of the entire world'),[33] as he stretches his arm and index finger towards Adam. His visage is more benign and his flight less tense, as his body and light tunic form an open arch that perfectly corresponds to the languid curve sketched in by man's body and the arms join God and Adam across space.

Michelangelo goes well beyond Giovanni di Paolo and Dante. Deeply inspired, as Edgar Wind has shown, by Saint Augustine, he conceived the primordial phases of Creation as a war of the elements, between darkness and light—a battle that prompts God to plunge into a 'contorted immersion into the recalcitrant substance he is about to split.'[34] Michelangelo's choice of God's whirling movement responds to his instinctively dramatic vocation, but also to the needs of theological complexity and mythical imagination. After thousands of years Michelangelo finally expressed the *ruaḥ 'ĕlōhîm*, God's *storm*, and thus paved the way to modernity.[35]

APPENDIX

The *Timaeus*

The Timaeus *for many hundreds of years exercised a wide and profound influence over men's minds. It is Plato's account of the creation of the universe, but it is more than an account, it is an explanation. To Plato the universe was intelligible and therefore how it came to be could be discovered by the searching intellect. In the first chapter of Genesis, "God said, Let there be light, and there was light." That is not Plato's way of dealing with the matter. He thinks out what light is and how it must have come about. The chapter in Genesis is poetry; the* Timaeus *has a great deal of poetry in it, but its aim is science.*

Plato sets himself to think out physics and astronomy and biology. His temper of mind nowhere even approaches the dogmatic, but in this dialogue it does so least of all. He hesitates and questions as he does in none of the ethical discussions in his earlier work. The statements he makes are possible, so he declares, even perhaps probable, but the only way to certainty about such matters would be to ask God and that is denied us. But at the very least it is better to use one's mind on these questions than to pass them by indolently without trying to think about them. Moreover, to do that kind of thinking, he says, is so diverting and refreshing—his prescription for resting a tired mind. "A man may sometimes set aside meditations about eternal things, and for recreation turn to consider the truths of generation, which are probable only; he will thus gain a pleasure not to be repented of, and secure for himself a wise and moderate pastime."

But when Plato's mind, never equaled for keenness and profundity, could not find a probable explanation to rest in, then he turned to the other realm where he was also at home, the realm of poetry. In the Timaeus *he says that truth is an eternal now, unchangeable, forever inexpressible. Time ever is, never has been, nor will be; it can be described as past or future only figuratively. It is "a moving image of eternity." What Plato said has been repeated by poets through the ages. Two thousand years later Vaughan wrote,*

I saw Eternity the other night,
Like a great Ring of pure and endless light,
  All calm, as it was bright;
And round beneath it, Time in hours, days, years,
  Driven by the spheres
Like a vast shadow moved . . .

That came straight out of the Timaeus.

We must read the dialogue with such thoughts in mind because most of it is no longer to us what it was to Plato and through him to the men for centuries after, up to and into the Middle Ages, a statement of scientific truth combined with mythical truth in which great spiritual truths could be found. Inevitably we read it, at least to begin with, as an account of the incredibilities antiquity believed. God creates the universe from innumerable triangles, described and compared with careful accuracy. When man is created the way breath is put into him is of an astounding complexity, also described in accurate and bewildering detail. No doubt, as Plato said, he had relaxed just then and was amusing himself by this kind of writing, but he was also feeling, as we no longer can, how reasonable it all was and quite possibly the very truth itself.

It is certain, however, that Plato would have taken with complete tranquillity our modern skepticism. He would have pointed out that science cannot be accurately true since it deals with the temporal, the finite, the forever changing, never with the eternal. But yet the visible world is a copy, an image, of what is eternal and true. It is a changing reflection of that which is changeless and therefore, imperfect though it is, in it can be found the truth, God the Creator, the all-good. That is the matter of importance, not scientific accuracy, but to catch a glimpse of "the beyond, which ever thereafter the soul will strive to reach."

Toward the close of the Timaeus *Plato says that death when it comes in old age is accompanied with pleasure, not pain. He was very old when he wrote that; he was near the end. The innumerable host of those who have learned from him and have loved him, who through the ages have found in him inspiration and guidance for life, vision to see "the beyond" and that the ultimate truth is God, our Creator and Father—all those whom he has taught so greatly have rejoiced that as death approached him he declared that he felt his soul "loosened from bonds and able to fly away with joy." Aristotle, who was best able to understand him, wrote that he had proved that the good man was the happy man. That is an aspect of Platonism which has been too little emphasized.*

SOCRATES: One, two, three, but where, my dear Timaeus, is the fourth of those who were yesterday my guests and are to be my entertainers today?

TIMAEUS: He has been taken ill, Socrates, for he would not willingly have been absent from this gathering.

SOCRATES: Then, if he is not coming, you and the two others must supply his place.

TIMAEUS: Certainly, and we will do our utmost not to disappoint you. Having been handsomely entertained by you yesterday, those of us who remain should be only too glad to return your hospitality.

SOCRATES: Do you remember what were the points of which I required you to speak?

TIMAEUS: We remember some of them, and you will be here to remind us of anything which we have forgotten, or rather, if we are not troubling you, will you briefly recapitulate the whole, and then the particulars will be more firmly fixed in our memories?

SOCRATES: To be sure I will. The chief theme of my yesterday's discourse was the state—how constituted and of what citizens composed it would seem likely to be most perfect.

TIMAEUS: Yes, Socrates, and what you said of it was very much to our mind.

SOCRATES: Did we not begin by separating the husbandmen and the artisans from the class of defenders of the state?

TIMAEUS: Yes.

SOCRATES: And when we had given to each one that single employment and particular art which was suited to his nature, we spoke of those who were intended to be our warriors, and said that they were to be guardians of the city against attacks from within as well as from without, and to have no other employment; they were to be merciful in judging their subjects, of whom they were by nature friends, but fierce to their enemies, when they came across them in battle.

TIMAEUS: Exactly.

SOCRATES: We said, if I am not mistaken, that the guardians should be gifted with a temperament in a high degree both passionate and philosophical, and that then they would be as they ought to be—gentle to their friends and fierce with their enemies.

TIMAEUS: Certainly.

SOCRATES: And what did we say of their education? Were they not to be trained in gymnastics and music and all other sorts of knowledge which were proper for them?

TIMAEUS: Very true.

From *The Dialogues of Plato,* translated with analyses and introductions by B. Jowett (4th edn., revised by order of the Jowett Copyright Trustees, Oxford, 1953; 1st edn., 1871).

SOCRATES: And being thus trained they were not to consider gold or silver or anything else to be their own private property. They were to be like hired troops, receiving pay for keeping guard from those who were protected by them—the pay was to be no more than would suffice for men of simple life—and they were to spend in common, and to live together in the continual practice of virtue, which was to be their sole pursuit.

TIMAEUS: That was also said.

SOCRATES: Neither did we forget the women, of whom we declared that their natures should be harmoniously developed by training, equally with those of the men, and that common pursuits should be assigned to them all both in time of war and in their ordinary life.

TIMAEUS: That, again, was as you say.

SOCRATES: And what about the procreation of children? Or rather was not the proposal too singular to be forgotten? For all wives and children were to be in common, to the intent that no one should ever know his own child, but they were to imagine that they were all one family; those who were within a suitable limit of age were to be brothers and sisters, those who were of an elder generation parents and grandparents, and those of a younger, children and grandchildren.

TIMAEUS: Yes, and the proposal is easy to remember, as you say.

SOCRATES: And do you also remember how, with a view of securing as far as we could the best breed, we said that the chief magistrates, male and female, should contrive secretly, by the use of certain lots, so to arrange the nuptial meeting that the bad of either sex and the good of either sex might pair with their like, and there was to be no quarreling on this account, for they would imagine that the union was a mere accident and was to be attributed to the lot?

TIMAEUS: I remember.

SOCRATES: And you remember how we said that the children of the good parents were to be educated, and the children of the bad secretly dispersed among the inferior citizens, and while they were all growing up the rulers were to be on the lookout, and to bring up from below in their turn those who were worthy, and those among themselves who were unworthy were to take the places of those who came up?

TIMAEUS: True.

SOCRATES: Then have I now given you all the heads of our yesterday's discussion? Or is there anything more, my dear Timaeus, which has been omitted?

TIMAEUS: Nothing, Socrates. The discussion was just as you have said.

SOCRATES: I should like, before proceeding further, to tell you how I feel about the state which we have described. I might compare myself to a person who, on beholding beautiful animals either created by the painter's art, or, better still, alive but at rest, is seized with a desire of seeing them in motion or engaged in some struggle or conflict to which their forms appear suited—this is my feeling about the state which we have been describing. There are conflicts which all cities undergo, and I should like to hear someone tell of our own city carrying on a struggle against her neighbors, and how she went out to war in a becoming manner, and when at war showed by the greatness of her actions and the magnanimity of her words in dealing with other cities a result worthy of her training and education. Now I, Critias and Hermocrates, am conscious that I myself should never be able to celebrate the city and her citizens in a befitting manner, and I am not surprised at my own incapacity; to me the wonder is rather that the poets present as well as past are no better—not that I mean to depreciate them, but everyone can see that they are a tribe of imitators, and will imitate best and most easily the life in which they have been brought up, while that which is beyond the range of a man's education he finds hard to carry out in action, and still harder adequately to represent in language. I am aware that the Sophists have plenty of brave words and fair conceits, but I am afraid that being only wanderers from one city to another, and having never had habitations of their own, they may fail in their conception of philosophers and statesmen and may not know what they do and say in time of war, when they are fighting or holding parley with their enemies. And thus people of your class are the only ones remaining who are fitted by nature and education to take part at once both in politics and philosophy. Here is Timaeus, of Locri in Italy, a city which has admirable laws, who is himself in wealth and rank the equal of any of his fellow citizens; he has held the most important and honorable offices in his own state, and, as I believe, has scaled the heights of all philosophy. And here is Critias, whom every Athenian knows to be no novice in the matters of which we are speaking, and as to Hermocrates, I am assured by many witnesses that his genius and education qualify him to take part in any speculation of the kind. And therefore yesterday when I saw that you wanted me to describe the formation of the state, I readily assented, being very well aware that, if you only would, none was better qualified to carry the discussion further, and that when you had engaged our city in a suitable war, you of all men living could best exhibit her playing a fitting part. When I had completed my task, I in return imposed this other task upon you. You conferred together and agreed to entertain me today, as I had entertained you, with a feast of discourse. Here am I in festive array, and no man can be more ready for the promised banquet.

HERMOCRATES: And we too, Socrates, as Timaeus says, will not be wanting in enthusiasm, and there is no excuse for not complying with your request. As soon as we arrived yesterday at the guestchamber of Critias, with whom we are staying, or rather on our way thither, we talked the matter over, and he told us an ancient tradition which I wish, Critias, that you would repeat to Socrates, so that he may help us to judge whether it will satisfy his requirements or not.

CRITIAS: I will, if Timaeus, who is our other partner, approves.

TIMAEUS: I quite approve.

CRITIAS: Then listen, Socrates, to a tale which, though strange, is certainly true, having been attested by Solon, who was the wisest of the seven sages. He was a relative and a dear friend of my great-grandfather, Dropides, as he himself says in many passages of his poems, and he told the story to Critias, my grandfather, who remembered and repeated it to us. There were of old, he said, great and marvelous actions of the Athenian city, which have passed into oblivion through lapse of time and the destruction of mankind, and one in particular, greater than all the rest. This we will now rehearse. It will be a fitting monument of our gratitude to you, and a hymn of praise true and worthy of the goddess, on this her day of festival.

SOCRATES: Very good. And what is this ancient famous action of the Athenians, which Critias declared, on the authority of Solon, to be not a mere legend but an actual fact?

CRITIAS: I will tell an old-world story which I heard from an aged man, for Critias, at the time of telling it, was, as he said, nearly ninety years of age, and I was about ten. Now the day was that day of the Apaturia which is called the Registration of Youth, at which, according to custom, our parents gave prizes for recitations, and the poems of several poets were recited by us boys, and many of us sang the poems of Solon, which at that time had not gone out of fashion. One of our tribe, either because he thought so or to please Critias, said that in his judgment Solon was not only the wisest of men, but also the noblest of poets.

The old man, as I very well remember, brightened up at hearing this and said, smiling, Yes, Amynander, if Solon had only, like other poets, made poetry the business of his life and had completed the tale which he brought with him from Egypt, and had not been compelled, by reason of the factions and troubles which he found stirring in his own country when he came home, to attend to other matters, in my opinion he would have been as famous as Homer or Hesiod or any poet.

And what was the tale about, Critias? said Amynander.

About the greatest action which the Athenians ever did, and which ought to have been the most famous, but, through the lapse of time and the destruction of the actors, it has not come down to us.

Tell us, said the other, the whole story, and how and from whom Solon heard this veritable tradition.

He replied, In the Egyptian Delta, at the head of which the river Nile divides, there is a certain district which is called the district of Sais, and the great city of the district is also called Sais, and is the city from which King Amasis came. The citizens have a deity for their foundress; she is called in the Egyptian tongue Neith, and is asserted by them to be the same whom the Hellenes call Athena. They are great lovers of the Athenians and say that they are in some way related to them. To this city came Solon and was received there with great honor; he asked the priests, who were most skillful in such matters, about antiquity, and made the discovery that neither he nor any other Hellene knew anything worth mentioning about the times of old. On one occasion, wishing to draw them on to speak of antiquity, he began to tell about the most ancient things in our part of the world—about Phoroneus, who is called 'the first man,' and about Niobe, and after the Deluge, of the survival of Deucalion and Pyrrha, and he traced the genealogy of their descendants and, reckoning up the dates, tried to compute how many years ago the events of which he was speaking happened.

Thereupon one of the priests, who was of a very great age, said, O Solon, Solon, you Hellenes are never anything but children, and there is not an old man among you.

Solon in return asked him what he meant.

I mean to say, he replied, that in mind you are all young; there is no old opinion handed down among you by ancient tradition, nor any science which is hoary with age. And I will tell you why. There have been, and will be again, many destructions of mankind arising out of many causes; the greatest have been brought about by the agencies of fire and water, and other lesser ones by innumerable other causes. There is a story which even you have preserved, that once upon a time Phaethon, the son of Helios, having yoked the steeds in his father's chariot, because he was not able to drive them in the path of his father, burned up all that was upon the earth, and was himself destroyed by a thunderbolt. Now this has the form of a myth, but really signifies a declination of the bodies moving in the heavens around the earth, and a great conflagration of things upon the earth which recurs after long intervals; at such times those who live upon the mountains and in dry and lofty places are more liable to destruction than those who dwell by rivers or on the seashore. And from this calamity we are preserved by the liberation of the Nile, who is our never-failing savior. When, on the other hand, the gods purge the earth with a deluge of water, the survivors in your country are herdsmen and shepherds who dwell on the mountains, but those who, like you, live in cities are carried by the rivers into the sea. Whereas in this land, neither then nor at any other time, does the water come down from above on the fields, having always a tendency to come up from below, for which reason the traditions preserved here are the most ancient. The fact is that wherever the extremity of winter frost or of summer sun does not prevent, mankind exist, sometimes in greater, sometimes in lesser numbers. And whatever happened either in your country or in ours, or in any other region of which we are informed—if there were any actions noble or great or in any other way remarkable, they have all been written down by us of old and are preserved in our temples. Whereas just when you and other nations are beginning to be provided with letters and the other requisites of civilized life, after the usual interval, the stream from heaven, like a pestilence, comes pouring down and leaves only those of you who are destitute of letters and education, and so you have to begin all over again like children, and know nothing of what happened in ancient times, either among us or among yourselves.

As for those genealogies of yours which you just now recounted to us, Solon, they are no better than the tales of children. In the first place you remember a single deluge only, but there were many previous ones; in the next place, you do not know that there formerly dwelt in your land the fairest and noblest race of men which ever lived, and that you and your whole city are descended from a small seed or remnant of them which survived. And this was unknown to you, because, for many generations, the survivors of that destruction died, leaving no written word. For there was a time, Solon, before the great deluge of all, when the city which now is Athens was first in war and in every way the best-governed of all cities, and is said to have performed the noblest deeds and to have had the fairest constitution of any of which tradition tells, under the face of heaven.

Solon marveled at his words, and earnestly requested the priests to inform him exactly and in order about these former citizens.

You are welcome to hear about them, Solon, said the priest, both for your own sake and for that of your city, and above all, for the sake of the goddess who is the common patron and parent and educator of both our cities. She founded your city a thousand years before ours, receiving from the Earth and Hephaestus the seed of your race, and afterward she founded ours, of which the constitution is recorded in our sacred registers to be eight thousand years old. As touching your citizens of nine thousand years ago, I will briefly inform you of their laws and of their most famous action; the exact particulars of the whole we will hereafter go through at our leisure in the sacred registers themselves. If you compare these very laws with ours you will find that many of ours are the counterpart of yours as they were in the olden time. In the first place, there is the caste of priests, which is separated from all the others; next, there are the artificers, who ply their several crafts by themselves and do not intermix, and also there is the class of shepherds and of hunters, as well as that of husbandmen. And you will observe, too, that the warriors in Egypt are distinct from all the other classes, and are commanded by the law to devote themselves solely to military pursuits; moreover, the weapons which they carry are shields and spears—a style of equipment which the goddess taught of Asiatics first to us, as in your part of the world first to you.

Then as to wisdom, do you observe how our law from the very first made a study of the whole order of things, extending even to prophecy and medicine which gives health, out of these divine elements deriving what was needful for human life, and adding every sort of knowledge which was akin to them. All this order and arrangement the goddess first imparted to you when establishing your city, and she chose the spot of earth in which you were born, because she saw that the happy temperament of the seasons in that land would produce the wisest of men. Wherefore the goddess, who was a lover both of war and of wisdom, selected and first of all settled that spot which was the most likely to produce men likest herself. And there you dwelt, having such laws as these and still better ones, and excelled all mankind in all virtue, as became the children and disciples of the gods.

Many great and wonderful deeds are recorded of your state in our histories. But one of them exceeds all the rest in greatness and valor. For these histories tell of a mighty power which unprovoked made an expedition against the whole of Europe and Asia, and to which your city put an end. This power came forth out of the Atlantic Ocean, for in those days the Atlantic was navigable, and there was an island situated in front of the straits which are by you called the Pillars of Heracles. The island was larger than Libya and Asia put together, and was the way to other islands, and from these you might pass to the whole of the opposite continent which surrounded the true ocean, for this sea which is within the Straits of Heracles is only a harbor, having a narrow entrance, but that other is a real sea, and the land surrounding it on every side may be most truly called a boundless continent. Now in this island of Atlantis there was a great and wonderful empire which had rule over the whole island and several others, and over parts of the continent, and, furthermore, the men of Atlantis had subjected the parts of Libya within the columns of Heracles as far as Egypt, and of Europe as far as Tyrrhenia. This vast power, gathered into one, endeavored to subdue at a blow our country and yours and the whole of the region within the straits, and then. Solon, your country shone forth, in the excellence of her virtue and strength, among all mankind. She was pre-eminent in courage and military skill, and was the leader of the Hellenes. And when the rest fell off from her, being compelled to stand alone, after having undergone the very extremity of danger, she defeated and triumphed over the invaders, and preserved from slavery those who were not yet subjugated, and generously liberated all the rest of us who dwell within the Pillars. But afterward there occurred violent earthquakes and floods, and in a single day and night of misfortune all your warlike men in a body sank into the earth, and the island of Atlantis in like manner disappeared in the depths of the sea. For which reason the sea in those parts is impassable and impenetrable, because there is a shoal of mud in the way, and this was caused by the subsidence of the island.

I have told you briefly, Socrates, what the aged Critias heard from Solon and related to us. And when you were speaking yesterday about your city and citizens, the tale which I have just been repeating to you came into my mind, and I remarked with astonishment how, by some mysterious coincidence, you agreed in almost every particular with the narrative of Solon, but I did not like to speak at the moment. For a long time had elapsed, and I had forgotten too much; I thought that I must first of all run over the narrative in my own mind, and then I would speak. And so I readily assented to your request yesterday, considering that in all such cases the chief difficulty is to find a tale suitable to our purpose, and that with such a tale we should be fairly well provided.

And therefore, as Hermocrates has told you, on my way home yesterday I at once communicated the tale to my companions as I remembered it, and after I left them, during the night by thinking I recovered nearly the whole of it. Truly, as is often said, the lessons of our childhood make a wonderful impression on our memories, for I am not sure that I could remember all the discourse of yesterday, but I should be much surprised if I forgot any of these things which I have heard very long ago. I listened at the time with childlike interest to the old man's narrative; he was very ready to teach me, and I asked him again and again to repeat his words, so that, like an indelible picture, they were branded into my mind. As soon as the day broke, I rehearsed them as he spoke them to my companions, that they, as well as myself, might have something to say. And now, Socrates, to make an end of my preface, I am ready to tell you the whole tale. I will give you not only the general heads, but the particulars, as they were told to me. The city and citizens, which you yesterday described to us in fiction, we will now transfer to the world of reality. It shall be the ancient city of Athens, and we will suppose that the citizens whom you imagined were our veritable ancestors of whom the priest spoke; they will perfectly harmonize, and there will be no inconsistency in saying that the citizens of your republic are these ancient Athenians. Let us divide the subject among us, and all endeavor according to our ability gracefully to execute the task which you have imposed upon us. Consider then, Socrates, if this narrative is suited to the purpose, or whether we should seek for some other instead.

SOCRATES: And what other, Critias, can we find that will be better than this which is natural and suitable to the festival of the goddess, and has the very great advantage of being a fact and not a fiction? How or where shall we find another if we abandon this? We cannot, and therefore you must tell the tale, and good luck to you, and I in return for my yesterday's discourse will now rest and be a listener.

CRITIAS: Let me proceed to explain to you, Socrates, the order in which we have arranged our entertainment. Our intention is that Timaeus, who is the most of an astronomer among us, and has made the nature of the universe his special study, should speak first, beginning with the generation of the world and going down to the creation of man; next, I am to receive the men whom he has created, and of whom some will have profited by the excellent education which you have given them; and then, in accordance with the tale of Solon, and equally with his law, we will bring them into court and make them citizens, as if they were those very Athenians whom the sacred Egyptian record has recovered from oblivion, and thenceforward we will speak of them as Athenians and fellow citizens.

SOCRATES: I see that I shall receive in my turn a perfect and splendid feast of reason. And now, Timaeus, you, I suppose, should speak next, after duly calling upon the gods.

TIMAEUS: All men, Socrates, who have any degree of right feeling, at the beginning of every enterprise, whether small or great, always call upon God. And we, too, who are going to discourse of the nature of the universe, how created or how existing without creation, if we be not altogether out of our wits, must invoke the aid of gods and goddesses and pray that our words may be above all acceptable to them and in consequence to ourselves. Let this, then, be our invocation of the gods, to which I add an exhortation of myself to speak in such manner as will be most intelligible to you, and will most accord with my own intent.

First then, in my judgment, we must make a distinction and ask, What is that which always is and has no becoming, and what is that which is always becoming and never is? That which is apprehended by intelligence and reason is always in the same state, but that which is conceived by opinion with the help of sensation and without reason is always in a process of becoming and perishing and never really is. Now everything that becomes or is created must of necessity be created by some cause, for without a cause nothing can be created. The work of the creator, whenever he looks to the unchangeable and fashions the form and nature of his work after an unchangeable pattern, must necessarily be made fair and perfect, but when he looks to the created only and uses a created pattern, it is not fair or perfect. Was the heaven then or the world, whether called by this or by any other more appropriate name—assuming the name, I am asking a question which has to be asked at the beginning of an inquiry about anything—was the world, I say, always in existence and without beginning, or created, and had it a beginning? Created, I reply, being visible and tangible and having a body, and therefore sensible, and all sensible things are apprehended by opinion and sense, and are in a process of creation and created. Now that which is created must, as we affirm, of necessity be created by a cause. But the father and maker of all this universe is past finding out, and even if we found him, to tell of him to all men would be impossible. This question, however, we must ask about the world. Which of the patterns had the artificer in view when he made it—the pattern of the unchangeable or of that which is created? If the world be indeed fair and the artificer good, it is manifest that he must have looked to that which is eternal, but if what cannot be said without blasphemy is true, then to the created pattern. Everyone will see that he must have looked to the eternal, for the world is the fairest of creations and he is the best of causes. And having been created in this way, the world has been framed in the likeness of that which is apprehended by reason and mind and is unchangeable, and must therefore of necessity, if this is admitted, be a copy of something. Now it is all-important that the beginning of everything should be according to nature. And in speaking of the copy and the original we may assume that words are akin to the matter which they describe; when they relate to the lasting and permanent and intelligible, they ought to be lasting and unalterable, and, as far as their nature allows, irrefutable and invincible—nothing less. But when they express only the copy or likeness and not the eternal things themselves, they need only be likely and analogous to the former words. As being is to becoming, so is truth to belief. If then, Socrates, amidst the many opinions about the gods and the generation of the universe, we are not able to give notions which are altogether and in every respect exact and consistent with one another, do not be surprised. Enough if we adduce probabilities as likely as any others, for we must remember that I who am the speaker and you who are the judges are only mortal men, and we ought to accept the tale which is probable and inquire no further.

SOCRATES: Excellent, Timaeus, and we will do precisely as you bid us. The prelude is charming and is already accepted by us—may we beg of you to proceed to the strain?

TIMAEUS: Let me tell you then why the creator made this world of generation. He was good, and the good can never have any jealousy of anything. And being free from jealousy, he desired that all things should be as like himself as they could be. This is in the truest sense the origin of creation and of the world, as we shall do well in believing on the testimony of wise men. God desired that all things should be good and nothing bad, so far as this was attainable. Wherefore also finding the whole visible sphere not at rest, but moving in an irregular and disorderly fashion, out of disorder he brought order, considering that this was in every way better than the other. Now the deeds of the best could never be or have been other than the fairest, and the creator, reflecting on the things which are by nature visible, found that no unintelligent creature taken as a whole could ever be fairer than the intelligent taken as a whole, and again that intelligence could not be present in anything which was devoid of soul. For which reason, when he was framing the universe, he put intelligence in soul, and soul in body, that he might be the creator of a work which was by nature fairest and best. On this wise, using the language of probability, we may say that the world came into being—a living creature truly endowed with soul and intelligence by the providence of God.

This being supposed, let us proceed to the next stage. In the likeness of what animal did the creator make the world? It would be an unworthy thing to liken it to any nature which exists as a part only, for nothing can be beautiful which is like any imperfect thing. But let us suppose the world to be the very image of that whole of which all other animals both individually and in their tribes are portions. For the original of the universe contains in itself all intelligible beings, just as this world comprehends us and all other visible creatures. For the deity, intending to make this world like the fairest and most perfect of intelligible beings, framed one visible animal comprehending within itself all other animals of a kindred nature. Are we right in saying that there is one world, or that they are many and infinite? There must be one only if the created copy is to accord with the original. For that which includes all other intelligible creatures cannot have a second or companion; in that case there would be need of another living being which would include both, and of which they would be parts, and the likeness would be more truly said to resemble not them, but that other which included them. In order then that the world might be solitary, like the perfect animal, the creator made not two worlds or an infinite number of them, but there is and ever will be one only-begotten and created heaven.

Now that which is created is of necessity corporeal, and also visible and tangible. And nothing is visible where there is no fire, or tangible which has no solidity, and nothing is solid without earth. Wherefore also God in the beginning of creation made the body of the universe to consist of fire and earth. But two things cannot be rightly put together without a third; there must be some bond of union between them. And the fairest bond is that which makes the most complete fusion of itself and the things which it combines, and proportion is best adapted to effect such a union. For whenever in any three numbers, whether cube or square, there is a mean, which is to the last term what the first term is to it, and again, when the mean is to the first term as the last term is to the mean—then the mean becoming first and last, and the first and last both becoming means, they will all of them of necessity come to be the same, and having become the same with one another will be all one. If the universal frame had been created a surface only and having no depth, a single mean would have sufficed to bind together itself and the other terms, but now, as the world must be solid, and solid bodies are always compacted not by one mean but by two, God placed water and air in the mean between fire and earth, and made them to have the same proportion so far as was possible—as fire is to air so is air to water, and as air is to water so is water to earth—and thus he bound and put together a visible and tangible heaven. And for these reasons, and out of such elements which are in number four, the body of the world was created, and it was harmonized by proportion, and therefore has the spirit of friendship, and having been reconciled to itself, it was indissoluble by the hand of any other than the framer.

Now the creation took up the whole of each of the four elements, for the creator compounded the world out of all the fire and all the water and all the air and all the earth, leaving no part of any of them nor any power of them outside. His intention was, in the first place, that the animal should be as far as possible a perfect whole and of perfect parts, secondly, that it should be one, leaving no remnants out of which another such world might be created, and also that it should be free from old age and unaffected by disease. Considering that if heat and cold and other powerful forces surround composite bodies and attack them from without, they decompose them before their time, and by bringing diseases and old age upon them make them waste away—for this cause and on these grounds he made the world one whole, having every part entire, and being therefore perfect and not liable to old age and disease. And he gave to the world the figure which was suitable and also natural. Now to the animal which was to comprehend all animals, that figure would be suitable which comprehends within itself all other figures. Wherefore he made the world in the form of a globe, round as from a lathe, having its extremes in every direction equidistant from the center, the most perfect and the most like itself of all figures, for he considered that the like is infinitely fairer than the unlike. This he finished off, making the surface smooth all around for many reasons—in the first place, because the living being had no need of eyes when there was nothing remaining outside him to be seen, nor of ears when there was nothing to be heard, and there was no surrounding atmosphere to be breathed, nor would there have been any use of organs by the help of which he might receive his food or get rid of what he had already digested, since there was nothing which went from him or came into him, for there was nothing besides him. Of design he was created thus—his own waste providing his own food, and all that he did or suffered taking place in and by himself. For the creator conceived that a being which was self-sufficient would be far more excellent than one which lacked anything, and, as he had no need to take anything or defend himself against anyone, the creator did not think it necessary to bestow upon him hands, nor had he any need of feet, nor of the whole apparatus of walking. But the movement suited to his spherical form was assigned to him, being of all the seven that which is most appropriate to mind and intelligence, and he was made to move in the same manner and on the same spot, within his own limits revolving in a circle. All the other six motions were taken away from him, and he was made not to partake of their deviations. And as this circular movement required no feet, the universe was created without legs and without feet.

Such was the whole plan of the eternal God about the god that was to be; he made it smooth and even, having a surface in every direction equidistant from the center, a body entire and perfect, and formed out of perfect bodies. And in the center he put the soul, which he diffused throughout the body, making it also to be the exterior environment of it, and he made the universe a circle moving in a circle, one and solitary, yet by reason of its excellence able to converse with itself, and needing no other friendship or acquaintance. Having these purposes in view he created the world a blessed god.

Now God did not make the soul after the body, although we are speaking of them in this order, for when he put them together he would never have allowed that the elder should be ruled by the younger, but this is a random manner of speaking which we have, because somehow we ourselves too are very much under the dominion of chance. Whereas he made the soul in origin and excellence prior to and older than the body, to be the ruler and mistress, of whom the body was to be the subject. And he made her out of the following elements and on this wise. From the being which is indivisible and unchangeable, and from that kind of being which is distributed among bodies, he compounded a third and intermediate kind of being. He did likewise with the same and the different, blending together the indivisible kind of each with that which is portioned out in bodies. Then, taking the three new elements, he mingled them all into one form, compressing by force the reluctant and unsociable nature of the different into the same. When he had mingled them with the intermediate kind of being and out of three made one, he again divided this whole into as many portions as was fitting, each portion being a compound of the same, the different, and being. And he proceeded to divide after this manner. First of all, he took away one part of the whole [1], and then he separated a second part which was double the first [2], and then he took away a third part which was half as much again as the second and three times as much as the first [3], and then he took a fourth part which was twice as much as the second [4], and a fifth part which was three times the third [9], and a sixth part which was eight times the first [8], and a seventh part which was twenty-seven times the first [27]. After this he filled up the double intervals [that is, between 1, 2, 4, 8] and the triple [that is, between 1, 3, 9, 27], cutting off yet other portions from the mixture and placing them in the intervals, so that in each interval there were two kinds of means, the one exceeding and exceeded by equal parts of its extremes [as for example, 1, 4/3, 2, in which the mean 4/3 is one third of 1 more than 1, and one third of 2 less than 2], the other being that kind of mean which exceeds and is exceeded by an equal number. Where there were intervals of 3/2, and of 4/3 and of 9/8 made by the connecting terms in the former intervals, he filled up all the intervals of 4/3 with the interval of 9/8, leaving a fraction over, and the interval which this fraction expressed was in the ratio of 256 to 243. And thus the whole mixture out of which he cut these portions was all exhausted by him. This entire compound he divided lengthwise into two parts which he joined to one another at the center like the letter X, and bent them into a circular form, connecting them with themselves and each other at the point opposite to their original meeting point, and, comprehending them in a uniform revolution upon the same axis, he made the one the outer and the other the inner circle. Now the motion of the outer circle he called the motion of the same, and the motion of the inner circle the motion of the other or diverse. The motion of the same he carried round by the side to the right, and the motion of the diverse diagonally to the left. And he gave dominion to the motion of the same and like, for that he left single and undivided, but the inner motion he divided in six places and made seven unequal circles having their intervals in ratios of two and three, three of each, and bade the orbits proceed in a direction opposite to one another. And three [sun, Mercury, Venus] he made to move with equal swiftness, and the remaining four [moon, Saturn, Mars, Jupiter] to move with unequal swiftness to the three and to one another, but in due proportion.

Now when the creator had framed the soul according to his will, he formed within her the corporeal universe, and brought the two together and united them center to center. The soul, interfused everywhere from the center to the circumference of heaven, of which also she is the external envelopment, herself turning in herself, began a divine beginning of never-ceasing and rational life enduring throughout all time. The body of heaven is visible, but the soul is invisible and partakes of reason and harmony, and, being made by the best of intellectual and everlasting natures, is the best of things created. And because she is composed of the same and of the different and of being these three, and is divided and united in due proportion, and in her revolutions returns upon herself, the soul, when touching anything which has being, whether dispersed in parts or undivided, is stirred through all her powers to declare the sameness or difference of that thing and some other, and to what individuals are related, and by what affected, and in what way and how and when, both in the world of generation and in the world of immutable being. And when reason, which works with equal truth, whether she be in the circle of the diverse or of the same—in voiceless silence holding her onward course in the sphere of the self-moved—when reason, I say, is hovering around the sensible world and when the circle of the diverse also moving truly imparts the intimations of sense to the whole soul, then arise opinions and beliefs sure and certain. But when reason is concerned with the rational, and the circle of the same moving smoothly declares it, then intelligence and knowledge are necessarily achieved. And if anyone affirms that in which these two are found to be other than the soul, he will say the very opposite of the truth.

When the father and creator saw the creature which he had made moving and living, the created image of the eternal gods, he rejoiced, and in his joy determined to make the copy still more like the original, and as this was an eternal living being, he sought to make the universe eternal, so far as might be. Now the nature of the ideal being was everlasting, but to bestow this attribute in its fullness upon a creature was impossible. Wherefore he resolved to have a moving image of eternity, and when he set in order the heaven, he made this image eternal but moving according to number, while eternity itself rests in unity, and this image we call time. For there were no days and nights and months and years before the heaven was created, but when he constructed the heaven he created them also. They are all parts of time, and the past and future are created species of time, which we unconsciously but wrongly transfer to eternal being, for we say that it 'was,' or 'is,' or 'will be,' but the truth is that 'is' alone is properly attributed to it, and that 'was' and 'will be' are only to be spoken of becoming in time, for they are motions, but that which is immovably the same forever cannot become older or younger by time, nor can it be said that it came into being in the past, or has come into being now, or will come into being in the future, nor is it subject at all to any of those states which affect moving and sensible things and of which generation is the cause. These are the forms of time, which imitates eternity and revolves according to a law of number. Moreover, when we say that what has become *is* become and what becomes *is* becoming, and that what will become *is* about to become and that the nonexistent *is* nonexistent—all these are inaccurate modes of expression. But perhaps this whole subject will be more suitably discussed on some other occasion.

Time, then, and the heaven came into being at the same instant in order that, having been created together, if ever there was to be a dissolution of them, they might be dissolved together. It was framed after the pattern of the eternal nature—that it might resemble this as far as was possible, for the pattern exists from eternity, and the created heaven has been and is and will be in all time. Such was the mind and thought of God in the creation of time. The sun and moon and five other stars, which are called the planets, were created by him in order to distinguish and preserve the numbers of time, and when he had made their several bodies, he placed them in the orbits in which the circle of the other was revolving—in seven orbits seven stars. First, there was the moon in the orbit nearest the earth, and the next the sun, in the second orbit above the earth; then came the morning star and the star said to be sacred to

Hermes, moving in orbits which have an equal swiftness with the sun, but in an opposite direction, and this is the reason why the sun and Hermes and Lucifer regularly overtake and are overtaken by each other. To enumerate the places which he assigned to the other stars and to give all the reasons why he assigned them, although a secondary matter, would give more trouble than the primary. These things at some future time, when we are at leisure, may have the consideration which they deserve, but not at present.

Now, when each of the stars which were necessary to the creation of time had come to its proper orbit, and they had become living creatures having bodies fastened by vital chains, and learned their appointed task—moving in the motion of the diverse, which is diagonal and passes through and is governed by the motion of the same—they revolved, some in a larger and some in a lesser orbit, those which had the lesser orbit revolving faster, and those which had the larger more slowly. Now by reason of the motion of the same, those which revolved fastest appeared to be overtaken by those which moved slower although they really overtook them, for the motion of the same made them all turn in a spiral, and, because some went one way and some another, that which receded most slowly from the sphere of the same, which was the swiftest, appeared to follow it most nearly. That there might be some visible measure of their relative swiftness and slowness as they proceeded in their eight courses, God lighted a fire, which we now call the sun, in the second from the earth of these orbits, that it might give light to the whole of heaven, and that the animals, as many as nature intended, might participate in number, learning arithmetic from the revolution of the same and the like. Thus, then, and for this reason the night and the day were created, being the period of the one most intelligent revolution. And the month is accomplished when the moon has completed her orbit and overtaken the sun, and the year when the sun has completed his own orbit. Mankind, with hardly an exception, have not remarked the periods of the other stars, and they have no name for them, and do not measure them against one another by the help of number, and hence they can scarcely be said to know that their wanderings, being of vast number and admirable for their variety, make up time. And yet there is no difficulty in seeing that the perfect number of time fulfills the perfect year when all the eight revolutions, having their relative degrees of swiftness, are accomplished together and attain their completion at the same time, measured by the rotation of the same and equally moving. After this manner, and for these reasons, came into being such of the stars as in their heavenly progress received reversals of motion, to the end that the created heaven might be as like as possible to the perfect and intelligible animal, by imitation of its eternal nature.

Thus far and until the birth of time the created universe was made in the likeness of the original, but inasmuch as all animals were not yet comprehended therein, it was still unlike. Therefore, the creator proceeded to fashion it after the nature of the pattern in this remaining point. Now as in the ideal animal the mind perceives ideas or species of a certain nature and number, he thought that this created animal ought to have species of a like nature and number. There are four such. One of them is the heavenly race of the gods; another, the race of birds whose way is in the air; the third, the watery species; and the fourth, the pedestrian and land creatures. Of the heavenly and divine, he created the greater part out of fire, that they might be the brightest of all things and fairest to behold, and he fashioned them after the likeness of the universe in the figure of a circle, and made them follow the intelligent motion of the supreme, distributing them over the whole circumference of heaven, which was to be a true cosmos or glorious world spangled with them all over. And he gave to each of them two movements—the first, a movement on the same spot after the same manner, whereby they ever continue to think consistently the same thoughts about the same things, in the same respect; the second, a forward movement, in which they are controlled by the revolution of the same and the like—but by the other five motions they were unaffected, in order that each of them might attain the highest perfection. And for this reason the fixed stars were created, to be divine and eternal animals, ever abiding and revolving after the same manner and on the same spot, and the other stars which reverse their motion and are subject to deviations of this kind were created in the manner already described. The earth, which is our nurse, clinging around the pole which is extended through the universe, he framed to be the guardian and artificer of night and day, first and eldest of gods that are in the interior of heaven. Vain would be the attempt to tell all the figures of them circling as in dance, and their juxtapositions, and the return of them in their revolutions upon themselves, and their approximations, and to say which of these deities in their conjunctions meet, and which of them are in opposition, and in what order they get behind and before one another, and when they are severally eclipsed to our sight and again reappear, sending terrors and intimations of the future to those who cannot calculate their movements—to attempt to tell of all this without a visible representation of the heavenly system would be labor in vain. Enough on this head, and now let what we have said about the nature of the created and visible gods have an end.

To know or tell the origin of the other divinities is beyond us, and we must accept the traditions of the men of old time who affirm themselves to be the offspring of the gods—that is what they say—and they must surely have known their own ancestors. How can we doubt the word of the children of the gods? Although they give no probable or certain proofs, still, as they declare that they are speaking of what took place in their own family, we must conform to custom and believe them. In this manner, then, according to them, the genealogy of these gods is to be received and set forth.

Oceanus and Tethys were the children of Earth and Heaven, and from these sprang Phorcys and Cronus and Rhea, and all that generation, and from Cronus and Rhea sprang Zeus and Hera, and all those who are said to be their brethren, and others who were the children of these.

Now, when all of them, both those who visibly appear in their revolutions as well as those other gods who are of a more retiring nature, had come into being, the creator of the universe addressed them in these words. Gods, children of gods, who are my works and of whom I am the artificer and father, my creations are indissoluble, if so I will. All that is bound may be undone, but only an evil being would wish to undo that which is harmonious and happy. Wherefore, since ye are but creatures, ye are not altogether immortal and indissoluble, but ye shall certainly not be dissolved, nor be liable to the fate of death, having in my will a greater and mightier bond than those with which ye were bound at the time of your birth. And now listen to my instructions. Three tribes of mortal beings remain to be created—without them the universe will be incomplete, for it will not contain every kind of animal which it ought to contain, if it is to be perfect. On the other hand, if they were created by me and received life at my hands, they would be on an equality with the gods. In order then that they may be mortal, and that this universe may be truly universal, do ye, according to your natures, betake yourselves to the formation of animals, imitating the power which was shown by me in creating you. The part of them worthy of the name immortal, which is called divine and is the guiding principle of those who are willing to follow justice and you—of that divine part I will myself sow the seed, and having made a beginning, I will hand the work over to you. And do ye then interweave the mortal with the immortal and make and beget living creatures, and give them food and make them to grow, and receive them again in death.

Thus he spoke, and once more into the cup in which he had previously mingled the soul of the universe he poured the remains of the elements, and mingled them in much the same manner; they were not, however, pure as before, but diluted to the second and third degree. And having made it he divided the whole mixture into souls equal in number to the stars and assigned each soul to a star, and having there placed them as in a chariot he showed them the nature of the universe and declared to them the laws of destiny, according to which their first birth would be one and the same for all—no one should suffer a disadvantage at his hands. They were to be sown in the instruments of time severally adapted to them, and to come forth the most religious of animals, and as human nature was of two kinds, the superior race was of such and such a character, and would hereafter be called man. Now, when they should be implanted in bodies by necessity and be always gaining or losing some part of their bodily substance, then, in the first place, it would be necessary that they should all have in them one and the same faculty of sensation, arising out of irresistible impressions; in the second place, they must have love, in which pleasure and pain mingle—also fear and anger, and the feelings which are akin or opposite to them. If they conquered these they would live righteously, and if they were conquered by them, unrighteously. He who lived well during his appointed time was to return and dwell in his native star, and there he would have a blessed and congenial existence. But if he failed in attaining this, at the second birth he would pass into a woman, and if, when in that state of being, he did not desist from evil, he would continually be changed into some brute who resembled him in the evil nature which he had acquired, and would not cease from his toils and transformations until he helped the revolution of the same and the like within him to draw in its train the turbulent mob of later accretions made up of fire and air and water and earth, and by this victory of reason over the irrational returned to the form of his first and better state. Having given all these laws to his creatures, that he might be guiltless of future evil in any of them, the creator sowed some of them in the earth, and some in the moon, and some in the other instruments of time. And when he had sown them he committed to the younger gods the fashioning of their mortal bodies, and desired them to furnish what was still lacking to the human soul, and having made all the suitable additions, to rule over them, and to pilot the mortal animal in the best and wisest manner which they could and avert from him all but self-inflicted evils.

When the creator had made all these ordinances he remained in his own accustomed nature, and his children heard and were obedient to their father's word, and receiving from him the immortal principle of a mortal creature, in imitation of their own creator they borrowed portions of fire and earth and water and air from the world, which were hereafter to be restored—these they took and welded them together, not with the indissoluble chains by which they were themselves bound, but with little pegs too small to be visible, making up out of all the four elements each separate body, and fastening the courses of the immortal soul in a body which was in a state of perpetual influx and efflux. Now these courses, detained as in a vast river, neither overcame nor were overcome, but were hurrying and hurried to and fro, so that the whole animal was moved and progressed, irregularly however and irrationally and anyhow, in all the six directions of motion, wandering backward and forward, and right and left, and up and down, and in all the six directions. For great as was the advancing and retiring flood which provided nourishment, the affections produced by external contact caused still greater tumult—when the body of anyone met and came into collision with some external fire or with the solid earth or the gliding waters, or was caught in the tempest borne on the air—and the motions produced by any of these impulses were carried through the body to the soul. All such motions have consequently received the general name of 'sensations,' which they still retain. And they did in fact at that time create a very great and mighty movement; uniting with the ever-flowing stream in stirring up and violently shaking the courses of the soul, they completely stopped the revolution of the same by their opposing current and hindered it from predominating and advancing, and they so disturbed the nature of the other or diverse that the three double intervals [that is, between 1, 2, 4, 8] and the three triple intervals [that is, between 1, 3, 9, 27], together with the mean terms and connecting links which are expressed by the ratios of 3:2 and 4:3 and of 9:8—these, although they cannot be wholly undone except by him who united them, were twisted by them in all sorts of ways, and the circles were broken and disordered in every possible manner, so that when they moved they were tumbling to pieces and moved irrationally, at one time in a reverse direction, and then again obliquely, and then upside down, as you might imagine a person who is upside down and has his head leaning upon the ground and his feet up against something in the air, and when he is in such a position, both he and the spectator fancy that the right of either is his left, and the left right. If, when powerfully experiencing these and similar effects, the revolutions of the soul come in contact with some external thing, either of the class of the same or of the other, they speak of the same or of the other in a manner the very opposite of the truth, and they become false and foolish, and there is no course or revolution in them which has a guiding or directing power. And if again any sensations enter in violently from without and drag after them the whole vessel of the soul, then the courses of the soul, though they seem to conquer, are really conquered.

And by reason of all these affections, the soul, when incased in a mortal body, now, as in the beginning, is at first without intelligence, but when the flood of growth and nutriment abates and the courses of the soul, calming down, go their own way and become steadier as time goes on, then the several circles return to their natural form and their revolutions are corrected, and they call the same and the other by their right names and make the possessor of them to become a rational being. And if these combine in him with any true nurture or education, he attains the fullness and health of the perfect man, and escapes the worst disease of all, but if he neglects education he walks lame to the end of his life and returns imperfect and good for nothing to the world below. This, however, is a later stage; at present we must treat more exactly the subject before us, which involves a preliminary inquiry into the generation of the body and its members, and how the soul was created—for what reason and by what providence of the gods—and holding fast to probability we must pursue our way.

First, then, the gods, imitating the spherical shape of the universe, enclosed the two divine courses in a spherical body, that, namely, which we now term the head, being the most divine part of us and the lord of all that is in us; to this the gods, when they put together the body, gave all the other members to be servants, considering that it must partake of every sort of motion. In order then that it might not tumble about among the high and deep places of the earth, but might be able to get over the one and out of the other, they provided the body to be its vehicle and means of locomotion, which consequently had length and was furnished with four limbs extended and flexible. These God contrived to be instruments of locomotion with which it might take hold and find support, and so be able to pass through all places, carrying on high the dwelling place of the most sacred and divine part of us. Such was the origin of legs and hands, which for this reason were attached to every man, and the gods, deeming the front part of man to be more honorable and more fit to command than the hinder part, made us to move mostly in a forward direction. Wherefore man must needs have his front part unlike and distinguished from the rest of his body. And so in the vessel of the head, they first of all put a face in which they inserted organs to minister in all things to the providence of the soul, and they appointed this part, which has authority, to be the natural front. And of the organs they first contrived the eyes to give light, and the principle according to which they were inserted was as follows. So much of fire as would not burn, but gave a gentle light, they formed into a substance akin to the light of everyday life, and the pure fire which is within us and related thereto they made to flow through the eyes in a stream smooth and dense, compressing the whole eye and especially the center part, so that it kept out everything of a coarser nature and allowed to pass only this pure element. When the light of day surrounds the stream of vision, then like falls upon like, and they coalesce, and one body is formed by natural affinity in the line of vision, wherever the light that falls from within meets with an external object. And the whole stream of vision, being similarly affected in virtue of similarity, diffuses the motions of what it touches or what touches it over the whole body, until they reach the soul, causing that perception which we call sight. But when night comes on and the external and kindred fire departs, then the stream of vision is cut off, for going forth to an unlike element it is changed and extinguished, being no longer of one nature with the surrounding atmosphere which is now deprived of fire, and so the eye no longer sees, and we feel disposed to sleep. For when the eyelids, which the gods invented for the preservation of sight, are closed, they keep in the internal fire, and the power of the fire diffuses and equalizes the inward motions; when they are equalized, there is rest, and when the rest is profound, sleep comes over us scarce disturbed by dreams, but where any greater motions still remain, according to their nature and locality, they engender within us corresponding visions in dreams, which are remembered by us when we awaken to the external world. And now there is no longer any difficulty in understanding the creation of images in mirrors and all smooth and bright surfaces. For from the communion of the internal and external fires, and again from the union of them and their numerous transformations when they meet in the mirror, all these appearances of necessity arise when the fire from the face coalesces with the fire from the eye on the bright and smooth surface. And right appears left and left right, because the visual rays come into contact with the rays emitted by the object in a manner contrary to the usual mode of meeting. But the right appears right, and the left left, when the position of one of the two concurring lights is reversed, and this happens when the mirror is concave and its smooth surface repels the right stream of vision to the left side, and the left to the right. Or if the mirror be turned vertically, then the concavity makes the countenance appear to be all upside down, and the lower rays are driven upward and the upper downward.

All these are to be reckoned among the second and co-operative causes which God, carrying into execution the idea of the best as far as possible, uses as his ministers. They are thought by most men not to be the second, but the prime causes of all things, because they freeze and heat, and contract and dilate, and the like. But they are not so, for they are incapable of reason or intellect; the only being which can properly have mind is the invisible soul, whereas fire and water, and earth and air, are all of them visible bodies. The lover of intellect and knowledge ought to explore causes of intelligent nature first of all, and, secondly, of those things which, being moved by others, are compelled to move others. And this is what we too must do. Both kinds of causes should be acknowledged by us, but a distinction should be made between those which are endowed with mind and are the workers of things fair and good, and those which are deprived of intelligence and always produce chance effects without order or design. Of the second or co-operative causes of sight, which help to give to the eyes the power which they now possess, enough has been said. I will therefore now proceed to speak of the higher use and purpose for which God has given them to us. The sight in my opinion is the source of the greatest benefit to us, for had we never seen the stars and the sun and the heaven, none of the words which we have spoken about the universe would ever have been uttered. But now the sight of day and night, and the months and the revolutions of the years have created number and have given us a conception of time, and the power of inquiring about the nature of the universe. And from this source we have derived philosophy, than which no greater good ever was or will be given by the gods to mortal man. This is the greatest boon of sight, and of the lesser benefits why should I speak? Even the ordinary man if he were deprived of them would bewail his loss, but in vain. Thus much let me say however. God invented and gave us sight to the end that we might behold the courses of intelligence in the heaven, and apply them to the courses of our own intelligence which are akin to them, the unperturbed to the perturbed, and that we, learning them and partaking of the natural truth of reason, might imitate the absolutely unerring courses of God and regulate our own vagaries. The same may be affirmed of speech and hearing. They have been given by the gods to the same end and for a like reason. For this is the principal end of speech, whereto it most contributes. Moreover, so much of music as is adapted to the sound of the voice and to the sense of hearing is granted to us for the sake of harmony. And harmony, which has motions akin to the revolutions of our souls, is not regarded by the intelligent votary of the Muses as given by them with a view to irrational pleasure, which is deemed to be the purpose of it in our day, but as meant to correct any discord which may have arisen in the courses of the soul, and to be our ally in bringing her into harmony and agreement with herself, and rhythm too was given by them for the same reason, on account of the irregular and graceless ways which prevail among mankind generally, and to help us against them.

Thus far in what we have been saying, with small exceptions, the works of intelligence have been set forth, and now we must place by the side of them in our discourse the things which come into being through necessity—for the creation of this world is the combined work of necessity and mind. Mind, the ruling power, persuaded necessity to bring the greater part of created things to perfection, and thus and after this manner in the beginning, through necessity made subject to reason, this universe was created. But if a person will truly tell of the way in which the work was accomplished, he must include the variable cause as well, and explain its influence. Wherefore, we must return again and find another suitable beginning—as about the former matters, so also about these. To which end we must consider the nature of fire and water and air and earth, such as they were prior to the creation of the heaven, and what was happening to them in this previous state, for no one has as yet explained the manner of their generation, but we speak of fire and the rest of them, as though men knew their natures, and we maintain them to be the first principles and letters or elements of the whole, when they cannot reasonably be compared by a man of any sense even to syllables or first compounds. And let me say thus much. I will not now speak of the first principle or principles of all things, or by whatever name they are to be called, for this reason—because it is difficult to set forth my opinion according to the method of discussion which we are at present employing. Do not imagine, any more than I can bring myself to imagine, that I should be right in undertaking so great and difficult a task. Remembering what I said at first about probability, I will do my best to give as probable an explanation as any other—or rather, more probable—and I will first go back to the beginning and try to speak of each thing and of all. Once more, then, at the commencement of my discourse, I call upon God and beg him to be our savior out of a strange and unwonted inquiry, and to bring us to the haven of probability. So now let us begin again.

This new beginning of our discussion of the universe requires a fuller division than the former, for then we made two classes; now a third must be revealed. The two sufficed for the former discussion. One, which we assumed, was a pattern intelligible and always the same, and the second was only the imitation of the pattern, generated and visible. There is also a third kind which we did not distinguish at the time, conceiving that the two would be enough. But now the argument seems to require that we should set forth in words another kind, which is difficult of explanation and dimly seen. What nature are we to attribute to this new kind of being? We reply that it is the receptacle, and in a manner the nurse, of all generation. I have spoken the truth, but I must express myself in clearer language, and this will be an arduous task for many reasons, and in particular because I must first raise questions concerning fire and the other elements, and determine what each of them is, for to say, with any probability or certitude, which of them should be called water rather than fire, and which should be called any of them rather than all or some one of them, is a difficult matter. How, then, shall we settle this point, and what questions about the elements may be fairly raised?

In the first place, we see that what we just now called water, by condensation, I suppose, becomes stone and earth, and this same element, when melted and dispersed, passes into vapor and air. Air, again, when inflamed, becomes fire, and, again, fire, when condensed and extinguished, passes once more into the form of air, and once more, air, when collected and condensed, produces cloud and mist—and from these, when still more compressed, comes flowing water, and from water comes earth and stones once more—and thus generation appears to be transmitted from one to the other in a circle. Thus, then, as the several elements never present themselves in the same form, how can anyone have the assurance to assert positively that any of them, whatever it may be, is one thing rather than another? No one can. But much the safest plan is to speak of them as follows. Anything which we see to be continually changing, as, for example, fire, we must not call 'this' or 'that,' but rather say that it is 'of such a nature,' nor let us speak of water as 'this,' but always as 'such,' nor must we imply that there is any stability in any of those things which we indicate by the use of the words 'this' and 'that,' supposing ourselves to signify something thereby, for they are too volatile to be detained in any such expressions as 'this,' or 'that,' or 'relative to this,' or any other mode of speaking which represents them as permanent. We ought not to apply 'this' to any of them, but rather the word 'such,' which expresses the similar principle circulating in each and all of them; for example, that should be called 'fire' which is of such a nature always, and so of everything that has generation. That in which the elements severally grow up, and appear, and decay, is alone to be called by the name 'this' or 'that,' but that which is of a certain nature, hot or white, or anything which admits of opposite qualities, and all things that are compounded of them, ought not to be so denominated. Let me make another attempt to explain my meaning more clearly. Suppose a person to make all kinds of figures of gold and to be always remodeling each form into all the rest; somebody points to one of them and asks what it is. By far the safest and truest answer is, 'That is gold,' and not to call the triangle or any other figures which are formed in the gold 'these,' as though they had existence, since they are in process of change while he is making the assertion, but if the questioner be willing to take the safe and indefinite expression, 'such,' we should be satisfied. And the same argument applies to the universal nature which receives all bodies—that must be always called the same, for, inasmuch as she always receives all things, she never departs at all from her own nature and never, in any way or at any time, assumes a form like that of any of the things which enter into her; she is the natural recipient of all impressions, and is stirred and informed by them, and appears different from time to time by reason of them. But the forms which enter into and go out of her are the likenesses of eternal realities modeled after their patterns in a wonderful and mysterious manner, which we will hereafter investigate. For the present we have only to conceive of three natures: first, that which is in process of generation; secondly, that in which the generation takes place; and thirdly, that of which the thing generated is a resemblance naturally produced. And we may liken the receiving principle to a mother, and the source or spring to a father, and the intermediate nature to a child, and may remark further that if the model is to take every variety of form, then the matter in which the model is fashioned will not be duly prepared unless it is formless and free from the impress of any of those shapes which it is hereafter to receive from without. For if the matter were like any of the supervening forms, then whenever any opposite or entirely different nature was stamped upon its surface, it would take the impression badly, because it would intrude its own shape. Wherefore that which is to receive all forms should have no form, as in making perfumes they first contrive that the liquid substance which is to receive the scent shall be as inodorous as possible, or as those who wish to impress figures on soft substances do not allow any previous impression to remain, but begin by making the surface as even and smooth as possible. In the same way that which is to receive perpetually and through its whole extent the resemblances of all eternal beings ought to be devoid of any particular form. Wherefore the mother and receptacle of all created and visible and in any way sensible things is not to be termed earth or air or fire or water, or any of their compounds, or any of the elements from which these are derived, but is an invisible and formless being which receives all things and in some mysterious way partakes of the intelligible, and is most incomprehensible. In saying this we shall not be far wrong; as far, however, as we can attain to a knowledge of her from the previous considerations, we may truly say that fire is that part of her nature which from time to time is inflamed, and water that which is moistened, and that the mother substance becomes earth and air, in so far as she receives the impressions of them.

Let us consider this question more precisely. Is there any self-existent fire, and do all those things which we call self-existent exist, or are only those things which we see or in some way perceive through the bodily organs truly existent, and nothing whatever besides them? And are those intelligible forms, of which we are accustomed to speak, nothing at all, and only a name? Here is a question which we must not leave unexamined or undetermined, nor must we affirm too confidently that there can be no decision; neither must we interpolate in our present long discourse a digression equally long, but if it is possible to set forth a great principle in a few words, that is just what we want.

Thus I state my view. If mind and true opinion are two distinct classes, then I say that there certainly are these self-existent ideas unperceived by sense, and apprehended only by the mind; if, however, as some say, true opinion differs in no respect from mind, then everything that we perceive through the body is to be regarded as most real and certain. But we must affirm them to be distinct, for they have a distinct origin and are of a different nature; the one is implanted in us by instruction, the other by persuasion; the one is always accompanied by true reason, the other is without reason; the one cannot be overcome by persuasion, but the other can; and lastly, every man may be said to share in true opinion, but mind is the attribute of the gods and of very few men. Wherefore also we must acknowledge that one kind of being is the form which is always the same, uncreated and indestructible, never receiving anything into itself from without, nor itself going out to any other, but invisible and imperceptible by any sense, and of which the contemplation is granted to intelligence only. And there is another nature of the same name with it, and like to it, perceived by sense, created, always in motion, becoming in place and again vanishing out of place, which is apprehended by opinion jointly with sense. And there is a third nature, which is space and is eternal, and admits not of destruction and provides a home for all created things, and is apprehended, when all sense is absent, by a kind of spurious reason, and is hardly real—which we, beholding as in a dream, say of all existence that it must of necessity be in some place and occupy a space, but that what is neither in heaven nor in earth has no existence. Of these and other things of the same kind, relating to the true and waking reality of nature, we have only this dreamlike sense, and we are unable to cast off sleep and determine the truth about them. For an image, since the reality after which it is modeled does not belong to it, and it exists ever as the fleeting shadow of some other, must be inferred to be in another [that is, in space], grasping existence in some way or other, or it could not be at all. But true and exact reason, vindicating the nature of true being, maintains that while two things [that is, the image and space] are different they cannot exist one of them in the other and so be one and also two at the same time.

Thus have I concisely given the result of my thoughts, and my verdict is that being and space and generation, these three, existed in their three ways before the heaven, and that the nurse of generation, moistened by water and inflamed by fire, and receiving the forms of earth and air, and experiencing all the affections which accompany these, presented a strange variety of appearances, and being full of powers which were neither similar nor equally balanced, was never in any part in a state of equipoise, but swaying unevenly hither and thither, was shaken by them, and by its motion again shook them, and the elements when moved were separated and carried continually, some one way, some another. As, when grain is shaken and winnowed by fans and other instruments used in the threshing of corn, the close and heavy particles are borne away and settle in one direction, and the loose and light particles in another. In this manner, the four kinds or elements were then shaken by the receiving vessel, which, moving like a winnowing machine, scattered far away from one another the elements most unlike, and forced the most similar elements into close contact. Wherefore the various elements had distinct places also before they were arranged so as to form the universe. At first, however, they were all without reason and measure. But when the world began to get into order, fire and water and earth and air did indeed show faint traces of themselves, but were altogether in such a condition as one may expect to find wherever God is absent. Such, I say, being their nature, God now fashioned them by form and number. Let it be consistently maintained by us in all that we say that God made them as far as possible the fairest and best, out of things which were not fair and good. And now I will endeavor to show you the disposition and generation of them by an unaccustomed argument which I am compelled to use. But I believe that you will be able to follow me, for your education has made you familiar with the methods of science.

In the first place, then, as is evident to all, fire and earth and water and air are bodies. And every sort of body possesses volume, and every volume must necessarily be bounded by surfaces, and every rectilinear surface is composed of triangles, and all triangles are originally of two kinds, both of which are made up of one right and two acute angles; one of them has at either end of the base the half of a divided right angle, having equal sides, while in the other the right angle is divided into unequal parts, having unequal sides. These, then, proceeding by a combination of probability with demonstration, we assume to be the original elements of fire and the other bodies, but the principles which are prior to these God only knows, and he of men who is the friend of God. And next we have to determine what are the four most beautiful bodies which could be formed, unlike one another, yet in some instances capable of resolution into one another, for having discovered thus much, we shall know the true origin of earth and fire and of the proportionate and intermediate elements. For we shall not be willing to allow that there are any distinct kinds of visible bodies fairer than these. Wherefore we must endeavor to construct the four forms of bodies which excel in beauty, and secure the right to say that we have sufficiently apprehended their nature. Now of the two triangles, the isosceles has one form only; the scalene or unequal-sided has an infinite number. Of the infinite forms we must again select the most beautiful, if we are to proceed in due order, and anyone who can point out a more beautiful form than ours for the construction of these bodies, shall carry off the palm, not as an enemy, but as a friend. Now, the one which we maintain to be the most beautiful of all the many triangles—and we need not speak of the others—is that of which the double forms a third triangle which is equilateral. The reason of this would be long to tell; he who disproves what we are saying, and shows that we are mistaken, may claim a friendly victory. Then let us choose two triangles, out of which fire and the other elements have been constructed, one isosceles, the other having the square of the longer side equal to three times the square of the lesser side.

Now is the time to explain what was before obscurely said. There was an error in imagining that all the four elements might be generated by and into one another; this, I say, was an erroneous supposition, for there are generated from the triangles which we have selected four kinds—three from the one which has the sides unequal, the fourth alone framed out of the isosceles triangle. Hence they cannot all be resolved into one another, a great number of small bodies being combined into a few large ones, or the converse. But three of them can be thus resolved and compounded, for they all spring from one, and when the greater bodies are broken up, many small bodies will spring up out of them and take their own proper figures. Or, again, when many small bodies are dissolved into their triangles, by their total number, they can form one large mass of another kind. So much for their passage into one another. I have now to speak of their several kinds, and show out of what combinations of numbers each of them was formed. The first will be the simplest and smallest construction, and its element is that triangle which has its hypotenuse twice the lesser side. When two such triangles are joined at the diagonal, and this is repeated three times, and the triangles rest their diagonals and shorter sides on the same point as a center, a single equilateral triangle is formed out of six triangles, and four equilateral triangles, if put together, make out of every three plane angles one solid angle, being that which is nearest to the most obtuse of plane angles. And out of the combination of these four angles arises the first solid form which distributes into equal and similar parts the whole circle in which it is inscribed. The second species of solid is formed out of the same triangles, which unite as eight equilateral triangles and form one solid angle out of four plane angles, and out of six such angles the second body is completed. And the third body is made up of one hundred and twenty triangular elements, forming twelve solid angles, each of them included in five plane equilateral triangles, having altogether twenty bases, each of which is an equilateral triangle. The one element [that is, the triangle which has its hypotenuse twice the lesser side], having generated these figures, generated no more, but the isosceles triangle produced the fourth elementary figure, which is compounded of four such triangles, joining their right angles in a center, and forming one equilateral quadrangle. Six of these united form eight solid angles, each of which is made by the combination of three plane right angles; the figure of the body thus composed is a cube, having six plane quadrangular equilateral bases. There was yet a fifth combination which God used in the delineation of the universe with figures of animals.

Now he who, duly reflecting on all this, inquires whether the worlds are to be regarded as indefinite or definite in number will be of opinion that the notion of their indefiniteness is characteristic of a sadly indefinite and ignorant mind. He, however, who raises the question whether they are to be truly regarded as one or five, takes up a more reasonable position. Arguing from probabilities, I am of opinion that they are one; another, regarding the question from another point of view, will be of another mind. But, leaving this inquiry, let us proceed to distribute the elementary forms, which have now been created in idea, among the four elements.

To earth, then, let us assign the cubic form, for earth is the most immovable of the four and the most plastic of all bodies, and that which has the most stable bases must of necessity be of such a nature. Now, of the triangles which we assumed at first, that which has two equal sides is by nature more firmly based than that which has unequal sides, and of the compound figures which are formed out of either, the plane equilateral quadrangle has necessarily a more stable basis than the equilateral triangle, both in the whole and in the parts. Wherefore, in assigning this figure to earth, we adhere to probability, and to water we assign that one of the remaining forms which is the least movable, and the most movable of them to fire, and to air that which is intermediate. Also we assign the smallest body to fire, and the greatest to water, and the intermediate in size to air, and, again, the acutest body to fire, and the next in acuteness to air, and the third to water. Of all these elements, that which has the fewest bases must necessarily be the most movable, for it must be the acutest and most penetrating in every way, and also the lightest as being composed of the smallest number of similar particles, and the second body has similar properties in a second degree, and the third body, in the third degree. Let it be agreed, then, both according to strict reason and according to probability, that the pyramid is the solid which is the original element and seed of fire, and let us assign the element which was next in the order of generation to air, and the third to water. We must imagine all these to be so small that no single particle of any of the four kinds is seen by us on account of their smallness, but when many of them are collected together, their aggregates are seen. And the ratios of their numbers, motions, and other properties, everywhere God, as far as necessity allowed or gave consent, has exactly perfected and harmonized in due proportion.

From all that we have just been saying about the elements or kinds, the most probable conclusion is as follows. Earth, when meeting with fire and dissolved by its sharpness, whether the dissolution take place in the fire itself or perhaps in some mass of air or water, is borne hither and thither until its parts, meeting together and mutually harmonizing, again become earth, for they can never take any other form. But water, when divided by fire or by air, on re-forming, may become one part fire and two parts air, and a single volume of air divided becomes two of fire. Again, when a small body of fire is contained in a larger body of air or water or earth, and both are moving, and the fire struggling is overcome and broken up, then two volumes of fire form one volume of air, and when air is overcome and cut up into small pieces, two and a half parts of air are condensed into one part of water. Let us consider the matter in another way. When one of the other elements is fastened upon by fire and is cut by the sharpness of its angles and sides, it coalesces with the fire, and then ceases to be cut by them any longer. For no element which is one and the same with itself can be changed by or change another of the same kind and in the same state. But so long as in the process of transition the weaker is fighting against the stronger, the dissolution continues. Again, when a few small particles, enclosed in many larger ones, are in process of decomposition and extinction, they only cease from their tendency to extinction when they consent to pass into the conquering nature, and fire becomes air and air water. But if bodies of another kind go and attack them [that is, the small particles], the latter continue to be dissolved until, being completely forced back and dispersed, they make their escape to their own kindred, or else, being overcome and assimilated to the conquering power, they remain where they are and dwell with their victors, and from being many become one. And owing to these affections, all things are changing their place, for by the motion of the receiving vessel the bulk of each class is distributed into its proper place, but those things which become unlike themselves and like other things are hurried by the shaking into the place of the things to which they grow like.

Now all unmixed and primary bodies are produced by such causes as these. As to the subordinate species which are included in the greater kinds, they are to be attributed to the varieties in the structure of the two original triangles. For either structure did not originally produce the triangle of one size only, but some larger and some smaller, and there are as many sizes as there are species of the four elements. Hence when they are mingled with themselves and with one another there is an endless variety of them, which those who would arrive at the probable truth of nature ought duly to consider.

Unless a person comes to an understanding about the nature and conditions of rest and motion, he will meet with many difficulties in the discussion which follows. Something has been said of this matter already, and something more remains to be said—which is that motion never exists in what is uniform. For to conceive that anything can be moved without a mover is hard or indeed impossible, and equally impossible to conceive that there can be a mover unless there be something which can be moved—motion cannot exist where either of these is wanting, and for these to be uniform is impossible; wherefore we must assign rest to uniformity and motion to the want of uniformity. Now inequality is the cause of the nature which is wanting in uniformity, and of this we have already described the origin. But there still remains the further point—why things when divided after their kinds do not cease to pass through one another and to change their place—which we will now proceed to explain. In the revolution of the universe are comprehended all the four elements, and this being circular and having a tendency to come together, compresses everything and will not allow any place to be left void. Wherefore also fire, above all things, penetrates everywhere, and air next, as being next in rarity of the elements, and the two other elements in like manner penetrate according to their degrees of rarity. For those things which are composed of the largest particles have the largest void left in their compositions, and those which are composed of the smallest particles have the least. And the contraction caused by the compression thrusts the smaller particles into the interstices of the larger. And thus, when the small parts are placed side by side with the larger, and the lesser divide the greater and the greater unite the lesser, all the elements are borne up and down and hither and thither toward their own places, for the change in the size of each changes its position in space. And these causes generate an inequality which is always maintained, and is continually creating a perpetual motion of the elements in all time.

In the next place we have to consider, first, that there are diverse kinds of fire. There are, for example, first, flame, secondly, those emanations of flame which do not burn but only give light to the eyes, and thirdly, the remains of fire, which are seen in red-hot embers after the flame has been extinguished. There are similar differences in the air, of which the brightest part is called the aether, and the most turbid sort mist and darkness, and there are various other nameless kinds which arise from the inequality of the triangles. Water, again, admits in the first place of a division into two kinds, the one liquid and the other fusile. The liquid kind is composed of the small and unequal particles of water, and moves itself and is moved by other bodies owing to the want of uniformity and the shape of its particles, whereas the fusile kind, being formed of large and uniform particles, is more stable than the other and is heavy and compact by reason of its uniformity. But when fire gets in and dissolves the particles and destroys the uniformity, it has greater mobility, and becoming fluid is thrust forth by the neighboring air and spreads upon the earth, and this dissolution of the solid masses is called melting, and their spreading out upon the earth flowing. Again, when the fire goes out of the fusile substance, it does not pass into a vacuum, but into the neighboring air, and the air which is displaced forces together the liquid and still movable mass into the place which was occupied by the fire, and unites it with itself. Thus compressed the mass resumes its equability, and is again at unity with itself, because the fire which was the author of the inequality has retreated, and this departure of the fire is called cooling, and the coming together which follows upon it is termed congealment. Of all the kinds termed fusile, that which is the densest and is formed out of the finest and most uniform parts is that most precious possession called gold, which is hardened by filtration through rock; this is unique in kind, and has both a glittering and a yellow color. A shoot of gold, which is so dense as to be very hard, and takes a black color, is termed adamant. There is also another kind which has parts nearly like gold, and of which there are several species; it is denser than gold, and it contains a small and fine portion of earth and is therefore harder, yet also lighter because of the great interstices which it has within itself, and this substance, which is one of the bright and denser kinds of water, when solidified is called copper. There is an alloy of earth mingled with it which, when the two parts grow old and are disunited, shows itself separately and is called rust. The remaining phenomena of the same kind there will be no difficulty in reasoning out by the method of probabilities. A man may sometimes set aside meditations about eternal things, and for recreation turn to consider the truths of generation, which are probable only; he will thus gain a pleasure not to be repented of, and secure for himself, while he lives, a wise and moderate pastime. Let us grant ourselves this indulgence and go through the probabilities relating to the same subjects which follow next in order.

Water which is mingled with fire, so much as is fine and liquid—being so called by reason of its motion and the way in which it rolls along the ground—and soft, because its bases give way and are less stable than those of earth, when separated from fire and air and isolated, becomes more uniform, and by their retirement is compressed into itself. And if the condensation be very great, the water above the earth becomes hail, but on the earth, ice, and that which is congealed in a less degree and is only half solid, when above the earth is called snow, and when upon the earth and condensed from dew, hoarfrost. Then, again, there are the numerous kinds of water which have been mingled with one another and are distilled through plants which grow in the earth, and this whole class is called by the names of juices or saps. The unequal admixture of these fluids creates a variety of species—most of them are nameless, but four which are of a fiery nature are clearly distinguished and have names. First, there is wine, which warms the soul as well as the body; secondly, there is the oily nature, which is smooth and divides the visual ray, and for this reason is bright and shining and of a glistening appearance, including pitch, the juice of the castorberry, oil itself, and other things of a like kind; thirdly, there is the class of substances which expand the contracted parts of the mouth, until they return to their natural state, and by reason of this property create sweetness—these are included under the general name of honey; and, lastly, there is a frothy nature which differs from all juices, having a burning quality which dissolves the flesh and is called *opos* [a vegetable acid].

As to the kinds of earth, that which is filtered through water passes into stone in the following manner. The water which mixes with the earth and is broken up in the process changes into air, and taking this form mounts into its own place. But as there is no surrounding vacuum it thrusts away the neighboring air, and this being rendered heavy, and, when it is displaced, having been poured around the mass of earth, forcibly compresses it and drives it into the vacant space whence the new air had come up, and the earth when compressed by the air into an indissoluble union with water becomes rock. The fairer sort is that which is made up of equal and similar parts and is transparent; that which has the opposite qualities is inferior. But when all the watery part is suddenly drawn out by fire, a more brittle substance is formed to which we give the name of pottery. Sometimes also moisture may remain, and the earth which has been fused by fire becomes, when cool, a certain stone of a black color. A like separation of the water which had been copiously mingled with them may occur in two substances composed of finer particles of earth and of a briny nature; out of either of them a half-solid body is then formed, soluble in water—the one, soda, which is used for purging away oil and earth, the other, salt, which harmonizes so well in combinations pleasing to the palate, and is, as the law testifies, a substance dear to the gods. The compounds of earth and water are not soluble by water, but by fire only, and for this reason. Neither fire nor air melts masses of earth, for their particles, being smaller than the interstices in its structure, have plenty of room to move without forcing their way, and so they leave the earth unmelted and undissolved, but particles of water, which are larger, force a passage and dissolve and melt the earth. Wherefore earth when not consolidated by force is dissolved by water only; when consolidated, by nothing but fire, for this is the only body which can find an entrance. The cohesion of water again, when very strong, is dissolved by fire only; when weaker, then either by air or fire—the former entering the interstices, and the latter penetrating even the triangles. But nothing can dissolve air, when strongly condensed, which does not reach the elements or triangles, or if not strongly condensed, then only fire can dissolve it. As to bodies composed of earth and water, while the water occupies the vacant interstices of the earth in them which are compressed by force, the particles of water which approach them from without, finding no entrance, flow around the entire mass and leave it undissolved, but the particles of fire enter into the interstices of the water and fire does to water what water does to earth. Such particles are the sole causes of the compound body of earth and water liquefying and becoming fluid. Now these bodies are of two kinds. Some of them, such as glass and the fusible sort of stones, have less water than they have earth; on the other hand, substances of the nature of wax and incense have more of water entering into their composition.

I have thus shown the various classes of bodies as they are diversified by their forms and combinations and changes into one another, and now I must endeavor to set forth their affections and the causes of them. In the first place, the bodies which I have been describing are necessarily objects of sense. But we have not yet considered the origin of flesh, or what belongs to flesh, or of that part of the soul which is mortal. And these things cannot be adequately explained without also explaining the affections which are concerned with sensation, nor the latter without the former, and yet to explain them together is hardly possible, for which reason we must assume first one or the other and afterward examine the nature of our hypothesis. In order, then, that the affections may follow regularly after the elements, let us presuppose the existence of body and soul.

First, let us inquire what we mean by saying that fire is hot, and about this we may reason from the dividing or cutting power which it exercises on our bodies. We all of us feel that fire is sharp, and we may further consider the fineness of the sides, and the sharpness of the angles, and the smallness of the particles, and the swiftness of the motion—all this makes the action of fire violent and sharp, so that it cuts whatever it meets. And we must not forget that the original figure of fire [that is, the pyramid], more than any other form, has a dividing power which cuts our bodies into small pieces (κερματίζει), and thus naturally produces that affection which we call heat, and hence the origin of the name (θερμός, κέρμα). Now, the opposite of this is sufficiently manifest; nevertheless we will not fail to describe it. For the larger particles of moisture which surround the body, entering in and driving out the lesser, but not being able to take their places, compress the moist principle in us, and this, from being unequal and disturbed, is forced by them into a state of rest which is due to equability and compression. But things which are contracted contrary to nature are by nature at war and force themselves apart, and to this war and convulsion the name of shivering and trembling is given, and the whole affection and the cause of the affection are both termed cold. That is called hard to which our flesh yields, and soft which yields to our flesh, and things are also termed hard and soft relatively to one another. That which yields has a small base, but that which rests on quadrangular bases is firmly posed and belongs to the class which offers the greatest resistance; so, too, does that which is the most compact and therefore most repellent. The nature of the light and the heavy will be best understood when examined in connection with our notions of above and below, for it is quite a mistake to suppose that the universe is parted into two regions, separate from and opposite to each other—the one a lower to which all things tend which have any bulk, and an upper to which things only ascend against their will. For as the universe is in the form of a sphere, all the extremities, being equidistant from the center, are equally extremities, and the center, which is equidistant from them, is equally to be regarded as the opposite of them all. Such being the nature of the world, when a person says that any of these points is above or below, may he not be justly charged with using an improper expression? For the center of the world cannot be rightly called either above or below, but is the center and nothing else, and the circumference is not the center, and has in no one part of itself a different relation to the center from what it has in any of the opposite parts. Indeed, when it is in every direction similar, how can one rightly give to it names which imply opposition? For if there were any solid body in equipoise at the center of the universe, there would be nothing to draw it to this extreme rather than to that, for they are all perfectly similar, and if a person were to go round the world in a circle, he would often, when standing at the antipodes of his former position, speak of the same point as above and below. For, as I was saying just now, to speak of the whole which is in the form of a globe as having one part above and another below is not like a sensible man. The reason why these names are used, and the circumstances under which they are ordinarily applied by us to the division of the heavens, may be elucidated by the following supposition. If a person were to stand in that part of the universe which is the appointed place of fire, and where there is the great mass of fire to which fiery bodies gather—if, I say, he were to ascend thither, and, having the power to do this, were to abstract particles of fire and put them in scales and weigh them, and then, raising the balance, were to draw the fire by force toward the uncongenial element of the air, it would be very evident that he could compel the smaller mass more readily than the larger, for when two things are simultaneously raised by one and the same power, the smaller body must necessarily yield to the superior power with less reluctance than the larger, and the larger body is called heavy and said to tend downward, and the smaller body is called light and said to tend upward. And we may detect ourselves who are upon the earth doing precisely the same thing. For we often separate earthy natures, and sometimes earth itself, and draw them into the uncongenial element of air by force and contrary to nature, both clinging to their kindred elements. But that which is smaller yields to the impulse given by us toward the dissimilar element more easily than the larger, and so we call the former light, and the place toward which it is impelled we call above, and the contrary state and place we call heavy and below, respectively. Now the relations of these must necessarily vary because the principal masses of the different elements hold opposite positions, for that which is light, heavy, below, or above in one place will be found to be and become contrary and transverse and every way diverse in relation to that which is light, heavy, below, or above in an opposite place. And about all of them this has to be considered—that in some cases the tendency of each toward its kindred element makes the body which is moved heavy, and the place toward which the motion tends below, but things which have an opposite tendency we call by an opposite name. Such are the causes which we assign to these phenomena. As to the smooth and the rough, anyone who sees them can explain the reason of them to another. For roughness is hardness mingled with irregularity, and smoothness is produced by the joint effect of uniformity and density.

The most important of the affections which concern the whole body remains to be considered—that is, the cause of pleasure and pain in the perceptions of which I have been speaking, and in all other things which are perceived by sense through the parts of the body, and have both pains and pleasures attendant on them. Let us imagine the causes of every affection, whether of sense or not, to be of the following nature, remembering that we have already distinguished between the nature which is easy and which is hard to move, for this is the direction in which we must hunt the prey which we mean to take. A body which is of a nature to be easily moved, on receiving an impression however slight, spreads abroad the motion in a circle, the parts communicating with each other, until at last, reaching the principle of mind, they announce the quality of the agent. But a body of the opposite kind, being immobile and not extending to the surrounding region, merely receives the impression and does not stir any of the neighboring parts, and since the parts do not distribute the original impression to other parts, it has no effect of motion on the whole animal, and therefore produces no effect on the patient. This is true of the bones and hair and other more earthy parts of the human body, whereas what was said above relates mainly to sight and hearing because they have in them the greatest amount of fire and air. Now we must conceive of pleasure and pain in this way. An impression produced in us contrary to nature and violent, if sudden, is painful, and, again, the sudden return to nature is pleasant, but a gentle and gradual return is imperceptible and vice versa. On the other hand, the impression of sense which is easily produced is most readily felt, but is not accompanied by pleasure or pain; such, for example, are the affections of the sight, which, as we said above, is a body naturally uniting with our body in the daytime, for cuttings and burnings and other affections which happen to the sight do not give pain, nor is there pleasure when the sight returns to its natural state; yet very clear and strong sensations arise for every affection of sight, whether the eye is passive or is deliberately turned upon an object. The reason is that no violence at all is involved in the separation and reunion of the visual ray. But bodies formed of larger particles yield to the agent only with a struggle, and then they impart their motions to the whole and cause pleasure and pain—pain when alienated from their natural conditions, and pleasure when restored to them. Things which experience gradual withdrawings and emptyings of their nature, and great and sudden replenishments, fail to perceive the emptying, but are sensible of the replenishment, and so they occasion no pain, but the greatest pleasure, to the mortal part of the soul, as is manifest in the case of perfumes. But things which are changed all of a sudden, and only gradually and with difficulty return to their own nature, have effects in every way opposite to the former, as is evident in the case of burnings and cuttings of the body.

Thus have we discussed the general affections of the whole body, and the names of the agents which produce them. And now I will endeavor to speak of the affections of particular parts, and the causes and agents of them, as far as I am able. In the first place, let us set forth what was omitted when we were speaking of juices, concerning the affections peculiar to the tongue. These too, like most of the other affections, appear to be caused by certain contractions and dilations, but they have besides more of roughness and smoothness than is found in other affections, for whenever earthy particles enter into the small veins which are the testing instruments of the tongue, reaching to the heart, and fall upon the moist, delicate portions of flesh—when, as they are dissolved, they contract and dry up the little veins, they are astringent if they are rougher, but if not so rough, then only harsh. Those particles which act upon these veins as an abstergent, and purge the whole surface of the tongue, if they do it in excess and so encroach as to consume some part of the flesh itself, like potash and soda, are all termed bitter. But the particles which are deficient in the alkaline quality, and which cleanse only moderately, are called salt, and having no bitterness or roughness are regarded as rather agreeable than otherwise. Bodies which share in and are made smooth by the heat of the mouth, and which are inflamed and again in turn inflame that which heats them, and which are so light that they are carried upward to the sensations of the head and cut all that comes in their way, by reason of these qualities in them, are all termed pungent. There are other particles which, previously refined by putrefaction, enter into the narrow veins, and being duly proportioned to the particles of earth and air which are there, set them whirling about one another, and while they are in a whirl cause them to dash against and enter into one another, and so form hollows surrounding the particles that enter. These watery vessels of air—for a film of moisture, sometimes earthy, sometimes pure, is spread around the air—are hollow spheres of water, and those of them which are pure are transparent and are called bubbles, while those composed of the earthy liquid, which is in a state of general agitation and effervescence, are said to boil or ferment. Of all these affections the cause is termed acid. And there is the opposite affection arising from an opposite cause, when the mass of entering particles, immersed in the moisture of the mouth, is congenial to the tongue, and smooths and oils over the roughness, and relaxes the parts which are unnaturally contracted, and contracts the parts which are relaxed, and disposes them all according to their nature—that sort of remedy of violent affections is pleasant and agreeable to every man, and has the name sweet. But enough of this.

The faculty of smell does not admit of differences of kind, for all smells are of a half-formed nature, and no element is so proportioned as to have any smell. The veins about the nose are too narrow to admit earth and water, and too wide to detain fire and air, and for this reason no one ever perceives the smell of any of them. But smells always proceed from bodies that are damp, or putrefying, or liquefying, or evaporating, and are perceptible only in the intermediate state, when water is changing into air and air into water, and all of them are either vapor or mist. That which is passing out of air into water is mist, and that which is passing from water into air is vapor, and hence all smells are thinner than water and thicker than air. The proof of this is that when there is any obstruction to the respiration and a man draws in his breath by force, then no smell filters through, but the air without the smell alone penetrates. Wherefore the varieties of smell have no name, and they have not many or definite and simple kinds, but they are distinguished only as painful and pleasant, the one sort irritating and disturbing the whole cavity which is situated between the head and the navel, the other having a soothing influence and restoring this same region to an agreeable and natural condition.

In considering the third kind of sense, hearing, we must speak of the causes in which it originates. We may in general assume sound to be a blow which passes through the ears, and is transmitted by means of the air, the brain, and the blood, to the soul, and that hearing is the vibration of this blow which begins in the head and ends in the region of the liver. The sound which moves swiftly is acute, and the sound which moves slowly is grave, and that which is regular is equable and smooth, and the reverse is harsh. A great body of sound is loud, and a small body of sound the reverse. Respecting the harmonies of sound I must hereafter speak.

There is a fourth class of sensible things, having many intricate varieties, which must now be distinguished. They are called by the general name of colors and are a flame which emanates from every sort of body, and has particles corresponding to the sense of sight. I have spoken already, in what has preceded, of the causes which generate sight, and in this place it will be natural and suitable to give a rational theory of colors.

Of the particles coming from other bodies which fall upon the sight, some are smaller and some are larger, and some are equal to the parts of the sight itself. Those which are equal are imperceptible, and we call them transparent. The larger produce contraction, the smaller dilation, in the sight, exercising a power akin to that of hot and cold bodies on the flesh, or of astringent bodies on the tongue, or of those heating bodies which we termed pungent. White and black are similar effects of contraction and dilation in another sphere, and for this reason have a different appearance. Wherefore we ought to term white that which dilates the visual ray, and the opposite of this black. There is also a swifter motion of a different sort of fire which strikes and dilates the ray of sight until it reaches the eyes, forcing a way through their passages and melting them, and eliciting from them a union of fire and water which we call tears, being itself an opposite fire which comes to them from an opposite direction—the inner fire flashes forth like lightning, and the outer finds a way in and is extinguished in the moisture, and all sorts of colors are generated by the mixture. This affection is termed dazzling, and the object which produces it is called bright and flashing. There is another sort of fire which is intermediate and which reaches and mingles with the moisture of the eye without flashing, and in this the fire, mingling with the ray of the moisture, produces a color like blood, to which we give the name of red. A bright hue mingled with red and white gives the color called auburn (ξανθόν). The law of proportion, however, according to which the several colors are formed, even if a man knew he would be foolish in telling, for he could not give any necessary reason, nor indeed any tolerable or probable explanation of them. Again, red, when mingled with black and white, becomes purple, but it becomes umber (ὄρφνινον) when the colors are burned as well as mingled and the black is more thoroughly mixed with them. Flame color (πυρρόν) is produced by a union of auburn and dun (φαιόν), dun by an admixture of black and white, and pale yellow (ὠχρόν) by an admixture of white and auburn. White and bright meeting, and falling upon a full black, become dark blue(κμανοῦυ), and when dark blue mingles with white, a light blue (γλαυκόν) color is formed, as flame color with black makes leek-green (πράσιον). There will be no difficulty in seeing how and by what mixtures the colors derived from these are made according to the rules of probability. He, however, who should attempt to verify all this by experiment would forget the difference of the human and divine nature. For God only has the knowledge and also the power which are able to combine many things into one and again resolve the one into many. But no man either is or ever will be able to accomplish either the one or the other operation.

These are the elements, thus of necessity then subsisting, which the creator of the fairest and best of created things associated with himself when he made the self-sufficing and most perfect god, using the necessary causes as his ministers in the accomplishment of his work, but himself contriving the good in all his creations. Wherefore we may distinguish two sorts of causes, the one divine and the other necessary, and may seek for the divine in all things, as far as our nature admits, with a view to the blessed life, but the necessary kind only for the sake of the divine, considering that without them and when isolated from them, these higher things for which we look cannot be apprehended or received or in any way shared by us.

Seeing, then, that we have now prepared for our use the various classes of causes which are the material out of which the remainder of our discourse must be woven, just as wood is the material of the carpenter, let us revert in a few words to our beginning, and hasten back to the point from which we set out on our road hither. We may then endeavor to crown our tale with a suitable conclusion.

As I said at first, when all things were in disorder, God created in each thing in relation to itself, and in all things in relation to each other, all the measures and harmonies which they could possibly receive. For in those days nothing had any proportion except by accident, nor was there anything deserving to be called by the names which we now use—as, for example, fire, water, and the rest of the elements. All these the creator first set in order, and out of them he constructed the universe, which was a single animal comprehending in itself all other animals, mortal and immortal. Now of the divine, he himself was the creator, but the creation of the mortal he committed to his offspring. And they, imitating him, received from him the immortal principle of the soul, and around this they proceeded to fashion a mortal body, and made it to be the vehicle of the soul, and constructed within the body a soul of another nature which was mortal, subject to terrible and irresistible affections—first of all, pleasure, the greatest incitement to evil; then, pain, which deters from good; also rashness and fear, two foolish counselors, anger hard to be appeased, and hope easily led astray—these they mingled with irrational sense and with all-daring love according to necessary laws, and so framed man. Wherefore, fearing to pollute the divine any more than was absolutely unavoidable, they gave to the mortal nature a separate habitation in another part of the body, placing the neck between them to be the isthmus and boundary, which they constructed between the head and breast, to keep them apart. And in the breast, and in what is termed the thorax, they incased the mortal soul, and as the one part of this was superior and the other inferior they divided the cavity of the thorax into two parts, as the women's and men's apartments are divided in houses, and placed the midriff to be a wall of partition between them. That part of the inferior soul which is endowed with courage and passion and loves contention, they settled nearer the head, midway between the midriff and the neck, in order that being obedient to the rule of reason it might join with it in controlling and restraining the desires when they are no longer willing of their own accord to obey the word of command issuing from the citadel.

The heart, the knot of the veins and the fountain of the blood which races through all the limbs, was set in the place of guard, that, when the might of passion was roused by reason making proclamation of any wrong assailing them from without or being perpetrated by the desires within, quickly the whole power of feeling in the body, perceiving these commands and threats, might obey and follow through every turn and alley, and thus allow the principle of the best to have the command in all of them. But the gods, foreknowing that the palpitation of the heart in the expectation of danger and excitement of passion must cause it to swell and become inflamed, formed and implanted as a supporter to the heart the lung, which was, in the first place, soft and bloodless, and also had within hollows like the pores of a sponge, in order that by receiving the breath and the drink, it might give coolness and the power of respiration and alleviate the heat. Wherefore they cut the air channels leading to the lung, and placed the lung about the heart as a soft spring, that, when passion was rife within, the heart, beating against a yielding body, might be cooled and suffer less, and might thus become more ready to join with passion in the service of reason.

The part of the soul which desires meats and drinks and the other things of which it has need by reason of the bodily nature, they placed between the midriff and the boundary of the navel, contriving in all this region a sort of manger for the food of the body, and there they bound it down like a wild animal which was chained up with man, and must be nourished if man was to exist. They appointed this lower creation his place here in order that he might be always feeding at the manger, and have his dwelling as far as might be from the council chamber, making as little noise and disturbance as possible, and permitting the best part to advise quietly for the good of the whole and the individual. And knowing that this lower principle in man would not comprehend reason, and even if attaining to some degree of perception would never naturally care for rational notions, but that it would be especially led by phantoms and visions night and day—planning to make this very weakness serve a purpose, God combined with it the liver and placed it in the house of the lower nature, contriving that it should be solid and smooth, and bright and sweet, and should also have a bitter quality in order that the power of thought, which proceeds from the mind, might be reflected as in a mirror which receives likenesses of objects and gives back images of them to the sight, and so might strike terror into the desires when, making use of the bitter part of the liver, to which it is akin, it comes threatening and invading, and diffusing this bitter element swiftly through the whole liver produces colors like bile, and contracting every part makes it wrinkled and rough, and twisting out of its right place and contorting the lobe and closing and shutting up the vessels and gates causes pain and loathing. And the converse happens when some gentle inspiration of the understanding pictures images of an opposite character, and allays the bile and bitterness by refusing to stir or touch the nature opposed to itself, but by making use of the natural sweetness of the liver corrects all things and makes them to be right and smooth and free, and renders the portion of the soul which resides about the liver happy and joyful, enabling it to pass the night in peace, and to practice divination in sleep, inasmuch as it has no share in mind and reason. For the authors of our being, remembering the command of their father when he bade them create the human race as good as they could, that they might correct our inferior parts and make them to attain a measure of truth, placed in the liver the seat of divination. And herein is a proof that God has given the art of divination not to the wisdom, but to the foolishness of man. No man, when in his wits, attains prophetic truth and inspiration, but when he receives the inspired word, either his intelligence is enthralled in sleep or he is demented by some distemper or possession. And he who would understand what he remembers to have been said, whether in a dream or when he was awake, by the prophetic and inspired nature, or would determine by reason the meaning of the apparitions which he has seen, and what indications they afford to this man or that, of past, present, or future good and evil, must first recover his wits. But, while he continues demented, he cannot judge of the visions which he sees or the words which he utters; the ancient saying is very true—that 'only a man who has his wits can act or judge about himself and his own affairs.' And for this reason it is customary to appoint interpreters to be judges of the true inspiration. Some persons call them prophets, being blind to the fact that they are only the expositors of dark sayings and visions, and are not to be called prophets at all, but only interpreters of prophecy.

Such is the nature of the liver, which is placed as we have described in order that it may give prophetic intimations. During the life of each individual these intimations are plainer, but after his death the liver becomes blind and delivers oracles too obscure to be intelligible. The neighboring organ [the spleen] is situated on the left-hand side and is constructed with a view of keeping the liver bright and pure—like a napkin, always ready-prepared and at hand to clean the mirror. And hence, when any impurities arise in the region of the liver by reason of disorders of the body, the loose nature of the spleen, which is composed of a hollow and bloodless tissue, receives them all and clears them away, and when filled with the unclean matter, it swells and festers, but, again, when the body is purged, shrinks and settles down into the same place as before.

Concerning the soul, as to which part is mortal and which divine, and how and why they are separated, and in what company they are placed, if God acknowledges that we have spoken the truth, then, and then only, can we be confident; still, we may venture to assert that what has been said by us is probable, and will be rendered more probable by investigation. Let us assume thus much.

The creation of the rest of the body follows next in order, and this we may investigate in a similar manner. And it appears to be very meet that the body should be framed on the following principles.

The authors of our race were aware that we should be intemperate in eating and drinking and take a good deal more than was necessary or proper, by reason of gluttony. In order then that disease might not quickly destroy us, and lest our mortal race should perish without fulfilling its end—intending to provide against this, the gods made what is called the lower belly, to be a receptacle for the superfluous meat and drink, and formed the convolution of the bowels, so that the food might be prevented from passing quickly through and compelling the body to require more food, thus producing insatiable gluttony and making the whole race an enemy to philosophy and culture, and rebellious against the divinest element within us.

The bones and flesh, and other similar parts of us, were made as follows. The first principle of all of them was the generation of the marrow. For the bonds of life which unite the soul with the body are made fast there, and they are the root and foundation of the human race. The marrow itself is created out of other materials. God took such of the primary triangles as were straight and smooth and were adapted to produce fire and water, and air and earth in the highest perfection—these, I say, he separated from their kinds, and mingling them in due proportions with one another, made the marrow out of them to be a universal seed of every mortal kind, and in this seed he then planted and enclosed the souls, and in the original distribution gave to the marrow as many and various forms as the different kinds of souls were hereafter to receive. That which, like a field, was to receive the divine seed, he made round every way, and called that portion of the marrow 'brain,' intending that, when an animal was perfected, the vessel containing this substance should be the head, but that which was intended to contain the remaining and mortal part of the soul he distributed into figures at once round and elongated, and he called them all by the name 'marrow.' And to these, as to anchors, fastening the bonds of the whole soul, he proceeded to fashion around them the entire framework of our body, constructing for the marrow, first of all, a complete covering of bone.

Bone was composed by him in the following manner. Having sifted pure and smooth earth he kneaded it and wetted it with marrow, and after that he put it into fire and then into water, and once more into fire and again into water—in this way, by frequent transfers from one to the other, he made it insoluble by either. Out of this he fashioned, as in a lathe, a globe made of bone, which he placed around the brain, and in this he left a narrow opening, and around the marrow of the neck and back he formed vertebrae which he placed under one another like pivots, beginning at the head and extending through the whole of the trunk. Thus wishing to preserve the entire seed, he enclosed it in a stonelike casing, inserting joints, and using in the formation of them the power of the other or diverse as an intermediate nature, that they might have motion and flexure. Then again, considering that the bone would be too brittle and inflexible, and when heated and again cooled would soon mortify and destroy the seed within—having this in view, he contrived the sinews and the flesh, that so binding all the members together by the sinews, which admitted of being stretched and relaxed about the vertebrae, he might thus make the body capable of flection and extension, while the flesh would serve as a protection against the summer heat and against the winter cold, and also against falls, softly and easily yielding to external bodies, like articles made of felt, and containing in itself a warm moisture which in summer exudes and makes the surface damp, would impart a natural coolness to the whole body, and again in winter by the help of this internal warmth would form a very tolerable defense against the frost which surrounds it and attacks it from without. He who modeled us, considering these things, mixed earth with fire and water and blended them, and making a ferment of acid and salt, he mingled it with them and formed soft and succulent flesh. As for the sinews, he made them of a mixture of bone and unfermented flesh, attempered so as to be in a mean, and gave them a yellow color; wherefore the sinews have a firmer and more glutinous nature than flesh, but a softer and moister nature than the bones. With these God covered the bones and marrow, binding them together by sinews, and then enshrouded them all in an upper covering of flesh. The more living and sensitive of the bones he enclosed in the thinnest film of flesh, and those which had the least life within them in the thickest and most solid flesh. So again on the joints of the bones, where reason indicated that no more was required, he placed only a thin covering of flesh, that it might not interfere with the flection of our bodies and make them unwieldy because difficult to move, and also that it might not, by being crowded and pressed and matted together, destroy sensation by reason of its hardness, and impair the memory and dull the edge of intelligence. Wherefore also the thighs and the shanks and the hips, and the bones of the arms and the forearms, and other parts which have no joints, and the inner bones, which on account of the rarity of the soul in their marrow are destitute of reason—all these are abundantly provided with flesh, but such as have mind in them are in general less fleshy, except where the creator has made some part solely of flesh in order to give sensation—as, for example, the tongue. But commonly this is not the case. For the nature which comes into being and grows up in us by a law of necessity does not admit of the combination of solid bone and much flesh with acute perceptions. More than any other part, the framework of the head would have had them if they could have coexisted, and the human race, having a strong and fleshy and sinewy head, would have had a life twice or many times as long as it now has, and also more healthy and free from pain. But our creators, considering whether they should make a longer-lived race which was worse, or a shorter-lived race which was better, came to the conclusion that everyone ought to prefer a shorter span of life, which was better, to a longer one, which was worse, and therefore they covered the head with thin bone, but not with flesh and sinews, since it had no joints, and thus the head was added, having more wisdom and sensation than the rest of the body, but also being in every man far weaker. For these reasons and after this manner God placed the sinews at the extremity of the head, in a circle round the neck, and glued them together by the principle of likeness and fastened the extremities of the jawbones to them below the face, and the other sinews he dispersed throughout the body, fastening limb to limb. The framers of us framed the mouth, as now arranged, having teeth and tongue and lips, with a view to the necessary and the good, contriving the way in for necessary purposes, the way out for the best purposes. For that is necessary which enters in and gives food to the body, but the river of speech, which flows out of a man and ministers to the intelligence, is the fairest and noblest of all streams. Still the head could neither be left a bare frame of bones, on account of the extremes of heat and cold in the different seasons, nor yet be allowed to be wholly covered and so become dull and senseless by reason of an overgrowth of flesh. The fleshy nature was not therefore wholly dried up, but a large sort of peel was parted off and remained over, which is now called the skin. This met and grew by the help of the cerebral moisture, and became the circular envelopment of the head. And the moisture, rising up under the sutures, watered and closed in the skin upon the crown, forming a sort of knot. The diversity of the sutures was caused by the power of the courses within the soul and of the food; the sutures were more numerous where these were strongly opposed to one another, fewer if the struggle were less violent. This skin the divine power pierced all round with fire, and out of the punctures which were thus made the moisture issued forth, and the liquid and heat which was pure came away, and a mixed part which was composed of the same material as the skin, and had a fineness equal to the punctures, was borne up by its own impulse and extended far outside the head, but, being too slow to escape, was thrust back by the external air and rolled up underneath the skin, where it took root. Thus the hair sprang up in the skin, being akin to it because it is like threads of leather, but rendered harder and closer through the pressure of the cold, by which each hair, while in process of separation from the skin, is compressed and cooled. Wherefore the creator formed the head hairy, making use of the causes which I have mentioned, and reflecting also that instead of flesh the brain needed the hair to be a light covering or guard which would give shade in summer and shelter in winter, and at the same time would not impede our quickness of perception. From the combination of sinew, skin, and bone, in the structure of the finger, there arises a triple compound which, when dried up, takes the form of one hard skin partaking of all three natures, and was fabricated by these second causes, but designed by mind which is the principal cause with an eye to the future. For our creators well knew that women and other animals would someday be framed out of men, and they further knew that many animals would require the use of nails for many purposes; wherefore they fashioned in men at their first creation the rudiments of nails. For this purpose and for these reasons they caused skin, hair, and nails to grow at the extremities of the limbs.

And now that all the parts and members of the mortal animal had come together, since its life of necessity consisted of fire and breath, and it therefore wasted away by dissolution and depletion, the gods contrived the following remedy. They mingled a nature akin to that of man with other forms and perceptions and thus created another kind of animal. These are the trees and plants and seeds which have been improved by cultivation and are now domesticated among us; anciently there were only the wild kinds, which are older than the cultivated. For everything that partakes of life may be truly called a living being, and the animal of which we are now speaking partakes of the third kind of soul, which is said to be seated between the midriff and the navel, having no part in opinion or reason or mind, but only in feelings of pleasure and pain and the desires which accompany them. For this nature is always in a passive state, and is not endowed by nature with the power of revolving in and about itself, repelling the motion from without and using its own, in such a way as to observe and reflect upon any of its own concerns. Wherefore it lives and does not differ from a living being, but is fixed and rooted in the same spot, having no power of self-motion.

Now after the superior powers had created all these natures to be food for us who are of the inferior nature, they cut various channels through the body as through a garden, that it might be watered as from a running stream. In the first place, they cut two hidden channels or veins down the back where the skin and the flesh join, which answered severally to the right and left side of the body. These they let down along the backbone, so as to have the marrow of generation between them, where it was most likely to flourish, and in order that the stream coming down from above might flow freely to the other parts, and equalize the irrigation. In the next place, they divided the veins about the head, and interlacing them, they sent them in opposite directions; those coming from the right side they sent to the left of the body, and those from the left they diverted toward the right, so that they and the skin might together form a bond which should fasten the head to the body, since the crown of the head was not encircled by sinews, and also in order that the sensations from both sides might be distributed over the whole body. And next, they ordered the watercourses of the body in a manner which I will describe, and which will be more easily understood if we begin by admitting that all things composed of lesser parts retain the greater, but those composed of greater parts cannot retain the lesser. Now of all natures fire has the smallest parts, and therefore penetrates through earth and water and air and their compounds, nor can anything hold it. And a similar principle applies to the human belly, for when meats and drinks enter it, it holds them, but it cannot hold air and fire because the particles of which they consist are smaller than its own structure.

These elements, therefore, God employed for the sake of distributing moisture from the belly into the veins, weaving together a network of fire and air like a creel, having at the entrance two lesser creels; further he constructed one of these with two openings, and from the lesser creels he extended cords reaching all round to the extremities of the network. All the interior of the net he made of fire, but the lesser creels and their cavity, of air. The network he took and spread over the newly formed animal in the following manner. He let the lesser creels pass into the mouth; there were two of them, and one he let down by the air pipes into the lungs, the other by the side of the air pipes into the belly. The former he divided into two branches, both of which he made to pass out at the channels of the nose, so that when the way through the mouth was not open, the streams of the mouth as well were replenished through the nose. With the other cavity [that is, of the greater creel] he enveloped the hollow parts of the body, and at one time he made all this to flow into the lesser creels, quite gently, for they are composed of air, and at another time he caused the lesser creels to flow back again. And the net he made to find a way in and out through the pores of the body, and the rays of fire which are bound fast within followed the passage of the air either way, never at any time ceasing so long as the mortal being holds together. This process, as we affirm, the namegiver named inspiration and expiration. And all this movement, active as well as passive, takes place in order that the body, being watered and cooled, may receive nourishment and life. For when the respiration is going in and out, and the fire, which is fast bound within, follows it, and ever and anon moving to and fro, enters through the belly and reaches the meat and drink, it dissolves them, and dividing them into small portions and guiding them through the passages where it goes, pumps them as from a fountain into the channels of the veins, and makes the stream of the veins flow through the body as through a conduit.

Let us once more consider the phenomena of respiration, and inquire into the causes which have made it what it is. They are as follows. Seeing that there is no such thing as a vacuum into which any of those things which are moved can enter, and the breath is carried from us into the external air, the next point is, as will be clear to everyone, that it does not go into a vacant space, but pushes its neighbor out of its place, and that which is thrust out in turn drives out its neighbor. And in this way everything of necessity at last comes round to that place from whence the breath came forth, and enters in there and following the breath fills up the vacant space, and this goes on like the rotation of a wheel, because there can be no such thing as a vacuum. Wherefore also the breast and the lungs, when they emit the breath, are replenished by the air which surrounds the body and which enters in through the pores of the flesh and is driven round in a circle, and again, the air which is sent away and passes out through the body forces the breath inward through the passage of the mouth and the nostrils. Now the origin of this movement may be supposed to be as follows. In the interior of every animal the hottest part is that which is around the blood and veins; it is in a manner an internal fountain of fire, which we compare to the network of a creel, being woven all of fire and extended through the center of the body, while the outer parts are composed of air. Now we must admit that heat naturally proceeds outward to its own place and to its kindred element, and as there are two exits for the heat, the one out through the body, and the other through the mouth and nostrils, when it moves toward the one, it drives round the air at the other, and that which is driven round falls into the fire and becomes warm, and that which goes forth is cooled. But when the heat changes its place, and the particles at the other exit grow warmer, the hotter air inclining in that direction and carried toward its native element, fire, pushes round the air at the other, and this being affected in the same way and communicating the same impulse, a circular motion swaying to and fro is produced by the double process, which we call inspiration and expiration.

The phenomena of medical cupping glasses and of the swallowing of drink and of the projection of bodies, whether discharged in the air or bowled along the ground, are to be investigated on a similar principle, and swift and slow sounds, which appear to be high and low, and are sometimes discordant on account of their inequality, and then again harmonic on account of the equality of the motion which they excite in us. For when the motions of the antecedent swifter sounds begin to pause and the two are equalized, the slower sounds overtake the swifter and then propel them. When they overtake them they do not intrude a new and discordant motion, but introduce the beginnings of a slower which answers to the swifter as it dies away, thus producing a single mixed expression out of high and low, whence arises a pleasure which even the unwise feel, and which to the wise becomes a higher sort of delight, being an imitation of divine harmony in mortal motions. Moreover, as to the flowing of water, the fall of the thunderbolt, and the marvels that are observed about the attraction of amber and the Heraclean stones—in none of these cases is there any attraction, but he who investigates rightly will find that such wonderful phenomena are attributable to the combination of certain conditions—the nonexistence of a vacuum, the fact that objects push one another round, and that they change places, passing severally into their proper positions as they are divided or combined.

Such, as we have seen, is the nature and such are the causes of respiration—the subject in which this discussion originated. For the fire cuts the food and following the breath surges up within, fire and breath rising together and filling the veins by drawing up out of the belly and pouring into them the cut portions of the food, and so the streams of food are kept flowing through the whole body in all animals. And fresh cuttings from kindred substances, whether the fruits of the earth or herb of the field, which God planted to be our daily food, acquire all sorts of colors by their intermixture, but red is the most pervading of them, a quality created by the cutting action of fire and by the impression which it makes on a moist substance, and hence the liquid which circulates in the body has a color such as we have described. The liquid itself we call blood, which nourishes the flesh and the whole body, whence all parts are watered and empty places filled.

Now the process of repletion and evacuation is effected after the manner of the universal motion by which all kindred substances are drawn toward one another. For the external elements which surround us are always causing us to consume away and distributing and sending off like to like; the particles of blood, too, which are divided and contained within the frame of the animal as in a sort of heaven, are compelled to imitate the motion of the universe. Each, therefore, of the divided parts within us, being carried to its kindred nature, replenishes the void. When more is taken away than flows in, then we decay, and when less, we grow and increase.

The frame of the entire creature when young has the triangles of each kind new, and may be compared to the keel of a vessel which is just off the stocks; they are locked firmly together and yet the whole mass is soft and delicate, being freshly formed of marrow and nurtured on milk. Now when the triangles out of which meats and drinks are composed come in from without, and are comprehended in the body, being older and weaker than the triangles already there, the frame of the body gets the better of them and its newer triangles cut them up, and so the animal grows great, being nourished by a multitude of similar particles. But when the roots of the triangles are loosened by having undergone many conflicts with many things in the course of time, they are no longer able to cut or assimilate the food which enters, but are themselves easily divided by the bodies which come in from without. In this way every animal is overcome and decays, and this affection is called old age. And at last, when the bonds by which the triangles of the marrow are united no longer hold and are parted by the strain of existence, they in turn loosen the bonds of the soul, and she, obtaining a natural release, flies away with joy. For that which takes place according to nature is pleasant, but that which is contrary to nature is painful. And thus death, if caused by disease or produced by wounds, is painful and violent, but that sort of death which comes with old age and fulfills the debt of nature is the easiest of deaths, and is accompanied with pleasure rather than with pain.

Now everyone can see whence diseases arise. There are four natures out of which the body is compacted—earth and fire and water and air—and the unnatural excess or defect of these, or the change of any of them from its own natural place into another, or, since there are more kinds than one of fire and of the other elements, the assumption by any of these of a wrong kind, or any similar irregularity, produces disorders and diseases. For when any of them is produced or changed in a manner contrary to nature, the parts which were previously cool grow warm, and those which were dry become moist, and the light become heavy, and the heavy light; all sorts of changes occur. For, as we affirm, a thing can only remain the same with itself, whole and sound, when the same is added to it, or subtracted from it, in the same respect and in the same manner and in due proportion, and whatever comes or goes away in violation of these laws causes all manner of changes and infinite diseases and corruptions. Now there is a second class of structures which are also natural, and this affords a second opportunity of observing diseases to him who would understand them. For whereas marrow and bone and flesh and sinews are composed of the four elements, and the blood, though after another manner, is likewise formed out of them, most diseases originate in the way which I have described, but the worst of all owe their severity to the fact that the generation of these substances proceeds in a wrong order; they are then destroyed. For the natural order is that the flesh and sinews should be made of blood, the sinews out of the fibers to which they are akin, and the flesh out of the clots which are formed when the fibers are separated. And the glutinous and rich matter which comes away from the sinews and the flesh, not only glues the flesh to the bones, but nourishes and imparts growth to the bone which surrounds the marrow, and there remains a part, consisting of the purest and smoothest and oiliest sort of triangles, which filters through the solid texture of the bones, from which it drops like dew and waters the marrow. Now when each process takes place in this order, health commonly results; when in the opposite order, disease. For when the flesh becomes decomposed and sends back the wasting substance into the veins, then an oversupply of blood of diverse kinds, mingling with air in the veins, having variegated colors and bitter properties as well as acid and saline qualities, contains all sorts of bile and serum and phlegm. For all things go the wrong way, and having become corrupted, first, they taint the blood itself, and then ceasing to give nourishment to the body they are carried along the veins in all directions, no longer preserving the order of their natural courses, but at war with themselves, because they receive no good from one another, and are hostile to the abiding constitution of the body, which they corrupt and dissolve. The oldest part of the flesh which is corrupted, being hard to decompose, from long burning grows black, and from being everywhere corroded becomes bitter, and is injurious to every part of the body which is still uncorrupted. Sometimes, when the bitter element is refined away, the black part assumes an acidity which takes the place of the bitterness; at other times the bitterness being tinged with blood has a redder color, and this, when mixed with black, takes the hue of grass, and again, an auburn color mingles with the bitter matter when new flesh is decomposed by the fire which surrounds the internal flame—to all which symptoms some physician, perhaps, or rather some philosopher who had the power of seeing in many dissimilar things one nature deserving of a name has assigned the common name of bile. But the other kinds of bile are variously distinguished by their colors. As for serum, that sort which is the watery part of blood is innocent, but that which is a secretion of black and acid bile is malignant when mingled by the power of heat with any salt substance, and is then called acid phlegm. Again, the substance which is formed by the liquefaction of new and tender flesh when air is present, if inflated and incased in liquid so as to form bubbles which separately are invisible owing to their small size, but when collected are of a bulk which is visible and have a white color arising out of the generation of foam—all this decomposition of tender flesh when intermingled with air is termed by us white phlegm. And the whey or sediment of newly formed phlegm is sweat and tears, and includes the various daily discharges by which the body is purified. Now all these become causes of disease when the blood is not replenished in a natural manner by food and drink, but gains bulk from opposite sources in violation of the laws of nature. When the several parts of the flesh are separated by disease, if the foundation remains, the power of the disorder is only half as great, and there is still a prospect of an easy recovery, but when that which binds the flesh to the bones is diseased, and no longer being separated off from the muscles and sinews, ceases to give nourishment to the bone and to unite flesh and bone, and from being oily and smooth and glutinous becomes rough and salty and dry, owing to bad regimen, then all the substance thus corrupted crumbles away under the flesh and the sinews and separates from the bone, and the fleshy parts fall away from their foundation and leave the sinews bare and full of brine, and the flesh again gets into the circulation of the blood and makes the previously mentioned disorders still greater. And if these bodily affections be severe, still worse are the prior disorders, as when the bone itself, by reason of the density of the flesh, does not obtain sufficient air, but becomes moldy and hot and gangrened and receives no nutriment, and the natural process is inverted, and the bone crumbling passes into the food, and the food into the flesh, and the flesh again falling into the blood makes all maladies that may occur more virulent than those already mentioned. But the worst case of all is when the marrow is diseased, either from excess or defect, and this is the cause of the very greatest and most fatal disorders, in which the whole course of the body is reversed.

There is a third class of diseases which may be conceived of as arising in three ways, for they are produced sometimes by wind, and sometimes by phlegm, and sometimes by bile. When the lung, which is the dispenser of the air to the body, is obstructed by rheums and its passages are not free, some of them not acting, while through others too much air enters, then the parts which are unrefreshed by air corrode, while in other parts the excess of air forcing its way through the veins distorts them and decomposing the body is enclosed in the midst of it and occupies the midriff; thus numberless painful diseases are produced, accompanied by copious sweats. And oftentimes when the flesh is dissolved in the body, wind, generated within and unable to escape, is the source of quite as much pain as the air coming in from without, but the greatest pain is felt when the wind gets about the sinews and the veins of the shoulders and swells them up, and so twists back the great tendons and the sinews which are connected with them. These disorders are called tetanus and opisthotonos, by reason of the tension which accompanies them. The cure of them is difficult; relief is in most cases given by fever supervening. The white phlegm, though dangerous when detained within by reason of the air bubbles, yet if it can communicate with the outside air, is less severe, and only discolors the body, generating leprous eruptions and similar diseases. When it is mingled with black bile and dispersed about the courses of the head, which are the divinest part of us, the attack, if coming on in sleep, is not so severe, but when assailing those who are awake it is hard to be got rid of, and being an affection of a sacred part, is most justly called sacred. An acid and salt phlegm, again, is the source of all those diseases which take the form of catarrh, but they have many names because the places into which they flow are manifold.

Inflammations of the body come from burnings and inflamings, and all of them originate in bile. When bile finds a means of discharge, it boils up and sends forth all sorts of tumors, but when imprisoned within, it generates many inflammatory diseases, above all when mingled with pure blood, since it then displaces the fibers which are scattered about in the blood and are designed to maintain the balance of rare and dense, in order that the blood may not be so liquefied by heat as to exude from the pores of the body, nor again become too dense and thus find a difficulty in circulating through the veins. The fibers are so constituted as to maintain this balance, and if anyone brings them all together when the blood is dead and in process of cooling, then the blood which remains becomes fluid, but if they are left alone, they soon congeal by reason of the surrounding cold. The fibers having this power over the blood, bile, which is only stale blood, and which from being flesh is dissolved again into blood, at the first influx coming in little by little, hot and liquid, is congealed by the power of the fibers, and so congealing and made to cool, it produces internal cold and shuddering. When it enters with more of a flood and overcomes the fibers by its heat, and boiling up throws them into disorder, if it have power enough to maintain its supremacy, it penetrates the marrow and burns up what may be termed the cables of the soul, and sets her free, but when there is not so much of it, and the body though wasted still holds out, the bile is itself mastered and is either exuded from the whole body, or is thrust through the veins into the lower or upper belly, and is driven out of the body like an exile from a state in which there has been civil war, whence arise diarrheas and dysenteries, and all such disorders. When the constitution is disordered by excess of fire, continuous heat and fever are the result; when excess of air is the cause, then the fever is quotidian; when of water, which is a more sluggish element than either fire or air, then the fever is a tertian; when of earth, which is the most sluggish of the four, and is only purged away in a fourfold period, the result is a quartan fever, which can with difficulty be shaken off.

Such is the manner in which diseases of the body arise; the disorders of the soul, which depend upon the body, originate as follows. We must acknowledge disease of the mind to be a want of intelligence, and of this there are two kinds—to wit, madness and ignorance. In whatever state a man experiences either of them, that state may be called disease, and excessive pains and pleasures are justly to be regarded as the greatest diseases to which the soul is liable. For a man who is in great joy or in great pain, in his unseasonable eagerness to attain the one and to avoid the other, is not able to see or to hear anything rightly, but he is mad and is at the time utterly incapable of any participation in reason. He who has the seed about the spinal marrow too plentiful and overflowing, like a tree overladen with fruit, has many throes, and also obtains many pleasures in his desires and their offspring, and is for the most part of his life deranged because his pleasures and pains are so very great; his soul is rendered foolish and disordered by his body; yet he is regarded not as one diseased, but as one who is voluntarily bad, which is a mistake. The truth is that sexual intemperance is a disease of the soul due chiefly to the moisture and fluidity which is produced in one of the elements by the loose consistency of the bones. And in general, all that which is termed the incontinence of pleasure and is deemed a reproach under the idea that the wicked voluntarily do wrong is not justly a matter for reproach. For no man is voluntarily bad, but the bad become bad by reason of an ill disposition of the body and bad education—things which are hateful to every man and happen to him against his will. And in the case of pain, too, in like manner the soul suffers much evil from the body. For where the acid and briny phlegm and other bitter and bilious humors wander about in the body and find no exit or escape, but are pent up within and mingle their own vapors with the motions of the soul, and are blended with them, they produce all sorts of diseases, more or fewer, and in every degree of intensity, and being carried to the three places of the soul, whichever they may severally assail, they create infinite varieties of ill temper and melancholy, of rashness and cowardice, and also of forgetfulness and stupidity. Further, when to this evil constitution of body evil forms of government are added and evil discourses are uttered in private as well as in public, and no sort of instruction is given in youth to cure these evils, then all of us who are bad become bad from two causes which are entirely beyond our control. In such cases the planters are to blame rather than the plants, the educators rather than the educated. But however that may be, we should endeavor as far as we can, by education and pursuits and learning, to avoid vice and attain virtue; this, however, is part of another subject.

There is a corresponding inquiry concerning the mode of treatment by which the mind and the body are to be preserved, about which it is meet and right that I should say a word in turn, for it is more our duty to speak of the good than of the evil. Everything that is good is fair, and the fair is not without proportion, and the animal which is to be fair must have due proportion. Now we perceive lesser symmetries or proportions and reason about them, but of the highest and greatest we take no heed, for there is no proportion or disproportion more productive of health and disease, and virtue and vice, than that between soul and body themselves. This however we do not perceive, nor do we reflect that when a weak or small frame is the vehicle of a great and mighty soul, or conversely, when a little soul is incased in a large body, then the whole animal is not fair, for it lacks the most important of all symmetries, but the due proportion of mind and body is the fairest and loveliest of all sights to him who has the seeing eye. Just as a body which has a leg too long, or which is unsymmetrical in some other respect, is an unpleasant sight, and also, when doing its share of work, is much distressed and makes convulsive efforts, and often stumbles through awkwardness, and is the cause of infinite evil to its own self—in like manner we should conceive of the double nature which we call the living being. And when in this compound there is an impassioned soul more powerful than the body, that soul, I say, convulses and fills with disorders the whole inner nature of man, and when eager in the pursuit of some sort of learning or study, causes wasting. Or again, when teaching or disputing in private or in public, and strifes and controversies arise, inflames and dissolves the composite frame of man and introduces rheums, and the nature of this phenomenon is not understood by most professors of medicine, who ascribe it to the opposite of the real cause. And once more, when a body large and too strong for the soul is united to a small and weak intelligence, then inasmuch as there are two desires natural to man—one of food for the sake of the body, and one of wisdom for the sake of the diviner part of us—then, I say, the motions of the stronger, getting the better and increasing their own power, but making the soul dull and stupid and forgetful, engender ignorance, which is the greatest of diseases. There is one protection against both kinds of disproportion—that we should not move the body without the soul or the soul without the body, and thus they will be on their guard against each other and be healthy and well balanced. And therefore the mathematician or anyone else whose thoughts are much absorbed in some intellectual pursuit, must allow his body also to have due exercise, and practice gymnastics, and he who is careful to fashion the body should in turn impart to the soul its proper motions and should cultivate the arts and all philosophy if he would deserve to be called truly fair and truly good. And the separate parts should be treated in the same manner, in imitation of the pattern of the universe, for as the body is heated and also cooled within by the elements which enter into it, and is again dried up and moistened by external things, and experiences these and the like affections from both kinds of motions, the result is that the body if given up to motion when in a state of quiescence is overmastered and perishes. But if anyone, in imitation of that which we call the foster mother and nurse of the universe, will not allow the body ever to be inactive, but is always producing motions and agitations through its whole extent, which form the natural defense against other motions both internal and external, and by moderate exercise reduces to order according to their affinities the particles and affections which are wandering about the body, as we have already said when speaking of the universe, he will not allow enemy placed by the side of enemy to stir up wars and disorders in the body, but he will place friend by the side of friend, so as to create health. Now of all motions that is the best which is produced in a thing by itself, for it is most akin to the motion of thought and of the universe, but that motion which is caused by others is not so good, and worst of all is that which moves the body, when at rest, in parts only and by some external agency. Wherefore of all modes of purifying and reuniting the body the best is gymnastics; the next best is a surging motion, as in sailing or any other mode of conveyance which is not fatiguing; the third sort of motion may be of use in a case of extreme necessity, but in any other will be adopted by no man of sense—I mean the purgative treatment of physicians, for diseases unless they are very dangerous should not be irritated by medicines, since every form of disease is in a manner akin to the living being, whose complex frame has an appointed term of life. For not the whole race only, but each individual—barring inevitable accidents—comes into the world having a fixed span, and the triangles in us are originally framed with power to last for a certain time beyond which no man can prolong his life. And this holds also of the constitution of diseases; if anyone regardless of the appointed time tries to subdue them by medicine, he only aggravates and multiplies them. Wherefore we ought always to manage them by regimen, as far as a man can spare the time, and not provoke a disagreeable enemy by medicines.

Enough of the composite animal and of the body which is a part of him, and of the manner in which a man may train and be trained by himself so as to live most according to reason, and we must above and before all provide that the element which is to train him shall be the fairest and best-adapted to that purpose. A minute discussion of this subject would be a serious task, but if, as before, I am to give only an outline, the subject may not unfitly be summed up as follows.

I have often remarked that there are three kinds of soul located within us, having each of them motions, and I must now repeat, in the fewest words possible, that one part, if remaining inactive and ceasing from its natural motion, must necessarily become very weak, but that which is trained and exercised, very strong. Wherefore we should take care that the movements of the different parts of the soul should be in due proportion.

And we should consider that God gave the sovereign part of the human soul to be the divinity of each one, being that part which, as we say, dwells at the top of the body, and inasmuch as we are a plant not of an earthly but of a heavenly growth, raises us from earth to our kindred who are in heaven. And in this we say truly, for the divine power suspends the head and root of us from that place where the generation of the soul first began, and thus makes the whole body upright. When a man is always occupied with the cravings of desire and ambition, and is eagerly striving to satisfy them, all his thoughts must be mortal, and, as far as it is possible altogether to become such, he must be mortal every whit because he has cherished his mortal part. But he who has been earnest in the love of knowledge and of true wisdom, and has exercised his intellect more than any other part of him, must have thoughts immortal and divine, if he attain truth, and in so far as human nature is capable of sharing in immortality, he must altogether be immortal, and since he is ever cherishing the divine power and has the divinity within him in perfect order, he will be singularly happy. Now there is only one way of taking care of things, and this is to give to each the food and motion which are natural to it. And the motions which are naturally akin to the divine principle within us are the thoughts and revolutions of the universe. These each man should follow, and by learning the harmonies and revolutions of the universe, should correct the courses of the head which were corrupted at our birth, and should assimilate the thinking being to the thought, renewing his original nature, so that having assimilated them he may attain to that best life which the gods have set before mankind, both for the present and the future.

Thus our original design of discoursing about the universe down to the creation of man is nearly completed. A brief mention may be made of the generation of other animals, so far as the subject admits of brevity; in this manner our argument will best attain a due proportion. On the subject of animals, then, the following remarks may be offered. Of the men who came into the world, those who were cowards or led unrighteous lives may with reason be supposed to have changed into the nature of women in the second generation. And this was the reason why at that time the gods created in us the desire of sexual intercourse, contriving in man one animated substance, and in woman another, which they formed, respectively, in the following manner. The outlet for drink by which liquids pass through the lung under the kidneys and into the bladder, which receives and then by the pressure of the air emits them, was so fashioned by them as to penetrate also into the body of the marrow, which passes from the head along the neck and through the back, and which in the preceding discourse we have named the seed. And the seed, having life and becoming endowed with respiration, produces in that part in which it respires a lively desire of emission, and thus creates in us the love of procreation. Wherefore also in men the organ of generation becoming rebellious and masterful, like an animal disobedient to reason, and maddened with the sting of lust, seeks to gain absolute sway, and the same is the case with the so-called womb or matrix of women. The animal within them is desirous of procreating children, and when remaining unfruitful long beyond its proper time, gets discontented and angry, and wandering in every direction through the body, closes up the passages of the breath, and, by obstructing respiration, drives them to extremity, causing all varieties of disease, until at length the desire and love of the man and the woman, bringing them together and as it were plucking the fruit from the tree, sow in the womb, as in a field, animals unseen by reason of their smallness and without form; these again are separated and matured within; they are then finally brought out into the light, and thus the generation of animals is completed.

Thus were created women and the female sex in general. But the race of birds was created out of innocent light-minded men who, although their minds were directed toward heaven, imagined, in their simplicity, that the clearest demonstration of the things above was to be obtained by sight; these were remodeled and transformed into birds, and they grew feathers instead of hair. The race of wild pedestrian animals, again, came from those who had no philosophy in any of their thoughts, and never considered at all about the nature of the heavens, because they had ceased to use the courses of the head, but followed the guidance of those parts of the soul which are in the breast. In consequence of these habits of theirs they had their front legs and their heads resting upon the earth to which they were drawn by natural affinity, and the crowns of their heads were elongated and of all sorts of shapes, into which the courses of the soul were crushed by reason of disuse. And this was the reason why they were created quadrupeds and polypods. God gave the more senseless of them the more support that they might be more attracted to the earth. And the most foolish of them, who trail their bodies entirely upon the ground and have no longer any need of feet, he made without feet to crawl upon the earth. The fourth class were the inhabitants of the water; these were made out of the most entirely senseless and ignorant of all, whom the transformers did not think any longer worthy of pure respiration, because they possessed a soul which was made impure by all sorts of transgression, and instead of the subtle and pure medium of air, they gave them the deep and muddy sea to be their element of respiration. And hence arose the race of fishes and oysters, and other aquatic animals, which have received the most remote habitations as a punishment of their outlandish ignorance. These are the laws by which all animals pass into one another, now, as in the beginning, changing as they lose or gain wisdom and folly.

We may now say that our discourse about the nature of the universe has an end. The world has received animals, mortal and immortal, and is fulfilled with them, and has become a visible animal containing the visible—the sensible God who is the image of the intellectual, the greatest, best, fairest, most perfect—the one only-begotten heaven.

SIGLA

BAC	Madrid: Biblioteca de Autores Cristianos
BL	Paris: Les Belles Lettres
BPO	Bompiani Pensiero Occidentale. Milan: Bompiani
CCCM	Corpus Christianorum Continuatio Medievalis. Turnhout: Brepols
CCSL	Corpus Christianorum Series Latina. Turnhout: Brepols
CUP	Cambridge: Cambridge University Press
DOML	Dumbarton Oaks Medieval Library Cambridge, MA: Harvard University Press
LCL	Loeb Classical Library. Cambridge, MA: Harvard University Press
OCT	Oxford Classical Texts. Oxford: Oxford University Press
OUP	Oxford: Oxford University Press
PG	J.-P. Migne, ed., Patrologia Graeca
PL	J.-P. Migne, ed., Patrologia Latina
SC	Sources Chrétiennes. Paris: CERF
VM	Fondazione Valla-Mondadori. Milan: Arnoldo Mondadori
VP	Paris: Librairie philosophique J. Vrin.

ABBREVIATIONS

ALTER Robert Alter, *The Hebrew Bible,* translation and commentary, 3 vols. New York: Norton, 2019.

DDC Dante Alighieri, *Divina Commedia,* 3 vols, edited by Anna Maria Chiavacci Leonardi. Milan: Mondadori, 1991 (*Inferno*); 1994 (*Purgatorio*); 1997 (*Paradiso*).

KJB *The Bible: Authorized King James Version,* with Introduction and notes by Robert Carroll and Stephen Prickett. Oxford: Oxford University Press, 1997.

PETRUCCI Platone, *Timeo,* edited by Federico Maria Petrucci. Milan: Fondazione Valla-Mondadori, 2022.

VULGATE *Biblia sacra iuxta Vulgatam versionem,* edited by Robert. Weber. Stuttgart: Deutsche Bibelgesellschaft, 2007.

NOTES

Chapter One: One, Two, Three

1. The latter theory, which returns for example in Cicero's *Somnium Scipionis* and, as we shall see, in Dante, was so successful in antiquity that it became part of popular belief and was mentioned in epitaphs on tombstones: see *Epitaffi greci*, ed. E. Lelli, trans. F. Mosino (BPO, 2019), for examples, see nos. 1097, 1163, 1777; *Iscrizioni funerarie, sortilegi e pronostici di Roma antica*, ed. L. Storoni Mazzolani (Turin: Einaudi, 1973), nos. 110, 112, 125 (which explicitly mentions the theme of the descent and return to the stars); *Iscrizioni funerarie latine: Sopravvivere alla morte*, ed. M.-P. Pieri, G. Danesi Marioni and C. Gabrielli (Milan: Rusconi, 2020), nos. 2.3, 2.16, 219, 3.17.

2. Petrucci, pp. xiii–xiv. For the reception of the cosmogony of the *Timaeus* in antiquity, see M. Baltes, *Die Weltentstehung des Platonischen Timaios nach den antiken Interpreten* (Leiden: Brill, 1976–78).

3. *Timaeus* 27d–28 (emphases added).

4. *Timaeus* 47a–b. Significantly combining Plato with the Bible, William of Conches interprets this passage in the light of Ecclesiasticus 1:1: 'omnis sapientia a Domino Deo est': Guillelmus de Conchis, *Glosae super Platonem*, ed. É. A. Jeauneau (CCCM 203, 2006), 151.1–10 (pp. 271–72) for the present passage.

5. *Timaeus* 28c–29a;, pp. 38–41 with the Greek text in the VM edition.

6. *Timaeus* 92c.

7. *Greater Hyppias* 304e; *Republic* 345c, 497d; *Cratylus* 384b. The expression was probably proverbial and seems to originate in Solon: Plutarch, *Life of Solon* 14.

8. *Timaeus* 29c.

9. *Timaeus* 29d–31b.

10. Friedrich W. J. Schelling, *Sullo spirito della filosofia platonica: Il 'Timeo' di Platone; Commento manoscritto (1794)* (Italian translation with facing original German text), ed. L. Follesa (Milan, Mimesis, 2022) pp. 84–85.

11. Aristotle, *De caelo* 280a, in *The Works of Aristotle Translated into English*, ed. W. D. Ross, vol. 2: *De caelo*, trans. J L. Stocks; *De generatione et corruptione*, trans. H. H. Joachim (OUP, 1922), p. 279.

Chapter Two: Emulator of Homer

1. Cicero, *Timaeus*, in *De divinatione, De fato, Timaeus*, ed. W. Ax (Leipzig: Teubner, 1938), pp. 154–87. Plato's *inconstantia* is pointed out in the *De natura deorum* 1.18. See V. Hösle, 'Cicero's Plato', *Wiener Studien* 121 (2008): 145–70.

2. F. M. Cornford, *Plato's Cosmology: The 'Timaeus' of Plato*, 2nd edn (London: Routledge, 1977), p. 31. Cf. L. Brisson, *Le Même et l'Autre dans la structure ontologique du 'Timée' de Platon: Un commentaire systématique du 'Timée' de Platon* (Paris: Klincksiek, 1974), pp. 17–25; A. E. Taylor, *A Commentary on Plato's 'Timaeus'*, 2nd edn (OUP, 1928), pp. 13–43.

3. Torquato Tasso, *Discorsi sul poema eroico*, in *Discorsi dell'arte poetica e del poema eroico*, ed. L. Poma (Bari: Laterza, 1964), *Libro primo*, p. 64.

4. Pseudo-Longinus, *On the Sublime*, ed. Stephen Halliwell (OUP, 2022), 12.4 (p. 25).

5. Pseudo-Longinus, *On the Sublime* 13.1 (p. 25). The reference is to *Republic* 9.586a–b, adapted here; cf. Halliwell's foundational commentary on chapters 12 and 13–14, pp. 204–32. See also the commentaries of G. Lombardo: *Il Sublime* (Palermo: Aesthetica, 1987), and C. M. Mazzucchi, *Del Sublime*, 2nd edn (Milan: Vita e Pensiero, 2010).

6. Pseudo-Longinus, *On the Sublime* 13.2 (p. 25).

7. Pseudo-Longinus, *On the Sublime* 13.3 (p. 25; italics mine).

8. Pseudo-Longinus, *On the Sublime* 13.4 (p. 27).

9. Adelard of Bath, *Conversations with His Nephew: 'On the Same and the Different', 'Questions on Natural Science', and 'On Birds'*, ed. and trans. C. Burnett (CUP, 1998): *De eodem et diverso*, pp. 20–21: 'mentis altitutidine elatus pennisque [. . .] nisus'. Adelard's image of the wings of the mind is drawn from Boethius, *Consolation of Philosophy* 4, pr. 1.

10. Pseudo-Longinus, *On the Sublime* 32.5 (pp. 51–52).

11. Hippocrates, *Ancient Medicine* 20.11, in LCL 147 (Hippocrates, vol. 1), trans. W.H.S. Jones (1923), pp. 52–53.

12. As he declares respectively in the fragment (668 Rose) of a letter believed today to be authentic, preserved in Demetrius's *On Style* (144), and in the *Metaphysics* 1.982b.11–12; for the latter, see P. Boyde, *Dante Philomythes and Philosopher: Man in the Cosmos* (CUP, 1981), pp. 43–62; P. Dronke, *Fabula: Explorations into the Use of Myth in Medieval Platonism* (Leiden: Brill, 1974), pp. 3–4.

13. Aristotle, *Poetics* 22.6.1459a.5–8, in LCL 199 (Aristotle, *Poetics*; Longinus, *On the Sublime*; Demetrius, *On Style*), trans. S. Halliwell (1995), pp. 114–15. Ezra Pound's creative translation in *The Spirit of Romance* (London: Dent, 1910) seems to come close to several aspects of Aristotle's words: 'The apt use of metaphor, arising, as it does, from a swift perception of relations, is the hall-mark of genius' (p. 166). The concepts expressed in the *Poetics* are present in more expanded form in *Rhetoric* 3.2.1405a.8–10.

14. Pseudo-Longinus, *On the Sublime* 32.3–4 (p. 51).

15. Plato, *Laws* 6.773c–d.

16. Pseudo-Longinus, *On the Sublime* 33.4–5 (p. 55).

17. Valerius Maximus, *Factorum et dictorum memorabilium libri IX*, ed. R. Faranda (Turin: UTET, 1971), 12, ext. 3; derived in its turn from the pseudo-Plutarchan life of Homer: see *De Homero*, ed. by J. F. Kindstrand (Leipzig: Teubner 1990), A.4.60.

18. Ioannis Saresberiensis [John of Salisbury], *Policraticus*, ed. C.C.I. Webb, 2 vols (OUP, 1909), 7.6.647a–c (vol. 2, pp. 110–11).

Chapter Three: Pythagorean and Socratic

1. The *Timaeus* is also at the centre of attention for the so-called Middle Platonists, both Greek and Latin, and in particular of Alcinous (or Albinus, for those who still prefer the latter attribution) in his *Didaskalikos*: Alcinoos, *Enseignement des doctrines de Platon*, ed. J. Whittaker, trans. (into Fr.) P. Louis, 2nd edn (BL, 2002); and of Apuleius in his various philosophical works, *De deo Socratis, De Platone et eius dogmate, De mundo, Peri hermeneias*, available in Latin and Italian in *Medioplatonici*, ed. E. Vimercati (BPO, 2015), pp. 585–709. See F. Ferrari, *Materia, movimento, anima e tempo prima della nascita dell'universo: Plutarco e Attico sulla cosmologia del Timeo*, in *De l'Antiquité tardive au Moyen Age: Études de logique aristotélicienne, de philosophie grecque, syriaque, arabe et latine offertes a Henri Hugonnard-Roche*, ed. E. Coda and C. Martini Bonadeo (VP, 2014), pp. 255–76. It would be interesting to know what Posidonius, a philosopher who had great influence on his contemporaries and successors, and who might have written a commentary on the *Timaeus*, thought on the subject, but the extant fragments of his works do not permit of any conclusion (not even that he did actually write a commentary on the *Timaeus*): see the four volumes of *Fragments, Commentary* and *Translations* edited by I. G. Kidd (the first with L. Edelstein) for Cambridge University Press between 1972 (2nd edn 1989) and 1999.

2. Proclus, *Commentary on Plato's 'Republic'*, ed. and trans. D. Baltzly, J. F. Finamore and G. Miles (CUP, 2022), 1.14–15 (pp. 62–64).

3. *Procli Diadochi in Platonis Timaevm Commentaria*, ed. G. Van Riel, 3 vols (OCT, 2022); translated into French by A. J. Festugière in 5 vols as *Commentaire sur le Timée* (VP, 1966–68), and into English by H. Tarrant in 6 vols as *Commentary on Plato's Timaeus* (CUP, 2007–17): see A. Lernould, *Physique et théologie: Lecture du 'Timée' de Platon par Proclus* (Lille: Presses Universitaires du Septentrion, 2001).

4. Proclus, *Commentary* 1.7–8 (p. 100). Proclus's attitude towards the 'style' of the *Parmenides* in his *In Platonis Parmenidem commentaria* is entirely different: see *Procli in Platonis Parmenidem commentaria*, ed. C. Steel (OCT, 2007–9); *Proclus' Commentary on Plato's 'Parmenides'*, trans. G. R. Morrow and J. M. Dillon (Princeton, NJ: Princeton University Press, 1987).

5. Proclus, *Commentary* 1.8.3–4 (pp. 100–101).

6. Proclus Diadochus, *On the Theology of Plato*, trans. W. Taylor (London: Longman & Golding, 1816), 1.5 (p. 15).

7. *Procli Diadochi in Platonis Timaevm* 64.12–21 (Festugière's vol. 1, p. 99).

8. *Procli Diadochi in Platonis Timaevm* 1.4 (p. 13). The *Timaeus* is also present in the treatise by Damascius, the last of the pagan thinkers: *Problems and Solutions Concerning First Principles*, ed. S. Ahbel-Rappe (OUP, 2010), as well as passing into Christian hands, as for example those of Origen: *On First Principles*, ed. J. Behr (OUP, 2017).

9. Schelling, *Sullo spirito*, pp. 88–89.

Chapter Four: *Parens, fabricator, artifex*: Demogorgon and Phaethon

1. Cicero, *Timaeus*, 6.16.156b; and see C. Hoenig, *Plato's 'Timaeus' and the Latin Tradition* (CUP, 2018), pp. 38–101.

2. In the concluding Book 15, Pythagoras's speech on the *primordia* is inspired by Empedocles: see P. Hardie, 'The Speech of Pythagoras in Ovid *Metamorphoses* 15: Empedoclean *epos*', now in his *Lucretian Receptions: History, the Sublime, Knowledge* (CUP, 2009), pp. 136–52.

3. Ovid, *Metamorphoses*, trans. A. D. Melville (OUP 1986), 1.83; see A. Barchiesi's commentary in his edition (Ovidio, *Metamorfosi*), vol. 1 (VM, 2005).

4. Apuleius, *De Platone et eius dogmate* 1.5–6.190–93, in Apulée, *Opuscules philosophiques*, ed. J. Beaujeu, 3rd edn (BL, 2018), pp. 63–65. On Apuleius, see Hoenig, *Plato's 'Timaeus'*, pp. 102–59.

5. See now *Ovide moralisés latins*, ed. J.-M. Fritz with C. Noacco (Paris: Garnier, 2022), pp. 94–95; cf. *The Vulgate Commentary on Ovid's 'Metamorphoses', Book 1*, ed. and trans. F. T. Coulson (Kalamazoo, MI: Western Michigan University Medieval Institute Publications, 2015), pp. 31–34. See. P. Dronke, 'Metamorphoses: Allegory in Early Medieval Commentaries on Ovid and Apuleius', *Journal of the Warburg and Courtauld Institutes* 72 (2009): 21–39 at 33–34.

6. *Integumenta Ovidii* 15, in *Ovide moralisés latins*, pp. 224–25.

7. *Mythographus Vaticanus tertius*, ed. G. C. Garfagnini (Spoleto: Fondazione Centro italiano di studi sull'Alto Medioevo, 2018), p. 48.

8. *Allegoriae librorum Ovidii 'Metamorphoseos'*, in *Ovide moralisès latins*, pp. 294–97.

9. Pierre Bersuire [Petrus Berchorius], *The Moralized Ovid*, ed. and trans. F. T. Coulson and J. Haynes (DOML 82, 2023), pp. 122–23.

10. Thomas Walsingham, *De archana deorum*, ed. R. A. van Kluyve, (Durham, NC: Duke University Press, 1968), 1a (p. 4).

11. G. Sandys, trans., *Ovid's Metamorphosis Englished, Mythologized, and Represented in Figures* ed. K. K. Hulley and S. T. Vandersall (Lincoln, NE: University of Nebraska Press, 1970), p. 48.

12. Sandys, *Ovid's Metamorphosis*, p. 48.

13. See the still useful C. G. Osgood, *Boccaccio on Poetry* (Princeton, NJ: Princeton University Press, 1939); and C. Mésoniat, *Poetica theologia: La 'Lucula noctis' di Giovanni Dominici e le dispute letterarie tra '300 e '400* (Rome: Edizioni di Storia e Letteratura, 1984).

14. Giovanni Boccaccio, *Genealogie deorum gentilium*, ed. V. Zaccaria, in *Tutte le opere di Giovanni Boccaccio*, gen. ed. V. Branca, vols 7–8 (Milan: Mondadori, 1998), 1, Proh. 2–3 (pp. 64–73).

15. Statius, *Thebaid* 4.516; Lucan, *Pharsalia* 6.744.

16. *Lactantii Placidi in Statii Thebaida commentum*, ed. R. D. Sweeney (Stuttgart: Teubner, 1997), 4.516–17 (p. 293).

17. C. S. Lewis, *The Discarded Image: An Introduction to Medieval and Renaissance Literature* (CUP, 1964), p. 40.

18. Francis Bacon, *De sapientia veterum*, in *Operum moralium et civilium tomus* (London: Edward Griffin, 1638), Praef. pp. 276–77: Bacon, *The Wisdom of the Ancients* (Altenmünster: Jazzybee Verlag Jurgen Beck, 2015), p. 3.

19. *Timaeus* 22c–d.

20. Guillelmus, *Glosae super Platonem* 26 (pp. 49–51).

Chapter Five: Descendants and Intermediaries

1. *Timaeus* 28c; Philo of Alexandria, *De opificio mundi* 2.7, in *On the Creation of the Cosmos According to Moses*, ed. and trans. D. T. Runia, (Leiden: Brill, 2001), pp. 48 and 51; also Runia's comment on p. 94. See F. Ferrari, *Poietes kai pater: Appunti sulla metafisica di Filone alla luce del medioplatonismo*, in *Similitudini, metafore e allegoria nel 'De opificio mundi' di Filone di Alessandria*, ed. L. De Luca (Rome: Edizioni di Storia e Letteratura, 2021), pp. 73–90.

2. See D. T. Runia, *Philo of Alexandria and the 'Timaeus' of Plato* (Leiden: Brill, 1986); L. De Luca, *Il dio architetto di Filone di Alessandria ('De opificio mundi' 17–20)* (Milan: Vita e Pensiero, 2021).

3. Lactantius, *Divinae institutiones*, ed. E. Heck and A. Wlosok (Munich: Teubner, 2005), 1.5; 4.4; 7.7: the references are to *Timaeus* 28c–29a, and to *Phaedrus* 245c via Cicero, *Tusculanae disputationes* 1.23.53.

4. See D. T. Runia, *Philo in Early Christian Literature: A Survey* (Minneapolis: Assenden, 1993).

5. Augustine, *City of God*, vol. 3 (Books 8–11), LCL 413, trans. D. S. Wiesen (1968), 8.11 (pp. 50–53).

6. *Timaeus* 90b–c.

7. Exodus 3:14.

8. Augustine, *City of God* 8.11 (pp. 54–55).

9. See H. Hagendahl, *Augustine and the Latin Classics* (Stockholm: Almqvist & Wiskell, 1967), pp. 131–38.

10. See Hoenig, *Plato's 'Timaeus'*, pp. 215–79.

Chapter Six: Rachel's Beauty

1. Genesis 12:11. All English translations in this chapter are from Alter.

2. Genesis 24:16.

3. Genesis 26:7. In both cases Jerome translates 'pulcherrima' and 'propter eius pulchritudinem'. Federico Giuntoli has given me crucial help with the Hebrew.

4. But there is a play here on the very name of Isaac, on which see Alter 1, p. 90n.

5. Genesis 28:11–13.

6. Genesis 29:4–12

7. Genesis 29:16–18.

8. L. N. Tolstoy, *War and Peace*, trans. R. Edmonds (Harmondsworth: Penguin, 1982), p. 1318.

9. Genesis 39:6; Genesis 39:7–20. It should be added that both Leah and Rachel will have a long life as allegories, generally of active and contemplative life respectively, but also of the Synagogue and the Church. Dante uses them both in the *Comedy*: *Purgatorio* 27 and elsewhere. The last time we encounter Rachel is in Melville's *Moby Dick*, where the whaler *Rachel* rescues the protagonist, Ishmael, after the destruction of the *Pequod*.

10. Esther 2:7.

11. 2 Samuel 11:2: 'and the woman was very beautiful'; Esther 1:11: 'she was comely to look at'.

12. 1 Samuel 9:2; 1 Samuel 17:42; 1 Kings 1:6.

13. Psalm 19:1–4.

14. Psalm 78:13–15.

15. Psalm 104:2–4.

16. Job 37:14 and 16, 'the wonders of the Perfect in Knowlege'. On this, see J.-P.Sonnet, '"He who makes wonders": God's *Mirabilia* in the Hebrew Bible Between Narrative and Poetry', in *Astonishment: Essays on Wonder for Piero Boitani*, ed. E. Di Rocco (Rome: Edizioni di Storia e Letteratura, 2019), pp. 31–47; W. P. Brown, *Wisdom's Wonder* (Grand Rapids MI: Eerdmans, 2014).

17. Job 38–39.

18. Giorgio Vasari, *Le vite de' più eccellenti architetti, pittori, et scultori italiani*, ed. L. Bellosi and A. Rossi (Turin, Einaudi, 1986), p. 894.

19. God's marvels are of course praised in the Book of Wisdom (or Wisdom of Solomon) and Ecclesiasticus (Sirach), but in Greek.

20. Song of Songs 4:1.

21. Indeed, Thomas Mann was clearly inspired by it: see Jacob's long speech to Rachel in *Joseph and his Brothers*, vol. 1: *The Stories of Jacob*, Part 5, 'Laban's Increasing Wealth', trans. J. E. Woods (New York: Knopf, 2005), pp. 221–22.

22. Isaiah 52:7.

23. H. Fisch, 'What is Beautiful?', in Fisch, *Poetry with a Purpose: Biblical Poetics and Interpretation* (Bloomington, IN: Indiana University Press, 1988), pp. 16–17.

24. F. M. Dostoevsky, *Idiot* (Moscow: Ėksmo, 2020), p. 524; *The Idiot* trans. D. Magarshack (Harmondsworth: Penguin, 1968), pp. 419–20.

Chapter Seven: The Lilies of the Field

1. Plotinus, *Enneads*, vol. 5, LCL 444, trans. A. H. Armstrong (1984), 8.2 (pp. 241–43).

2. Plotinus, *Enneads*, vol. 4, LCL 443, trans. A. H. Armstrong (1984), 8.1 (p. 397)

3. Plotinus, *Enneads*, vol. 5, 8.1 (pp. 239–41).

4. Plotinus, *Enneads*, vol. 1, LCL 440, trans. A. H. Armstrong (1961), 6.8 (p. 257). For Plotinus's disciple Porphyry, in *On the Cave of the Nymphs* (34–35) Ulysses is a figure of the mystic, who abandons the sea (matter) and sits under the olive tree, discussing with Athena how to get rid of all passions. In her splendid commentary to *L'antro delle Ninfe* (Milan: Adelphi, 1986), Laura Simonini points out how Ulysses incarnates some of the deepest themes of Neoplatonic ethics (p. 249), and quotes on this both Proclus's commentary on Plato's *Parmenides* and Hermias's commentary on *Phaedrus* 259a. See also K. N. Akçay, *Porphyry's 'On the Cave of the Nymphs' in Its Intellectual Context* (Leiden, Brill, 2019).

5. Plotinus, *Enneads*, vol. 5, 8.2 (pp. 243–45).

6. A. Grabar, *Les origines de l'esthétique médiévale* (Paris : Macula, 2001); *Plotinus and the Origins of Medieval Aesthetics*, trans. A. Palladino, 2nd edn (Rome : Viella, 2018); see D. Guastini, *Immagini cristiane e cultura antica* (Brescia: Morcelliana, 2021).

7. Matthew 6:25–30.

8. See G. Lingua, 'Come vestono i gigli del campo: Trasformazioni dell'immaginario floreale nei primi secoli cristiani', *Ocula* 21 no. 23 (2020): 79–89.

9. Clément d'Alexandrie, *Le Pédagogue, Livre II*, ed. H.-I. Marrou, trans. C. Mondésert (SC 108, 1991), 102.5–103.1 (pp. 194–97).

10. Genesis 27:27.

11. Psalm 49:11.

12. Sant'Ambrogio, *Exameron: I sei giorni della creazione*, ed. and trans. G. Banterle (Milan: Biblioteca Ambrosiana/Rome: Città Nuova, 1979), 3.5.8.35–36 (pp. 146–49). Saint Ambrose, *Hexameron, Paradise, and Cain and Abel*, trans. J. J. Savage (New York: Catholic University of America Press, 1961), *Hexameron* 3.8.36 (pp. 94–95).

13. Plotinus, *Enneads*, vol. 3, LCL 442, trans. A. H. Armstrong (1967), 2.13 (pp. 83–85).

14. Augustine, *City of God* 10.14 (pp. 314, 315).

Chapter Eight: 'Mira profunditas'

1. Augustine, *De musica*, ed. M. Jakobson (Berlin: De Gruyter, 2017); Boethius, *Traité de la musique*, ed. C. Meyer (Turnhout: Brepols, 2004). See E. De Bruyne, *Études d'esthétique médiévale*, vol. 1: *De Boèce à Jean Scot Erigène* (Bruges: De Tempel, 1946), pp. 3–34; and, in quite a different direction, H. U. von Balthasar, *The Glory of the Lord: A Theological Aesthetics*, vol. 2: *Studies in Theological Style: Clerical Styles*, ed. J. Riches, , trans. A. Louth, F. McDonagh and B. McNeil (Edinburgh: T. & T. Clark, 1984).

2. The title of this chapter mirrors the beautiful title of the first section of chapter 2 of *Exégèse médiévale*, vol. 1, by Henri De Lubac (Paris: Aubier, 1959): full of important quotations from an almost unlimited number of authors.

3. E. Auerbach, 'Sacrae Scripturae sermo humilis', in Auerbach, *Gesammelte Aufsätze zur romanischen Philologie* (Bern: Francke, 1967), pp. 21–26 (in French); it first appeared in German in Auerbach's *Neue Dantestudien* (Istanbul: I. Horoz, 1944); also Auerbach, 'Sermo humilis', in *Literatursprache und Publikum in der lateinischen Spätantike und im Mittelalter* (Bern: Francke, 1958), pp. 25–53; in English, *Literary Language and its Public in Late Latin Antiquity and the Middle Ages, trans Ralph Manheim (Princeton, NJ: Princeton University Press, 1965)*. For Augustine, see *De Trinitate* 1.2; *De doctrina christiana* 2.41–42; Ep. 137.18.

4. Augustine, *De doctrina christiana*, ed. and trans. R.P.H. Green (OUP, 1995; italics mine). Biblical references in Exodus 12:35–36 (but the stripping or spoliation of the Egyptians is already announced in Exodus 3:21–22 and 11:2); 2 Chronicles 9:11–24 (1 Kings 10:11–24); 1 Corinthians 8:1 for 'scientia inflat, charitas vero aedificat'. In his letter to Gregory Thaumaturgus (Grégoire le Thaumaturge, *Remerciement a Origène: Lettre d'Origène à Grégoire*, ed. H. Crouzel [SC 148, 1969]) Origen sees this episode as an example of how 'gentile learning' may be preparatory to the study of the Holy Scripture.

5. Pseudo-Longinus, *On the Sublime* 9.9 (pp. 14–15).

6. Robert Lowth, *De sacra poesi hebraeorum*, 2nd edn (OUP, 1821), cites Longinus; for Coleridge's dictum, *Specimens of the Table Talk of Samuel Taylor Coleridge* (London, John Murray, 1836), p. 178: see *Coleridge's Writings on the Sublime*, ed. D. Vallins (New York, Palgrave Macmillan, 2003).

7. Augustine, *De doctrina christiana*, 3.5.9; 3.7.18–20; 3.18.26 (pp. 335–36). It is well known that Augustine owes some of the principles of his interpretation of the Bible to Tychonius's *Liber*

regularum, which he summarises in *De doctrina christiana* 3.30–37. But Tychonius's work, the first of Biblical hermeneutics to appear in the West, never mentions questions of style, although he opens the way to the allegorical and figural interpretation of Scripture. See *Le livre des règles*, ed. J.-M. Vercruysse (SC 488, 2004), and P. Bright, *The Book of Rules of Tyconius: Its Purpose and Inner Logic* (Notre Dame, IN, University of Notre Dame Press, 1988).

8. Augustine, *Confessions*, vol. 2 (Books 9–13), LCL 27, ed. and trans. C. J.-B. Hammond (2016), 12.14.17 (pp. 282–83).

9. Agostino, *Confessioni*, ed. M. Simonetti and J. Pépin (VM, 1997), vol. 5, comment to 12.14.17.

10. See J. J. O'Donnell, *Augustine, 'Confessions'*, vol. 3: *Commentary, Books 8–13*, (OUP, 1992), p. 316.

11. Plotinus, *Enneads*, vol. 1, 6.7 (p. 253).

12. Von Balthasar, *Glory of the Lord*, vol. 2, p. 141.

13. Augustine, *Confessions*, vol. 2, 11.1.1–11.6.8. Augustine is naturally not the only Church Father to discuss the problems raised by Scripture; see, for example, Origène, *Philocalie, 1–20: Sur les Écritures*, ed. M. Harl (SC 302, 1983).

14. Jerome, *In Ezechielem*, Book 14, praef.: PL 25, 448D.

15. For references see H. de Lubac, *Exégèse médiévale: Les quatre sens de l'Écriture, Première Partie*, t. 1 (Paris: Aubier, 1959), pp. 119–20 and notes.

16. Origene, *Omelie sulla Genesi*, ed. M. Simonetti (Rome, Città Nuova, 2002), 9.1 (p. 246), for the Latin text; in English, *The Homilies on Genesis*, in *Origen: Homilies on Genesis and Exodus*, trans. R. E. Heine (Washington, DC: The Catholic University of America Press, 1982), p. 148.

Chapter Nine: Compunction and Transfiguration

1. Grégoire le Grand [Gregory the Great], *Homélies sur Ézéchiel* (SC 327, 1986), 8.11–12 (pp. 290–93).

2. Grégoire le Grand, *Homélies* 8.16–19 (pp. 296–303).

3. J. Leclercq, *L'amour des lettres et le désir de Dieu* (Paris : CERF, 2008 [1957]), pp. 30–39.

4. Gregory the Great, *Moralia in Iob* 27.40–41.

5. See Leclercq, *L'amour*, p. 35.

6. Leclercq, *L'amour*, p. 38. See Gregory the Great, *On the Song of Songs*, ed. M. DelCogliano (Collegeville, MN: Cistercian Publications Liturgical Press, 2012), 10, 14, 18, 26 and 27.

7. *The Dialogues of Gregory the Great*, ed. E. G. Gardner (Merchantville, NJ: Evolution Publishing, 2010): see Gregorio Magno, *Storie di santi e di diavoli (Dialogi)*, ed. M. Simonetti and S. Pricoco, 2 vols (VM, 2005).

8. Exodus 3:7–12.

9. R. Alter, comment to 1 Samuel 3, in Alter 2, p. 187; see also P. K. McCarter, Jr., ed. and trans., *1 Samuel: A New Translation with Introduction, Notes, and Commentary* (The Anchor Bible, 8) (New York: Doubleday), p. 199.

10. *Commento al Primo Libro dei Re*, ed. G. I. Gargano, vol. 1: *I–III, 37* (Rome: Città Nuova, 2007), 2.139 (pp. 234–35; my translation).

Chapter Ten: 'O qui perpetua mundum ratione gubernas'

1. In his edition of the *Consolation* for VM (2023), pp. 303–4, Peter Dronke regards Calcidius as the main source.

2. Lev Shestov, *Athens and Jerusalem*, ed. R. Fotiade, trans. B. Martin, 2nd edn (Athens, OH: Ohio University Press, 2016), p. 235.

3. Boethius, *The Consolation of Philosophy*, LCL 74, trans. H. E. Stewart, E. K. Rand and S. J. Tester (1973), 3 pr. 9 (pp. 268–69).

4. Boethius, *Consolation* 3 pr. 9 (pp. 268–71).

5. Boethius, *Consolation* 3 m. 9 (pp. 270–75). Dante refers to this metre in *Convivio* 3.2.17, where he translates lines 6–8. It is also cited in the *Epistle to Cangrande* 33 [89]: 'Il fine è vedere te'.

6. The metre was already considered 'veluti quandam *epitomen* primae partis Timaei' by Renato Vallino: see F. Klingner, *De Boethii Consolatione philosophiae*, 2nd edn (Zurich: Weidmann, 1966), p. 39; J. Gruber, *Kommentar zu Boethius, 'De consolatione philosophiae'*, 2nd edn (Berlin: De Gruyter, 2006), p. 275. On the *Consolation*, see also P. Dronke, *The Spell of Calcidius: Platonic Concepts and Images in the Medieval West* (Florence: SISMEL Edizioni del Galluzzo, 2008), pp. 35–69, which I often follow here, as also Dronke's 'Introduction' and commentary in the VM edition of the *Consolation*.

7. Guillelmus de Conchis, *Glosae super Boetium*, ed. L. Nauta (CCCM 158, 1999), 3 m. 9, 1–735 (pp. 144–79).

8. Wisdom 7:27 in the Vulgate: 'et in se permanens omnia innovat'.

9. Boethius uses images from the *Timaeus* in 1 m. 5, 'Stelliferi conditor orbis', and above all in 2 m. 8, 'Quod mundus stabili fide', where, however, he introduces the fundamental notion of *amor*, absent in Plato except as *philia*. King Alfred's version, an adaptation of 'O qui perpetua', in which he transforms the original twenty-eight hexameters into 281 couplets of alliterative hemistichs, possesses a quite remarkable imaginative originality and verve; see Dronke, *Spell*, pp. 58–67.

Chapter Eleven: Beauty

1. See H. U. von Balthasar, *Cosmic Liturgy: The Universe According to Maximus the Confessor*, trans. B. E. Daly (San Francisco, Ignatius Press, 2003); and (at least) Y. De Andia, 'Pseudo-Dionysius the Areopagite and Maximus Confessor', in *The Oxford Handbook of Maximus Confessor*, ed. P. Allen and B. Neil (OUP, 2015), pp. 177–93; in general, E. J. Rybarczyk, *For Him Who Has Eyes to See: Beauty in the History of Theology* (Eugene, OR: Cascade Books, 2016).

2. Acts 17:32–34.

3. See E. Bellini, in *Dionigi Areopagita: Tutte le opere*, ed. P. Scazzoso and E. Bellini, (BPO, 2009), p. 33. The references are to *De divinis nominibus* 681A, 684D, 681C–D and *Letter Seven*, 1081B–C. See P. Rorem and J. C. Lamoureaux, *John of Scythopolis and the Dionysian Corpus* (OUP, 1998), pp. 106–7.

4. Eusebius of Caesarea, *Ecclesiastical History* 3.4.10; 4.23.3.

5. The *Passio Sancti Dionysii* may be found in PL 106, 13–50. But see the recent, splendid edition by M. Lapidge, *Hilduin of Saint Denis: The Passio Sancti Dionysii in Prose and Verse* (Leiden: Brill, 2017), which also contains the documents preceding Hilduin.

6. And many others: see *The Oxford Handbook of Dionysius the Areopagite*, ed. M. Edwards, D. Pallis and G. Steiris (OUP, 2022) for all questions concerning the *Corpus Dionysiacum*, its roots and influence.

7. See E. Panofsky, *Abbot Suger on the Abbey Church of St-Denis and Its Art Treasures*, 2nd edn, ed. G. Panofsky-Soergel (Princeton, NJ: Princeton University Press, 1979); the original was reprinted as chapter 3 in Panofsky's *Meaning and the Visual Arts* (New York: Doubleday, 1955), pp. 108–45. Suger's *Œuvres* in Latin accompanied by facing French translation are edited by F. Gasparri (BL, 1996–2001). An earlier translation of the *Gesta Ludovici regis* is Suger, *Vie de Louis VI le Gros*, ed. and trans. H. Waquet (BL, 1964). After Panofsky, art historians have analysed the Victorine aspects of Suger's aesthetics: see, for example, C. Rudolph, 'Inventing the Gothic Portal: Suger, Hugh of St. Victor and the Construction of a New Public Art at Saint-Denis', *Art History* 33 (2010): 568–95; Rudolph, 'Inventing the Exegetical Stained-Glass Window: Suger, Hugh, and a New Elite Art', *The Art Bulletin* 93, no. 4 (2011): 399–422; above all, *L' abbé Suger, le manifeste gothique de Saint-Denis et la pensée victorine*, ed. D. Poirel (Turnhout: Brepols, 2001). Hugh is the one author who, following Dionysius and John Scotus, develops a highly original aesthetics: see ch. 14 below.

8. The first mediator between Platonism and Christian mysticism was Gregory of Nyssa, well before Dionysius: see J. Daniélou, *Platonisme et théologie biblique* (Paris: Aubier, 1944); the introduction by C. Moreschini to Gregorio di Nissa, *Opere dogmatiche* (BPO, 2014), pp. 7–194; the introductory essay and additional essays by I. Ramelli to Gregorio di Nissa, *Sull'anima e la resurrezione* (BPO, 2007), pp. 7–341, 735–1151; the introduction and comment by M. Simonetti to Gregorio di Nissa, *Vita di Mosè* (VM, 1984). The chain of sources is, however, unending, for behind Gregory is Origen; see also L. Pertile, *La punta del disio: Semantica del desiderio nella Commedia* (Florence: Cadmo, 2005).

9. Dionysius, *The Mystical Theology* in *Pseudo-Dionysius: The Complete Works*, trans. C. Luibheid, with notes by P. Rorem (New York: Paulist Press, 1988), 3.1032D–1033B (pp. 138–39).

10. Dionysius, *Mystical Theology* 3.1033B–C (p. 139).

11. Dionysius, 'The Letters', in *Pseudo-Dionysius: The Complete Works* (cited above), Letter 9, 1105D (p. 283).

12. Dionysius, 'The Letters', Letter 9, 1104C–1105B (pp. 281–82); for biblical references see the footnotes.

13. Dionysius, 'The Letters', Letter 9, 1108A (p. 283).

14. Dionysius, 'The Letters', Letter 9, 1105B (p. 282); Letter 7, 1080B (p. 267).

15. Dionysius, *The Divine Names*, in *Pseudo-Dionysius: The Complete Works* (cited above), 596A (p. 54), referring to Genesis 32:29.

16. Dionysius, *Divine Names* 596A, referring to Exodus 3:14. The translation 'I am being' (Ho ón), is in the Septuagint; the Hebrew original, ''ehyeh 'ăšer 'ehyeh' was translated by Jerome for the Vulgate as 'Ego sum qui sum' (I am that I am).

17. Dionysius, *Divine Names* 596B (pp. 55–56).

18. Dionysius, *Divine Names* 597B (pp. 56–57). All this is repeated, amplified and explained in Letter 9, 1104C–1113C (pp. 281–88).

19. Song of Songs 1:16; Psalms 45 (44):2; 1 John 4:8–16; 1 Peter 1:17.

20. Referring to Plato, *Symposium* 211a–b

21. Dionysius, *Divine Names* 701C–704A (pp. 76–77; translation slightly altered).

22. Dionysius, *Divine Names* 704B–C (pp. 414–17).

23. Marsilio Ficino, *On Dionysius the Areopagite*, vol. 1: *'Mystical Theology' and 'The Divine Names' Part I'*, ed. and trans. M.J.B. Allen (Cambridge, MA: Harvard University Press, 2015), pp. 4–5.

24. Printed in parallel with the text in the two volumes of the *Dionysiaca: Recueil donnant l'ensemble des traductions latines des ouvrages attribués au Denys de l'Aréopage*, ed. P. Chevallier et al. (Bruges: Desclée de Brouwer, 1937; facsimile edition in four volumes published by Frommann-Holzboog [Stuttgart], 1989). For John Scotus's translation, see also PL 122, 1029–1194.

25. Now *Dionysii Areopagitae De mystica theologia, De divinis nominibus; interprete Marsilio Ficino*, ed. P. Podolak (Naples: D'Auria, 2011).

26. Grosseteste translated and commented on the *Celestial Hierarchy*: *Versio Caelestis hierarchiae Pseudo-Dionysii Areopagitae cum scholiis ex Graeco sumptis necnon commentariis notulisque eiusdem Lincolniensis*, ed. D. A. Lawell (CCCM 268, 2015), and composed a commentary on the *Mystical Theology*: see *Il commento di Roberto Grossatesta al 'De Mystica Theologia' del pseudo-Dionigi l'Areopagita*, ed. U. Gamba (Milan: Vita e Pensiero, 1942). Thomas Gallus, the author of a paraphrase of the *Angelic Hierarchy* (*Dionysiaca* 3.1043–66) and glosses to the *Angelic Hierarchy*, also composed an *Explanatio* of the entire *Corpus dionysiacum*: *Glose super angelica hierarchia, Explanatio in libros Dionysii*, ed. D. Lawell (CCCM 223A and 223, 2011). Hugues de Balma composed a *Mystical Theology* towards the end of the thirteenth century, the *Viae Sion lugent: Théologie mystique*, ed. F. Ruello, trans. and notes by J. Barbet, 2 vols (SC 408 and 409, 1995–96). On Eckart's works, both Latin and vernacular, see E. Rubino, 'Pseudo-Dionysius the Areopagite and Eckart', in *A Companion to Meister Eckart*, ed. J. M. Hackett (Leiden: Brill, 2013), pp. 299–309. Jean Gerson's *De mystica theologia* (1408–22) is also notable: the critical edition is by A. Combes (Lugano: Thesaurus Mundi, 1958); English translation in Gerson, *Early Works*, ed. B. P. McGuire (New York: Paulist Press, 1998). For Bonaventure, Albert and Thomas Aquinas, see below.

27. *'The Cloud of Unknowing' and 'The Book of Privy Counselling'*, ed. P. Hodgson (EETS 218) (OUP, 1944); *'Deonise Hid Divinite' and Other Treatises on Contemplative Prayer Related to 'The Cloud of Unknowing'*, ed. P. Hodgson (EETS 231) (OUP, 1955).

28. As by J. Grosfillier in the introduction to his edition of Richard de Saint-Victor, *De contemplatione (Beniamin maior)* (Turnhout: Brepols, 2013), pp. 25–26.

29. Maximus the Confessor, *De theologia* 7.83 (PG 90, 1383; my translation).

Chapter Twelve: *Metaphorá*

1. See W. Beierwaltes, *Platonismus in Christentum*, 3rd edn (Frankfurt am Main: Klosterman, 2001), pp. 44–84.

2. Dronke, *Fabula*. For the *Timaeus* in the Middle Ages, see (at least) E. De Bruyne, *Études d'esthétique médiévale*, vol. 2: *L'époque romane* (Bruges: De Tempel, 1946), pp. 255–301; E. Garin, *Studi sul platonismo medievale* (Florence:, Le Monnier, 1958); W. Wetherbee, *Platonism and Poetry in the Twelfth Century* (Princeton, NJ: Princeton University Press, 1972), pp. 28–77;

T. Gregory, *Anima Mundi: La filosofia di Guglielmo di Conches e la Scuola di Chartres* (Florence: Sansoni, 1955); Gregory, *Platonismo medievale: Studi e ricerche* (Rome: Istituto storico italiano per il Medio Evo, 1958), pp. 53–134; and more recently, Gregory, *Mundana sapientia: Forme di conoscenza nella cultura medievale* (Rome: Edizioni di Storia e Letteratura, 1992), pp. 145–73.

3. John Scotus Eriugena, *Sulle nature dell'universo (Periphyseon)*, ed. P. Dronke, vol. 1 (VM, 2012), p. xl.

4. John Scotus Eriugena, *Periphyseon (The Division of Nature)*, trans. I. P. Sheldon-Williams, rev. J. J. O'Meara (Montreal: Bellarmin; Washington, DC: Dumbarton Oaks: 1987), 1.511c–512a (pp. 108–9).

5. Similarly to Theology, personified as a poetess: see P. Dronke, 'Theologia veluti quaedam poetria: Quelques observations sur la fonction des images poétiques chez Jean Scot', in *Jean Scot Erigène et l'histoire de la philosophie*, ed. R. Roques (Colloques internationaux du CNRS 561) (Paris: Éditions du CNRS, 1977), pp. 243–52; later reprinted in *The Medieval Poet and his World* (Rome: Edizioni di Storia e Letteratura, 1984), pp. 39–53.

6. Scotus translated Gregory of Nyssa's *De opificio hominis* on man's creation in his *De imagine*, and wrote poems on it in his *Carmina*, ed. in a single volume by M. Herren, A. Dunning, C. Tommasi and G. Mandolino (CCCM 167, 2020).

7. Eriugena, *Periphyseon*, 3.705a–706b (pp. 336–37).

8. *Timaeus* 29c.

9. Eriugena, *Periphyseon*, 3.668a; 3.671c (pp. 292; 296).

10. Iohannes Scotus Eriugena, *Expositiones in hierarchiam coelestem*, ed. J. Barbet (CCCM 31, 1975), pp. 34, 48, 52 and passim to p. 195: 'Et ut breuiter colligam omnia que de laude ignis predicantur, pulchre per metaphoram de Deo predicari possunt'.

11. Giovanni Scoto [Eriugena], *Il Prologo di Giovanni*, ed. M. Cristiani (VM, 1987), 1 and 4 (pp. 8–15).

Chapter Thirteen: *Integumenta; Esthétique du Timée*

1. Guillelmus, *Glosae super Platonem* 49.16–18 (citing *De divinis nominibus* 4.23); 118.13–15. On William, see *Guillaume de Conches: Philososophie et science au XIIe siècle*, ed. B. Obrist and I. Caiazzo (Florence: SISMEL Edizioni del Galluzzo, 2011).

2. Guillelmus, *Glosae super Platonem*, and *Glosae super Boetium* 119–20 (pp. 213–16). The two commentaries intersect each other continuously.

3. Guillelmus, *Glosae super Platonem* 6.11–14 (p. 12); Uguccione da Pisa [Hugutio of Pisa], *Derivationes*, ed. E. Cecchini et al., 2 vols (Florence: SISMEL Edizioni del Galluzzo, 2004), T108 (vol. 2, pp. 1221–22). The first part of the etymology, *thymus* = 'flower', is already present as *thymum* in Isidore, *Etymologiae* 4.12, 2; 17.9.9; in English in *The 'Etymologies' of Isidore of Seville*, ed. and trans. S. A. Barney, W. J. Lewis, J. A. Beach and O. Berghof (CUP, 2006), pp. 115; 310. The world in a Platonic key, with various references to the *Timaeus*, is also discussed by Honorius of Autun in his *Imago mundi*, ed. V.I.J. Flint in *Archives d'histoire doctrinale et littéraire du Moyen Âge* 49 (1982): 1–153; and in his *Clavis physicae*, ed. P. Lucentini (Rome: Edizioni di Storia e Letteratura, 1974).

4. Dronke, *Spell*, pp. 118–21.

5. P. Dronke, *Dante e le tradizioni latine medievali*, 2nd edn (Bologna: Il Mulino, 2022), pp. 80–81, where he quotes Gregory's translation in the latter's *Platonismo medievale*, pp. 98–102.

6. According to the *Thesaurus linguae latinae* the word *integumentum* is used already by Plautus and Cicero. The earliest instances with a 'philosophical-theological' meaning come from Ambrose and Martianus Capella. The definition in the commentary to the first six books of the *Aeneid* 'commonly', but by no means with any certainty, attributed to Bernardus Silvestris, states rather dryly, 'genus demonstrationis sub fabulosa narratione veritatis involvens intellectum, unde etiam dicitur involucrum': 'a kind of demonstration that wraps up the understanding of truth in a fabled narrative—that is why it is also called "a wrapping"' (trans. Dronke, *Fabula*, p. 25 n. 3). And see *The Commentary on the First Six Books of the 'Aeneid' Commonly Attributed to Bernardus Silvestris*, ed. J. W. Jones and E. F. Jones (Lincoln, NE: University of Nebraska Press, 1977), pp. 3, 14–15.

7. Not Scripture, but rather Jerome, *Epistulae* 126.1. See Jeauneau's notes in Guillelmus, *Glosae super Platonem*, p. 213, for all of William's sources, together with parallels in his other works.

8. Guillelmus, *Glosae super Platonem* 102.5 (p. 216), quoted in English in Dronke, *Dante and Medieval Latin Traditions* (CUP, 1986), p. 28. See Guillelmus, *Glosae super Boetium* 3 m. 9, 620–65 (pp. 174–75). Far less imaginative and much more scientifically oriented is William's earlier work, *Philosophia*, ed. M. Albertazzi, Lavis, 2010. Once attributed to both Honorius of Autun and Bede, this is not to be confused with William's later *Dragmaticon philosophiae*, in Guillelmus de Conches, *Dragmaticon philosophiae, Summa de philosophia in vulgari*, ed. I. Ronca, L. Badia and J. Pujol (CCCM 152, 1997).

9. Thomas Aquinas, *In Aristotelis librum De anima commentarium*, ed. A. M. Pirotta, 3rd edn (Turin: Marietti, 1948), 1.8.107 (p. 31). The passage had already been quoted by Dronke in *Fabula*, pp. 3–5. But see below for Thomas's commentary on Job.

10. Albertus Magnus, *De natura et origine animae*, in *B. Alberti Magni opera omnia*, ed. A. Borgnet and É. Borgnet, vol. 11 (Paris: Vivès, 1891), 2.7 (pp. 416–17), as quoted by Bruno Nardi in Nardi, *Saggi di filosofia dantesca*, 2nd edn (Florence, La Nuova Italia, 1967), p. 70; more recently in *Alberti Magni opera omnia*, vol. 12, ed. B. Geyer (Münster: Monasterii Westfalorum, Aschendorff, 1955), p. 31; but the whole of the seventh chapter of Albert's treatise is fascinating, set within an overview of of the 'status animarum post mortem' that examines in addition to the theory of Plato, those of the Brahmins, the Egyptians and Chaldeans, of Socrates (7), Pythagoras (8), Anaxagoras and Averroes (9), of Avicenna and Al-Ghazali (10), of the Epicureans (11), and an unknown 'opinio novella' based on Democritus and 'Orpheus' that assures the permanence of the soul after death for all animals (12).

11. De Bruyne, *Études*, vol. 2, pp. 255–30, at p. 256; see also R. Assunto, *La critica d'arte nel pensiero medioevale* (Milan: Il Saggiatore, 1961). A biography of Plato rich in details derived from different sources, and full of quotations from the *Timaeus*, was composed by John of Salisbury for the *Policraticus* (7.5–7). Hugh of Saint-Victor begins his *Didascalicon* by quoting the *Timaeus*.

12. Gregory, *Anima mundi*, pp. 212–18; see, more recently, Gregory, *Mundana sapientia*.

13. Guillelmus, *Glosae super Platonem* 71.3–5 (pp. 123–24): see G. Spinosa, '*Ornatus mundi*: Nota di terminologia filosofica medievale', *Archivum latinitatis medii aevi* 66 (2008): 201–12;

C. Martello, *I princìpi e le cause: Le 'Glosae super Platonem' di Guglielmo di Conches*, 2 vols (Palermo: Officina di Studi Medievali, 2014 and 2018).

14. De Bruyne *Études*, vol. 2, p. 256; see Richard of St. Victor, *The Mystical Ark*, in *The Twelve Patriarchs; The Mystical Ark; Book Three of the Trinity*, trans. G. A. Zinn (New York: Paulist Press, 1979), 6 (p. 161); Richard de Saint-Victor, *De contemplatione* 1.6 (pp. 104–5).

15. See De Bruyne, *Études*, vol. 2, pp. 280–301. Together with William's commentaries on Plato and Boethius and his *Dragmaticon philosophiae*, due consideration should be paid to the works of Theodoric (Thierry) of Chartres, especially the *Commentaries on Boethius by Thierry of Chartres and his School*, ed. N. M. Häring (Toronto: Pontifical Institute of Mediaeval Studies, 1971), and his *De sex dierum operibus* (or *Hexaemeron*), also edited by Häring: see Haring [*sic*], 'The Creation of the World According to Thierry of Chartres and Clarenbaldus of Arras', *Archives d'histoire doctrinale et littéraire du Moyen Age* 30 (1955): 137–216.

16. Alain de Lille, *De planctu naturae/The Plaint of Nature*, in Alan of Lille, *Literary Works: Alan*, ed. and trans. W. Wetherbee (DOML 22, 2013), p. 107.

17. Included in Alan of Lille, *Literary Works*.

18. B. Stock, *Myth and Science in the Twelfth Century* (Princeton, NJ: Princeton University Press, 1972); Wetherbee, *Platonism and Poetry*.

19. Bernardus Silvestris, *Cosmographia*, ed. and trans. W. Wetherbee, in Bernardus Silvestris, *Poetic Works* (DOML 38, 2015), 3.1–13 (pp. 30–31).

20. Bernardus Silvestris, *Cosmographia*, 3.35–55 (pp. 32–35).

21. Bernardus Silvestris, *Cosmographia*, 2.1–21 (pp. 82–85).

22. Guillaume de Lorris and Jean de Meun, *Le roman de la rose*, vol. 2, 16729–16753, ed. F. Lecoy (Paris: Champion, 1966); *The Romance of the Rose*, trans. C. Dahlberg (Princeton, NJ: Princeton University Press, 1972), 16729–16751 (pp. 281–82). See De Bruyne, *Études*, vol. 2, pp. 278–78.

23. The pioneering work was done by Pietro Toesca: Toesca, 'Gli affreschi della cattedrale di Anagni', *Le gallerie nazionali italiane* 5 (1902): 116–87.

24. On which see now C. Quattrocchi, *Un martire inglese alla curia di Roma: L'oratorio di San Thomas Beckett di Canterbury nella Cattedrale di Anagni* (Rome: Campisano Editore, 2018).

25. The best explanation is to be found in Lorenzo Cappelletti, *Gli affreschi della cripta anagnina: Iconologia* (Rome: Editrice Pontificia Università Gregoriana, 2002), esp. chs 3–5 and 8.

26. Bibliography on the Crypt is not very extensive, and authors differ in their interpretations. I cite here the most relevant titles: *Un universo di simboli: Gli affreschi della cripta nella cattedrale di Anagni*, ed. G. Giammaria (Rome: Viella, 2001); D. Angelucci and C. Coladarci, *Il Museo della Cattedrale di Anagni*, 2nd edn (Rome: Efesto, 2021); M. Q. Smith, 'Anagni: An Example of Medieval Typological Decoration', *Papers of the British School at Rome* 33 (1965): 1–47; A. Cesaro, 'Il potere magico di Federico I, Signore del mondo e degli elementi: Ideologia del sapere e ideologia del potere negli affreschi della cripta della Cattedrale di Anagni', *Orbis Idearum* 7, no. 1 (2019): 31–62; L. Pressouyre, 'Le cosmos platonicien de la cathédrale d'Anagni', *Mélanges de l'École française de Rome* 78, no. 2 (1966): 551–93; *Il restauro della cripta di Anagni*, ed. A. Bianchi (Rome: Artemide, 2003). Three essays by Marie-Thérèse D'Alverny must moreover be considered particularly relevant: 'Le cosmos symbolique du XII siècle', *Archives d'histoire doctrinale et littéraire du Moyen Age* 28 (1953) : 31–81; 'L'homme comme symbole: Le microcosme',

in *Simboli e simbologia nell'Alto Medioevo* (Spoleto: Fondazione Centro italiano di studi sull'Alto Medioevo, 1976), pp. 123–95 ; and 'La Sagesse et ses sept filles : Recherches sur les allégories de la philosophie et des arts libéraux au XII siècle', in *Mélanges dédiés à la mémoire de Félix Grat*, vol. 1 (Paris: Pecqueur-Grat, 1946), pp. 245–78.

27. Precise passages seem to be referred to from both: for instance, Calcidius 1.22–25, 'De genitura mundi' (Calcidius, *On Plato's 'Timaeus'*, ed. and trans. J. Magee [DOML 41, 2016], pp. 152–59); *Timaeus* 31d–32c, 42c–44a, 48b–d, 49c–50a. Also Hippocrates, who actually appears with Galen in one of the frescoes, is relevant to their meaning, for his theory of the four humours. The ancient classics would of course be known through medieval intermediaries: see Smith, 'Anagni', and Cappelletti, *Gli affreschi*, ch. 2, 'Redire ad fontes', pp. 19–36, and 4, 'Il ciclo scientifico', pp. 43–79.

Chapter Fourteen: The Three Days

1. The Patrologia Latina volumes are 175, 176 and 177. Critical editions exist of the *Super Hierarchiam Dionysii*, ed. D. Poirel (CCCM 178, 2015); of the *De archa Noe* and the *Libellus de formatione archae*, ed. P. Sicard (CCCM 176, 2001)); of the *De vanitate rerum mundanarum* and the *Dialogus de creatione mundi*, ed. C. Giraud (CCCM 269, 2015)); of the *De tribus diebus*, ed. D. Poirel (CCCM 177, 2002). Several volumes of *L'œuvre de Hugues de Saint-Victor* with critical Latin text and facing French translation have been published by Brepols, two at least including the *De arrha animae* and the *Super canticum Mariae*. *Six opuscules spirituels*, ed. R. Bacon, were published by CERF in 2016 (SC 155). For the *Didascalicon*, we have the BAC volume of 2001, ed. C. Munoz Gamero and L. Arribas Hernaez; the 'Fontes Christiani' Latin–German edition published by Herder (Freiburg, 1997); and the Latin–Italian volume, ed. M. Sannelli (Lavis: La Finestra, 2011).

2. CCCM 177, mentioned in n. 1 above.

3. *De tribus diebus* 1.1. Translation from *Trinity and Creation: A Selection of Works of Hugh, Richard and Adam of St Victor*, ed. B. T. Coolman and D. M. Coulter (Turnhout: Brepols, 2010), p. 61.

4. Romans 1:20.

5. Psalm 92:6–7; Isaiah 40:12, trans. Alter; *De tribus diebus* 4.88–93, 4.120–24.

6. *De tribus diebus* 12.409–18.

7. *De tribuus diebus* 12.419–27.

8. *De tribus diebus* 3.70–76 (italics mine). See R. Palmén, 'Beyond Hope and Above Expectation: Wonder in Hugh and Richard of St Victor's Writings', in *La scuola di San Vittore e la letteratura medievale*, ed. C. Bologna and C. Zacchetti (Pisa: Edizioni della Normale, 2022), altogether an important collection of essays.

9. The Introductions to the *Trinity and Creation* volume quoted above are very valuable. D. Poirel, *Hugues de Saint Victor* (Paris, CERF, 1998), and his *Des symboles et des anges: Hugues de St Victor et le reveil dionysien du XIIe siècle* (Turnhout: Brepols, 2013), are indispensable. The best works on Hugh's aesthetics are W. Cizewski, 'Reading the World as Scripture: Hugh of St Victor's *De tribus diebus*', *Florilegium* 9 (1987): 65–88; and L. Karfíková, *'De esse ad pulchrum esse': Schönheit in der Theologie Hugos von St. Viktor* (Turnhout: Brepols, 1998).

Chapter Fifteen: Towards the *altitudo terribilis*

1. *Paradiso* 11.57–59, trans. A. Mandelbaum (Berkeley, CA: University of California Press, 1984. All Italian quotations from the *Paradiso* are from A. M. Chiavacci Leonardi's edition (Milan: Mondadori, 1997). Except where otherwise indicated, as here, English translations are by R. Kirkpatrick (London: Penguin, 2007).

2. This is Claudio Leonardi's thesis in the introduction to the first volume of the Letteratura Francescana series edited by him for the Fondazione Valla and Mondadori (Milan, 2004), *Francesco e Chiara d'Assisi*, 'Introduzione', pp. xiii–clxxvii. The text of the 'Canticle' (lines 5–19) that follows is quoted from the same volume, pp. 217–19 (the translation is mine); the commentary in that volume by Daniele Solvi (pp. 451–60) is essential for a correct understanding of the poem.

3. The adjective 'bello' itself is repeated three times in the 'Canticle', but the entire description underlines the extraordinary beauty, preciousness, clarity (and usefulness) of the created world with a typically Pseudo-Dionysian insistence.

4. The echoes include Daniel, the Epistle of James, the Acts of the Apostles and Revelation.

5. In Romance languages, 'death'—*morte, mort, muerte*—is feminine.

6. Francis concludes by threatening 'woe to those who die in mortal sin' and by praising those who live by God's wishes, because, he says, 'second death' will do them no harm. He projects human life eschatologically to the final Judgment.

7. Von Balthasar, *Glory of the Lord*, vol. 2, pp 260–61: see H. Pouillon, 'La Beauté, proprieté transcendantale chez les Scolastiques (1220–1270)', *Archives d'histoire doctrinale et littéraire du Moyen Age* 15 (1946): 263–329. Of fundamental importance for the aesthetics of Bonaventure is E. De Bruyne, *Études d'esthétique médièvale*, vol. 3: *Le XIIIe siècle*, pp. 189–226.

8. Two of the authors included in the *Summa universae theologiae* or *Summa halensis* published in five volumes by Quaracchi (Rome: Collegio S. Bonaventura, 1924–48). The *Summa halensis* is strongly influenced by the writings of Dionysius the Areopagite both as regards its conception of Scripture (4.516b: *De coelesti hierarchia* 2.2) and its ideas of *pulchrum* and *pulchritudo*, to both of which it returns very often and the latter of which it considers a transcendental: see J. S. Coyle, 'Beauty Among the Transcendentals in the *Summa Halensis*', *Nova et Vetera* (English edition) 18, no. (2020): 1–33.

9. Bonaventure, *Legenda maior*, ed. C. Leonardi in the Letteratura Francescana series: vol. 4 (VM, 2013).

10. Included in the *Opera omnia* (Rome: Ad Claras Aquas [Quaracchi], 1882–1902). For an outline of these works, see C. Leonardi's introduction to *La letteratura francescana*, vol. 3: *Bonaventura: La perfezione cristiana* (VM, 2012), pp. xv–c. Quotations in Latin from the *Itinerarium* are taken from this volume.

11. See Bonaventure, *Collationes in Hexaemeron* 6.1–5; in English, *Conferences on the Six Days of Creation: The Illuminations of the Church*, trans. with notes by J. M. Hammond (New York: The Franciscan Institute, St. Bonaventure University, 2018). See E. Gilson, *La philosophie de Saint Bonaventure* (VP, 1924); J. Ratzinger, *Die Geschichtstheologie des heiligen Bonaventura* (Munich: Schnell und Steiner, 1959).

12. Bonaventure, *Itinerarium* 1.1 and 8.3: for both, Dionysius, *Theologia mystica* 1.1: PG 3, 997A–B; PL 122, 1171C–1173A. Bonaventure cites Dionysius in several works, from the

Itinerarium to the *Breviloquium* and the *Collationes in Hexaemeron*: see J.-G. Bougerol, *Saint Bonaventure: Études sur les sources de sa pensée* (Northampton: Variorum Reprints, 1989).

13. Von Balthasar, *Glory of the Lord*, vol. 2, p. 144. The so called 'radical Averroists', all contemporaries of Bonaventure and Thomas Aquinas and all operating in the same Paris schools—Boethius of Dacia and Siger of Brabant—are not interested at all in the theme of beauty and tend to ignore Plato. Siger alone, in his commentary on the *Liber de causis*, naturally deals with the Platonic tradition, and even refers to the *Timaeus*: see *Les 'Quaestiones super librum de causis' de Siger de Brabant: Édition critique*, ed. A. Marlasca (Louvain: Publications Universitaires/ Paris: Béatrice Nauwelaerts, 1972), e.g., p. 76.

14. Bonaventure, *De triplici via* 3.12: St. Bonaventure of Bagnoregio, *The Triple Way, or The Kindling of Love*, ed. and trans. P.D.M. Fehlner (New Bedford, MA, Academy of the Immaculate, 2012;), pp. 187–88 (italics mine). On the qualification of this passage as 'sublime', see P. Boitani, *The Tragic and the Sublime in Medieval Literature* (CUP, 1989), pp. 252–53.

15. *Soliloquium*, Prologue 1 and 4; *Breviloquium*, Prologue 3; each dimension is discussed in the subsequent chapters, with references to Ephesians 3:14–18.

16. Bonaventure, *Legenda maior* 9.6–7; *The Life of St. Francis*, trans. E. Cousins, in Bonaventure, *The Soul's Journey into God; The Tree of Life; The Life of St. Francis* (New York, Paulist Press, 1978), at p. 263.

17. Ecclesiastes 1:8.

18. Bonaventure, *De reductione artium ad theologiam*, trans. E. T. Healy, rev. Z. Hayes, in *Works of Saint Bonaventure*, vol. 1 (New York: The Franciscan Institute, St. Bonaventure University, 1996), 10 (p. 49).

19. Assunto, *La critica d'arte*, p. 237.

20. Bonaventure, *Itinerarium* 2.10.8–9; *The Journey of the Mind to God*, trans. P. Boehner and Z. Hayes, in *Works of Saint Bonaventure*, vol. 2 (New York: The Franciscan Institute, St. Bonaventure University, 2002), p. 12.

21. Bonaventure, *Breviloquium*, in *The Works of Bonaventure: Cardinal Seraphic Doctor and Saint*, vol. 1, trans. J. de Vinck (New York: St. Anthony's Guild Press, 1963), Prologue 3.3 (p. 13).

22. Bonaventure, *Breviloquium*, Prologue 2.4 (p. 13).

23. Bonaventure, *Collationes in Hexaemeron/Conferences on the Six Days* 20.8.

24. See De Bruyne, *Études*, vol. 3, pp. 131–35, 199–207.

25. U. Eco, *Art and Beauty in the Middle Ages* (New Haven, CT: Yale University Press, 1986)], pp. 93–96.

26. Bonaventure, *Collationes in Hexaemeron/Conferences on the Six Days* 13.1–2.

27. Ecclesiastes (Qohelet) 1:7.

28. Psalm 92:3.

29. Psalm 92:4.

30. Psalm 106:23.

31. Ecclesiastes (Qohelet) 7:24; Ecclesiasticus (Sirach) 24:4–5.

32. Luke 26:45.

33. The *Collationes* (here, no. 13) are published in volume 5 of Bonaventure's *Opera omnia* (Rome: Quaracchi, 1893). The English translation by J. M. Hammond is to be found in *Works of Saint Bonaventure*, vol. 18 (New York: The Franciscan Institute, St. Bonaventure University, 2018.

Chapter Sixteen: The Names of God

1. A Dionysian programme to the full, in other words: *Super Dionysium De ecclesiastica hierarchia*, ed. M. Burger, P. Simon and W. Kübel (1999); *Super Dionysium De caelesti hierarchia*, ed. P. Simon and W. Kübel (1993); *Super Dionysii Mysticam theologiam et Epistulas*, ed. P. Simon (1978); all published in *Opera omnia* (Münster: Monasterii Westfalorum, Aschendorff).

2. See W. J. Hankey, 'Dionysius in Albertus Magnus and His Student Thomas Aquinas', in *Oxford Handbook of Dionysius the Areopagite*, pp. 394–416. It should be remembered that Thomas transcribed by hand all Albert's comments on Dionysus: see Manuscript I B 54 in the Biblioteca Nazionale di Napoli.

3. See Thomas d'Aquin, *Super Librum de causis expositio*, ed. H.-D. Saffrey, 2nd edn (VP, 2002), 'Proemium', p. 3 and 'Introduction', pp. xxxvi–xxxvii; English translation: Thomas Aquinas, *Complete Works*, vol. 59 (2024), available at https://aquinas.cc/la/en/~LibCaus

4. U. Eco, *Il problema estetico in Tommaso d'Aquino* (Milan: Bompiani, 1956); Eco, *Arte e bellezza nell'estetica medievale* (Milan: La nave di Teseo, 2016), pp. 54–60, 131–40, 149–68: both, together with his *Metafora e conoscenza nel Medioevo* (with a section devoted to Dionysius), in Eco, *Scritti sul pensiero medievale*, 3rd edn (BPO, 2016); English translations: *The Aesthetics of Thomas Aquinas*, trans. H. Bredin (Cambridge, MA: Harvard University Press, 1988); *Art and Beauty* (cited above).

5. Albertus Magnus, *Super De divinis nominibus*, ed. P. Simon (Münster: Monasterii Westfalorum, Aschendorff, 1972), 4.72 (p. 182).

6. Thomas Aquinas, *In librum beati Dionysii De divinis nominibus expositio, Commentary on the Book on the Divine Names of Blessed Denys/Exposition of Dionysius' On the Divine Names* (bilingual Latin/English edition), trans. U. Hannon (Aquinas Institute/Emmaus Press online bilingual Latin/English edition, 2024, https://aquinas.cc/en/el/~DeDivNom), 4.5.349.

7. Albertus, *Super De divinis nominibus* 4.72 (p. 182).

8. Eco, *Art and Beauty*, p. 25.

9. Albertus, *Super De divinis nominibus* 4.84 (p. 190); 4.74 (p. 183); my translation.

10. Albertus, *Super De divinis nominibus* 4.77 (p. 186); 4.114 (p. 211) (repeated more than once); 4.78 (p. 187); my translation.

11. Albertus, *Super De divinis nominibus* 454.71.

12. Aquinas, *In librum beati Dionysii* 4.5.37: Dionysius, *Divine Names* 701C–D (pp. 414–15), quoting *Symposium* 211a.

13. Aquinas, *In librum beati Dionysii* 4.5.353.

14. Thomas Aquinas, *Summa Theologiae*, trans. L. Shapcote (Aquinas Institute/Emmaus Press online bilingual Latin/English edition, 2018: https://aquinas.cc/la/en/~ST.I), I.q5.a4, ad 1.

15. Aquinas, *In librum beati Dionysii* 4.21.554.

16. James Joyce, *A Portrait of an Artist as a Young Man*, ed. S. Deane (London, Penguin, 1992 [1916]), p. 229.

17. Aquinas, *Summa Theologiae*, I.q39.a8 resp.

18. Albertus, *Super De divinis nominibus* 4.38–59 (pp. 143–67). Albert is also widely attributed with the authorship of a consistent *Speculum astronomiae*: see P. Zambelli, *The 'Speculum astronomiae' and Its Enigma* (Dordrecht: Kluwer, 1992).

19. Aquinas, *In librum beati Dionysii* 4.3.306: Malachi 4:2.

20. Albertus Magnus, *Super Dionysii Mysticam theologiam et Epistulas*, ed. P. Simon, (Münster: Monasterii Westfalorum, Aschendorff, 1978), 40–65 (p. 504).

21. Albertus, *Super Dionysii Mysticam theologiam*, 71–80 (p. 529).

22. Aquinas, *Summa Theologiae* I.q1.a9.

23. Aquinas, *Summa Theologiae* I-II.q101.a2.

24. Aquinas, *Summa Theologiae* I.q1.a9.

Chapter Seventeen: *Decor, altitudo, gloria*

1. Thomas Aquinas, *Expositio super Iob ad Litteram/Literal Commentary on Job* (bilingual edition based on the Editio Leonina), ed. Aquinas Institute, trans. B.T.B. Mullady (Lander,WY: Aquinas Institute, 2016), C.37.

2. A particularly relevant passage.

3. Aristotle, *De caelo* 2.14.290b12.

4. Job 38:38.

5. Aquinas, *Expositio super Iob* C.38.

6. Aquinas, *Expositio super Iob* C.38.

7. Aquinas, *Expositio super Iob* C.40.529.

Chapter Eighteen: *Philomythía* and Poetry

1. See Boyde, *Dante Philomythes*, and Dronke, *Fabula*, both quoted here several times. I anticipated some of the views I uphold here in my *Verso l'incanto: Lezioni sulla poesia* (Rome: Laterza, 2021).

2. Aristotle, *Metaphysics Volume 1: Books 1–9*, LCL 271, trans. H. Tredennick (1933), 1.2.982b11–21 (pp. 12–13).

3. Albertus Magnus, *Metaphysica*, t. 1, ed. B. Geyer (Münster: Monasterii Westfalorum, Aschendorff, 1960), 2.6 (p. 23): the whole of Albert's discussion in chapters 6–11 is remarkable, as also his discussion of art later in the *Metaphysica*: 10.20; 13.10–50; 15.13–16, 15.50; 11.6–13; 12.74; 13.69–75, etc.; and of *poiesis* and *poetica*, starting with 23.49–63, and then in 277.55; 345.10.

4. In his commentaries on the *Analytica posteriora* and the *Ethica Nicomachea*: see M. O. Boyle, 'The Wonder of the Heart: Albert the Great on the Origin of Philosophy', *Viator* 45, no. 2 (2014): 149–72; and Boyle, *Cultural Anatomies of the Heart in Aristotle, Augustine, Aquinas, Calvin, and Harvey* (London, Palgrave Macmillan, 2018).

5. Albertus, *Metaphysica* 1.2.6 (p. 23)

6. S. Thomae Aquinatis, *In duodecim libros metaphysicorum Aristotelis expositio*, ed. M. R. Cathala and R. Spiazzi, 2nd edn (Turin: Marietti, 1971), 1.3.55 (p. 18).

7. See S. J. Broadie, 'A Science of First Principles', in *Aristotle's Metaphysics Alpha: Symposium Aristotelicum*, ed. C. Steel (OUP, 2012), pp. 43–67 at 63.

8. Aristotle, *Metaphysics* 7.6.1071b26–27 (pp. 142–43).

9. Aquinas, *In metaphysicorum* 12.6.2502 (p. 586). Orpheus is an addition by Thomas, who does not, however, introduce Aristotle's Empedocles and his theory of Love and Strife, although he mentions them in 1.1.132 at line 8 (p. 38).

10. Aquinas, *In metaphysicorum* 12.6.2502–4 (p. 586).

11. Aristotle, *Metaphysics* 1.4.984b (p. 23) Thomas borrows from Aristotle, but devotes much greater space to *Amor*: Aquinas, *In metaphysicorum* 1.5.101–2 (p. 29).

12. Aristotle, *Metaphysics* 1.4.984b (pp. 24–27): as if both Parmenides and Hesiod were 'implying that there must be in the world some cause to move things and combine them'.

13. Aquinas, *In metaphysicorum* 1.5.102 (p. 29): 'Quod autem amor congreget, ex hoc patet; quia ipse amor est unio quaedam amantis et amati, dum amans amatum quasi se reputat': the last sentence of a discussion of over twenty-five lines.

14. The same attitude is shared in the fourteenth century by the Oxford *magister* Robert Holcot in his commentary on the Book of Wisdom (M. Roberti Holkoth, *In librum Sapientiae regis Salomonis praelectiones CCXIII* [Basel: Sebastianus Henricpetri, 1586]), who, when it comes to Creation, follows Augustine's *City of God* (11.21) and hence the *Timaeus* in Calcidius's translation (lectio 13). For a thorough examination of Holcot's Creation theory, see E. Di Rocco, 'The Wonder of Creation: Robert Holcot's Commentary to the Book of Wisdom', in *Myths of Origins. Literary and Cultural Patterns*, ed. E. Di Rocco and C. Lombardi (Leiden: Brill, 2024), pp. 39–53.

15. Maximus of Tyre, *The Philosophical Orations*, trans. M. B. Trapp (OUP, 1997), 4.1 (p. 33).

16. Marcus Aurelius, *Meditations*, in *Marcus Aurelius*, LCL 58, ed. and trans. C. R. Haines (1916), 1.7 (p. 5).

17. Tasso, *Discorsi*, p. 71 (my translation).

18. John Keats, 'Ode on a Grecian Urn' (orig. 'On a Grecian Urn', *Annals of Fine Arts*, 1819), in Keats, *Lamia, Isabella, The Eve of St Agnes, and Other Poems* (London: Taylor and Hessey, 1820).

Chapter Nineteen: 'I love those who love me'

1. *Timaeus* 39e.

2. Petrucci, p. 293 (my translation).

3. *Timaeus* 40d–41a.

4. Cicero, *On the Nature of the Gods* (*De natura deorum*) LCL 268, trans. H. Rackham, (1933), 268.1.25–31 (pp. 28–35). See M. Tullii Ciceronis, *De natura deorum libri tres*, with Introduction and commentary by J. B. Mayor, 3 vols (CUP, 1880–85).

5. Wisdom (*KJB* Apocrypha) 13:1–6 (the Book of Wisdom is not included in either the Hebrew or Protestant Bibles). The purely mythological account of Genesis 6:1–4 should be borne in mind, with the narration of the generations between the divine beings and the daughters of men. For similar reflections in the New Testament, see Romans 1:20–23. Deuteronomy and the Prophets strongly oppose empty idols created from elements of creation (wood, stone, etc.): Deuteronomy 4:28; 28:36 and 64; 29:16; 2 Kings 19:18; Isaiah 37:19; Jeremiah 2:27; Ezekiel 20:32.

6. Wisdom 7:22–30, *KJB* translation (italics mine).

7. L. Mazzinghi, in the three-volume *Bibbia* (Bible) prepared under the direction of Enzo Bianchi (Turin: Einaudi, 2022), vol. 2, p. 1001n. Mazzinghi is the author of an excellent, extensive commentary on Wisdom in *Libro della Sapienza*, Analecta Biblica 13 (Rome: Pontifical Biblical Institute, Gregorian and Biblical Press, 2020), which mentions but is also superior to that of C. Larcher, *Le livre de la sagesse, ou La sagesse de Salomom*, 3 vols (Paris: Gabalda,

1983–85); to the three volumes of the *Libro della sapienza* by G. Scarpat, (Brescia: Paideia, 1996–2000); and to *The Wisdom of Solomon*, ed. D. Winston, New Haven, CT: Yale University Press, 1979).

8. *Timaeus* 29c–29a.

9. Philo of Alexandria, *On the Unchangeablenss of God*, in *Philo*, vol. 3, LCL 247, trans. F. H. Colson and G. H. Whittaker (1939), 108.23 (pp. 64–65).

10. Seneca, *Epistles, Volume 1: 1–65*, LCL 75, trans. R. M. Gummere (1917), 65.10 (pp. 450–51).

11. Proverbs (*KJB*) 8:1; 8:11; 8:22–31: See R. Imbach, '"Le sage qui écoute sera plus sage". Bible et philosophie:. Perspectives d'un historien de la philosophie médiévale', *Revue de théologie et de philosophie* 151, no. 2 (2019): 87–126.

12. Proverbs 8:8, 8:11, 8:16.

13. Dante, *Convivio* 3.5.4–7. English translations of the *Convivio* here and below are from Dante Alighieri, *Il Convivio (The Banquet)*, trans. R. H. Lansing (New York: Garland, 1990), available at https://digitaldante.columbia.edu/text/library/the-convivio/

14. 'Amor che ne la mente mi ragiona', ll. 55–60, in Dante Alighieri, *Convivio*, in *Opere minori*, t. 1.2, ed. C. Vasoli and D. De Robertis (Milan: Ricciardi, 1988; henceforth: *Convivio*), p. 284. On 'Amor che ne la mente mi ragiona', see also A. Frisardi's notes in his edition of the *Convivio* (CUP, 2018), pp. 457–64.

15. Acts 2; for Guinizzelli, see *Convivio*, p. 286n (Vasoli).

16. 'Amor che ne la mente mi ragiona', ll. 65–67; see K. Foster and P. Boyde, *Dante's Lyric Poetry*, vol. 2: *Commentary* (OUP, 1967), p. 174: 'Dante [. . .] delighted in an intermittent contemplation of ideal wisdom as such, universally considered in all its lucid and yet mysterious beauty; and it is contemplation of this sort that the present canzone aims at expressing. It is exquisitely appropriate that, to evoke a like contemplative "moment" at the foot of Mount Purgatory, this canzone will be sung by Dante's friend Casella (*Purg.* II, 106–17)'.

17. *Convivio* 3.15.1–5.

18. Wisdom 8:2.

19. *Convivio* 4.25.5: Aristotle, *Metaphysics* 1.2.982b12–19. See K. Foster, 'The Mind in Love: Dante's Philosophy', in *Dante*, ed. J. Freccero (Englewood Cliffs, NJ: Prentice Hall, 1965), pp. 43–60 at 50.

20. Ecclesiasticus (Sirach) 42:21.

21. Proverbs 8:17.

22. *Convivio* 3.11.12.

23. Vasoli, ad *Convivio* 3.11.12 (pp. 428–29; italics mine).

24. Song of Solomon 1:15–17.

25. *Convivio* 2.15.12.

26. Ecclesiasticus (Sirach) 24:1–9; Song of Solomon 4:9.

27. *Purgatorio* 29.85–87: Luke 1:28, from Judith 13:23.

28. *Convivio* 2.14.20.

29. In one of the best books I know about this controversial procession, *La puttana e il gigante: Dal 'Cantico dei Cantici' al Paradiso Terrestre di Dante* (Ravenna: Longo, 1998), pp. 206–17, Lino Pertile reconstructs the exegetical tradition in particular of the giant who appears in

Purgatorio 32.152, and identifies him with the bridegroom of the Song via a well-established view which associated him with the giant of Psalm 19: 'in them hath he set a tabernacle for the sun, / Which is as a bridegroom coming out of the chamber (Vulgate, *thalamo*), and rejoiceth as a strong man (Vulgate: *gigas*) to run a race'. Thus the cosmic theme is linked with those of love, beauty, and wisdom.

Chapter Twenty: 'What Timaeus argues about the souls'

1. In A. E. Taylor's classic work, *Commentary on Plato's 'Timaeus'*, 2nd edn (OUP, 1928), Dante is mentioned a good ten times.

2. *Convivio* 2.12.2.

3. See P. Boitani, 'Dante da Boezio a Chartres', in *Convegno: La biblioteca di Dante (Roma, 7–9 ottobre 2021)*, Atti dei Convegni Lincei 345 (Rome: Bardi, 2022), pp. 343–64.

4. *Paradiso* 28.130–39. But Dionysius's penetration is considerably deeper, as perhaps I first realised while studying *Paradiso* 33 in 'The Sibyl's Leaves', *Dante Studies* 96 (1978): 83–126, and as D. Sbacchi later demonstrated more extensively in his *La presenza di Dionigi Areopagita nel Paradiso di Dante* (Florence: Olschki, 2006).

5. See S. Vanni Rovighi, 'Il canto IV del Paradiso visto da uno studioso di filosofia medievale', *Studi danteschi* 48 (1971): 67–82; P. Giannantonio, 'La poesia dottrinale (*Paradiso* IV)', *Critica letteraria* 8 (1980): 3–23; P. Boyde, *Perception and Passion in Dante's Commedia* (CUP, 1993), pp. 193–209; A. Raffi, 'Dante e il *Timeo*: Nota sugli aspetti metaletterari del IV canto del *Paradiso*', *Campi immaginabili* 34/35 (2007).

6. Here (*Paradiso* 4.39), however, instead of 'celestial' as Kirkpatrick has it, translating from Petrocchi's edition, I agree with Chiavacci Leonardi's reading of the word as 'spiritual', following E. Parodi, *Poesia e storia nella Divina Commedia* (Vicenza: Neri Pozza, 1965), pp. 377–78.

7. *Paradiso* 4.22–63.

8. Calcidius, *On Plato's 'Timaeus'*, ed. and trans. Magee, pp. 71–85; Macrobius, *Commentary on the Dream of Scipio*, trans. W. H. Stahl (New York: Columbia University Press, 1952), pp. 171–81.

9. See *Vedere l'invisibile: Nicea e lo statuto dell'Immagine*, ed. L. Russo, 2nd edn (Palermo: Aesthetica, 1999).

10. Dionysius, *De divinis nominibus*, 1.6–8, 596A–597B; Aquinas, *In librum beati Dionysii*, 3.97–98.

11. Aquinas, *Summa Theologiae* I.q1.a9 resp. ad 1–3; q1.a10, ad 3.

12. Isidore, *Etymologiae* 1.32.22.

13. See the essays published in *Dante and the Human Body*, ed. J. C. Barnes and M. Sonzogni (Dublin: Irish Academic Press, 2005).

14. See M. Ariani, 'Le stelle di Timeo e le metafore dell'ineffabile', in Ariani, *Lux inaccessibilis : Metafore e teologia della luce nel 'Paradiso' di Dante* (Rome: Aracne, 2010), pp. 151–58.

15. A. M. Chiavacci Leonardi, *DDC*, comment to *Paradiso* 4.58–60 (p. 115).

16. *Epistole* 13.28–29 (77–84), Princeton Dante Project, Testo critico della Società Dantesca Italiana (Florence: Società Dantesca Italiana, 1960), ed. E. Pistelli, trans. P. Toynbee; quotation from 83–84.

17. See the comment by L. Azzetta, ad loc., in Dante Alighieri, *Epistole; Eglcge; Questio de aqua et terra*, ed. M. Baglio and L. Azzetta, M. Pettoletti and M Rinaldi (Rome: Salerno Editrice, 2021); and the fundamental and exhaustive essay by M. Ariani, 'I "metaphorismi" di Dante', in *Dante e la metafora*, ed. Ariani (Florence: Olschki, 2009), pp. 1–57; also, in the same volume, Ariani, '"Metafore assolute": Emanazionismo e sinestesie della luce fluente', pp. 193–219.

Chapter Twenty-One: 'The hall-mark of genius'

1. Pound, *Spirit of Romance*, p. 144. To have a fuller idea of Pound's conception of Dante, see the collection of material in E. Pound, *Dante (dalle carte Scheiwiller)*, ed. C. Bologna and L. Fabiani (Venice: Marsilio, 2015).
2. In particular, *Phaedrus* 247c–d.
3. Pound, *Spirit of Romance*, pp. 144–45.
4. Pound, *Spirit of Romance*, p. 147 (italics mine).
5. Pound, *Spirit of Romance*, p. 166.
6. According to Ariani, the quotation of *Paradiso* 4.49, refers to Timaeus the person, not the title of the dialogue: Ariani, 'I "metaphorismi"', p. 10 n. 31

Chapter Twenty-Two: 'We must lose ourselves'

1. See V. Albi, *Sotto il manto delle favole: La ricezione di Fulgenzio nelle opere di Dante e negli antichi commenti alla 'Commedia'* (Ravenna: Longo, 2021).
2. *Inferno* 4.135.
3. *Purgatorio* 3.34–39.
4. *Purgatorio* 3.37–45.
5. *Epistole* 13.29, Princeton Dante Project.

Chapter Twenty-Three: 'Those things that cannot die and those that can'

1. *Epistole* 13.89, Princeton Dante Project.
2. John 17:3; Boethius, *Consolation* 3 m. 9, 27.
3. This is a procedure typical of Dante: the passages combining usefulness and pleasure are in Horace's *Ars poetica* 333–34 and 343–44.
4. Cassiodorus, *Variae* 1.45, *Variarum libri XII*, ed. Å. J. Fridh (CCSL 96, 1973), p. 49.
5. *Paradiso* 7.64–69.
6. Boethius, *Consolation* 3 m. 9, 6. See Boyde, *Dante Philomythes*, pp. 235–47.
7. *Paradiso* 13.52–60.

Chapter Twenty-Four: 'To new loves Love Eternal opened out'

1. The third time Dante speaks of Creation, with the image from Proverbs 8:27–29, of God who 'turned His compass, around the reaches of the universe' (the passage from Proverbs is already used in *Convivio* 3.15.16, but without the image of God with a compass), in *Paradiso* 19.40–45, is the only occurrence that does not contain Neoplatonic elements.

2. *Convivio*, explicitly ('Libro de le Cagioni') at 3.2.4, 3.6.4, 3.7.2 and 4.21.9; but Vasoli in his commentary on the *Convivio* (Dante, *Opere minori*, t. 1.2) suggests far more occurrences: see A. Raffi, 'Dante e il *Liber De causis*: Il problema della creazione nella "teologia" della *Commedia*', *Campi immaginabili* 40/41 (2009).

3. *Paradiso* 29.13–18.

4. See P. Boitani, 'The Poetry and Poetics of the Creation', in *Dante's 'Commedia': Theology as Poetry*, ed. V. Montemaggi and M. Treherne (Notre Dame, IN, University of Notre Dame Press, 2010), pp. 95–130.

5. Augustine, *De Genesi ad litteram* 1.15.29, already speaks of 'informis materia' and 'res formatae', using the expression 'concreatum' employed in this passage by Dante: 'Non quia informis materia formatis rebus tempore prior est, cum sit utrumque simul concreatum et unde factum est, et quod factum est'.

6. Thomas Aquinas, *Summa contra Gentiles* 2.19, *Quod in creatione non sit successio*: 'Relinquitur igitur quod creatio sit in instanti. Unde simul aliquid, dum creatur, creatum est: sicut illuminatur et illuminatum est' (BAC, 1968), p. 427.

7. Hieronymus, *In Epist. ad Titum* 1.2.

8. *Paradiso* 29.13–45.

Chapter Twenty-Five: 'That deep mind'

1. *Paradiso* 2.127–32.

2. Boethius, *Consolation* 3 m. 9, 13–17 (italics mine).

3. Boethius, *Consolation* 3 m. 11 (italics mine).

4. Boethius, *Consolation* 3 pr. 12, 1.

Chapter Twenty-Six: 'Amor quo caelum regitur'

1. Boethius, *Consolation* 2 m. 8.

2. See C. J. De Vogel, 'Amor quo caelum regitur', *Vivarium* 1 (1963): 2–34, and P. Dronke, 'L'amor che move il sole e l'altre stelle', reprinted in Dronke, *Medieval Poet*, pp. 439–75. Dronke's introduction and comment to the VM (2023) edition of the *Consolation* are magnificent. See also Gruber, *Kommentar zu Boethius*, pp. 228–32.

3. As well as on the Boccaccio of *Filostrato* 3.74–79, and on the Chaucer of *Troilus*, 3.1–49 and 3.1744–80.

4. *Inferno* 1.37–40; *Paradiso* 33.145 (italics mine).

5. As again, closely linked to 2 m. 8, and in counterpoint to 1 m. 5, in 6 m. 6, where Boethius speaks of 'cunctis communis amor', and concludes the song by writing, ' This is the love common to all things, /And they seek to be bound by their end, the good, / Since in no other way could they endure, / If the causes that gave them being did not flow back / Under the power of returning love.'

6. Dronke, ad loc., 3 m. 9, 6–9, also finds a biblical reminiscence here, as too had Bieler before him: *Sap.* 7.27: 'et in se permanens omnia innovat' (and remaining in herself, she maketh all things new).

Chapter Twenty-Seven: 'He laughed, self-mockingly'

1. Gregory, *Moralia in Iob* 32.23.41–43

2. *Paradiso* 28.135: 'di sé medesmo rise'.

3. Even if Gregory himself changed his mind about the angelic hierarchies, adopting a model very close to that of Dionysius: see *Homiliae in evangelia* 2.34.7.

4. *Paradiso* 28.51–57.

5. Chiavacci Leonardi, *DDC*, ad *Paradiso* 28.67–72 (pp. 777–78).

6. *Paradiso* 28.79–87.

7. *Paradiso* 29.142–45.

8. *Paradiso* 30.61–69.

Chapter Twenty-Eight: 'This reason moved Augustine'

1. Lewis, *Discarded Image*, p. 45.

2. *Inferno* 11.64–65; *Inferno* 24.110–11: *Somnium* 4.3; Macrobius's *Commentary* 1.22.4–8.

3. *Inferno* 1.79–80: Macrobius, *Saturnalia, Volume 2: Books* 3–5, LCL 511, ed. and trans. R. A. Kaster (2011), 5.1.10 (pp. 218–19).

4. *Convivio* 1.2.12–15: *Convivio*, trans. Lansing.

5. Throughout the book, but see also his 'Dante e la tradizione del Timeo', *Atti e memorie dell'Accademia nazionale di scienze, lettere e arti di Modena* 6, no. 4 (1962): 107–23.

6. Augustinus, *Contra academicos, De beata vita, De ordine*, ed. T. Fuhrer and S. Adam (Berlin: De Gruyter, 2017); Augustine, *On the Happy Life*, in *St. Augustine's Cassiciacum Dialogues*, vol. 2, trans. M. P. Foley (New Haven, CT: Yale University Press, 2019), p. 17. See *De moribus ecclesiae* 2.21.

Chapter Twenty-Nine: 'Fountain of light, seedbed of life'

1. For the original texts in Latin, see Guillelmus, *Dragmaticon philosophiae, Summa de Philosophia in Vulgari*; Guillelmus, *Glosae super Boetium*;Guillelmus, *Glosae super Platonem*; *Commentaries on Boethius by Thierry of Chartres* (ed. Häring); N. M. Häring, *Life and Works of Clarembald of Arras* (Toronto: Pontifical Institute of Mediaeval Studies, 1965). On the school of Chartres, see Wetherbee's classic *Platonism and Poetry*.

2. For the works of William of Saint-Thierry, Ivo, Aelred, Saint Bernard and Richard, see *Trattati d'amore cristiani del XII secolo*, ed. F. Zambon, 2 vols (VM, 2007–2008); for Hildegard, at least the *Liber divinorum operum*, ed. A. Derolez and P. Dronke (CCCM 92, 1996), and *Scivias*, ed. A. Führkötter (CCCM 43, 1978). On Richard, see the important work by M. Mocan, *L'arca della mente: Riccardo di San Vittore nella 'Commedia' di Dante* (Florence: Olschki, 2012).

3. The *Mathematicus* is published in Latin and English, ed. D. M. Stone, in *Archives d'histoire doctrinale et littéraire du Moyen Age* 63 (1996): 209–83. If Bernard, or Bernardus, Silvestris (of Tours) is the same person as Bernard of Chartres (but the two have been considered distinct writers for a while now), his works also include the *Glosae super Platonem* (ed. P. E. Dutton [Toronto: Pontifical Institute of Mediaeval Studies, 1991]), attributed to the latter. To Bernard

of Chartres is attributed the authorship of a comment on Martianus Capella published in *Tutti i commenti a Marziano Capella*, ed. I. Ramelli (BPO, 2006).

4. Bernardus Silvestris, *Cosmographia*, pp. 3–5.

5. See P. Dronke, 'The Background of the Cosmographia: Some Testimonies', in Bernardus Silvestris, *Cosmographia*, ed. Dronke (Leiden: Brill, 1978), pp. 70–91.

6. The copy of the *Cosmographia* transcribed by hand by Boccaccio is contained in the Laurenziana manuscript n. XXXIII 31 in the Biblioteca Laurenziana, Florence; the quotation is from the *Esposizioni sopra la Comedia di Dante* 2.2.30–31, ed. G. Padoan, in *Tutte le opere di Giovanni Boccaccio*, ed. V. Branca, vol. 6 (Milan: Mondadori, 1965).

7. See above, p. 225.

8. Trans. Wetherbee, pp. 24–27.

9. In *The Commentary on the First Six Books of the Aeneid of Vergil Commonly Attributed to Bernardus Silvestris*, ed. J. W Jones and E. F. Jones (Lincoln, NE, University of Nebraska Press, 1977). For the attribution to Bernardus, see P. Dronke, 'Bernardo Silvestre' in *Enciclopedia Virgiliana*, vol. 1 (Rome: Istituto dell'Enciclopedia Italiana, 1997), pp. 497–500.

10. The classic edition of Fulgentius is edited by R. Helm, containing in a single Teubnerian volume (Leipzig, 1898), the works of Fabius Fulgentius Planciades, Fabius Claudius Gordianus Fulgentius and Saint Fulgentius bishop.

11. See H. T. Silverstein, 'Dante and Vergil the Mystic', *Harvard Studies and Notes in Philology and Literature* 34 (1932): 51–82; D. Thompson, 'Dante and Bernard Silvestris', *Viator* 1 (1971): 201–6. See also S. Italia, *Dante e l'esegesi virgiliana: Tra Servio, Fulgenzio e Bernardo Silvestre* (Acireale: Bonanno, 2013).

Chapter Thirty: 'Beings and accidents and modes of life'

1. See S. Barsella, *In the Light of the Angels: Angelology and Cosmology in Dante's 'Divina Commedia'* (Florence: Olschki, 2010).

2. *Paradiso* 33.85–90.

3. Pseudo-Dionysius, *The Divine Names*, in *Pseudo-Dionysius: The Complete Works*, trans. C. Luibheid (Mahwah, NJ: Paulist Press, 1987), 820D (p. 99).

4. Eriugena, *Periphyseon*, trans. Sheldon-Williams. Greek text and Italian translation of Dionysius in *Dionigi Areopagita: Tutte le opere*. Latin text of Dionysius in Aquinas, *In librum beati Dionysii*, pp. 230–31; or, in the translation by Johannes Scotus cited here, in PL 122, 1149; *Periphyseon* 1.470b–472c, which I read in P. Dronke's edition in five volumes, *Sulle nature dell'universo* (VM, 2012–17).

5. Aquinas, *In librum beati Dionysii* 5.1.640–41.

Chapter Thirty-One: The Moon Smiles Among the Eternal Nymphs

1. Polycarp Leyser, *Historia poetarum et poematum medii aevi* (Halae Magdeb. [Halle]: Novi Bibliopolii, 1721).

2. *Alani Magni de Insulis Opera moralia, paraenetica, et polemica*, 'opere et stvdio R. D. Caroli De Visch' ('Antverpiae [Antwerp]: 'apud Gvilielmvm Lesteenivm et Engelbertvm Gymnicvm', 1654).

3. The most complete edition of Alan's works to date is PL 210. W. Wetherbee edited his *Literary Works* for DOML 22 (2013). Many *Textes inédits* were edited by M.-Th. D'Alverny (VP, 1965). The classic edition of the *Anticlaudianus* is by R. Bossuat (VP, 1955); of *De planctu naturae* by N. M. Häring in *Studi medievali* 3rd series 19 (1978): 797–879.

4. See C. Vasoli, 'La "Theologia Apothetica" di Alano di Lilla', *Rivista critica di storia della filosofia* 16, no. 3 (1961): 153–87.

5. The most complete edition available is that of F. Hudry (VP, 2009); a partial English translation by Juan Acevedo is available on the website of The Matheson Trust: https://www.themathesontrust.org/papers/metaphysics/XXIV-A4.pdf

6. Aquinas, *Super Librum de causis*, p. 3: Aquinas, *Complete Works*, vol. 59 (2024), https://aquinas.cc/la/en/~LibCaus. In his *De causis*, Albert the Great had already expressed doubts as to the Aristotelian authorship: Albertus Magnus, *De causis et processu universitatis a prima causa*, ed. W. Fauser (Münster: Monasterii Westfalorum, Aschendorff, 1993; Albertus, *Buch über die Ursachen und den Hervorgang von allem aus der ersten Ursache: Erstes Buch*, ed. H. Möhle, Philosophische Bibliothek 580 (Hamburg: Meiner, 2018).

7. *Epistole* 13.57, Princeton Dante Project. See B. Nardi, 'Le citazioni dantesche del *Liber de causis*', in Nardi, *Saggi*, pp. 82–109.

8. *Epistole* 13.58–61, Princeton Dante Project; Dionysius, *De coelesti hierarchia* 3.2; *Liber de causis* 10.

9. *Liber de causis*, 1 and 10.

10. C. Vasoli, 'Alano di Lilla' in *Enciclopedia dantesca*, vol. 1 (Rome: Istituto dell'Enciclopedia Italiana, 1970).

11. Vasoli, 'Alano di Lilla'.

12. E. R. Curtius, *European Literature and the Latin Middle Ages*, trans. W. R. Trask, (London: Routledge, 1953), p. 360.

13. P. Dronke, 'Boethius, Alanus and Dante', in Dronke, *Medieval Poet*, pp. 431–38, at 432 n. 4. *Contra* Dronke and much of the criticism mentioned here, see a recent essay by Z. G. Barański, 'Dante e Alano di Lilla: Problemi di metodo storico-critico', in *Studi e problemi di critica testuale* 103 (2021): 57–71. Barański denies the possibility of claiming with any certainty, on the basis of the evidence put forward up to now, the existence of a direct textual relationship between Dante and Alan.

14. A. Ciotti, 'Alano e Dante', *Convivium* n.s. 3 (1960): 257–88. See studies by S. Prandi: 'Teologia come pittura: Alain de Lille e Dante (*Purg.* X–XII)', in *La parola e l'immagine: Studi in onore di Gianni Venturi*, ed. M. Ariani et al. (Florence: Olschki, 2011), vol. 1, pp. 99–116; and '"Ad intuitum supercelestium formarum": Alain de Lille e la *Commedia*', in *Dante poeta cristiano e la cultura religiosa medievale: In ricordo di Anna Maria Chiavacci Leonardi*, ed. G. Ledda (Ravenna: Centro dantesco dei Frati minori conventuali, 2018), pp. 117–35.

15. Ciotti, 'Alano e Dante', p. 284.

16. See Dante, *Paradiso*, trans. Kirkpatrick, p. 431 nn. 25–27.

17. Allen Mandelbaum's translation. *The Divine Comedy* (New York: Knopf, 1995).

18. Alan of Lille, *Anticlaudianus*, in *Literary Works*, pp. 362–63 (prose translation arranged as verse).

19. *Iliad* 8.555–59; Sappho 34, in *Poetarum lesbiorum fragmenta*, ed. E. Lobel and D. Page (OUP, 1955), p. 33; translation by M. L. West: *Greek Lyric Poetry* (OUP, 1993), p. 39; Ecclesiasticus (Sirach) 50:6.

20. Accius, *Atreus* 678–80, in *Scaenicae Romanorum poesis fragmenta*, ed. O. Ribbeck, 2nd edn (Leipzig: Teubner, 1871). Accius's source is with all probability the description of the garments and tapestries in Euripides, *Ion* 1146–58, woven with depictions of stars mustered to embellish the circle of the sky; the difference, however, is that in Euripides the images of the starry sky are woven into fabrics, whereas later it is the stars that adorn or 'paint' the sky. Boccaccio uses the same phrase—'come nei lucidi sereni sono le stelle ornamento del cielo' (as in the bright serene are the stars adorning the sky)—twice in the *Decameron* (1.10.3–4 and 6.1.2).

21. Manilius, *Il poema degli astri*, ed. S. Feraboli, E. Flores and R. Scarcia (VM, 1996; italics mine); my translation from the family MSS O.

22. Manilius, *Astronomica*, LCL 469, ed. and trans. G. P. Goold (1977), p. 41 (italics mine).

23. Seneca, *Medea*, in Seneca, *Tragedies, Volume 1: Hercules; Trojan Women; Phoenician Women; Medea; Phaedra*, LCL 62, ed. and trans. J. G. Fitch (2018), 309–11 (310) (pp. 344–45). See A. Traina, '[Review of] Boezio, *La consolazione della filosofia*, [. . .] a cura di Raffaello Del Re (Scriptores Latini, 8) Roma, edizioni dell'Ateneo 1968', *Rivista di filologia e di istruzione classica* 3rd series 98 (1970): 97–99, at p. 98 n. 2.

24. Seneca, *Thyestes*, in Seneca, *Tragedies, Volume 2: Oedipus; Agamemnon; Thyestes; Hercules on Oeta; Octavia*, LCL 78, ed. and trans. J. G. Fitch (2018), 833–34 (834) (pp. 302–3).

25. Trans. E. Gee, from Avienus, 'Proem', in *Aratus and the Astronomical Tradition* (OUP, 2013; Latin and English parallel texts), Appendix C, p. 237, from Aviénus, *Les phénomènes d'Aratos*, ed. J. Soubiran (BL, 1981), 77–78 (p. 97). The same editions published the poetic fragments of Cicero's *Aratea*, ed. J. Soubiran (2002), and Germanicus's *Les phénomènes d'Aratos*, ed. A. Le Bœuffle (2003). The expression in question is found neither in Aratos nor in any of the Latin versions before Festus Avienus. In *Aratos* (451–453) there is mention of certain stars as 'agalmata', 'figures of the passing night, well fixed / in the sky just as they are': Aratus, *Phaenomena*, ed. and trans. D. Kidd (CUP, 2008), 452–53 (pp. 104–7).

26. Boethius, *Consolation* 4 m. 1, 13.

Chapter Thirty-Two: 'Splendour of God!'

1. K. Foster, 'Dante as a Religious Poet', *Blackfriars* 35, no. 417 (1954): 506–15, reprinted in Foster, *God's Tree: Essays on Dante and Other Matters* (London: Blackfriar's Publications, 1957), with the title 'Dante as a Christian Poet', pp. 1–14, quotation at 13–14. Foster's discussion was followed up by John Took, first in his *Conversations with Kenelm* (London: Ubiquity Press, 2013), then in his *Dante* (Princeton, NJ: Princeton University Press, 2020).

2. B. Croce, *La poesia di Dante* (Bari: Laterza, 1921).

3. *Paradiso* 33.43, 54, 66, 67–68, 83, 100, 110, 116, 124, 128. I showed the precise correspondences in my *Tragic and the Sublime*, pp. 231–33 and 306–7, indicating also the sources in Scripture, in Dionysius and in Thomas's commentary on the *Divine Names*.

4. *Paradiso* 33.54, 79, 86, 81, 103–5, 124–26.

5. See ch. 34 below.

6. Chiavacci Leonardi, *DDC*, ad *Paradiso* 30.40–42.

7. Chiavacci Leonardi, *DDC*, ad *Paradiso* 30.40–42.

8. *Paradiso* 30.55–60 and 100–5.

9. *Paradiso* 30.97–99.

Chapter Thirty-Three: 'The beauty I saw'

1. *Purgatorio* 31.139–44.

2. *Purgatorio* 22.65.

3. *Purgatorio* 28.141.

4. *Purgatorio* 21.136: this is not just what Statius says to Virgil when he wants to embrace his knees, but I think a general indication of Dante's poetics: see my '"Trattando l'ombre come cosa salda": Fisiologia, poetica e metafisica dell'ombra', now in P. Boitani, *Dante e il suo futuro* (Rome: Edizioni di Storia e Letteratura, 2013), pp. 63–74.

5. *Paradiso* 30.76–78.

6. *Paradiso* 30.16–33 (italics mine).

7. The 'dolce riso' of l. 26 is the same as that of 'Amor che ne la mente mi ragiona' (57) in the *Convivio*—speaking there of his new Donna Gentile, Philosophy (see above, ch. 19). 'Dal primo giorno ch"i'vidi il suo viso / in questa vita' is a clear reference to the *Vita nuova*: Dante fuses the images of his entire poetic career—and of his life—to speak of one single shining beauty, the beauty of Beatrice.

8. *Paradiso* 30.16–18. The poetry and poetics of *loda* had been announced in chapter 18 of the *Vita nuova* and in the canzone 'Donne ch'avete intelletto d'amore' of chapter 19.

9. *Paradiso* 30.46–51.

10. The presence of the various stages is essential in the *Paradiso*'s last cantos, as in contemporary books of mysticism.

11. *Paradiso* 30.61–69.

12. See Dante, *Paradiso*, trans. Kirkpatrick, pp. 456–61.

Chapter Thirty-Four: Neptune and Lethargy

1. Foster, 'Mind in Love', p. 52. The *Paradiso* is literally a wrestling match, as Dante calls it the 'aringo rimaso', 'the arena that's left over' in *Paradiso* 1.18.

2. *Paradiso* 33.52–54, 97–99, 76–78, 100–2, 79–80, 112–13, 80–84, 132: see my *Tragic and the Sublime*, pp. 226–228.

3. Boitani, *Tragic and the Sublime*, p. 228; see here chs 30–31.

4. *Paradiso* 33.55–57, 106–9, 121–23.

5. *Paradiso* 33.67–75, 82–84, 124–26.

6. *Paradiso* 33.91–93.

7. *Paradiso* 33.58–66

8. *Paradiso* 33.91–93.

9. *Anticlaudianus* 6.74–75.

10. E. R. Curtius, *Dante und Alanus ab Insulis* (1950), in *Gesammelte Aufsätze zur Romanischen Philologie* (Bern: Francke, 1960), pp. 28–31; E. Auerbach, *Typologische Motive in der mittelalterlichen Literatur* (Krefeld: Scherpe, 1953), , in *Gesammelte Aufsätze zur romanischen Philologie*, ed. M. Bormuth and M. Vialon, 2, extended edition (Tübingen: Narr, 2021), pp. 107–12; translated as 'Typological Symbolism in Medieval Literature', *Yale French Studies* 9 (1952): 3–10; Dronke, 'Boethius, Alanus and Dante'. For Curtius's consideration of Alan in *European Literature and the Latin Middle Ages*, see there ch. 30 n. 12.

11. Boethius, *Consolation* 1 pr. 2, 5.

12. Dronke, 'Boethius, Alanus and Dante', pp. 432–33.

13. *Paradiso* 33.94–99.

14. Richard de Saint-Victor, *De contemplatione* 1.4 (pp. 96–98); in English, Richard of St. Victor, *Mystical Ark*, p. 158. There are parallels to the sequence of *gradus* in Richard's own *De Trinitate*, Prol. 50–65, ed. J. Braillier (VP, 1958), pp. 82–83, and in the *De IV gradibus violentae charitatis*, in *Trattati d'amore cristiani del XII secolo*, ed. F. Zambon, vol. 2 (VM, 2008), 31 (pp. 510–13 and n. 108, pp. 637*ff.*).

15. *Paradiso* 17.17–18.

16. G. Contini, *Un'idea di Dante* (Turin: Einaudi, 1976), pp. 205–6.

17. Uguccione [Hugutio], *Derivationes* L49 (vol. 2, pp. 666–67): once more, I remind readers of Boethius, *Consolation* 1 pr. 2: 'He is in no real danger, but suffers only from lethargy, a sickness common to deluded minds. He has for a little forgotten his real self. He will soon recover—he did, after all, know me before—and to make this possible for him, let me for a little clear his eyes of the mist of mortal affairs that clouds them.'

18. Dronke, 'Boethius, Alanus and Dante', p. 435.

19. *Paradiso* 29.12.

20. Uguccione [Hugutio], *Derivationes* L49 (vol. 2, pp. 666–67): Ovid, *Remedia amoris* 789–90, trans. A. S. Kline (in Ovid, *The Love Poems, Poetry in Translation*, 2001, https://www.poetryintranslation.com/PITBR/Latin/CuresforLove.php).

21. *Convivio* 4.25.5.

22. T. S. Eliot, *Dante* (London: Faber, 1929), p. 55. One would inevitably think that Eliot's 'power of establishing relations' owes something to Pound's theories: see ch. 21 above.

23. *Paradiso* 2.16–18. Ploughing is also an image for writing: see Curtius, *European Literature*, p. 313.

24. S. Mallarmé, *Œuvres complètes*, ed. Bertrand Marchal, vol. 2 (Paris: Gallimard, 2003), p. 213: English translation in *Collected Poems*, trans. Henry Weinfield (Berkeley, CA: University of California Press, 1994), p. 67. Neither Weinfield nor M. A. Caws in his edition of *Selected Poetry and Prose* (New York: New Directions Books, 1982), p. 76, actually translates the key word *oublié*, the various forms of which I have italicised in the three French quotations.

25. Mallarmé, *Œuvres complètes*, vol. 2, p. 36: English translation by E. H. Blackmore and A. M. Blackmore, in Mallarmé, *Collected Poems and Other Verse* (OUP, 2006), p. 66.

26. Mallarmé, *Œuvres complètes*, vol. 1 (Paris:, Gallimard, 1998), pp. 96, 387.

27. Ovid, *Metamorphoses* 6.721.

28. H. Rahner, *Symbole der Kirche : Die Ekklesiologie der Väter* (Salzburg : Otto Müller, 1964), pp. 314–15, 345, 370, 451; E. R. Curtius, 'Das Schiff der Argonauten', in *Kritische Essays zur europäischen Literatur*, 2nd edn (Bern: Francke, 1954), pp. 412–37, in English in Curtius, *Essays on European Literature*, trans. M. Kowal (Princeton, NJ: Princeton University Press, 1973), pp. 465–96; G. Stabile, *Dante e la filosofia della natura: Percezioni, linguaggi, cosmologie* (Florence: SISMEL Edizioni del Galluzzo, 2007), pp. 85–136.

29. Cicero, *Aratea* (BL, 2006), 390, 396 (p. 188).

30. Virgil, *Eclogues* 4.34.

31. Seneca, *Medea* 364–89.

32. C. Colón, *Textos y documentos completos*, ed. C. Varela (Madrid: Alianza, 1989), p. 287.

33. T. S. Eliot, *Four Quartets*, 4: *Little Gidding* 5.37–38.

Chapter Thirty-Five: The Last Simile: The Geometer

1. The parallel was already mentioned by Dronke, *Fabula*, pp. 152–53.

2. My translation, based on *Works*, ed. Wetherbee, p. 540.

3. *Paradiso* 33.133–45.

4. See M. Mocan, *La trasparenza e il riflesso: Sull'alta fantasia in Dante e nel pensiero medievale* (Milan: Bruno Mondadori, 2007).

5. A reminiscence of the *Liber viginti quatuor philosophorum* may have acted on the image of the three 'giri' and on that of the 'cerchio': see P. Lucentini, 'Il *Liber Viginti Quatuor Philosophorum* nei poemi medievali: Il *Roman de la Rose*, il *Granum Sinapis*, la *Divina Commedia*', in *Poetry and Philosophy: A Festschrift for Peter Dronke*, ed. J. Marenbon (Leiden: Brill, 2001), pp. 131–53. As Lucentini indicates, both Benvenuto da Imola, *Comentum super Dantis Aldigherji Comoediam* (Florence: Barbera, 1887), 5, pp. 523–24, and C.Landino, *Comento sopra la Comedia*, ed. P. Procaccioli, vol. 4 (Rome: Salerno Editrice, 2001), pp. 2025–26, already saw this possibility. The best editions of the *Liber* are by F. Hudry: *Le Livre des vingt-quatre philosophes: Résurgence d'un texte du IV*[e] *siècle* (VP, 2009); and P. Lucentini: *Il libro dei ventiquattro filosofi*, 2nd edn (Milan: Adelphi, 1999); in English as 'Book of the Twenty-Four Philosophers', in *Hermetica II: The Excerpts of Stobaeus, Papyrus Fragments, and Ancient Testimonies in an English Translation with Notes and Introduction*, ed. M. D. Litwa (CUP, 2018), 320–21.

6. *Inferno* 1.39–40. The rhyme 'stelle'–'belle' is also present in *Inferno* 34.137–39, when Dante and Virgil emerge from hell onto the shores of Purgatory.

Chapter Thirty-Six: Epilogue: Descent from Heaven, Ascent to Art and Science

1. See E. H. Gombrich, 'Raphael's *Stanza della Segnatura* and the Nature of Its Symbolism', in his *Symbolic Images: Studies in the Art of the Renaissance II* (London: Phaidon, 1972), pp. 85–101; M. Marinacci, *Raffaello e la biblioteca di Giulio II: Esegesi della Stanza della Segnatura*, (Genoa: Marietti 1820, 2010); H. von Einem, *Das Programm der Stanza della Segnatura im Vatikan: 160. Sitzung am 15. Juli 1970 in Düsseldorf* (Opladen: Westdeutscher Verlag), 1971; C. L. Joost-Gaugier, *Raphael's Stanza della Segnatura: Meaning and Invention* (CUP, 2002).

2. See Joost-Gaugier, *Raphael's Stanza della Segnatura*, pp. 164–71. The 'programme' of the Stanza may have been important for Milton in his construction of *Paradise Lost*: see M. A. Treip, *'Descend from Heav'n, Urania': Milton's 'Paradise Lost' and Raphael's Cycle in the 'Stanza della Segnatura'* (Victoria, B.C.: University of Victoria: 1985).

3. This is of course an oversimplification, because the ideas and the images displayed on the Sistine Chapel ceiling represent indeed another *summa* of doctrines both Neoplatonic and Scholastic: see E. Wind, *The Religious Symbolism of Michelangelo: The Sistine Ceiling*, ed. E. Sears (OUP, 2000); also Wind, *Die Bildsprache Michelangelos*, ed. P. Schneider, (Berlin: De Gruyter, 2017).

4. Maurice Scève's *Microcosme*, = Scève, *Œuvres complètes*, vol. 5, ed. M. Clément (Paris: Garnier, 2013), 1.103–16 (p. 154; my translation).

5. *Timaeus* 90a.

6. The situation is clearly different for intellectuals such as Montaigne, who, following Cicero's *De natura deorum*, underlines Plato's contradictions on the origins of the universe: M. de

Montaigne, 'Apologie de Raimond de Sebonde', in *Montaigne: Les Essais*, ed. J. Balsamo, M. Magnien and C. Magnien-Simonin (Paris: Gallimard, 2007), 2.12 (pp. 543–45).

7. E. van Wolde, *Stories of the Beginning: Genesis 1–11 and Other Creation Stories*, trans. J. Bowden (London: SCM Press, 1996).

8. P. Sarmiento de Gamboa, *Historia de los Incas* (Madrid: Miraquano/Polifemo, 2007), chs 6 and 7. See S. MacCormack, *Religion in the Andes: Vision and Imagination in Early Colonial Peru* (Princeton, NJ: Princeton University Press, 1991); MacCormack, *On the Wings of Time: Rome, the Incas, Spain, and Peru* (Princeton, NJ: Princeton University Press, 2007). Other ethno-anthropological observations on the Beginning are scattered in several accounts of the European *conquistadores*. The *primordia rerum* of Sumerian, Babylonian and Egyptian versions are known exclusively through Greek sources. In his *Il vero significato del 'Signore del Cielo'*, ed. A. Chiricosta (Vatican City: Urbaniana University Press, 2006), Matteo Ricci has a Western and a Chinese man of letters discuss the Christian Creation.

9. Montaigne, 'Apologie', p. 526: Plato, *Timaeus* 28c; Cicero, *Timaeus* 2.

10. Luis de Camões, *Os Lusíadas* 10.79. The best edition, from which I quote, is now that coordinated by R. Marnoto, *I Lusiadi* (Milan: Bompiani, 2022), with the original text, Italian translation by R. Gigliucci and extensive commentary. The English translation I use is R. F. Duff's *The Luciad of Camoens Translated into English Spenserian Verse* (Lisbon: M. Lewtas, 1880). On Camões and creation, see now G. Berchi's excellent doctoral dissertation, 'Chaos and Epic: Dante, Camões, Tasso, Milton' (Yale University, 2024).

11. See Marnoto's n. 377 in her edition (p. 1238), and L. Thorndike, *The Sphere of Sacrobosco and Its Commentators* (Chicago: The University of Chicago Press, 1949).

12. Alonso de Acevedo, *De la creación del mundo*, ed. C. Barbolani (Caceres: Institución Cultural 'El Brocense' El Brocense' de la Excma, 1984).

13. *Timaeus* 31b–33a (quotation at 31b).

14. *Timaeus* 32b.

15. Guillaume Salluste Du Bartas, *La Sepmaine, ou Creation du monde*, vol. 1, ed. J. Céard (Paris: Garnier, 2011), 2.919–38 (pp. 154–55).

16. *Du Bartas his deuine weekes and workes translated: and dedicated to the Kings most excellent Maiestie by Iosuah Syluester* (London: Humfrey Lounes, 1611 [University of Michigan Library]), pp. 51–52.

17. Torquato Tasso, *Il mondo creato* 2.93–103 (my translation).

18. Tasso, *Il mondo creato* 2.110–50. Tasso denies that the Demiurge selected only the best material for the creation of the heavens (*Timaeus* 32a*ff.*) and interprets Pythagoras and the Pythagoreans according to the treatment they receive in the *Timaeus* 53a*ff.*

19. Tasso, *Il mondo creato* 7.1111–16 (my translation). The invocation continues for another fifteen lines.

20. Proverbs 8:27–28.

21. John Milton, *Paradise Lost* 7.210–42. The best editions of *Paradise Lost* are by A. Fowler, 2nd edn (London: Longman, 1998), and by G. Teskey, 2nd edn (New York: W. W. Norton, 2020). I use Fowler's here for quotation.

22. I still think E. C. Baldwin, 'Milton and Plato's *Timaeus*', *PMLA* 35 (1920): 210–17 had the right perspective on this.

23. See I. Montori, 'Representing Creation, Experiencing the Sublime: The Longinian Tradition in Tasso and Milton', *Sederi* 30 (2020): 69–89; K. Lehtonen, *Heroic Awe: The Sublime and the Remaking of Renaissance Epic* (Toronto: University of Toronto Press, 2023).

24. In which the *Timaeus* is mentioned as a scientific source at least three times: see Nicolas Copernic, *De revolutionibus orbium coelestium*, critical edition by M.-P. Lerner, A.-P. Segonds and J.-P. Verdet, vol. 2 (BL, 2015), pp. 23, 329, 476. Copernicus read Plato in Ficino's translation (1484).

25. See C. Baumgardt, *Johannes Kepler: Life and Letters* (with an Introduction by Albert Einstein) (New York: Philosophical Library, 1951).

26. Baumgardt, *Johannes Kepler*, p. 24.

27. Johannes Kepler, *Gesammelte Werke*, ed. M. Caspar, vol. 1: *Mysterium cosmographicum* (Munich: Beck, 1938), pp. 23–24.

28. Kepler, *Mysterium*, p. 26.

29. Galileo Galilei, *Il Saggiatore*, critical edition by O. Besomi and M. Helbing (Padua: Antenore, 2005), pp. 119–20; excerpts published in English as 'The Assayer', trans. S. Drake, in *Discoveries and Opinions of Galileo*, ed. Drake (New York: Doubleday, 1957), pp. 229–81 (quotation at 234). Since A. Koyré's 1943 essay on 'Galileo and Plato', *Journal of the History of Ideas* 4 (1943): 400–428, discussion on Galileo's Platonism has been constant: see T. R. Girill, 'Galileo and Platonistic Methodology', *Journal of the History of Ideas* 31, no. 4 (1970): 501–20; B. Bartocci, 'Paolo Beni and Galileo Galilei', *Rivista di storia della filosofia* 71, no. 3 (2016): 423–52.

30. F. Ferrari, in Petrucci, p. cxlii: Kepler, *Mysterium*, pp. 82, 192.

31. Kepler, *Mysterium*, p. 80.

32. Johannes Kepler, *Gesammelte Werke*, ed. M. Caspar, vol. 6: *Harmonice mundi* (Munich: Beck, 1940), p. 221.

33. Marsilio Ficino, *Compendium in Timaeum*, translated into English as *All Things Natural: Ficino on Plato's 'Timaeus'*, trans. A. Farndell (London: Shepheard-Walwyn, 2010), p. 3.

34. See *The Cambridge Platonists*, ed. C. A. Patrides CUP 1980.

35. See *Brill's Companion to German Platonism*, ed. A. Kim (Leiden: Brill, 2019).

36. See F. Dastur, 'Hölderlin and the Orientalisation of Greece', *Pli* 10 (2000): 155–73.

37. Giacomo Leopardi, *Zibaldone: The Notebooks of Leopardi*, ed. M. Caesar and F. D'Intino, (London: Penguin, 2013), 928, 2331, 2150, 3245. Leopardi evidently studied the *Timaeus* (in Cicero's translation as well) very carefully, since he returns to it in the *Pensieri*, and many times in the *Zibaldone*, examining both its philosophical importance and its stylistic perfection.

38. A. N. Whitehead, *Process and Reality: An Essay in Cosmology*, corrected edition, ed. D. R. Griffin and D. W. Sherburne (New York: The Free Press, 1978), p. 39.

39. Whitehead, *Process and Reality*, p. 93.

40. Whitehead, *Process and Reality*, p. 94.

41. Whitehead, *Process and Reality*, pp. 94–95.

42. Milton, *Paradise Lost* 2.891–97.

43. Whitehead, *Process and Reality*, p. 96.

44. W. Heisenberg, *Physics and Philosophy: The Revolution in Modern Science* (New York: Harper, 1958), p. 65.

45. Heisenberg, *Physics and Philosophy*, p. 66.

46. Diogenes Laertius 9.40, quoting the Peripatetic Aristoxenus of Tarentum as source of the anecdote. *Lives of the Eminent Philosophers, Volume 2: Books 6–10*, LCL 185, trans. R. D. Hicks (1925), pp. 448–49.

47. Heisenberg, *Physics and Philosophy*, p. 67.

48. Heisenberg, *Physics and Philosophy*, p. 69.

49. Heisenberg, *Physics and Philosophy*, pp. 72–73. Franco Ferrari, in Petrucci, pp. cxlvi–cxlvii, goes on to examine Guido Tonelli's *Genesi: Il grande racconto delle origini* (Milan: Feltrinelli, 2019); in English, *Genesis: The Story of How Everything Began*: trans. E. Segre and S. Carnell (London: Picador, 2022).

50. Heisenberg, *Physics and Philosophy*, p. 168.

51. The translation of *Faust* used in *Physics and Philosophy* is the late nineteenth-century one by Anna Swanwick, published by, for instance, George Bell of London in 1879.

52. W. Heisenberg, 'Sprache und Wirklichkeit in der modernen Physik', in Heisenberg, *Schritte über Grenzen: Gesammelte Reden und Aufsätze* (Munich: Piper, 1971), pp. 160–81; English translation in Heisenberg, *Physics and Philosophy*, pp. 167–86.

53. W. Heisenberg, *Across the Frontiers*, ed. R. N. Anshen (New York: Harper & Row, 1974), pp. 166–83, quotation at p. 182.

54. Ovid, *Metamorphoses* 15.60–478: see commentary by P. Hardie in *Ovidio: Metamorfosi*, vol. 6: *Libri XIII–XV* (VM, 2015), pp. 486–547.

55. The Italian publisher Raffaello Cortina is the only one to have brought out a selection of Dirac's essays and speeches, under the title *La bellezza come metodo*, ed. V. Barone (Milan, 2019). I met Paul Dirac in September 1979 over dinner, coffee and port at St John's College, Cambridge. The subject of the conversation, mostly between him and a young Florentine astrophysicist, was the first three seconds of the life of the universe. Patrick Boyde and I were able to follow them for about two seconds.

56. P.A.M. Dirac, 'The Evolution of the Physicist's Picture of Nature', *Scientific American* 208, no. 5 (1963): 45–53. I have dealt briefly with the historical and literary relevance of beauty to modern physics in my *The Machine of the World: The Modern Cosmos*, trans. A. Weston (New York: Nova, 2018), pp. 208–10. This is the second part of my *Il grande racconto delle stelle*, 2nd edn (Bologna: Il Mulino, 2019). The first had appeared, also published by Nova, in 2017 as *Looking Upwards: Stars in Ancient and Medieval Culture*.

Chapter Thirty-Seven: Afterword: The Unmoved Mover Begins to Move: Literary and Visual Renderings of the Christian Bible

1. This chapter reproduces with permission, and with a minor change of title, my contribution to *Interpreting Scriptures in Judaism, Christianity, and Islam: Overlapping Inquiries*, ed. M. Z. Cohen and A. Berlin (CUP, 2016).

2. See the entries *'āmar* (S. Wagner), *'ôr* (S. Aalen), and *dābār* (J. Bergman e W. H. Schmidt) in the *Theological Dictionary of the Old Testament*, ed. G. J. Botterweck and H. Ringgren, rev. edn (Grand Rapids, MI: Eerdmans, 1974); the entry λέγω (G. Kittel) in the *Theological Dictionary of the New Testament*, ed. G. Kittel (Grand Rapids, MI: Eerdmans, 1964); and C. Westermann,

Genesis 1–11: A Continental Commentary (Minneapolis: Augsburg Fortress Publishers, 1994), n. 2 to Genesis 1:3 (pp. 110–12).

3. On Creation, see Van Wolde, *Stories of the Beginning*; G. Steiner, *Grammars of Creation* (London: Faber & Faber, 2001); P. Conrad, *Creation: Artists, Gods and Origins* (London: Thames & Hudson, 2007); *Divine Creation in Ancient, Medieval, and Early Modern Thought. Essays Presented to the Rev'd Dr Robert D. Crouse*, ed. M. Treschow, W. Otten and W. Hannam (Leiden: Brill, 2007); M. C. Steenberg, *Irenaeus on Creation: The Cosmic Christ and the Saga of Redemption* (Leiden: Brill, 2008); Westermann, *Genesis 1–11*.

4. Basilio di Cesarea, *Sulla Genesi (Omelie sull'Esamerone)*, ed. M. Naldini (VM, 1990), 2.7.2–3 (pp. 58–59); see Commentary, p. 327. See also A. Rasmussen, *Genesis and Cosmos: Basil and Origen on Genesis 1 and Cosmology* (Leiden: Brill, 2019).

5. On the history of exegesis on this verse, see K. Smoroński, 'Et Spiritus Dei ferebatur super aquas: Inquisitio historico-exegetica in interpretationem textus Gen. 1. 2c', *Biblica* 6, nos 2–4 (1925): 140–56, 275–93, 361–95; A. Tarabochia Canavero, *Esegesi biblica e cosmologica: Note sull'interpretazione patristica e medioevale di Genesi 1, 2* (Milan: Vita e Pensiero, 1981); M. Naldini, 'Sull'interpretazione esamerale di Gen. 1, 2 "Spiritus Dei ferebatur super aquas"', in *Mémorial Dom Jean Gribomont (1920–1986)*, Studia Ephemeridis Augustinianum 27 (Rome: Istituto Patristico Augustinianum, 1988), pp. 446–49; T. Gregory, 'Le acque sopra il firmamento: Genesi e tradizione esegetica', in *L'acqua nei secoli altomedievali: Spoleto, 12–17 aprile 2007* (Spoleto: Fondazione Centro italiano di studi sull'Alto Medioevo, 2008), pp. 1–41.

6. Hesiod, *Theogony* 116–38.

7. Ovid, *Metamorphoses* 1.5–86.

8. Plato, *Timaeus* 29e–31b.

9. Aristotle, *Metaphysics* 6.1072a23–35, 1073a24–38.

10. See ch. 10 above.

11. Iohannis Scotti seu Eriugenae, *Periphyseon*, ed. É. A. Jeauneau, 3 (CCCM 163, 1999), 632B, 577–80 (p. 22).

12. Psalm 147:15 (Alter).

13. *Periphyseon* 1 (CCCM 161, 1996), 452A–D, 436–53, (pp. 18–19; my translation); cf. 505A: 'At si amat deus quae fecit, profecto videtur moveri; suo enim amore movetur.'

14. *Periphyseon* 3, 690D, 2974–75 (p. 102). It is probably from Eriugena (but the immobile movement of the divine intellect goes back to Marius Victorinus, *Adversus Arium* 4.17) that the *Liber XXIV philosophorum* (19) picks up the formulation (*Libro dei ventiquattro filosofi*, ed. P. Lucentini, [Milan: Adelphi, 1999], p. 90): 'Immobilis dicitur Deus quia est secundum unam dispositionem semper, et hoc est esse in quiete. Movens semper est, quia vivens in se, tamen sine alteratione.'

15. In the church of Bishop Sergius at Umm-al-Rasas in Jordan (eighth century), however, there is a mosaic with the representation of the cosmos, the earth, and the abyss that may have been part of an illustration of Creation.

16. On the 'Tapiz', see F. Revilla, 'Riqueza iconológica del "Tapiz de la Creación"', *Annals de l'Institut d'Estudis Gironins* 35 (1995): 69–96. Italicised Latin words in the paragraphs that follow here reproduce the inscriptions on the 'Tapiz'.

17. Hebrews 1:1–4.

18. On the Monreale mosaics, see E. Kitzinger, *I mosaici di Monreale* (Palermo: Flaccovio, 1991).

19. See Westermann, *Genesis 1–11*, pp. 104–10.

20. On San Clemente's mosaic, see S. Riccioni, *Il mosaico absidale di S. Clemente a Roma: Exemplum della chiesa riformata* (Spoleto: Fondazione Centro italiano di studi sull'Alto Medioevo, 2006).

21. On the San Marco mosaics, see E. Forlati, *Mosaici di S. Marco* (Milan: Silvana, 1957); O. Demus, *The Mosaic Decoration of San Marco, Venice*, ed. H. L. Kessler (Chicago: The University of Chicago Press, 1988); M. Da Villa Urbani, *La basilica di San Marco* (Venice: Storti, 2001); N. Panciera and M. D'Agostino, *Il mistero della salvezza nei mosaici di San Marco* (Castel Bolognese: Itaca, 2005).

22. See Y. Delaporte, *La Cathédrale de Chartres et ses vitraux* (Paris: Éditions du Chêne, 1943); Delaporte, *Les trois Notre-Dame de la cathédrale de Chartres* (Chartres: É. Houvet, 1955); E. Mâle, *Notre-Dame de Chartres* (Paris: Flammarion, 1992).

23. See ch. 24 above.

24. *Convivio* 3.7.3. Compare *Liber de causis*, ed. A. Pattin, *Tijdschrift voor filosofie* 28 (1966): 90–203, Prop. 20.157: Dante's term *discorrimento* replaces the original *influxio*: see B. Nardi, 'Lo discorrer di Dio sovra quest'acque', in his *Nel mondo di Dante* (Rome: Edizioni di Storia e Letteratura, 1944), pp. 307–13; and J. Pépin, *Théologie cosmique et théologie chrétienne* (Paris: PUF, 1964), pp. 390–422.

25. Augustine, *De Genesi contra Manichaeos* 1.7.12; Peter Lombard, *Sententiae in IV Libris Distinctae* 2.12.c.3; Aquinas, *Summa Theologiae* I.q66.I ad 2.

26. *Paradiso* 24.130–32 (italics mine).

27. On Giovanni di Paolo, see J. Pope-Hennessy, *Giovanni di Paolo, 1403–1483* (London: Chatto & Windus, 1937).

28. Raphael will paint in the Vatican Loggias several scenes of Creation following Michelangelo's model: his God there is mobile although at times he looks like a caricature of the 'terrible' Creator of the Sistine vault.

29. On Lotto and the tarsias of Santa Maria Maggiore in Bergamo, see B. Berenson, *Lorenzo Lotto*, ed. L Vertova (Milan: Abscondita, 2008); P. Humfrey, *Lorenzo Lotto* (New Haven, CT: Yale University Press, 1997); J. Bonnet, *Lorenzo Lotto* (Paris: Adam Biro, 1998); M. Zanchi, *Lorenzo Lotto e l'immaginario alchemico: Le 'imprese' nelle tarsie del coro della basilica di Santa Maria Maggiore in Bergamo* (Clusone: Ferrari, 1997).

30. On the Sistine vault, see C. de Tolnay, *The Art and Thought of Michelangelo*, trans. N. Buranelli (New York: Pantheon Books, 1964); H. Pfeiffer, *La Sistina svelata* (Milan: Jaca Book, 2007); T. Verdon, *Michelangelo teologo* (Milan: Ancora, 2005); Wind, *Religious Symbolism*.

31. On the 'terribility' of Michelangelo's Creator, see Vasari, *Le vite*, p. 894; Wind, *Religious Symbolism*, p. 39 and n. 29.

32. 'Posteriora' is Jerome's translation in the Vulgate of the Hebrew expression *'ăḥōrāy*, Exodus 33:23: 'And I will take away mine hand, and thou shalt see my back parts: but my face shall not be seen.' Edgar Wind (*Religious Symbolism*, p. 80) thinks that Michelangelo showed God's face and back in an allusion to Paul, 1 Corinthians 13:12: 'videmus nunc per speculum in

aenigmate, tunc autem facie ad faciem' (we see now through a glass darkly, but then face to face). Thus, Michelangelo would, as in all Christian tradition, have played on the opposition between Old and New Testaments, considering the latter to be the former's fulfilment: Moses could see—*per speculum in aenigmate*—only God's *posteriora*; Christians see his *faciem*.

33. Vasari, *Le vite*, p. 895.

34. Wind, *Religious Symbolism*, p. 77.

35. Thus, as we saw in the Epilogue above, pointing the way to Du Bartas, Tasso, Acevedo and Milton.

FURTHER READING

Allen, Don Cameron. *Mysteriously Meant: The Rediscovery of Pagan Symbolism and Allegorical Interpretation in the Renaissance*. Baltimore: The Johns Hopkins Press, 1970.

Amoroso, Leonardo. *Per un'estetica della Bibbia* Pisa: ETS, 2008.

Antonelli, Roberto. *Dante poeta-giudice del mondo terreno*. Rome: Viella, 2021.

Ariani, Marco. 'Abyssus luminis: Dante e la veste di luce'. *Rivista di letteratura italiana* 11 (1993): 9–71.

Ariani, Marco. 'E sì come di lei bevve la gronda / de le palpebre mie (*Par*. XXX, 88): Dante e lo Pseudo-Dionigi l'Areopagita', in *Leggere Dante*, edited by L. Battaglia Ricci, pp. 131–52. Ravenna: Longo, 2002.

Ariani, Marco. 'La forma universal di questo nodo: *Paradiso* XXXIII, 58–105', in *Lectura Dantis Scaligera 2005–2007*, edited by E. Sandal, pp. 137–81. Rome: Antenore, 2008.

Asbaugh, Anne Friere. *Plato's Theory of Explanation: A Study of the Cosmological Account in the Timaeus* Albany, NY: State University of New York Press, 1988.

Babut, Daniel. *La religion des philosophes grecs: De Thales aux Stoiciens*. Paris: Les Belles Lettres, 2019.

Baxter, Jason M. *The Infinite Beauty of the World: Dante's Encyclopedia and the Names of God*. Oxford: Peter Lang, 2020.

Beierwaltes, Walter. *Catena Aurea: Plotin Augustinus Eriugena Thomas Cusanus*. Frankfurt am Main: Klostermann, 2017.

Bodei, Remo. *Le forme del bello*, 2nd edn. Bologna: Il Mulino, 2017.

Brisson, Luc, and F. Walter Meyerstein. *Inventer l'Univers: Le problème de la connaissance et les modèles cosmologiques*. Paris: Les Belles Lettres, 1991.

Brumble, H. David. *Classical Myths and Legends in the Middle Ages and Renaissance: A Dictionary of Allegorical Meanings*. Westport, CT, Greenwood Press, 1998.

Cambiano, Giuseppe. *Filosofia greca e identità dell'Occidente: Le avventure di una tradizione*. Bologna: Il Mulino, 2022.

Carruthers, Mary. *The Craft of Thought: Meditation, Rhetoric, and the Making of Images, 400–1200*. Cambridge: Cambridge University Press, 1998.

Carruthers, Mary. *The Experience of Beauty in the Middle Ages*. Oxford: Oxford University Press, 2013.

Carruthers, Mary. 'Terror, Horror and the Fear of God, or, Why There Is No Medieval Sublime', in *'Truthe is the beste': A Festschrift in Honour of A.V.C. Schmidt*, edited by N. Jacobs and G. Morgan, pp. 17–36. Oxford: Peter Lang, 2014.

Carruthers, Mary, ed. *Rhetoric Beyond Words: Delight and Persuasion in the Arts of the Middle Ages*. Cambridge: Cambridge University Press, 2010.

Cassirer, Ernst. *Sulla filosofia antica* [German–Italian parallel texts], edited by G. Borbone. Milan: Bompiani, 2023.

Celia, Francesco, and Angela Ulacco, eds. *Il Timeo: Esegesi greche, arabe, latine*. Pisa: Pisa University Press, 2015.

Cerri, Giovanni. *La poetica di Platone*, 3rd edn. Lecce: Argo, 2007.

Chadwick, Henry. *Boethius: The Consolations of Music, Logic, Theology, and Philosophy*. Oxford: Oxford University Press, 1990.

Chadwick, Henry. *Early Christian Thought and the Classical Tradition*. Oxford: Oxford University Press, 1966.

Chiodo, Simona. *La bellezza: Un'introduzione al suo passato e una proposta per il suo futuro*. Milan: Bruno Mondadori, 2015.

Cornford, Francis M. *Principium Sapientiae: The Origins of Greek Philosophical Thought*. Cambridge: Cambridge University Press, 1952.

Courcelle, Pierre. *La consolation de philosophie dans la tradition littéraire: Antécédents et postérité de Boèce*. Paris: Études Augustiniennes, 1967.

Curi, Umberto. *L'apparire del bello: Nascita di un'idea*. Turin: Bollati Bornghieri, 2013.

Daniélou, Jean. *A History of Early Christian Doctrine Before the Council of Nicaea*, 3 vols, edited and translated by J. A. Baker and D. Smith: vol. 1: *The Theology of Jewish Christianity*; vol. 2: *Gospel Message and Hellenistic Culture*; vol. 3: *The Origins of Latin Christianity*. London: Darton, Longman & Todd, 1964–77.

Daniélou, Jean. *Mythes païens, mystère chrétien*. Paris: Fayard, 1966.

Das, Aileen R. *Galen and the Arabic Reception of Plato's 'Timaeus'*. Cambridge: Cambridge University Press, 2020.

De Bruyne, Edgar. *The Esthetics of the Middle Ages*, translated by E. B. Hennessy. New York: Frederick Ungar, 1969).

Del Bo, Beatrice. *L'età del lume: Una storia della luce nel Medioevo*. Bologna: Il Mulino, 2023.

Dronke, Peter, ed. *A History of Twelfth-Century Western Philosophy*. Cambridge: Cambridge University Press, 1988.

Ferrari, Franco, ed. *I miti di Platone*. Milan: Rizzoli, 2006.

Ferrari, Franco. *La via dell'immortalitò: Percorsi platonici*. Turin: Rosenberg & Sellier, 2019.

Ferrucci, Franco. *Le due mani di Dio: Il cristianesimo e Dante* Rome: Fazi, 1999.

Florensky, Pavel. *Beyond Vision: Essays on the Perception of Art*, ed. N. Misler. London: Reaktion, 2002.

Florensky, Pavel. *Iconostasis*. Crestwood, NY: St. Vladimir's Seminary Press, 1996.

Fowler, Ryan C., ed. *Plato in the Third Sophistic*. Berlin: De Gruyter, 2014.

Funkenstein, Amos. *Theology and the Scientific Imagination from the Middle Ages to the Seventeenth Century*, 2nd edn. Princeton, NJ: Princeton University Press, 2018.

Garelli, Gianluca. *La questione della bellezza*. Turin: Einaudi, 2016.

Gersh, Stephen. *Middle Platonism and Neoplatonism: The Latin Tradition*, 2 vols. Notre Dame, IN: University of Notre Dame Press, 1986.

Gerson, Lloyd P., ed. *The Cambridge Companion to Plotinus*. Cambridge: Cambridge University Press, 2006.

Ghisalberti, Alessandro. *Medioevo teologico: Categorie della teologia razionale nel Medioevo*. Rome: Laterza, 1990.

Glunz, Hans H. *Die Literarästhetik des europäischen Mittelalters*, 2nd edn. Frankfurt am Main: Klostermann, 1963.

Gmirkin, Russell E. *Plato's 'Timaeus' and the Biblical Creation Accounts: Cosmic Monotheism and Terrestrial Polytheism in the Primordial History*. Abingdon: Routledge, 2022.

Grau, Donatien, and Pietro Pucci. *La parole au miroir: Dans la poésie grecque archaïque et classique*. Paris : Les Belles Lettres, 2022

Hadot, Pierre. *Plotinus, or the Simplicity of Vison*, translated by M. Chase. Chicago: University of Chicago Press, 1998.

Halliwell, Stephen. *The Aesthetics of Mimesis: Ancient Texts and Modern Problems*. Princeton, NJ: Princeton University Press, 2002.

Horky, Philip Sidney, ed. *Cosmos in the Ancient World*. Cambridge: Cambridge University Press, 2019.

Hunter, Richard. *Plato and the Traditions of Ancient Literature: The Silent Stream*. Cambridge: Cambridge University Press, 2012.

Jaeger, Stephen. *Enchantment: On Charisma and the Sublime in the Arts of the West*. Philadelphia: University of Pennsylvania Press, 2012.

Jaeger, Stephen, ed. *Magnificence and the Sublime in Medieval Aesthetics; Art, Architecture, Literature, Music*. New York: Palgrave Macmillan, 2010.

Jaeger, Werner. *Humanism and Theology*. Marquette, IN: Marquette University Press, 1943.

Janka, Markus, and Christian Schäfer, eds. *Platon als Mythologe: Interpretationen zu den Mythen in Platons Dialogen*, 2nd edn. Darmstadt: Wissenschaftliche Buchgesellschaft, 2014.

Kingsley, Peter. *Ancient Philosophy Mystery, and Magic: Empedocles and Pythagorean Tradition*. Oxford: Oxford University Press, 1995.

Köckert, Charlotte. *Christliche Kosmologie und kaiserzeitliche Philosophie: Die Auslegung des Schöpfungsberichtes bei Origenes, Basilius und Gregor von Nyssa vor dem Hintergrund kaiserzeitlicher Timaeus-Interpretationen*. Tübingen: Mohr, 2009.

Liebeschütz, Hans. *Fulgentius Metaforalis: Ein Beitrag zur Geschichte der antiken Mythologie im Mittelalter*. Leipzig: Teubner, 1926.

Lire le monde au Moyen Âge: Signe, symbole et corporéité: Revue des sciences philosophiques et théologiques 95, no. 2 (2011). Special review issue presented by E. Falque.

MacCormack, Sabine. *The Shadows of Poetry: Vergil in the Mind of Augustine*. Berkeley, CA: University of California Press, 1998.

Magee, John. 'Boethius: Last of the Romans'. *Carmina Philosophiae* 16 (2007): 1–22 (special issue, Part 1).

Marenbon, John, ed. *The Cambridge Companion to Boethius*. Cambridge: Cambridge University Press, 2009.

Marenbon, John, ed. *The Oxford Handbook of Medieval Philosophy*. Oxford: Oxford University Press, 2012.

Moore, Christopher, ed. *Plato in Medieval England: Pagan, Scientist, Alchemist, Theologian*. Turnhout: Brepols, 2024.

Moreschini, Claudio. *A Christian in Toga: Boethius, Interpreter of Antiquity and Christian Philosopher*. Göttingen: Vandenhoek & Ruprecht, 2014.

O'Brien, Carl Séan. *The Demiurge in Ancient Thought: Secondary Gods and Divine Mediators*. Cambridge: Cambridge University Press, 2015.

Orgel, Stephen, ed. *Allegoriae poeticae* (reprint of the 1520 Paris edition). New York: Garland, 1976.

Panofsky, Erwin. *Gothic Architecture and Scholasticism*. London: Thames and Hudson, 1957.

Pertile, Lino. *Dante controcorrente*. Ravenna: Longo, 2023.

Poirel, Dominique, ed. *L'abbé Suger, le manifeste gothique de Saint-Denis et la pensée victorine*. Turnhout: Brepols, 2001.

Porter, James I. *The Origins of Aesthetic Thought in Ancient Greece: Matter, Sensation, and Experience*. Cambridge: Cambridge University Press, 2010.

Pouillon, Henri. 'La Beauté, propriété transcendentale chez les Scholastiques (1220–1270)'. *Archives d'histoire doctrinale et littéraire du Moyen Age* 15 (1946): 263–328.

Reydams-Schils, Gretchen. *Calcidius on Plato's Timaeus: Greek Philosophy, Latin Reception and Christian Contexts*. Cambridge: Cambridge University Press, 2020.

Rutherford, R. B. *The Art of Plato: Ten Essays in Platonic Interpretation*. Cambridge, MA: Harvard University Press, 1995.

Sequeri, Pierangelo. *L'estro di Dio: Saggi d'estetica*. Milan: Glossa, 2000.

Shestov, Lev. 'On the Philosophy of the Middle Ages (*Concupiscentia irresistibilis*)', in Shestov, *Athens and Jerusalem*, translated by B. Martin, 2nd edn, pp. 207–80. Athens, OH: Ohio University Press, 2016.

Snell, Bruno. *The Discovery of the Mind: The Greek Origins of European Thought*, translated by T. G. Rosenmeyer.. Oxford: Basil Blackwell, 1953.

Soldini, Ida. *Il trascendentale del bello, causa della razionalità: Estetica drammatica in Platone e in Hans Urs von Balthasar*. Lugano: EU Press-Edizioni Cantagalli, 2024.

Stock, Brian, *Augustine the Reader: Meditation, Self-Knowledge, and the Ethics of Interpretation*. Cambridge, MA: Harvard University Press, 1996.

Stock, Brian. *Augustine's Inner Dialogue: The Philosophical Soliloquy in Late Antiquity*. Cambridge: Cambridge University Press, 2010.

Stock, Brian, *The Integrated Self: Augustine, the Bible, and Ancient Thought*. Philadelphia: University of Pennsylvania Press, 2016.

Strauss, Leo. *On Plato's Symposium*, edited by S. Benardete. Chicago: University of Chicago Press, 2001.

Tambling, Jeremy. *The Poetry of Dante's Paradiso: Lives Almost Divine, Spirits that Matter*. London: Palgrave Macmillan, 2023.

Tofighian, Omid. *Myth and Philosophy in Platonic Dialogues*. London: Palgrave Macmillan, 2016.

Tofighian, Omid. 'Rethinking Plato's Theory of Art: Aesthetics and the *Timaeus*'. *Literature & Aesthetics* 19, no. 2 (2009): 25–40.

Took, John. *Dante*. Princeton, NJ: Princeton University Press, 2020.

Took, John F. *L'Etterno Piacer: Aesthetic Ideas in Dante*. Oxford: Oxford University Press, 1985.

Valentini, Natalino, ed. *Cristianesimo e bellezza: Tra Oriente e Occidente*. Milan: Paoline, 2002.

Vasilou, Ansa, and Elsa Grasso. *Platon et la pensée de l'image*. Paris: Vrin, 2023.

Vercellone, Federico. *Oltre la bellezza*, Bologna: Il Mulino, 2008.

Whitman, Jon. *Allegory: The Dynamics of an Ancient and Medieval Technique*. Cambridge, MA: Harvard University Press, 1987.

Whitman, Jon, ed. *Interpretation and Allegory: Antiquity to the Modern Period*. Leiden: Brill, 2000.

Zambon, Francesco. *Allegoria: Una breve storia dall'antichità a Dante*. Rome: Carocci, 2021.

ILLUSTRATION CREDITS

1. Giovanni di Paolo, *Paradiso* 4, illuminated probably 1438–44 for King Alfonso V of Naples. London, British Library, MS Yates-Thompson 36
2. Plato's *Timaeus* in Calcidius's Latin translation, with diagrams, first half of the tenth century. Vatican City, Vatican Library, MS Reg. lat 1308
3. Mattia Preti, *Boethius and Philosophy*, ca. 1680. La Valletta, Malta, Grand Master's Palace
4. West facade of the basilica of Saint-Denis, Paris, built ca. 1135–40. Photo by Thomas Clouet, licenced under CC-BY-SA-4.0 from Wikimedia Commons.
5. Ambulatory of Abbot Suger in Saint-Denis, built ca. 1140–44. Photo by Pierre Poschadel, licenced under CC-BY-SA-3.0 from Wikimedia Commons.
6. William of Conches, frontispiece of the *Dragmaticon philosophiae*, early thirteenth century. Geneva, Fondation Bodmer, MS Bodmer 188
7. View of the crypt of Anagni Cathedral, twelth–thirteenth centuries: frescoes by the three 'Masters' illustrating the doctrine of the Timaeus, and Old Testament and apocalyptic scenes. essevu / Shutterstock.com
8. Crypt of Anagni Cathedral, the Zodiac. https://treeaveller.it/wp-content/uploads/2020/04/Cripta_zodiaco-900.jpg

9. Crypt of Anagni Cathedral, the Four Ages of Man. Photo by Diego Baglieri, licenced under CC-BY-SA-4.0 from Wikimedia Commons
10. Crypt of Anagni Cathedral. On the upper right hand side of the picture the figures of Hippocrates and Galen are visible. Immediately to their left, on the pillar the elements of the Timaeus. The circle with the Four Ages of Man of Plate 9 lies immediately above. Photo by Rovalf licenced under CC-BY-SA-4.0 from Wikimedia Commons.
11. Crypt of Anagni Cathedral: Elijah ascends to heaven in his chariot of fire.
12. Crypt of Anagni Cathedral: the Philistines return the Ark to Israel.
13. Crypt of Anagni Cathedral: story of Samuel. Photo by Acquario51, licenced under CC-BY-SA-4.0 from Wikimedia Commons.
14. Crypt of Anagni Cathedral: the Cherubim.
15. Anagni Crypt series of three vaults with scenes from the Ark's history; bottom wall with St. Peter and two lady saints. Photo by Diego Baglieri licenced under CC-BY-SA-4.0 from Wikimedia commons.
16. The Elders of the Apocalypse, 13th century fresco. The Crypt of St Magnus, St Mary Cathedral, Anagni. Italy, 13th century. Photo by Diego Baglieri licenced under CC-BY-SA-4.0 from Wikimedia commons
17. Giovanni di Paolo, *Paradiso* 10. London, British Library, MS Yates-Thompson 36
18. Giovanni di Paolo, *Paradiso* 12. London, British Library, MS Yates-Thompson 36
19. Giovanni di Paolo, *Paradiso* 33: Neptune and the *Argo*. London, British Library, MS Yates-Thompson 36

20. Guglielmo Giraldi and workshop, 'The Celestial Rose of the Blessed', from Dante's *Divina Commedia* (made for Federico da Montefeltro, Duke of Urbino), ca. 1474–1478. Vatican City, Biblioteca Apostolica Vaticana, MS Urb. lat. 365, fol. 286v. Album / Art Media / Heritage Images
21. Raphael, *School of Athens* fresco: Plato holding the *Timaeus* under his arm, ca. 1509–11. Vatican City, Vatican Museums: Stanza della Segnatura
22. Raphael: the creation of the universe by Wisdom as Prime Mover or Demiurge. Vatican City, Vatican Museums: vault of the Stanza della Segnatura
23. Girona Cathedral: 'Tapiz de la Creación', eleventh century. Photo by Kippelboy, licenced under CC-BY-SA-3.0 from Wikimedia Commons.
24. Monreale Cathedral: mosaic, the beginning of Creation, twelfth century. From Maria Franca Tricarico e Maria Mazzarello, *I mosaici della Creazione nel Duomo di Monreale. Il luogo dove la Storia della salvezza è resa visibile*, (Turin, Elledici, 2017), p. 16.
25. Basilica of San Marco, Venice: 'Genesis' dome, ca. 1220–40. Photo by amberapparently, licensed under CC-BY-2.0 from Wikimedia Commons.
26. Basilica of San Clemente, Rome: Mosaics of the apse, c. 1100: the 'New Creation' of Christianity. Photo by Jastrow from Wikimedia Commons.
27. Giovanni di Paolo, *Creation of the World and Expulsion from Paradise*, ca. 1450. New York, Metropolitan Museum of Art. https://www.metmuseum.org/art/collection/search/458971

28a–b. Lorenzo Lotto (designer), 'Magnum Chaos' (28a) and Creation (28b), with wood inlay by Giovan Francesco Capoferri, 1524, in the choir of Santa Maria Maggiore, Bergamo

29. Lucas Cranach the Elder, 'Creation', woodcut in the 1534 *Lutherbibel.*
30. Michelangelo, 'Separation of Light and Darkness', ceiling of the Sistine Chapel, 1508–12 (detail). Vatican City, Vatican Museums
31. Michelangelo, 'Creation of Sun and Moon', ceiling of the Sistine Chapel, 1508–12 (detail). Vatican City, Vatican Museums
32. J.M.W. Turner, *Light and Colour (Goethe's Theory), The Morning after the Deluge, Moses Writing the Book of Genesis,* 1843. Tate, London. https://www.tate.org.uk/art/artworks/turner-light-and-colour-goethes-theory-the-morning-after-the-deluge-moses-writing-the-book-n00532

INDEX OF NAMES

A NOTE ON THE TYPE

This book has been composed in Arno, an Old-style serif typeface in the classic Venetian tradition, designed by Robert Slimbach at Adobe.